Voices from the Yiddish

VOICES
FROM THE YIDDISH
Essays, Memoirs, Diaries

edited by
Irving Howe and Eliezer Greenberg

Ann Arbor
The University of Michigan Press

Grateful acknowledgment is made to the following for permission to reprint materials:

YIVO Institute for Jewish Research, for "Swislocz: Portrait of a Shtetl," by Abraham Ain, and "Yiddish Literature in the United States," by Joseph Opatashu. Reprinted by permission of YIVO Institute for Jewish Research, New York.

McGraw-Hill Book Company, for *Notes from the Warsaw Ghetto: The Journal of Emmanuel Ringelblum*, edited by Jacob Sloan. Copyright © 1958 by Jacob Sloan. Abridged with permission of McGraw-Hill Book Company.

Vallentine, Mitchell & Co. Ltd., for *A Warsaw Diary*, by Michael Zylberberg. Copyright © 1969 Vallentine, Mitchell & Co. Ltd.

The editors wish to thank Lucy Dawidowicz for her remarkably generous help in regard to a number of editorial and technical problems. They take pleasure in again acknowledging the aid of the librarian at the YIVO Institute for Jewish Research, Miss Dina Abramovich.

Contents

Introduction

by Irving Howe and Eliezer Greenberg

I

The essays in this book share a common historical matrix and, despite frequent differences of opinion, a common historical purpose. All were written in Yiddish during the last eighty years; all are intended for an "internal" audience to whom Biblical, Talmudic and perhaps even Cabbalistic references can be assumed to be transparent; and all emerge out of an assumption that, once unity of religious belief has been challenged while unity of nationhood is not yet regained, the fate of the Jews must remain not merely perilous— for that it has always been—but in new and severe ways, problematic.

The range of subjects covered by our authors is wide: from a sociological investigation of an east European *shtetl* to a survey of modernist influences on Yiddish poetry in America; from a social-psychological gloss on the experience of Sabbatai Zevi, the seventeenth-century false messiah, to a critical study of Moses Hess, the nineteenth-century German Jewish socialist; from immigrant memoirs of New York life during the 1880's to the last words of a Jewish historian trapped in Warsaw during the Nazi holocaust. In the end, however, each Yiddish writer finds himself turning back, whether through statement or suggestion, to the over-arching problem of Jewish destiny: the meaning, the mystery, the possibility of Jewish survival. It cannot be otherwise.

The rise of Yiddish literature in the mid-nineteenth century— first in fiction and poetry, and a bit later, in literary and social criticism—must be seen as a direct consequence of the break-up of the traditional world of east European Judaism. As long as the authority

1

of the rabbis was supreme and east European Jewry remained self-sufficient in its religious and spiritual life, a secular literature, whether imaginative or discursive, could not flourish. It could hardly be envisaged. But under the impact of the European Enlightenment, especially that of Germany; after internal fissures produced by competing movements for Jewish revival, one a campaign by the learned and prosperous to bring together strands of popular enlightenment with a modernized faith (Haskala), another that great popular upsurge of pietist enthusiasm known as Hasidism; through the appearance of such worldly movements as Zionism, socialism and various blends of the two at the end of the nineteenth century; in short, as a result of the confluence of these and other forces the east European Jews turned to the *idea* of secular expression. Turned, one might even say, with religious intensity to the idea of secular expression.

Through the last third of the nineteenth century and into our own time, first in eastern Europe, then the immigrant centers of America, and finally throughout the world, there blossomed that version of Jewish culture which we call *yidishkayt*. (This term signifies "Yiddishness," the moment and substance of devotion to cultural values associated with Yiddish.) It is a period in which the opposing impulses of faith and skepticism stand poised, one fiercely opposed to the other yet both sharing a community of culture. It is a period in which Jewish intellectuals find themselves torn by conflicting claims: those of the alien world, whether in the guise of accomplished cultures or revolutionary movements, and those of their native tradition, as it tugs upon their loyalties and their hopes for national renewal. It is a period of extreme restlessness, feverish collective dreaming, pretentious ideological effort. The sufferings of an oppressed people rub against, and contribute to, utopian expectation and secularized messianic fervor.

In the first decade of our century, the life of the east European Jews boils over with movements, parties, associations, many of them feeble and short-lived, but others—like socialism, Zionism, Yiddishism—soon to become the major forms of Jewish public life in Europe and America. We make distinctions between religious and secular ideologies, and we are right to make them; but in the heated actuality of Jewish life at that moment, the two had a way of becoming intertwined, with the imagery of religious aspiration and struggle finding strange hospitality in secular speech. (The word *kherem*, in its religious context signifying "excommunication," came to be employed by the Jewish socialists to mean "boycott.") Religious Jews enter reluctantly into political life and sometimes borrow the rhetoric of militancy from their secular opponents; Jewish socialists celebrate the rising working class of Warsaw and Lodz as a reincarnation of ancient Jewish heroes. Among all the competing groups polemics are fierce and differences of opinion seem acute; but to us, from the vantage point of time, it is clear that the energies of collective resurgence that held the Jews together were more important by far than the vocabularies of political sectarianism that drove them apart.

There had been a long history in Jewish life of movements coming to Yiddish for reasons of expedience, usually a wish to reach the masses who could read nothing else, and then remaining with the language out of love. Only Hasidism, arising out of the very depths of folk experience, had never condescended to Yiddish or supposed that God cared in which language men offered their devotion. The *maskilim* (enlighteners) of the Haskala had at first looked down on Yiddish and had often written it quite badly, with heavy admixtures of Hebrew and adulterations of German; yet they had been driven by need to employ Yiddish, otherwise how enlighten the unenlightened? The early Jewish socialists, as if to validate their revolutionary credentials, were hostile not merely to Yiddish as a language but to everything having to do with Jewish culture or religion. The major Jewish socialist movement, the Bund, at first showed little concern for the cultural resources of Yiddish, using the language because it was the natural medium for speaking to the Jewish proletariat; but after a while the Bundists recognized that their task was not merely economic and political but cultural as well, so that despite their strict secularism they could not avoid an often unacknowledged relationship to traditional Jewishness. For them, too, Yiddish became a language to be loved, the very marrow of their experience. By contrast Zionism, especially before it became a mass movement almost as powerful as the Bund, was for a time hostile to both traditional Jewish ways and those who sought to build a lasting Jewish culture within the Diaspora or *galut*. This hostility seemed to the early Zionists a logical conclusion of their passionate wish to do away with the evils of *galut*. As Lucy Dawidowicz writes:

> The Zionists chose to revolutionize their own Jewish society, to 'normalize' the Jewish people, make it like all other peoples, and, above all, to repudiate Israel's chosenness . . . they came to loathe the Jewish Diaspora, the good and bad without distinction: the inflexibility of religious tradition, the Yiddish language and its folk culture, the Jewish gift of accommodation and non-violent resistance. . . . The philosophical concept of the negation of the *galut* became, among many Zionists, a negation of Jewish creativity in the Diaspora.

Yet, just as the Jewish socialists modified their crude anti-religious propaganda, so the Zionists softened their hostility to the culture of *galut*. The various Jewish parties and factions would survive for decades, and gradually it became clear to many of them that their differences had slowly been rubbed away by time. In the culture of *yidishkayt* they found a basis of existence deeper than any politics.

The spokesmen and artists of *yidishkayt*, while always aware of its precarious condition and trained to sharpen their gift for irony on the grindstones of this awareness, had nevertheless to assume as a premise of their existence that the survival of Yiddish culture was not in question. The cultural milieu they created, both in eastern Europe and the immigrant quarters of America, was one in which all the competing intellectual tendencies of Jewish life were brought together under maximum pressure. That the centuries-long reign of the rabbinate had been challenged with at least some success, so much so that the more vital rabbis began to search for new modes of belief—this led to a release of energies, a seething intellectual ferment. That this release nevertheless occurred under conditions both economically cramped and socially humiliating—this gave the writings of the Yiddish novelists, poets and critics an occasional touch of unreality, that mocking awareness of being no more than passionate *luftmentshn* dealing in ideas without substance.

Today we know that the survival of Yiddish culture was very much in question. For insofar as the Yiddish writers continued in the path of their own tradition, they could not open themselves sufficiently to the surrounding cultures of Europe and America, nor engage themselves sufficiently with the style and values of modernity to which they now and again aspired. Yet insofar as they accepted the secular cultures of their time, they risked the loss of historical identity, a rupture with that sacred past which could still stir the skeptics quite as much as the believers. The culture of *yidishkayt*—at once deep-rooted and precarious, brilliant and short-breathed—had always to accept dilemma as the very ground of its existence. It had always to accept the burden of being at home neither entirely with its past nor entirely with the surrounding nations. Out of its marginality it made a premise for humaneness and out of its strivings to elevate Yiddish into a literary language, an experience of intellectual beauty.

One condition for the rise of Yiddish literature—we use the term "literature" in its broadest sense—was that to the rising young intelligentsia of Warsaw, Lodz, Vilna and the numerous *shtetl* peripheries the traditional religious system should remain a powerful force yet seem more and more inadequate. The winds of the Enlightenment, sweeping across the airless streets of the Pale, promised secular freedom but were not strong enough to bring it in. The past remained vivid, even beautiful to many of those who found themselves attacking it as obsolete, while the future enticed, almost against their will, many of those who declared themselves defenders of the past. You could denounce religion as superstition and worse, but the Yom Kippur service shook the heart and the voices of the Talmud lured the mind. You could decry the secular writers as apostates and worse, but no one with a scrap of Yiddish could resist Mendele's acrid satires or Sholom Aleichem's sadly ironic stories.

It was a condition of east European Jewish life that every idea emerging out of it be brought to absolute extreme and raging climax, even while, and no doubt because, few of its ideas could be realized in social actuality. And while the thrust of historical energy which *yidishkayt* represented for the east European Jews would in the long run be exhausted in mid-twentieth-century America, the immigrant Jews of the Lower East Side and other such settlements would nevertheless continue for some decades to act upon the vision of an indigenous Yiddish culture, one retaining its ties with the national-religious past of the Jews yet dedicated to a humanitarian, perhaps even universalist present. It was not, in our century, the least noble of ideas.

The rhetoric of this period seems at times a little overblown, a little grandiose, but deep down the Yiddish writers knew perfectly well how precarious their culture, their very existence, really was. Abraham Reisen, the most folk-like of Yiddish poets, once wrote a lovely little quatrain reflecting the dominant mood among his contemporaries: *My life I would compare/ To a lamp with a bit of kerosene:/ The lamp continues to flicker,/ But it hasn't the strength to flare.*

At the center of this culture was a loving attachment to Yiddish as a language. In the east European milieu Yiddish had always suffered an anomalous existence. It had been treated as both spoiled darling and neglected stepchild; it had been loved for its pithiness and folk-strength yet regarded as unworthy when compared with the sacred tongue of Hebrew or the learned one of German. Yiddish was the language that sprang first to a Jew's lips, a language crackling with cleverness and turmoil, ironic to its bones; yet decades of struggle were required before the learned and the orthodox could be convinced—some never would be—that this mere *zhargon*, this

street tongue, this dissheveled creature wearing the apron of the
Jewish week, this harum-scarum of a language recklessly jumbling
bits of German, Hebrew, Russian, Polish, Provençal, English and
God alone knows what, could become the bearer of a literature that
might gain the admiration of the world and serve as the medium
through which Jewish life would regain its bearing. Today it seems
almost impossible to imagine (unless, of course, one looks at what
has since happened to Yiddish in America) that there was a time
when in both eastern Europe and America the lovers of Yiddish had
to create a *movement* for its defense within the Jewish world. Calling
themselves *yidishistn*—some fervent if aging representatives can still
be found in every Jewish community of the world—they organized
a conference in Czernowitz, Romania, in 1908, at which writers, intellectuals and public figures came together to declare a programmatic adherence to Yiddish, not merely as a language meriting its
quotient of respect but as the agent of a national-cultural idea. "The
first conference devoted to the Yiddish language," they declared,
"recognizes Yiddish as a national tongue, the language of the Jewish
people, and demands for it political, communal and cultural equality. . . . " As if only through the declamations of conference-rhetoric
could status be accorded to what in reality was pulsingly alive!

A contributing ideology was developed in the 1890's by the distinguished historian Simon Dubnow. He saw the Jewish people as a
spiritual community held together by historical, cultural and religious
ties, despite the absence of a common homeland or territory, and he
urged the Jews to struggle for cultural and religious autonomy in
whichever country they happened to find themselves. In opposition
to the Bundists he stressed the unity of the Jewish people, and in
opposition to the Zionists he desired the preservation of Jewish identity within the Diaspora. The ultimate experience of *yidishkayt*, as
distinct from its momentary ideological tendencies, would in fact
come close to Dubnow's prescription:

> perennial struggle for communal autonomy—autonomy of the
> cells that make up the body of the nation—in a form that is
> appropriate to the conditions of the time; a struggle for national
> education at home and in schools established for this purpose—
> education in the ancient national language and the vernacular
> languages developed in the Diaspora which unite the entire
> people or large sections of it; a struggle for the cultivation of all
> basic national possessions and their adaptation to universal cul-
> ture without damaging their own individuality.

The center of Jewish learning in eastern Europe was Vilna, but for the culture of *yidishkayt* all roads led to the home in Warsaw of I. L. Peretz, one of the founding masters of Yiddish literature. Peretz lacked the incandescent genius of Sholom Aleichem or the corrosive wit of Mendele Mokher Sforim, the two other masters of the literature. But insofar as the culture of *yidishkayt* took on intellectual coherence, Peretz stood at the center. He opened his house and his heart to the younger Yiddish writers and intellectuals, often the sons of rabbis and learned men, often themselves *yeshive-bokherim* (yeshiva students) in both physical and cultural flight from their youth. He was familiar with the thought of the West, for one strand of his creative self would always be cosmopolitan and skeptical. In his passionate little essay "Hope and Fear" (page 22) he composed a remarkable anticipation of a central intellectual experience of this century, warning that the gods of secular progress might fail long before leading European writers would announce that their gods had indeed failed. At the same time Peretz turned back lovingly to the half-buried cultural past of the east European Jews, discovering a treasure of legend in folk and Hasidic sources. He came to these materials before Martin Buber, more intimately and surely than Buber, and without Buber's philosophical embellishments.

Jacob Glatstein, himself a major Yiddish poet, writes (page 53) that Peretz created "single-handed a Jewish nineteenth century." By this striking phrase Glatstein means that Peretz succeeded in yoking together the worldly culture of Europe with the religious tradition of the Jews, or more precisely, that Peretz rediscovered and refined the Jewish tradition so that, on its own, it could enter the era of intellectual modernism which begins in the nineteenth century. To bring together the folk voice of the past with a vision of Jewish renaissance; to place, in Glatstein's words, "the inner nature of the Jewish spirit upon the world calendar of the nineteenth century" by unearthing "the finest Jewish treasures and illuminating them with the first electric light"—this was Peretz's great achievement. He cast an eye westward, releasing his "hope and fear" for socialism and a harmonious ordering of nations, but most of all he cared for the strengthening of the Jewish community itself. With a unique generosity of spirit he became the leading figure of *yidishkayt*, yet he could be stern in holding the line against those who would either yield themselves uncritically to alien cultures or would try to draw back into ghettos of the mind. (See "What Our Literature Needs," page 25.) The influence of Peretz upon almost all later Yiddish writers is enormous, comparable to that of Pushkin upon Russian and Emerson upon

American culture. When Peretz died in 1915, more than a hundred thousand Jews poured out to his funeral in Warsaw, a response all but unimaginable in any culture of the West.

II

The conditions under which Yiddish-writing intellectuals lived and worked, both in eastern Europe and to a lesser extent America, were notably different from those we associate with Western intellectuals. To grasp some of the nuances and finer points of the essays in this book, one must know at least a little about those conditions.

Traditional Jewish life had given a place of honor to a caste of the learned, and the *shtetl* economy, no matter how threadbare, usually managed to support a number of men who devoted themselves entirely to religious study. But when modern intellectuals began to appear in the nineteenth century, the Jewish community proved hostile—from its point of view, rightly so. For between the values of religious orthodoxy and those of modern intellectuality there could be no lasting peace, only an occasional common defense against external enemies.

By now a good many of the main actors are no longer alive and the issues that roused them have come to seem a little distant. But we should remember that these conflicts were enacted by men of the most passionate convictions, men to whom disputes over the nature of Jewishness signified the future of the earth. The clash between fathers and sons that forms so vivid a theme in the work of late nineteenth century Russian and English novelists seems mild by comparison to the crises—with their thunderings of anathema, their outcries against encrusted superstition, their wounds of loving combatants—which now begin to occur among east European Jews. (Shlomo Bickel's "Three Generations," page 109, touches upon this estrangement of young from old.) For a youth in a Lithuanian or Ukrainian *shtetl* to choose a career as writer or intellectual meant a break from family and home, a total wrenching of his life: which may be one reason that such decisions were often justified in the name of a socialist conversion.

There were two main possibilities for the young Jewish intellectuals once they abandoned orthodoxy. They could throw themselves into the revolutionary movements of Russia, which usually led to a total repudiation of their Jewish identity, or they could attach themselves to one or another of the political movements and cultural groupings within the secular Yiddish world. A few who broke away would come back repentant, shocked to discover that anti-Semitism was by no means absent among the Russian revolutionists or persuaded that the hope for Jewish liberation through world-wide socialism was utopian. A good many brilliant young men —Trotsky, Martov, many others—left the Jewish community forever: Trotsky never felt any attachment to Jewishness though Martov had for a while been close to the Bund. For the east European Jews this trend brought a major depletion of talent, one that would continue deep into the twentieth century and become especially acute during the later stages of the emigration to America. But those aspiring young intellectuals who did remain within the arena of Yiddish lived under the shadow of their fathers and the faith of their fathers, even as they tried to improvise some principle of Jewishness, some "essence" transcending religion or nationality or even culture, that could survive in the secular world. Ultimately this could only be a doomed hope, but for the moment it proved to be enormously fruitful.

The immediate situation of these intellectuals was both enviable and deplorable. Behind them they usually had a Jewish education as intense as it was specialized: the Bible remained a vibrant presence, endlessly yielding in metaphors of drama, the substance of ethics, the music of poetry and even some guidance to the world; the Talmud and numerous attendent commentaries had trained them in the agilities of dialectic as well as standards of conduct; and Hebrew both as language and cultural resource was still available to them. By the late nineteenth century almost every Yiddish writer or intellectual had also received a smattering of worldly education, either at Jewish schools or the Russian and Polish schools they occasionally went to; a very few had even been allowed to enter the sacred grounds of the Russian universities.

Yet if the Yiddish writers were the direct heirs of a great tradition, they were also in the uncomfortable position of having to start from the beginning. Through a passion for collective renewal, and sometimes the sheer will to personal assertion, they were putting together the very terms of *yidishkayt*. The bounds and norms of Yiddish as a language had to be established each day; strong efforts were made to "purify" the language, ridding it of portentous and alien Germanisms, even as philosophical and scientific terms had also to be borrowed from the German. Nor was there any clear agreement as to the possibilities or even appropriate genres of Yiddish literature; much energy would be wasted in efforts to copy the massive family-novel popular in Western Europe at the turn of the century, even though the culture and society of the Yiddish writers favored other forms; and those developments in style and period which in other cultures have spread across centuries had here to be telescoped into a few decades. Yiddish-writing intellec-

tuals met with scorn and ridicule not only within the Jewish world,
but often among the intellectuals of surrounding cultures who smiled
at the idea that a little Jew with sideburns, the son of a Vilna tailor,
should today have something valuable to say about Spinoza or
compose a poem worth translating into German. Is it then surprising that Yiddish intellectuals often felt uneasy in relation to the
external world? Or that some compensated by ritualistic invocations
of Hebraic supremacy while others aped the mannerisms of European high culture?

Many of the institutions we take for granted in the Western
intellectual milieu were not available to Jews: there were no Jewish
symphonies in Vilna, no Jewish art museums in Warsaw, though
plenty of brilliant musicians and some gifted painters did emerge
from eastern Europe. Two of the main settings in which Western intellectuals have done their work—the university and bohemia—were
rarely accessible to those writers who chose to remain within the
Jewish community. The absence of universities in the east European
Jewish community meant that its scholarship had necessarily to be
unsystematic and its intellectual life erratic. It meant that young
Jewish writers had either to attend gentile universities, which bristled
with hostility and alien concepts, or undergo the trials of the auto-
didact. That YIVO, the outstanding Yiddish center of learning, was
not founded until 1925, is a sign of how late it was before substantial
institutions could be created in the culture of Yiddish.

As for bohemia, that classical setting for romantic writers, cities
like Warsaw, Kiev and Vilna could only occasionally provide the
social space or cultural ease. Yiddish literary groups were formed
of course, with their own meeting places and hang-outs, but the kind
of bohemia we have known in Paris and New York, coherent neighborhoods in which artists and writers establish a distinctive milieu
and improvise a life-style of their own, were beyond the resources,
perhaps beyond the imagining of the east European Jews. Even in
New York during the early years of this century, when there was a
concentration of writers on the lower East Side and Yiddish intellectual life flourished, only the most fragile approximation of bohemia
could be set up. The poignant recollection by the Yiddish poet and
critic Reuben Iceland holds for more than the group of poets (*Di
yunge*) about whom he writes:

> The majority of the young writers were shop workers. To miss a
> day's pay often meant not to have money to buy a pair of shoes
> for your child or be short three dollars toward the rent . . .
> Several of *Di yunge* were paper-hangers and painters, and it

wasn't unusual for them to get off the ladders in the middle of a job and come into the café in spattered work-clothes . . . For a long time I used to have my lunch in the shop, fearful that if I went down to a restaurant I would not have the strength of will to complete the day's work.

The Yiddish-writing intellectuals of New York were too poor to venture on the programmatic poverty of bohemia, and most of them still clung to the firm, even puritanical family-patterns of Jewish tradition. For better or worse, these intellectuals were thrown in with the masses of their people, sharing their poverty, their work, their tenements. They never could nor wished to experience that estrangement which in Western Europe and America has become a major fact of cultural survival.

In certain areas of secular thought, the Yiddish writers began to work without much of a sustaining tradition of their own. Yiddish linguistic study, it is true, has been very strong in the research of scholars like Shtif, Joffe and Weinreich. In the writings of Dubnow, Balaban, Shatzky, Zinberg, and Mahler beginnings were made toward a serious Jewish historiography, yet it is significant that Dubnow wrote in Russian and Balaban in Polish and Hebrew, languages presumed to be more appropriate for scholarship. In disciplines such as sociology Yiddish has been weak—in Europe because the very idea of sociology was first being developed and could hardly be expected to take root quickly in Poland or Russia, and in America because those Jews who did turn to sociological studies usually found themselves trained in American universities and writing in English. Which is one explanation for the relative paucity of sociological material in Yiddish about the American immigrant experience; the impulse to analyze this experience was very strong among second and third generation Jews, but they wrote mostly in English and hence their work does not qualify for inclusion in this volume.

In literary criticism, by contrast, Yiddish has some substantial achievements to its credit. By the early years of the century there were already major texts by Mendele, Peretz and Sholem Aleichem requiring scrutiny and demanding appreciation. The pioneering Yiddish critics, having no models in their own language to go by, were strongly influenced by the work of mid-nineteenth century Russian critics like Bielinski or French critics like Taine, whose strong emphasis on the social component of literature they found congenial. For both Yiddish literature itself and the criticism devoted to it have always been completely caught up with the historical immediacies of Jewish life. There was not yet enough space between experience and imagination to allow the luxury of estheticism to flourish: there could not be such space in the cramped conditions of eastern Europe or even for a time in the urban ghettos of America. When a pioneer critic like Ba'al Makhshoves writes about Mendele (see page 32), he is necessarily led, by the text itself, into reflections about the very nature of Jewish existence in the Pale—though Ba'al Makhshoves could also respond to the purely literary values of the authors he discussed. Only in recent decades, however, have there appeared critics, notably S. Niger, A. Tabachnik, and S. Bickel, whose approach to Yiddish writing has given appropriate emphasis to esthetic analysis and judgment.

One could continue to list the disadvantages under which the Yiddish writers worked, yet real as these were, they fade into insignificance when the entirety of *yidishkayt* is examined. Individual careers were often unfulfilled; many went astray through the parochialism of local color or the portentousness of cosmic reflection; and with a few exceptions, Yiddish cannot boast of essayists as polished as those of Western literature.

But no matter! For the Yiddish writers had enormous advantages of a spiritual and ethical nature which other writers might well envy. Their relationship to their people was close and firm. Their common involvement in the Jewish experience shielded them from those sins of snobbism and indulgences of reaction, those postures of pseudo-aristocratism, which have often marred Western culture. Yes, the Yiddish essayists and intellectuals lacked university and bohemia, institutions and publishing houses, mass markets and foundations; but they found their way, they managed to be heard. They transformed the Yiddish newspaper into colleges of their own, where they struggled with varying success to articulate their ideas and educate their readers. They published their books by themselves, paying the printers out of their own wages and selling a few copies on occasional lecture trips. And somehow they found it possible to survive without literary cocktail parties.

Disadvantages? To be sure. In reading the Yiddish essayists one often feels that, precisely because of their intimate relationship with their readers, they feel obliged always to start from scratch, explaining references that might more gracefully be slid over, offering a quick historical review of the subject under discussion which an educated reader may find gratuitous. But as against these handicaps, the Yiddish writers were blessed with historical passion and ethical security. They wrote out of a deep conviction as to the centrality of their material; they sensed behind them the vitality of folk energy and folk martyrdom; they were men *chosen* for a task greater than themselves; they did not need to hunt and fish for subjects—their inescapable subject had already found them once and for all. Grant the superior polish of Western intellectual life, grant its greater resources and sophistication. Who nevertheless will not feel for these Yiddish writers, living out their sense of mission, at least some moments of envy?

III

The essay as a literary genre did not find a quick or easy fulfillment in Yiddish. It is, after all, a genre that signifies a measure of cultural assurance and ease on the part of the writer, a sense that he belongs to an advanced culture in which the communication of taste, the exchange of ideas, even the display of eccentricity all contribute to the life of cultivation. It is a genre that suggests a playfulness of sophistication, and can assume the presence of an audience prepared to appreciate the play. These were precisely the attitudes that could not easily flourish in the atmosphere of *yidishkayt* and would come only with the development of a greater cultural security.

Among the essayists included in this volume two may be said to have become masters of the essay as a genre, Peretz and Hayim Greenberg. Of the two Peretz was the more original figure. One hears in his prose a nervous and vibrant voice, full of intelligence and a certain impatience too, which recognizes the need to make up for lost cultural time and speaks to its audience with an urgent directness. As for the audience, it is *there*, without question or doubt. Peretz writes face to face, unwilling to let literary elaborations stand in his way. His pithy idiomatic Yiddish, extremely difficult to translate, not only advances, but by its richness of allusion, embodies his central idea. What Peretz did was to mold for himself a distinctive form: brief, pungent, stripped to the essence of his matter. For he could still write with a complete confidence that his audience would immediately see his point.

Hayim Greenberg, the most accomplished formal essayist in Yiddish, belongs to a later moment. Though active all his life as a Labor Zionist, he was the kind of figure who would be at home in any modern intellectual community: at once eloquent and ironical in style, taking pleasure in spinning a web of allusion through his exposition, and gifted at molding the essay into a compact form. A modern sensibility, Greenberg could no longer expect to command from an audience the rapport that Peretz had; his writings sometimes constitute a musing for the walls. But the meeting of tradition and modernity Peretz had called for finds a rich embodiment in Greenberg's work: see for example his study of Sabbatai Zevi, the seventeenth-century false messiah, page 148, which is both a fine historical reconstruction and a muted reverie on the torments and glories of *galut*.

Falling somewhere in time and type between Peretz and Greenberg is Hayim Zhitlowsky, a once-influential ideologist of Yiddishism. His prose lacks the lightness and muscularity of Peretz's and Greenberg's; there is a touch of the library in everything he writes; his importance is less as a writer than an ideologist in whom the component elements of Yiddish thought converge. Zhitlowsky was a socialist who all of his life resisted the trend toward assimilation that has troubled Jewish life for the last two hundred years. Proposing to transform *yidishkayt* from a cultural value to a social program, he believed that the Yiddish language was not merely a folk expression but served as the linguistic medium of the class struggle within the Jewish world. Yiddish, he argued, was peculiarly the property of the proletarian masses who formed the bulk of the Jewish community. Iconoclastic as he may have been toward Jewish tradition, Zhitlowsky developed a theory of Jewish cultural nationality which served for a time to keep many antitraditionalists within the Jewish framework. His prose is often rather heavy, suggesting the difficulties of a writer who by inclination should have been a professor but by obligation became a publicist.

Some of the other contributors to this volume are what is called in Yiddish "library people," scholars like Zinberg and Weinreich, who bring modern standards of research to distinctively Jewish themes. Others like Niger, Koralnik, Bickel, Glatstein and Tabachnik are closer to our own concept of the man of letters. Niger was the most influential and authoritative literary critic in Yiddish, if by no means always the most brilliant. Koralnik, among Yiddish writers, came closest to the kind of informal essayist in English who ranges widely and impressionistically over many subjects. Bickel and Tabachnik were literary critics in the stricter sense of the term. Glatstein is a poet who has also written valuable criticism.

Except perhaps for the specialized scholars, all wrote for an "internal" audience, the more cultivated segment of the Yiddish-reading public. But we do not mean to invoke the image of an elite or avant garde coterie. The Yiddish writers directed their voices to the Yiddish audience because they shared a total concentration on common problems and a tacit assumption that no one beyond the Jewish boundary would care much about their work or ideas. There are, consequently, internal references in these essays which an uninstructed reader may not immediately grasp—some are clarified in the glossary at the end of the book. In the main, however, these essays ought to be accessible to readers, Jewish and non-Jewish, who have enough historical imagination to recognize the parallels and be concerned with the differences between the world of *yidishkayt* and the one we live in now. As for the clashes in outlook that are normal in any such collection—say, that between A. Ain's soberly sociological portrait of the *shtetl* and Abraham Heschel's rhapsodic celebration—we trust the reader will recognize elements of truth to be found in each. Even those literary essays dealing with individual Yiddish writers whom an American reader may not know, should prove to have themes of larger interest. What has been brought together in this volume are a few characteristic voices from one of the most vibrant and humane of modern cultures. For some of us they are like lights flickering onto the world of our fathers.

The date at the end of each essay is that of the first Yiddish book or magazine publication.

I

The Founding Fathers

*In the development of a distinctive Yiddish culture and conscious-
ness, Yiddish literature has played a central role; and in the development of Yiddish literature, the central figures have been
three "founding fathers," Mendele Mokher Sforim, I. L. Peretz and
Sholom Aleichem, who wrote in the late nineteenth and early twentieth centuries. Of these writers, Peretz was distinguished not only
for his fiction but also for essays that proved to be enormously influential within the Jewish world. Here, in this opening section, we
offer a few short essays by Peretz himself, as well as evaluations of
the historical and literary achievements of the three "founding fathers." It is pleasing that the authors of these essays on Mendele,
Peretz, and Sholom Aleichem should themselves be important figures in the development of Yiddish literary criticism.*

Advice to the Estranged

by I. L. Peretz

Translated by Solomon Liptzin

Two electric balls with opposite charges are suspended not far from each other on two separate threads in mid-air. They alternately attract and repel each other.

At one moment they rush towards each other with love and longing. They want to unite. The next moment they leap away from one another in disgust and hate, seeking to put the maximum distance between themselves.

Similar reactions are observable among peoples.

"There is a time for everything," says Solomon.

There are alternating periods of attraction, of pushing towards each other, and periods of retreat, of mutual repulsion.

There are alternating historical periods: thesis and antithesis.

In periods of attraction, general humanitarian feelings develop. Hearts spin the golden threads of common human ideals and weave the web of common human interests.

In periods of repulsion each people retreats into itself, seeks solitude, takes stock of its own spiritual resources, digs into the deepest layers of its soul for buried treasures, works out its own internal growth, develops its own specific traits, spins and weaves the garment of its own intimate national life.

Thesis and antithesis! What is the synthesis?

Humanity of the future, consisting of free, independent, and culturally differentiated peoples.

This future is remote. The historic process of mutual attraction and repulsion will last a long time. The cycles are speeding up, but even so they are still of considerable duration and human life is brief, so very brief.

A human being, whose short life with its short memories is contained within a single moment of history, regards such a moment as eternal. If this period comes to an end during his lifetime and if he himself is incapable of changing his modes of thought and his habits of reacting, then this fossilized individual wants to prolong the existing historic moment by force. He cannot succeed! Human hands are too weak to arrest the wheel of time. Such a person therefore sits down, closes his eyes, and refuses to look at the changes that, despite his own will, take place all around him. He sits with folded hands and dreams the dream of his generation with its obsolete thesis.

This is the position in which you, assimilationists, find yourselves. Now it is rumored that you have at last awakened and opened your eyes. Now you want to work with us.

This is our triumph!

We have been aware for some time that the springtide in the relations between peoples is over and gone. Winter is in the air. Evil winds are its harbingers. And so we have hastened home.

The gusts of winter will soon be in full blast and there is work for all hands. Walls must be sealed, the roof repaired, windows inspected, fuel restored, lights held in reserve, and—bread! We have been active for some time in our own workshop.

You remained in the houses of others; you tarried in the halls of strangers; you followed in the footsteps of foreigners.

You found their homes so bright, so rich, and our home so dark, so poor.

You therefore lived for them, worked for them, until they hinted to you that you were not welcome and that they did not need your help. You thereupon dispersed, in the hope that the fewer there were of you in one spot, the more likelihood there was of your being tolerated.

If two of you found yourself in the same place, one got away from the other. Two in one spot at one time might be more than the others would welcome. If one of you happened to look into a mirror and to see his own face there, he jumped aside, he did not recognize his own mask, he thought there was another person in his way.

But even the single individual was felt to be superfluous and no knives or forks were set for him at the table of the others. Coughing failed to attract their attention. Then you moved to one side, sat down in an obscure corner, closed your eyes, dreamed your daydreams, and drowsed off.

Now you have awakened. You want to come back. You want to work with us.

This is our triumph. But see, the victors shall not put our foot on your necks; we shall not close our doors to you. There is no lack of work for you in our workshop. We shall admit you as one of us, but we shall watch you carefully. We shall make sure that you do not sow the wrong seed-mixture, that you do not spin and weave threads of diverse qualities, that you do not introduce into our midst foreign contraband.

With us this is now a time for spiritual accounting and stock-taking, for holy work; and all hands that participate must be clean.

Times change! Formerly there was jubilation when one of the estranged returned to our midst. We pointed to him with pride and we held him up for all to see.

We are no longer so poor!

If you want to take from us, we shall gladly let you have of our own, our warmth, our intimacy.

If you want to give to us, however, we should like to know what you are giving. Is it gold or spurious currency?

Times change!

1910

Hope and Fear

by I. L. Peretz

Translated by Nathan Halper

My heart is with you.

My eye cannot have enough of your flaming banner; my ear does not tire when it listens to your mighty song.

My heart is with you. Man must be fed. He must have light. He should be free, should be able to control his labor and himself. He should have it in his power to create.

And if you bite the fist that would take your cry, your burning protest and force it down your throat, so that nobody should hear it—I feel jubilation. May God sharpen your teeth! When you march on old Sodom, intending to attack it, my soul marches with you. The confidence that you must win fills me, warms me, takes my senses like old wine.

Yet—

I fear for you.

I fear for the oppressed when they are victorious. They may turn into oppressors. An oppressor sins against the human spirit.

You keep saying that Mankind must march like an army to battle: you—playing the tune.

Man is not like an army.

The strong are in front. The passionate feel more deeply. The proud are taller. Will you fell the cedars so they shan't outgrow the grass?

22

Won't you spread your wing over mediocrity? Won't you give armor to the indifferent? Will you protect only the colorless, only cattle who are shorn in the same fashion?

I worry.

As victors, you may become the bureaucracy: apportioning to each his morsel, as to inmates in a poorhouse: alloting work, like a sentence of hard labor. You will destroy that creator of new worlds—the human spirit. You will fill the purest well of human happiness—initiative—the force that is able to pit one man against thousands. You will mechanize life. To improve it, you will command it to be burned.

You will be occupied with regulations: with writing, assessing, making notations. You'll be busy prescribing: how strongly, how often, a pulse is permitted to beat: how far an eye may see: how much an ear may take: what kind of dream is permitted to a yearning heart?

With deep joy, I watch you tear down the towers of old Sodom. But my heart trembles, lest on its ruins you build a worse one—colder and more dark.

There will be no house without windows; but the soul will be smothered in fog.

No stomach will be empty; yet the mind will be faminished. No cry of misery will sound. But the eagle, the spirit—its wings cut off—will stand, harnessed in the chariot, with the cow and with the ox.

Justice, your companion on the thorny way to victory, is going to leave you. You will not notice it. Winners and rulers are blind to such things. You will be the winner, the ruler. You will sink into injustice. You will not feel the swamp beneath your feet. A ruler feels secure—until he has fallen.

You will build prisons for those who show you the depth to which you sink. You will tear out the tongues of any who warn you of those who are coming to destroy you and your injustice.

Cruelly will you defend the equal rights of the herd—to grass beneath its feet. Your enemy will be the individual: the superior man, prophet, emancipator, poet, artist.

All that happens, happens in time and space.

Space represents what has happened already: the stagnant,

inert. Therefore, the paralyzed and frozen. The present day, which is fated to end.

Time is change. It develops, transforms: it is growth and blossoming—eternal tomorrow.

When your morrow, that to which you aspire, will turn into today, you will be defender of yesterday: the dying and dead. You will stamp on the shoots, destroy the blossoms. You will extinguish the radiance of prophecy, of dreams and new hope.

The present day is never ready to die. The sun sinks in blood.

I wish: I hope for your triumph. I dread: I tremble for your triumph.

You are my hope! You are my fear!

1906

What Our Literature Needs

by I. L. Peretz

Translated by Nathan Halper

I

First of all, tradition.

Our orthodox materialist smiles. Let him.

The icicle is unaware that he himself is melting. He looks for new symbols, holidays, party politics. He keeps looking—and melts.

"Art"—how alien, how extravagant this word sounds in Yiddish. But we have no other: I am forced to use it. Art is the soul of a people, the personality of a nation. Universal art will be created after we have a common humanity; meanwhile it doesn't exist. And the personality, the spirit of a people, is shaped by tradition.

Take a lantern and search our literature for tradition. You will find nothing. Nowhere will you hear the echo of the voices on Mt. Sinai, nor see the reflection of the Shekhina on the cherubim. The voice of prophecy is dumb. Our renaissance has barely reached back to Reb Nachman of Bratzlav.

"Transform old cultural values." "Old wines in new bottles." "Recreate the Bible." These were the slogans at Czernowitz.[1] The reality: a poorly translated European literature.

An old people, the oldest—and a young literature, the youngest.

Who are you, young Jewish writer? A child without mother or father.

Yiddish must be created, and for this we need a tradition. Everything can be found among us: a slice of life—in boots and galoshes; a shrewd, sickly side-glance (I don't get involved, I'm too smart) *à la* Chekhov; a garbled Maupassant, *via* Russian translation; a caricature of a talentless Sanin. Whatever you will!

[1] See page 6 of the Introduction.

But where is Jewish thought, where is the Shekhina?

Take a nation, one that changes its languages, a wandering nation with no established boundaries, no economic system of its own. It lives, suffers, and does not succumb. Weak and oppressed by the mighty, it does not surrender. Such a people will see and feel in a different way, it will have its own view of experience and its own notion of the future of the universe, of life and man. Is this reflected in our writing?

Who among us sees with Jewish eyes? Feels with a Jewish heart? Where do you hear a word from the Jewish soul?

People come from Berlin (never fewer than two of them). My, they were in Berlin. Saw Bismarck—granite and tin boots. Walked through the Sieges Allee—marble statues of noblemen. Feasted their eyes on wax-tipped Kaiserly moustaches, on royal coaches, white and plated with gold. They were enthralled by the power that radiates from policeman and Junker. These fellows come back to our ghetto and demand—Europe.

But it's not Europe we are lacking, it's Yiddish. And Hebrew.

II

Our literature is young, and frequently childish.

Children make faces and we call it "thinking." Children babble and we treat it as a quest for God.

In Chelm boys try to lure the moon into a barrel and it becomes a sign of the Kabbala.

Our young men have talent, but they don't know how to distinguish between near and far, shallow and deep, their own strength and that of others. They are reckless, and play with fire. At the fires of strangers, spirits have been burned.

Children, when left alone, look in drawers and closets, dress up as their elders and go parading in the street. Father's hat down over the ears; coat-tails swim in mud; a little girl puts on her mother's wig, the oldest sister's dress, the trinkets of a sister who's engaged. Our orphan-children wear the old clothes of strangers.

Is there nothing original?

An old people: a radiant past: a martyr-filled journey to the prophesied future. In the middle of the journey, we produce a trifle, a moue, a glow-worm's dance, the shadow of a mood.

A dispersed people, a wandering race, universal and eternal; a literature of the moment, topical, unable to get out of the Polish or Lithuanian *shtetl*. And if our turkey-gobbler really wants to get out of his narrow environment, he starts to imitate—the gentiles.

Suddenly there is activity, a ferment in the Pale. From women's prayer books and *Tsene-rene*,[2] we get the tales of I. M. Dik in Vilna. Mendele shows up in Odessa, replacing the hitherto undifferentiated Jewish masses with individual Jews, men and women with marrow. He shows them in the bathhouse, the poorhouse, the house of study. Dineson from Zhagory brings quiet domestic dramas, muted tragedies of young folks in the Jewish home. Sholom Aleichem from Kiev brings the comic traveling-salesman, naive and too clever, who in search of livelihood is forever moving from a small town to a larger one—or he brings us the tragi-comedy of Tevye the Dairyman. Soon there breaks out a revolt of the brighter students, the younger writers rush in with new themes as through an open door. Asch presents the Vistula, Kola Street, emigrants, a brothel. Nomberg—the defeated intellectual. Weissenberg—the village. He finds a father and sons in the outlying districts; sandy places, a forest, water, clouds. The still younger ones come with brighter colors, introduce the sea, sunrise, and sunset: peasants, gypsies, thieves.

The novel is born.

But where are the Sephardic Jews? The diamond cutters of Amsterdam? The colonists in Argentina? Or those in Palestine? How is Rothschild faring in Paris? Luzzatto in Rome?

A wandering people, and its literature like stagnant water.

A high point is needed from which to look upon all this. The prophet stands on a height. He sees countries unroll at his feet. Armies, nations march through—but not our own.

He sees the future; we see the next day—through the eyes of liberal reformers, the glasses of Social Democrats.

III

Let there be no misunderstanding.

I am not proposing that we lock ourselves in a spiritual ghetto. We must leave it—but with our own soul, our own spiritual wealth. We must make exchanges. Give and take. Not beg.

Ghetto means impotence. Interchange of culture is the only hope for human growth. Man, the complete man, will be the synthesis of all the varied forms of national culture and experience.

To take yet continue to be oneself—that is the important thing. It is also difficult, especially for nations that are weak and not inde-

[2] *Tsene-rene* (Ze'ena ure'ena = Go forth and gaze), a Yiddish translation of the Bible, embellished with explanations, legends, and moral sayings, widely used by women in Central and Eastern Europe from the seventeenth century on.

pendent. That is why we must be more demanding with the Yiddish writer. He has something that is unique.

He should not do what others have already done. Leave the ghetto, see the world—yes, but with Jewish eyes. He should consider his problem from a point of view that's Jewish. The ethical light in which he sees it must be Jewish. To have Jewish art, you need Jewish artists.

This does not mean that it is forbidden for us to use *kelev, pies* or *sobaka*, the Hebrew, Polish or Russian word for dog; nor that you must use the specifically Yiddish *hunt,* or for that matter, must pronounce it in the accent of your own district.

I am not addressing myself to those who are fighting for the right to correspond in Yiddish, to conduct a trial in Yiddish: those whose aim it is to have Yiddish in the mails, the court, local government: those who fight against the use of any word derived from Hebrew—who shudder when they hear the Hebrew for "soul" or go into a sweat when they hear "community of Israel." I am speaking to those who battle for cultural rights, for the freedom to create, for Yiddish cultural values. For it is not enough to speak Yiddish, you must have something to say.

If you haven't, you may speak it from the cradle to the grave. In all places, the home, the street, the synagogue during the reading of the Torah, at the Philharmonic, even the middle of the opera. (For some this is the height of their ambition!) What you will be saying will still be *goyish.*

And banal. Imitative and dead. A tragi-comedy. We stand like a stone wall in behalf of Yiddish. We make sacrifices for Yiddish. We fight against alien speech forms, both the old and new. Yet in front of our eyes, Jewish content dries up, the Jewish spirit becomes extinguished. We are flooded by imitations, false money, spurious goods. And some say with delight, "Oh! How European!"

Where is the original? the Yiddish?

You cannot survive unless your spirit is your own. You may be influenced, you may take suggestions, may be moved. But living with an alien will—that is impossible.

Which is why so much is planted and so little is reaped, why our sheaves have so much straw and so little grain. Why so many hopes are unfulfilled and so many stars keep falling from the sky.

When Negro children go to a European school, they show remarkable ability—in the early grades. As long as it's enough to pick up what the teacher says, to learn by heart, repeat what is written in the book, they stand at the head of the class. But when they reach the fourth or fifth grade—stop! Here you need your own intelligence, wide-awake and alive. Your own intuition and mental energy. In the alien school the children have lost it. They have learned to imitate for so long that their natural well-spring has gone dry. The subconscious process has stopped functioning. From the school there comes out a spiritual dwarf, a eunuch: black but dressed in European clothes, with top hat, frock coat and gloves. European manners, but underneath—it's skinny and naked.

This is the curse of our writing. A band of retarded geniuses. Pushkins, Goethes, Shakespeares—who never grow up to be people.

IV

Without a god, one goes looking for idols. Idols do not give a Torah.

One then is merely able to record or describe, not to create. The act of creating is religious. And if that is so, one needs a sense of the universe. Reason cannot give it. It must be intuitive—creative.

If one has no sense of the universe, one has no universe. Only torn and scattered facts, but no chain of phenomena. You are playing in sand. (As some esthetes tell us, "That's what Art is—Play.") You have no sense of the causality of time. Today does not emerge from yesterday, or tomorrow from today.

You have no ideal but that of self-interest. Without a higher view, there is no perspective, so that all is flat. Nature dead, life mechanical. Everything of equal value. Anything as a subject. If a light or shadow trembles, you get a couple of phrases or a rhyme.

No past, no future. A foundling in the world, without parents or tradition. Having no obligation to the future, the eternal, you have nothing but yourself. Nothing to which you can aspire. You are the measure, the single touchstone.

I am what I am. I must try everything and enjoy everything. The key word is "enjoy."

You have whims but no character. Desires but no will. No great love or hate, only superficial relationships.

Take the matter of women. In the Bible we had a Shulamite. In Proverbs, "a virtuous woman." And she who "waits" and "captures," a woman "loud and stubborn."

With us, however, a mother has to be solemn. Her beauty isn't considered a proper literary subject. We must be respectful toward the wife-mother. We must build her a temple.

Emphasize the nest. Forget the Shulamite: she is too healthy, too honest, too straightforward. We need maidenly modesty, the shy charm of a bride—dust on a butterfly's wings.

In the eyes of our writers, women do not care for love. All they want is domestic bliss.

Why isn't this situation exposed by our critics?

Because we have no critics.

We have a garden but no gardener. It grows wild, there is no one to pluck the weeds. No one fosters what is good, supports what is weak, gives water to the thirsty.

Young people are seekers, but no one shows them the way.

We have a public. It knows little, but is hungry for God's word. Thirsty, but no one shows it the difference between pure and impure.

It can only get poisoned.

And if once in a lifetime there is something bigger, deeper, more significant, nobody will explain it. One speaks only when able to pose as a cosmopolitan esthete, only when able to show someone else's mistakes.

Withered, yellow, jealous—their hostile impotence shows itself. If it sees a child with rosy cheeks, it pinches them—with malice.

Still, the earth moves.

This is not the last word in the Jewish tragedy.

We will come back to the Bible.

v

"Back to the Bible" is not the same as stopping at the Bible. Jewish faith is not a stagnant water. The Torah has been called "the Water of Life." What was given on Mt. Sinai had in it "all that a serious student may bring out"—all that the Jewish spirit may be able to evolve.

Being Jewish is dynamic. Everywhere in the Jewish world and at all times: not a single authentically Jewish moment should ever be erased.

Being Jewish is our approach, our only approach to Man. To the godly man. To the human god. To the Superman, if you will. (Even this is possible to Jews.)

No misfortune, not the most cruel edict, the most violent pogrom, need, hunger, shame, scorn—none is a justification for reaction. We must show still more character. Strike the stone: it will give water. Squeeze the olive: it offers its oil. Such is our lot—to live and work under the worst conditions. Not to leave our path.

Other ways are for other people.

No single place, no minute in time, no class in our nation has an exclusive right to Yiddish. Every thing, everywhere belongs to it.

Blind religious obedience, ignorant attitudes toward commandments and transgressions, the awe and fear of our lower classes toward words in antiquated books—erudite worship, rabbinical study of the Torah, with its understanding of commandments and avoidance of transgression—purity of spirit, the cabbalist's devotion to the body of precepts interpreted as symbols, unadorned Hasidic spirituality—the pure, philosophical, monistic world of the true Jewish intellectual—all these are facets of one faith, a coarser or a finer manifestation of the Jewish soul.

To find the heart, the essence of Jewishness in all places and times, in all parts of this scattered, dispersed yet universal people; to find the soul and see it illuminated with the prophetic dream of the future—this is the task of the Jewish artist.

Creation is an exaltation of the spirit. For the Jewish artist only a Jewish soul, his specifically Jewish soul, can be his Shekhina, his glory, enthusiasm, creative force.

This must be the way he looks at the world, its past, present, future.

He must not shut himself off from the universe. Only a little solitude, a moment of spiritual stock-taking, just enough to discover himself and disentangle himself from the alien and superfluous.

That is to say: back to the Bible.

Back to the most reliable point: from there, to become a human being. And on a Jewish path.

1910

Mendele, Grandfather of Yiddish Literature

by Ba'al Makhshoves

Translated by Ronald Sanders

There are writers who gently take hold of the reader's soul. With a witty or homely phrase, they soothe his brain with their quiet words. A profound change comes over him; hope and despair, sadness and joy, mingle in his heart. A divine spark enters into him and he begins to contemplate mankind and the world with the spirit of a poet.

But there are also writers—including some of the very best—who drag the reader into their imaginative world as if by violence. The road to their mountaintop is covered with dust. Their hills and valleys are full of ditches and bogs, and they must strain constantly, for at any moment the reader is likely to stiffen up and refuse to budge.

Mendele Mokher Sforim belongs to the latter group. Even before one has read a book of his from cover to cover, one can perceive the ditches and valleys of his literary talent. The critic is likely to see his faults before anything else. It takes hard work to begin to enjoy him and to sense what is really going on in his work.

He comes to us in disguise, wearing a pious countenance as his mask and intoning a little prayer—some verse from Bible or prayer-book is ever accompanying Reb Mendele like a faithful friend and constantly distracting him. In this guise he will latch onto somebody, and only then begin to let on that he is not at all what he seems. When, at length, he feels like letting some tears flow and revealing the bitterness of his heart, he will allow a witticism or bit of mockery to spring from his lips, like the devil in his story, *Di Kliatche* ("The Nag").

32

His diction is overly cultivated. One senses that Mendele wanted to create an eternal monument to the Yiddish language and strove to get its essence into his prose. And, except for a scattered few, Mendele's characters come to seem, despite all the differences between them and him, projections of his own dignified self. As a result, his work loses some of its potential vitality: one grows weary of swallowing the rather high-toned diction of Reb Mendele in so many different characters; it gets to be a little bit like drinking pure brew without an occasional drop of water—one wishes for a moment's rest, a chance to catch one's breath and look around a little.

Mendele is a poor architect who constructs without giving shape or direction. A story by him struggles onward like a wagon on a bumpy country road. He writes his longer works episodically, linking one set of events to another in succession, but the construct is not an organic whole; it is just strung together, often reminding the reader only at the very end of some plot scheme long since forgotten.

Mendele had a natural inclination to place double meanings in the speeches of his characters. Except when talking about the homeliest matters, their words would tend to assume larger implications hinting at the condition of the Jewish people in general. When the blind wife of Fishke the Lame pushes another man away and says, "Go on! I'm a married woman, thank heaven, and have someone to take me around visiting," we hear in her words an elegant hint at the general situation of the Jewish people. Such passages are everywhere in Mendele's works. This produces an ambiguity which constantly thrusts the reader from the particular to the general and back again, jarring him and interfering with his pleasure.

Like a true son of his people—who are eternally enamored of the sharp phrase—Mendele has an unfortunate habit of ruining a mood he has striven to evoke with a good deal of care and artistry, all for the sake of some clever epigram. At times the witticism he cannot help making is even a good one, yet inappropriate in the context.

All these faults are such significant elements in Mendele's art that we would probably never have had his work without them. But the shortcomings of a great talent are worth studying no less than its virtues. In a great writer the spirit of his people manifests itself as if through a magnifying glass—everything seems larger and more pronounced. And if we can achieve some understanding of the sources from which our greatest Jewish writers have drawn both their virtues and their faults, we can then understand something of the soul of the Jewish people with all its virtues and faults.

Mendele was the offspring of a generation that produced a new

type of Jew, the *maskilim,* or "enlightened ones," men who secretly
sought in their reading of Bible and Talmud justification for the rationalism they had recently imbibed from the general European
Enlightenment. Outwardly there was little distinguishing them from
previous generations of pious, learned Jews. They too spent their
years going about in long gaberdines and fringed garments, wearing
this traditional garb like a disguise. They prayed three times a day,
performed all the *mitzvas,* and whenever they ventured some innovation, this would perhaps consist of skipping a few of the minor
prayers in the service, or of combing out their beards a little more
often and shortening their forelocks just slightly. They gave no outward indication of what the Good Lord had wrought within. A holy
Jewish fire was burning in their hearts, a love for the whole world.
They felt that a new era of freedom and enlightenment was beginning, a paradise on earth. Among themselves they quietly lived as
brothers, like a group of followers of the same Hasidic rebbe. Their
chief source of inspiration was beautiful Hebrew writing, whether
that of a sacred prophet of old, or of some modern writer of elegant
prose compositions.

These were the days when Jews were still so deeply immersed
in Judaism they had nothing to do with people from other groups.
They could not conceive of life apart from the Jewish community;
they knew nothing yet of social or political rank; they settled all disputes of a civil nature among themselves, through the institutions of
the Jewish community. In effect, the community leaders were the
government and what they established as a general standard became
so. Whenever the Tsarist government tried to intervene in Jewish
affairs, this was looked upon as a terrible calamity, which had to be
warded off with prayers, acts of charity, and a hand extended toward
some uniformed official, bearing gifts.

The only people left unhappy by this way of doing things were
these secret followers of the Enlightenment. Ineffectually they stood
aside and sighed for better times, like Jewish women sighing over
their prayerbooks. There was really no clear picture of what they
longed for in their minds, which had been shaped by the works of
elegant and largely meaningless Hebrew prose that were so popular
among them. Their preeminent ideal was to live in a more dignified,
more European manner; they liked the outward virtues of the European way of life. They longed for a little more freedom, but their
notion of freedom was actually rather selfish and infantile: what
they sought to be free of were community meetings, long prayer
services, unhygienic public baths, foul-smelling synagogues, and the
like. They founded all their views upon their notion of reason, and

firmly believed that all problems could be coped with and solved by logical processes. But their logic wasn't worth a fig. Reason as they understood it was something that never troubled itself with facts, indeed did not even know how to deal with facts, for most of them never left the *shtetl*, and they tended to conceive of "education" as though it were some princess in an alabaster palace. Any discrepancies they perceived between their own ideals and Jewish life were at the expense of Jewish life, which they considered to be quite ugly, and they constantly strove to introduce more refinement and decorum, more grace, into their own lives. With these superficial pretensions regarding Jewish life, and their exalted notion of reason, they were of course utterly unable to arm themselves against the hostility of the surrounding world. They simply did not feel the Jewish plight deeply, the way we do today. With no better ideal than that of not being different from other educated Europeans, they tended to aim rather low. Working with their notion of reason—which did, after all, have its heretical tendencies—they secretly sought out new meanings in the sacred texts, which they then quietly tried to impose upon friends and relatives.

This was the generation into which Mendele Mokher Sforim was born, and its failings as well as its refinements always clung to him. To be sure, no one better understood its inadequacies than he did. The best passages in *Di Kliatche* were written about them and to them. But Mendele was ever aware that it was men of this sort who had guided his first steps into the alabaster palace of the Enlightenment. Even after he came to owe them very little intellectually, he continued to love them and to borrow many things from them in his work. In *Dos vintchfingerl* ("The Magic Ring") he calls them the "young old fools," who with all their education have not yet learned any of that lore of the modern world which is founded in the wisdom of the marketplace and the knowledge that money talks; and in both this book and *Dos kleyne mentchele* ("The Little Man") the *maskilim* are depicted as well-scrubbed puppets. But all this is done lovingly, like a father addressing a son. This same generation that had made Mendele into a dissembler also taught him to perfect his literary diction. In Mendele the writer of homely Yiddish there also dwelt the old writer of elegant Hebrew prose who would sit up all night composing a love letter. With his passion for precision, purity and reason, the *maskil* of that day awakened among Jews a taste for mathematics and grammar; it is likely that high-toned Hebrew grammatical works were then read by Jews with greater pleasure than that with which they would later read the stories of Mendele and the essays of Ahad Ha-Am. Envying the traditionally pious Jew with his purely Biblical

mode of discourse while trying to be outwardly indistinguishable
from the German Jew, the *maskil* was somewhat ashamed of Yiddish, a language full of the homely usages of everyday life and daring
to approach common sense in its structure. This fastidiousness about
language was transferred by Mendele from Hebrew to Yiddish. Re-
fining and polishing, purifying and simplifying, he became the creator of modern Yiddish. And this is what makes for the enormous
difference between Mendele and the writer of elegant but empty
Hebrew prose, the kind who skipped over passages in the Prayerbook
and trimmed his beard just a little. When he took up his pen Mendele shared in the faults of such men, but by the time he put it down
he had created a body of work reflecting the experience of an oppressed people in a pure and noble language.

The gentiles think very highly of Jewish fish and of Jewish wit.
Take up any collection of their witticisms and you will soon find a
joke or epithet that originated in some synagogue courtyard or bathhouse of Vilna. No other people so well remembers its great jokesters
—its Sheyke Feffers, its Mottke Habads, its Hershele Ostropoliers—
the way Jews do. A joke or a witty turn of phrase plays a very important role among us Jews—it can get someone through a fast day,
for example; and when two Jews get together it does not take long
for a witticism to pass between them.

When was it that we became afflicted with this trait, which is
after all a plague not even to be found among the punishments of
Leviticus? Is this "Jewish wit" a kind of flower of the Diaspora, which
has adhered to us the way the yellow patch once did? Or is it in fact
an inheritance from our earliest forefathers? But it would almost
seem that the latter *never* made jokes.

The real reason the Jew became such a wiseacre is something I
first began to discover when I studied the writings of Mendele. Not
that Mendele talks about this anywhere, but anyone who has gone
deeply into his work will be able to understand as a matter of course
why the Jew has become such a wit, heaven help him.

First of all, we see that poverty is visible everywhere in the Jewish milieu that Mendele describes. Jewish poverty is a kind of marvel
to him, for no parallel to it can be found anywhere. This is not the
poverty of the great European cities, nor is it the poverty of the Russian peasant. The poor people in the large cities are usually unemployed workers, people whom the factories have thrown off like
shavings from a lathe, forlorn, weak, drunk, the offshoot of a society
that dies without leaving any legacy to the future. Whatever strength
remains in them is consumed by sweatshops and by the bosses of all
kinds of illicit enterprises. But Jewish poverty has no idea what a

factory looks like, for it exists in the *shtetl*, where it has its origins in fathers and grandfathers who have been wretchedly poor since time immemorial. The Russian peasant, poor as he may be, is the proprietor of a small piece of land. And his condition is not hopeless—one feels that sooner or later it will improve. The well-being of the land itself is at stake in the improvement of his condition, and so the government is concerned about him. But Jewish poverty is utterly without a cure; the Jew has no available means for improving his condition, which will remain abject as long as he lives among alien peoples. In villages where life should have brought him closer to the earth, he lives as though he were in the city, and so he goes hungry while the fields do not bloom.

Secondly, this Jewish community has a remarkable past. It walks around with two thousand years of history on its back, living with the spirits of its grandfathers and following the pathways of bygone generations. It is separated from the outside world as though it were an island in the middle of an ocean, and what goes on in that world is like a splashing of surf that never reaches higher than the ankles. The members of this community are bound and shackled to one another, and should one of them wish to break away, he has no choice but to cast himself into the waves, which will carry him apart from the Jewish world forever.

Thirdly, this attachment to a dead past, to poverty, and this separateness from the life of the world around them, have made the members of this community into something like anchorites and have bred in their hearts a contempt for the ordinary pleasures of the world. They live in constant fear lest they stray out of the narrow cage into which their forefathers had directed them, heaven forbid, and they tend even to forsake whatever pleasures Jewish law allows them. They are constantly placing new yokes upon themselves. They hide their natural impulses. They renounce the darker elements in their nature. They have ears only for the reading of the law, eyes only for scrutinizing sacred texts, voices only for crying "Hear, O Israel."

Along with its asceticism, this Jewish community carries with it two conceptions of an eternal life. With unshakable faith it believes itself to be the glory of the world, and that the Jewish people will never die. It also believes that each individual Jew, after he dies, receives some portion of the world to come, and that he will achieve eternal life through the resurrection of the dead.

These Jews despise the joys of life and revere the Bible, in which there is to be found a people who were opposed to asceticism and who absorbed life with all their senses. They regard themselves as a chosen people, and they live worse than dogs; they believe in an eternal life after death, and yet it is a sufficient ideal to them to see marriage as only for making children, and to prepare to be buried with a bit of earth from the Land of Israel and a patch of linen on their shroud. They dream of an eternal life and their worries begin and end with the problems of family and of making a living. "The Eternal People" in Mendele's world who live by plucking chicken feathers and furnishing holy items for the Jewish religious institutions of Glupsk, die three times a day from hunger. They barely survive until the arrival upon the scene of some wealthy gentile from whom they can earn a bit of change. The stomach cannot be satisfied solely upon the collective memory of an eternal people. These anchorites have not yet even departed for the desert, but their frail bodies have already arrived at the firm resolve that they will separate themselves from the sinful world at some later date, if possible. But even when thus cast off from the world, his senses dormant and dust-covered, the anchorite remains a living intelligence, which continues to search and dig for meanings. And since it is still of some use to maintain the body, only one way of doing so remains: by sharpening the mind to such an extent that it can fashion satisfactions for itself that no stranger could ever take away, even with the utmost guile.

This poverty, separateness, contempt for the simple pleasures of life, this certainty of survival for all eternity, this mixture of repressed senses and sharp mind—all these factors have brought about a Jewish community that lives in a constant state of war with itself and with its feelings, running into contradictions at every step and hence presenting to the world at large the image of a people who harbor a profound and unique disharmony. But long before the world began to perceive this, the Jew, with his sharp intelligence, had sensed it himself. He then realized there were only two ways of expressing himself. If his senses had still been fresh, he could have tried, in his bitter disillusionment, to make something better of his life, to break out of his cage and create an ideal for which to fight. But among his atrophied senses there remained vivid only the sixth one: an overly sharp intelligence which tended to laugh and jeer at the contradictions of the life he was leading. And so a mood of waggishness and of jeering laughter took hold of the Jewish folk spirit. For critics of Jewish life, Sheyke Feffer and Mottke Habad were no less Jewish heroes than were the poets of the Enlightenment.

A sharply critical intelligence that hangs suspended over a dead body feels the agonies of life as though in a dream; they pass through the dust-covered senses and reach the mind like some distant flicker of lightning without thunder. This, however, is not the case for women and children, who experience the sad and happy events of life with less critical intelligence but with more passion than the men; they are not so good at making jokes or understanding witty turns of phrase. A yeshiva student sitting by a stove, who keeps his body nourished with a bit of herring now and then, is better at mocking life than a wealthy man or busy merchant. It is only old men, or long-oppressed peoples, or those who have been rejected by life and have suffered from a weakening of their natural senses, who turn to joking and making fun of even the most sacred and most terrible things. In Jewish wit one can hear the voice of self-contempt, of a people who have lost touch with the ebb and flow of life. In Jewish mockery one can hear the utter nihilism of a man who has never known the good things of life, the sick despair of a people whose existence has become an endless array of contradictions, a permanent witticism.

Even before Mendele Mokher Sforim presents as a gift to the Jewish people his story *Dos vintchfingerl*, he laughs at it and cries out in his preface: "Mazl-tov, mazl-tov to you, Jews of Kabtsansk." Every preface he wrote is soaked in Jewish wit, an air of mockery hangs over all his work. Mendele walked through the Jewish community with open eyes that saw in the smallest act of each individual the foolish contradictions of the Jewish spirit. The mere fact that he himself went about on beautiful summer days, through splendid fields of wheat, bearded and wearing a prayer-shawl and phylacteries, fasting all day and staring thus upon God's lovely world; the mere fact that God's lovely world is reflected in a soul so outwardly besmirched as Mendele's—this shows that the thousand contradictions in the life of his Jew are manifested in every move he makes.

We have seen what are the sources of the principal flaws in Mendele's work, and we have seen how these flaws were transmuted by him—perhaps the sole great talent of the Jewish Enlightenment— into a means of penetrating into the spirit of his time and his people. The disguised *maskil* does not emerge unscathed in Mendele's writings: in *Di Kliatche* he laughed at this figure and showed how narrow his life really was. But Mendele was not prepared to set forth a new teaching, a new ideal. He was, after all, born into a narrow world, and without a powerful voice.

We have also seen how this student of writers of elegant but empty Hebrew prose polished and ennobled our mother-tongue, and thereby became the creator of modern Yiddish. And we have seen how the artist Mendele Mokher Sforim, who in other times would probably have settled for simply describing individual characters and types, became instead the poet of the Jewish community of his day.

Finally, we have tried to show the hidden sources from which Mendele drew his icy wit, the quality in him that often repels men of natural feelings. In this wit, which is also called satire, the tragic contradictions of Jewish life are clearly reflected. In Mendele's satire one can hear a cold despair and the downtrodden spirit of a people whose natural feelings have atrophied.

Mendele's work is one of the few means of access we have into the soul of the Jewish masses. Those who argue that Mendele is passé because he describes a world that is now gone, the dead Judaism of another day, are right only as long as they seek in the artist someone who can awaken national ideals. But if they want to penetrate into the depths of the old Jewish ghetto soul—which had had a significant influence upon the life of the Jewish people to this day—and are seeking the artist who has captured it through a poetic vision, they must turn to Mendele Mokher Sforim, and most of all to *Fishke der Krumer* ("Fishke the Lame") and *Dos vintchfingerl*, the first great works of Yiddish literature.

1902

The Humor of Sholom Aleichem

by Shmuel Niger

Translated by Ruth Wisse

The strength of Samson lay in his hair. There are writers whose greatness is similarly concentrated. Sholom Aleichem is one of these: his strength lies in his humor.

The humorist is not satisfied with the world, but he knows that his dissatisfaction is no more than a part of the world with which he is dissatisfied. The humorist is a child of the pessimist, but a smiling child who can smoothe out the wrinkles on the troubled face of his father. He tells him: "You take the world too seriously. You believe in it, and demand from it more than it has to offer. Look at these trifles from a distance—from the proper distance that makes everything look insignificant—and you'll see that there is more cause for laughter than for tears. You are justified in your displeasure with the world, but even greater than justice is compassion. You are pessimistic because you are too much of an optimist. You think that the world deserves to be punished, whereas it deserves no more than forgiveness . . ." So concludes the consistent and therefore happy pessimist, laughing because he has made himself foolish in trying to make someone wiser. He laughs because he forgives his own foolish deeds as readily as those of another . . .

Forgiveness is both the bitterest root and the sweetest fruit of humor.

The most valuable, most human trait of Tevye the Dairyman, one of Sholom Aleichem's most wonderful characters, is precisely the ability of this common man to understand and forgive everything. To understand and forgive is a virtue of philosophers. And in every authentic humorist there is also something of the philosopher. Tevye

the Dairyman is a philosopher, though of the heart, not the head,
which is even better.

Though his head is the head of an ignorant and not overly sophisticated village Jew, he has the splendid philosophical ability to
turn everything inside out, so as to discover the standpoint from
which everything may be justified.

He tells, for example, of a conversation with his daughter,
Tsaytl, about Lazar Wolf, the wealthy widower whose offer of marriage she is unwilling to accept: "So, my daughter, you weren't
meant to fall into the lap of luxury and become mistress of a rich
household, and we weren't meant to see a little happiness in our old
age after all these years of work, I said, harnessed to the wheelbarrow day and night, knowing not a minute's peace, only poverty and
misery and bad luck everywhere you turn . . ." He speaks to her
softly, tenderly, and with his usual sympathy, but it almost seems as
though he is offended and on the point of anger. Yet when he hears
Tsaytl's tearful plea: "Papa, I'll hire myself out as a maid, I'll carry
clay, I'll dig ditches"; when he hears this outburst of his daughter's,
he understands *her* feelings too. A deeply human, fatherly compassion can be heard as he continues his story: "Why are you crying,
silly girl, I said to her. Am I blaming you, silly child? Am I com-
plaining about you? It's just that when things are bitter and gloomy
I like to get them off my chest and have a talk with the Lord of the
Universe about his treatment of me. I tell Him He's a Merciful Father, who takes pity on me and lords it over me—may He not punish
me for my words—He gives me all the joys that a father may expect,
and go complain to the wall! So it is, and so it probably has to be.
He is up there on high, and we are down here on the ground, deep,
deep in the ground. We might as well admit that He is right and His
Judgment is right, because if you want to look at it the other way
around, aren't I a silly fool? Why am I shouting? Why am I raising
a fuss? Who am I, but a tiny worm crawling around on earth? The
slightest wind, if God wished it, could put an end to me in one blink
of the eye. Who am I in my ignorance to give Him advice on how to
run His world? If He wants it this way, it probably ought to be this
way. Anyway, what good does it do to complain?"

In this delicate but penetrating irony of Tevye's, when the
philosopher in him suddenly speaks out, we recognize not the pious
but the knowing Jew, not the man of faith but the cheerful pessimist
who knows that you can find an answer for everything if you want
to, or no answer to anything if you want not to, so that it is better to
pose no questions and admit no complaints against the Lord. "Anyway, what good does it do to complain?" Just be sure not to wallow

like a fool in your own resentment; don't take it too seriously—
which can be avoided if you set your own sufferings and joys before
a higher authority than usual, and place yourself in the hands of
fate, not because you doubt your own powers but because you set
yourself above them.

The exceptional delicacy and complexity of feeling in Tevye—
who is, after all, a simple, ordinary Jew—derive from his hidden
store of humor, thanks to which he can transcend the pressure of
immediate influences and surrender to life on terms that are not
forced or slavish, but liberating. His liberating attitude of "taking it
as it comes" creates a cloak of peace, tolerance, and submissiveness
in which Tevye envelops his behavior, and which extends to his
relations with other people.

At one point he is approached by Motl Kamzoyl, a young tailor
from Anatevke. After a lengthy chat, filled with various insinuations,
the tailor speaks out bluntly: "The story of the matter is as follows:
your daughter Tsaytl and I gave each other our pledge over a year
ago that we would get married." Tevye is angry, and even later,
when he lets himself be won over, he still resents the outrage: "How
could they give each other their pledge? What is the world coming
to?" ". . . But when I looked at Motl, standing there with his head
bowed like a sinner, perfectly serious, not wanting to take advantage
of anyone, I reconsidered: If we look at it the other way around,
what am I making such a fuss about? Who am I to put on airs?"
And after considering it *the other way around,* everything seems
right. Motl Kamzoyl now appears to be "quite a fine young man, a
workingman who would provide for his wife, and an honest lad
besides. So what do I have against him?—Tevye, I say to myself,
don't make any lame excuses, and just give your blessing, as it says
in the prayer, 'I have forgiven according to thy word'.—So, con-
gratulations!'"

This is Tevye's way of translating the sacred texts, and of "looking at things the other way around." He would be the unhappiest
man in the world if he lacked this ability to smile down calmly on
his own bitter fate; he would be another Job cursing the day of his
birth were he not able to combine, as Ecclesiastes does, the ancient
"vanity of vanities" with the later, wiser, and more pious verse,
"Fear God, and keep his commandments."

"Whatever God ordains, His ways are best"—in this pious tone
of "God giveth, God taketh," Tevye begins the sad story of his
daughter Chava. But he immediately deepens the naive, common-
prayerbook tone and says, "That is to say, His ways have to be best,
because just try to be clever and improve on them! I tried to be

smart, I tried twisting the verse this way and that, but when I saw
it was of no use, I took my hand off my chest and said to myself:
'Tevye, you're a fool! You won't change the world. God has given
us "the pain of bringing up children" which means, children will
bring you trouble, but you had better make the best of it.'"

It is a mistake to think that the diaspora-Jew speaks through
Tevye's mouth, or the *nebbish,* the humble man, the character
whose formula is "this-too-is-for-the-best." Not at all. Tevye's
healthy human instincts have been neither dulled nor weakened. He
knows what is good in this world, and feels very keenly the misery
of life. But since he cannot control it from the outside, he uses
humor to sweeten it from the inside. Only in this delicate humor-
ously-sarcastic sense does he put up with the "world as it is." Only
after conquering it from within does he submit to it outwardly.

Here, for example, he is stopped on the road by his daughter,
Chava, who has run off with Khvedke, a gentile writer from the
local village. She wants to speak to Tevye, and a terrible inner struggle begins between the devout Jew and the devoted father. The insulted pride and stubborn determination of the God-fearing Jew
gain ascendency for a minute, and Tevye drives his horse with wild
vehemence, fleeing from his own flesh and blood. All the while we
feel that "Tevye is not a woman," as might sometimes appear, but a
man of firm character who, when occasion demands, can be stronger
than iron. Yet a moment later something occurs to him: "Tevye!
You're taking too much on yourself! What harm would it do to stop
for a while and listen to what she has to say? Maybe—who knows—
maybe she is sorry, and wants to return? Maybe he has buried her
six feet under and she needs your help to escape from hell? Maybe
and maybe and a lot more maybes fly through my head, and I imagine her as a child and remember the passage—'As a father is merciful to his children'—to a father there is no bad child; I torment
myself and accuse myself of being merciless and not worth the
ground I walk on. What is at issue? What are you stewing about,
you stubborn fool? What are you raising such a fuss over? Turn your
wagon around, you brute, and make your peace with her. She is
your child, not someone else's."

So Tevye argues with himself, wavering in his emotions, deeply
moved, but not altogether ruled by them—neither their victor nor
their victim. Even as his smile wrinkles into a deep crease of tragedy, he is illumined by the soft, elegiac shimmer of divinely inspired
humor . . .

Although he is beset by one disaster after another we don't insult him with our small feelings of pity because we see that his trou-

bles do not oppress or discourage him, but merely deepen his humanity.

Tevye has been seen by many as a representative of the old-fashioned, small-town Jewish masses; only the Jew in him was recognized. It seems to me, however, that precisely in the depiction of this simple villager Sholom Aleichem has also transcended that which is specifically Jewish. Tevye does have certain typical Jewish traits and mannerisms, including the characteristic Jewish ability to laugh out of one side of his mouth. Yet he also embodies something appreciably richer and fresher than the cold, angry, embittered Jewish irony, and he stands ten heads taller than the average ordinary small-town Jew.

If you see in this an idealization of Tevye, you must bear in mind that Sholom Aleichem himself idealized Tevye. He treats him quite differently from the other Kasrilevkites. Most of the men and women who people his stories are comic characters, objects of laughter, but Tevye is humorous. Sholom Aleichem stoops to the other characters in describing them, but Tevye he raises to his own level. He endows him with his own most beautiful talent—the ability to laugh. . . .

I have called Tevye Sholom Aleichem's beloved hero. I might have said his *most beloved hero*. Sholom Aleichem was not unfond of the other heroes of his novels, like Stempenyu, Yosele Solovey, Rafalesco of *Wandering Stars*. But whereas his love for them is of the "heroic" kind, his love for Tevye could be called simply "human." The above-mentioned and other romanticized heroes of Sholom Aleichem's works overshadow those around them because they are novelistic heroes—heroes by profession. God has blessed them with exceptional virtues and talents: one is a magnificent violinist, another a famous singer, the third an inspired actor. But Tevye is an everyday Jew, a common woodcarter, a simple villager. Thanks only to Sholom Aleichem's pen did Tevye become Tevye. When the heroes of the romances set out on their great adventures, when they soar to great heights and "speak poetry," it is no wonder; but Tevye had to be instructed by the author in what to say and what to think when he is alone with nature, or alone with himself. To Tevye the Dairyman the author entrusted his own role, the role of humorous story-teller, psychologist, portraitist, jokester, master of language—in short, the role of the writer. Consequently *Tevye the Dairyman* is not only the most moving and most likeable, but also the most intimate of Sholom Aleichem's books.

Tevye may have no match among the adults in Sholom Aleichem's cast of characters, but the children of Kasrilevke are por-

trayed with an equal measure of love and poetic tenderness. Like
that great child, Tevye, the small children are poignant but never
funny. And there is something else to be noted about them: Tevye,
after all, is not utterly unique in Yiddish literature. No matter how
refined his stories may be through humor, they are still sad, mourn-
ful stories; and sadness is the dominant mood of all Yiddish literature before Sholom Aleichem. Besides, if we really wanted to
quibble, we could find several familiar traits in Tevye reminiscent of
our old friend, Reb Mendele Mokher Sforim. With the children's
stories, however, Sholom Aleichem brought an entirely new atmosphere into Yiddish fiction.

Who knows if we adults have not done an injustice by taking
Sholom Aleichem away from the children? Who knows if he should
not have written for them and no one else:

-*Pay attention, children, and I'll tell you a story about a pen-
knife; not an imaginary story but a real story that actually happened to me. . . .*

or:

-*Today, children, I'll play something for you on the fiddle.
I don't think there is anything better or more beautiful than
to be able to play the fiddle. . . .*

or:

-*Children, guess which holiday is the best holiday of all?
Hanukka! . . .*

or:

-*Let me tell you a story about a flag. . . .*

You have to have something of the child in you to be able to
speak with children so simply and directly. You must still feel the
boy in yourself in order to sense the profound difference between
him and the adult Jew who has already taken upon himself the
burden of the diaspora, the burdens of Torah and *mitzvas*, the pain
of raising children and the worries of making a living; you must still
keenly feel the boy you were to be able to set him up as a protest
against the adult diaspora-Jew.

-*Why do you keep turning around like a corkscrew?—says my
father as we all walk together to grandfather Meir's Purim feast,
and I catch sight of the gang of masqueraders in the distance.*

-*You're a grown boy already, praise God, can't you walk a
little faster,—says my mother,—God willing, on the Sabbath
before Passover you'll be eight years old, may you live to be a
hundred and twenty.*

-Go on, go on!—Says my teacher, Reb Itzi, my angel of death, poking me from behind. . . .

Thus the old fashioned Jew trains his *eight-year-old* son, wanting to "make a man," that is, a little old Jew, out of him. But the little old Jew is not at all pleased at the prospect. He lowers his eyes to the mud on the ground, and keeps pace with the others, engrossed in miserable and gloomy thoughts: "Always with the grown-ups! Always with my teacher! . . . Morning, evening, Sabbath, and holidays! With Reb Itzi's big red tobacco nose, may it sink into the ground!" He isn't permitted to visit "the gang, King Ahasuerus—otherwise known as Kopel the Tailor wearing a golden crown." But the temptation is too great: when his childish heart, accustomed to yielding, can bear it no longer, he finally steals away from his grandfather's house and goes to join the masqueraders. He simply mounts a rebellion against the strict, boring regimen of the grown-ups. Nor is this the only rebellion.

"May my father in the world beyond forgive me," another of Sholom Aleichem's young boys tells us, "I could never understand what sort of a man he was. According to my mother he used to either study or pray all day long. In the first place, wasn't he ever tempted, as I am, to go outside on a summer morning before the sun is too strong, when it first begins to climb the sky? . . . What flavor can ordinary weekday prayers have on a glorious morning like that, can you tell me? Or sitting and studying in a dingy little room afterwards? . . ." The son cannot capture the feeling of his father's studying and praying because he lives in another world, without crowding or dinginess, without diaspora and its heavy burden, without Jew and gentile. When cheder boys fight with the gentile boys (as in the story, *Lag b'Omer*) it is only because the others, the gentiles, are "The Philistines," so they, "the Israelites," are obliged to wage war against them. How could it be otherwise? But elsewhere, Feitl plays very amicably with Fedka, and when spring comes they break out together into "God's great world, and taking each other by the hand they race towards the hill that beckons to them both: 'Come here, children!' They leap towards the sun that sends its greeting down to both: 'Come here, children!' And when they grow tired of running, they sit down on God's earth that knows no distinction between Jew and gentile, 'Come here, children, here to me!'" (*A Country Passover*). Let their fathers and mothers back there invent lies, blood libels, about one another; let them tremble in fear of one another; what does it have to do with them? The children, not having tasted the poisoned apples of the tree of knowledge, remain pure and healthy, as in the Garden of Eden. And if we grown-ups *are* poisoned by that knowledge, should we not desire at least the heart to feel and the eye to see again the innocence of children?

Sholom Aleichem is capable of childlike feeling and insight. When a gloomy Lithuanian rationalist, the nineteenth century writer, Moishe-Aaron Shatskes, described the Jewish Pre-Passover, he made of it a real tragedy, from which may Heaven preserve us! Whereas in Sholom Aleichem it appears as the "Pre-Passover Emigration," one of his merriest, happiest stories. Why? Again, because the enlightened Shatskes, the unbeliever, ultimately looked at the world with the uneasy, weary, preoccupied, and argued-out eyes of the study-house-and-tenant-Jews, of the marketplace-and-kitchen women with their angry, haggard, overworked faces. He shared their attitudes, except that he was more critical. But Sholom Aleichem saw not only the father, the gloomy Jew who is angry at the forced emigration from alcove to kitchen and from kitchen to cellar and from cellar to attic, not only the mother, the Jewish housewife, frightfully absorbed in cleaning and preparing for Passover—he saw also the child, the schoolboy, the mischief-maker, for whom the pre-Passover migration is a great festivity, a real holiday.

As he says, "I would favor having Passover every week so that every week I could crawl up to the attic. First of all, the climb itself is an event. At any other time, even if I got down on my knees, would they let me climb up to the attic? And here I'm able to march up the steps, bold as you please. Down below my father follows my progress, and says, 'Slowly, take your time.' Why slowly? Why take my time? I feel as though I've sprouted wings, and can fly, fly!" A moment later, when he has an accident, and flies toward the attic door and . . . "goes crashing head first down all the steps," the fall is not ominous either! "As you can see," he tells us, "I'm fine and well. May I never be any worse—except for this scar on my face [he concludes in Tevye's, or Sholom Aleichem's style] and some short-windedness that dates back from then, and this blinking of the eyes whenever I speak . . ." You can't help laughing when you read it, though the passage is quite sad. You feel that the Jew telling the story, were he still a boy, would go climbing up to the attic again, still marveling at his father who considers it a chore. Children pass so quickly from tears to laughter!

How precious a gift is this childish laughter for us chronic groaners. Not surprisingly it is Sholom Aleichem and no other who brings us this precious gift. The humorist and the child have one great virtue in common: their innermost carefreeness. The child *does not know* about life's cares, the humorist chooses to ignore them. That is why they understand each other so well, and why all humorists are writers for children.

It is interesting that with the exception of Tevye, Sholom Aleichem endowed only one of his other major characters with a humorous approach to life—Motl, Peysi the Cantor's Son.

In the book by that name, subtitled, "Writings of an Orphan," most of the characters are comic or tragi-comic. Only Motl is humorous; only he looks down upon the others with a gentle smile that suggests either simple childish innocence or a deep but rarified pain; he alone is set apart, at a slight distance from the others. We feel pity for the Kasrilevkites whose pain and suffering is described in these writings, but we feel nothing more than pity. Though Motl endures as much, if not more, than the others, we do not pity him at all. We love him. We love him because he doesn't need our help. In fact, with his bright and comforting smile, he may be able to help us in *our* need. His superb, calm humor enables him to tell us of many indescribable migrations, anxieties, and hardships, all in the tone of an idyll.

When Motl grows up he will become a Tevye. There is already something of Tevye in his nature, but for the time being he is still a boy, so his natural humor is not as overcast as that of Tevye, who is the father of children, with all the problems of raising them. Motl's humor is as yet much more innocent, pure, and bright than that of his close relative, Tevye. "I don't know," he says, "why mother cries so much over the children. The children seem very happy! When their mother begins to talk nonsense, they laugh aloud." And like all children, he too can laugh, not merely smile, as Tevye does.

Were we to ask ourselves whether Sholom Aleichem himself stood closer to Tevye or to Motl, we would say, to the latter. Like Motl, Sholom Aleichem cannot be satisfied with the tragic. Like Motl, he loves to laugh, simply and effortlessly. "Laughter is healthy; doctors prescribe laughter" is the motto of his writing.

The God of Laughter who reveals himself in H. D. Nomberg's Yiddish legend had two faces: one that laughed, and the other that grieved. There is of course a grieving face in Sholom Aleichem too, but it is hidden. Only the face that laughs and inspires laughter is revealed. Other writers have been able to tell happy tales; but no one else would take sad, often tiresome stories, and tell them for our pleasure, so that in our delight we might forget what is really going on, and like a child, ask no questions. Though his stories about Jewish life are almost always sad, they evoke not a sigh but a smile, and often a hearty laugh. He is always able to add something to the narrative that will ease our pain or dull it, or something to hide it from us so that we can forget. We thank Sholom Aleichem not because he awakens new ideas but to the contrary, because he is able for a moment to banish the thoughts that disturb our peace. We thank him for making the child his reader, but also for teaching his reader again to be a child.

1926

Peretz and the Jewish Nineteenth Century

(Fragments from a Larger Study)

by Jacob Glatstein

Translated by Ronald Sanders

I

Among our principal writers Peretz is the most conscious stylist. In "The Magician," one of his folklorist tales, he takes a familiar story about Elijah the Prophet and reworks it in a manner that bears close examination, for it provides a key to his unique qualities.

The story is told more in the manner of colloquial speech than of formal narrative. No sooner are the protagonists sketched in than the couple, Chaim Yone and Rivke-Beyle, become involved in a pantomime dance with the magician. They perform dramatic sketches in stylized movements, after the fashion of Vakhtangov's rendition of *The Dybbuk* (if one may be permitted so anachronistic an example). Hardly a word passes among them, as the strange, emaciated figure of the magician dances between the hungry and embarrassed couple. This naive flesh-and-bones story, which secretes nothing beyond its simple moral that the good Lord helps those who have faith, can still be read with great pleasure today, because Peretz depicted its remarkable pantomime with a rare artistic consciousness. The husband, the wife and the magician represent various Hasidic attitudes in their dance. Peretz has captured a *moment musical* of poverty.

I do not know whether Peretz is our greatest artist, but he is certainly our most durable artist, one who will live as long as Yiddish literature lives. His work will not require close reading and explication, nor will it need a mass of footnotes explaining a different way of life. Peretz's name will be immortal because he grasped Jewish life in its unchanging fundamentals.

His memoirs give evidence of the fact that this artist who could treat the Yiddish language as though it had just been born, as though it had barely yet been noticed and was just opening its mouth to utter its first words (to make a blessing, of course), could also use it as a language of the intellect. There is nothing soggy or sentimental about his vocabulary; his words can not only be heard and seen, they can also be used as tools for thinking. Sholom Aleichem's vocabulary can be savored by reading aloud and laughing over it; Mendele Mokher Sforim's vocabulary calls for scholarly research; but with Peretz's vocabulary you could think. And not only is one able to think with Peretz's Yiddish, one can also think swiftly and ingeniously. In Peretz's prose a word is a short cut to larger ideas, and between the words lurk the nuances of a highly cultivated mind. He never offends his readers by spelling out every point for them in great detail; he talks to a reader who can play along with him, who has the power quickly to grasp an idea and understand the nuance of a word.

Though he began writing in Yiddish out of pity for the starving Jewish masses, though he purposely chose to be a popularizer and educator who rolled up his sleeves and wrote scientific treatises under the name of Dr. Shtitser [Dr. Supporter], Peretz speaks to his readers as an equal and spares them nothing. And if this cultivated audience proves merely to be the product of his own wishful thinking, it reflects the optimism of an artist with a deep faith in the resonance of Yiddish.

For Peretz, to live is to think, to write is to think, and Jewish life means Jewish thought. The entire *oeuvre* of this Jewish thinker is a unified conception of the Jewish past, the Jewish present, and the ever-approaching Jewish future. Later writers will never need to be embarrassed by this father of modern Jewish literature. People will be proud to bring this rare man into the salons of the brightest society and say: we are his descendants.

Peretz can be read with the same fresh delight today as fifty years ago, because he was able to preserve the past with all of its piquancy. This folk-teacher, who educated his people as he told them stories, never treated them as mere raw beginners; he placed upon them the burden of crossing the bridge that he himself had spanned towards the future. He demanded of them that they catch every glimmer of an idea.

Peretz's Europeanisms of diction are not charming or coquettish little quirks, but a necessity, as we can see today, that sprang out of the very nature of his thought. When he employs such an expression as *grayzike topografye* ("faulty topography"), this is not some blemish resulting from an overdose of learning, but the best and most exact thing he could say. His imagery was original, and consequently it is still a pleasure to come across such an expression as *fargesenish-vasserl* ("water of oblivion"), or to read that a *vasser-shmeykhl* ("water-smile") floated at the bottom of a well into which he had nearly fallen. One has to look for a long time before finding a banal turn of phrase in Peretz. Indeed, his sedulous avoidance of banality was often at the expense of content. This was the case with him despite the fact that he lived at a time when Yiddish folk-poetry was still alive, and when Jewish sadness and Jewish laughter came in readily available stylistic forms. Many an eminent Jewish artist employed these established forms when he had material that was susceptible to them. But Peretz was never willing merely to use established forms. The author of folklorist tales, he naturally sought out the folk, but as one seeking to gain the refined folk-ear. Sholom Aleichem listened to the folk-voice, but Peretz cultivated the folk-ear and demonstrated that thoughts expressed in Yiddish can harbor a rhythm unique to that language.

II

Peretz came forth not merely as a creative artist, but as creator of a world that had not existed before his arrival. *From the outset, his task was that of creating single-handed a Jewish nineteenth century.* Perhaps this will sound paradoxical, but the fact is that, since the advent of the general calendar, Jews have not had centuries of their own; rather, they have been victims of alien calendars marking off alien centuries. With the possible exception of the Golden Age in Spain, Jews have not carried the centuries on their shoulders as equal partners with other peoples. For them, every century was a thousand-year nightmare, with its own terrifying joys and sorrows.

The nineteenth century, in its feverish preparation for the twentieth, was the ultimate point of inquietude and restless seeking in the history of human civilization. It saw a great hunger of the spirit, and a degree of human daring that challenged the very heavens. The century sang and blasphemed, steeped itself in belief, inquired, refuted, and then inquired again into the answers. It came with a deepening social conscience, a shaping of great problems. It rushed to a climax, driven by a powerful impetus toward the twentieth century, which it thought would be the millennium. The nineteenth century was to be a visionary preparation for the redemption of man, for the apotheosis of the human spirit, the embodiment of spirit and the spiritualization of body, the marvelous synthesis of man and God.

Thus spoke the nineteenth century through its poets, painters, sculptors and men of the spirit: Tolstoy, Dostoevsky, Rodin, Karl Marx, Heine, Debussy, Zola, Cézanne, Zamenhof, and Edison. And Theodor Herzl, too, was a product of the worldly nineteenth century, pursuing a vision of rescuing the Jews from a century that seemed in no way related to them. The nineteenth century brought with it a great examination of the conscience, a re-evaluation of values and a broadening of mankind's scope so that it would be capable of striding forward in common into the era of universal good.

Only the Jews had no nineteenth century. The fever and electricity of that agitated century had not yet begun to spread through Jewish life. Even the more worldly Jews, who had already added to the Jewish date one from the gentile calendar, did not really live spiritually in that century. To be sure, there were those who had stepped out into the world and closed the door of Jewish life behind them, entering into the general march of the time; but they had entered it as strangers, and soon they were devoured by the alien world. Deep down, Jewish life had not yet shaken out of its long slumber—at least not until Peretz consciously set out to create *a Jewish nineteenth century* shortly before the century was over. In Yiddish he reconstituted its general inquietude and fever, its mass of problems. And in that consists his strength and achievement, for Peretz brought us into the marching ranks of the world as conscious Jews. He joined us to the great ebb and flow of the world at large. Creating a whole Jewish century, he wove it into the cultural history of the world.

By the close of the nineteenth century Peretz had begun to write his Hasidic and folklorist tales. These were the dome and the cornices of the enormous structure he erected in the course of a few years. Peretz brought consolation to a lost generation, a generation that did not by itself have the strength to transform itself in the terms of the century that stormed and thundered around it. He, the father of modern Yiddish literature, was able to take hold of that generation in the midst of its lonely wanderings and give it national aspirations. This defining of national aspirations was a subtle process, making its appearance only gradually. But the strength of Peretz's commanding personality enabled him to impose that process of definition upon his generation, which now could suddenly find the outer world reflected within itself.

In evaluating Peretz's work for its place not only in Yiddish literature but in Jewish life, one cannot help but use grandiose terms. *He placed the inner nature of the Jewish spirit upon the world-calendar of the nineteenth century, he unearthed the finest Jewish treasures and illuminated them with the first electric light.* He was also one of the first Yiddish writers to win the confidence of the Jewish student youth, who obtained from Peretz a key to the understanding of themselves, and thereby began to perceive that a thirst for education did not necessarily mean a flight from oneself but could rather be a means of entry into the world through one's self and back to one's self. Peretz was thus the first Yiddish writer to deliver a powerful blow against assimilation and make it stand with bowed head before the Jewish past. For he showed that our past can enrich our life in the modern world, and that the nineteenth century, with all its troubles, problems, speculations, and guests, lies deeply within us. He discerned the outlines of a new kind of Jew, proud and the bearer of a freshly created language. To that language he gave the tone, the color, and the nuance of the nineteenth century mind. And to the Jewish worker he gave a pedigree, enabling him to stride into the era of one for all and all for one.

It would therefore not be an exaggeration to say that Peretz, as European Jew, was the Maimonides of the nineteenth century. Maimonides, our great medieval codifier, perceived in his own day that foreign ways of thought would have swallowed us up completely had we not adapted them to our own spiritual heritage. He therefore grabbed hold of Aristotelianism and harnessed it to normative Judaism. He was the great harmonizer of the worldliness of that epoch with Judaism, and he quite boldly introduced order into the disarray of the Jewish conception of the world. Maimonides demonstrated that the Torah was in fact the ethic that Aristotle had been seeking. In this way he renewed and updated all of Jewish thought, and rearranged it with such wisdom that there was no longer any need to look outside it, because the outside was now within ourselves.

Maimonides was above all a worldly man, but he spoke with the authority of one who, despite his worldliness, had not cut himself off from the Jewish tradition. He merely brought to light the innate rationality of the Jewish tradition and gave it method and system. Aristotelianism was reflected everywhere in the Middle Ages, but Maimonides brought to it the refinement of a thinker steeped in Jewish life.

Equipped with an all-encompassing "Aristotelianism" of the nineteenth century—if I may be permitted this extension of the meaning of the term—Peretz also turned to Jewish life and its spiritual treasures. He did this as a man of the highest moral concerns, as a man of logic and as a poet of the spirit. A *maskil*, a son of the Enlightenment, he turned to a mocked and derided Hasidism and uncovered the timeless Jewish beauty and luminosity that lay within it. And he gave Jewish life wings, lifting it up high and saying: "For you there are no limits, no obstacles in the way of your spirit. Fly high, if not higher, to the unattainable." By giving method, system, and new depth and direction to a lost generation, he became the Maimonides of the Jewish nineteenth century as it was reconstructed within the fabric of his own imagination.

III

Peretz cast about in search of an audience for a long time, until he finally came to the conclusion that his ideal reader was someone so close to himself that he could not write any books for him until he had first tried them out on himself. He quickly perceived that his was too perturbed a spirit to satisfy itself merely with art. In both Mendele Mokher Sforim and Sholom Aleichem there was a faint touch of condescension, a tendency to talk down to the reader and give him an occasional derisive pat on the cheek. But Peretz sought, with unusual austerity, to give of all of himself straightforwardly, down to the very bone; what he sought was the essence, both of himself and of imagined hundreds and thousands of I.L. Peretzes. He was a point of equilibrium between the other two classic Yiddish writers. After Mendele's satire and Sholom Aleichem's humor, he came forth with a tragic vision—not in the sense of hopelessness, but of exaltedness. His reader, in the last analysis he himself, was no longer able to live by the bread of humor and satire alone. His reader, he himself, had become too perturbed to be satisfied merely with reading books. He sought, instead, a new orientation for Jewish life because he could not view that life with utter resignation.

He saw what was coming with great acuteness. Himself a Jew who had broken away from traditional Judaism, he sought within himself a solution to the problem of a great rupture in Jewish continuity. And as the prototype of all his readers, he strove to make a minimal Judaism into a maximum Judaism; this was what led him directly to Hasidism, which is, in its very essence, a minimal Judaism elevated to the most passionate faith.

This is not the place to dwell upon Peretz's creative process in the task he had assigned himself, that of taking upon his shoulders the burden of ensuring the immortality of Yiddish and Judaism, without a home country and faced by the growing danger of assimilation and alienation. We know that he did not succeed, but we also know that, as long as he lived, he strove to check the process of assimilation with all his strength. And we know that, some years after his death, people were still able to gain sustenance from his legacy and bring it to bear in the fight against the kind of alienation which sought to rationalize its removal from Jewishness with one summary question: what was the need of it all? Peretz created a spiritual bulwark strong enough to withstand even this kind of skepticism. As for the skeptic's son and grandson, now that they live in another country, the magic of Peretz's legacy—which had influenced two generations of worldly Jews—no longer works so well.

Peretz was our guide in the midst of a desperate struggle for cultural survival that is still being waged. That is why he could not come to Jewish life with the calmness of the artist who seeks his private vision of the world. Rather, he was a truly altruistic artist who sacrificed everything upon the altar of a great and consoling answer, in behalf of a generation that demanded an answer. And this is what drove him to the Hasidic tale, into which he sought to pour the essence of a lyrical Judaism—a melodious Judaism that would be able to sing by itself, without lips and without words, and yet would impart to the modern Jew the feeling that an old and joyous sort of Judaism is insinuating its song into his bones.

Not for nothing did Peretz dwell so much upon melody in his Hasidic tales. In "Between Two Mountains" the Bialer Rebbe's Hasidim toss at him "a beginning of a melody. They burst into song and continue on their way singing." In "The Teaching of Hasidism" the Nemirover Rebbe's son-in-law discusses Torah, but his lesson is about the enthusiasm of the Rebbe's singing and dancing. In "Cabbalists" the yeshiva student dies after a voiceless spiritual melody begins singing within him; he is called aloft to the court of the heavenly host "because a singer is missing there." In "A Conversation" between two Hasidim the secret of why the Haggada is intoned with a tragic melody is brought out. Peretz sought the melody of Judaism in its very essence, a melody that not only needed no words, no spoken Torah, but could dispense with song itself.

There is a tragic quality in these Hasidic tales, with their super-human effort to provide a lost generation with something more than literature—something like a new guide for the perplexed. But at least Peretz's companions in perplexity still stood near the basic sources of Judaism; for them, Peretz's marvelous tales were winged variants of an old greatness. The time is soon coming, however, when people will have to study these tales solely as literature, and not as the guide for the perplexed that they were to Peretz's generation; and when one thinks of them exclusively as literature, it is only then that one can perceive the intensity with which they were written and feel the breath of a great artist. I cannot imagine a single generation of Jewish readers, even in the most distant future, ever renouncing so great a legacy as Peretz's Hasidic tales. Yet even now, our own lost generation is beyond the point where it can achieve salvation through the melody of Peretz's Judaism. Even those among us who are perhaps still able to hear the song do not know how to pass it on to our children. Still, Peretz's Hasidic tales comprise a book that was meant for the ages and that remains immortal. And why immortal? Because in it Peretz sounded out the depths of our moral heritage, the poetry of our existence.

Every one of Peretz's Hasidic tales is a poem, written in a dramatic rhythm. Physical descriptions are at a minimum, for they would take away from the spiritualized atmosphere that gives life to the stories. The Torah, singing out from every story, is truly the melody of Judaism. All will be well at the advent of the day when people will really be able to live with the melody itself. The moral of each tale, which raises it to a height of universality, is always a deeply Jewish one. It is never a candy-coated message; it always calls for effort—for straightforward Jewish endeavor.

In Peretz's Hasidic tales we sense the common bond between individuals who in an alien world have become a people by virtue of their acts. This still applies to us today, for we too must learn how to live with a Judaism that has become diluted, and how to live by Jewish deeds—because it is not enough merely to see one's own reflection in the glow of the past and to settle for humming a melody from that past. A melody uprooted from its source is a reincarnation without redemption.

Where today are those poor and virtuous people who populate Peretz's Hasidic tales, and who perceive a great light during their course? These are not ragged cripples full of religious fanaticism, but simply poor people able to enjoy life amidst their poverty, who settle for their lot and are able even to rejoice, because they can bear the yoke of their Judaism more easily for not having been burdened with the cares that come with wealth and power. Where—among what alien people and language—can one find today those good women who found it sufficient wealth in life that their husbands were studying Torah, and who joyously brought them their repast each day in the house of study? Where today is that simple, unassuming love, that noble harmony of soul?

In his Hasidic tales Peretz sought to give the poetry of Judaism without the prose of Jewish existence, even though this meant changing the priorities of diction that came naturally to him. Indeed, one cannot live by the soul alone, stripped of the body; this is why the road Peretz marked out cannot provide an everlasting solution for us. Each generation must find its own kind of Judaism—and must do with the same passion as that with which Peretz sought and almost found it for his own.

Peretz was, in effect, the Reb Levi Yitzkhok[1] of the agnostics. Through his marvelous Hasidic tales, he sought to give the agnostic legitimacy and to preserve Jewish life for him. There is a story among Peretz's works called "Joy of Joys," which tells how Reb Levi Yitzkhok snatched from the afterworld all the bundles of sins that the devil had collected and threw them into the fire. The devil caught him by the hand and was going to take him to be an oven-keeper in Gehenna. Paradise offered an enormous ransom for him, but no matter how much Paradise would offer it was nothing at all alongside the treasures that the devil tossed onto the table along with his devilish crown. Until finally the Lord of the World was able to ransom Reb Levi Yitzkhok from bondage by giving in exchange for him—the whole world.

IV

The crisis of the nineteenth century; the ladder of holiness that learned men clamber upon only to be overtaken by the inarticulate; grotesque heresies suspended from cobwebs of doubt; social unrest and the prophetic surge towards equality—it is not that Peretz forced these problems into the terms of Jewish life, but that he derived them from those terms.

In his "Bridal Portion," Peretz not only lifted a pauper out of the rubbish heap, he even made him into a lord and a commander. Into the midst of the wealth, comfort, and privileged doubting of Reb Uzzer Hoffenstand enters Poverty in the form of a bent old Jew "with a white, wind-blown beard that was tangled up in the threads of his worn-out old gaberdine, and with a pale face under a shabby cap."

Poverty himself has entered, Peretz tells us in an aside.

And how does Jewish-Hasidic Poverty make his entrance before Reb Uzzer Hoffenstand?

"Shalom Aleichem, Mendel," the millionaire says to him. "Aleichem Shalom, Uzzer," answers Mendel-Poverty.

The truth is, that Uzzer wraps his hand in a napkin before

[1] Levi Yitzkhok of Berdichev (ca. 1740–1809), Hasidic rebbe, noted for his elevation of the common man over the scholar and his preference for faith over learning.

extending it in greeting to Poverty, but Poverty is not at all taken aback at this bent for hygiene on the part of a fastidious rich man. He is not embarrassed in the slightest; rather, he goes right on to request—to demand even—a drop of brandy and a bite to eat. The two classes have met, and the poor is not at all fazed by the rich. In his *Memoirs* Peretz says somewhere that darkness is "only the lack of light." So also is the poverty of Mendel-Poverty only a "lack" of wealth; but for this small variation, it is, like wealth, a positive thing, and one that Mendel wears with great dignity. To Uzzer God has given riches, and to Mendel he has given poverty in abundance, and both men readily accept the burden of their respective legacies. It is not within Mendel's powers to meddle in God's ways of apportionment. How can he and why should he have the audacity to offer God an opinion in the matter? But there is one thing Mendel is sure of—that Uzzer owes him a dowry for his daughter. This is not strictly a matter of begging; he brandishes a Jewish bill of exchange in front of Uzzer and Uzzer feels that the note is sound.

But when Uzzer—Reb Uzzer, rather—is about to give a twenty-five and Mendel says "Don't make me laugh", the rich man begins to haggle. He knows quite well that he owes a debt, but he thinks he can bring the amount down a little, and he appeals to Poverty's sense of justice.

"All of it from me, then? . . . Why don't you also go to Berlin, to Chaim?"

But Mendel does not let himself be fooled. He is fully aware of what the rich man's obligations are.

"Please," he says, "what do you want from my life? Do you think I have the strength left for all those stony streets and stairs? I am an old man, I'm suffering from asthma—and you want me to go. You go! Or give me what's coming to me. I've given everything I ever had in the form of worries."

Poor Mendel is called a pauper, but he is thoroughly familiar with the rules of Jewish charity; he may stand far below the heights of glory, but the crown of humanity has not been taken from him. He enters like a king demanding what is his rightful due. He even takes over Uzzer's house—and Uzzer's couch; he washes his hands of him and he washes himself for dinner, then he sleeps a peaceful sleep. But Uzzer does not lose his patience and throw Mendel out— on the contrary, he does feel indebted to him because he feels that he himself has had abundance showered upon him by God, and that he has been given many things only in trust.

Two Jews have encountered one another as equals, and what is this equal to? The new proletarian implications of Hasidism. And

who is it that perceived this and gave the situation artistic embel-
lishment? The father of modern Yiddish literature, the man who
gave dramatic form to the whole body of Jewish folk tales and
found Jewish wisdom in every Hasidic tale.

v

With all the strength of his artistic personality, Peretz sought the
ideal of artistic anonymity in his folkloric tales. He wanted, as it
were, to give these tales back to the people, but in the process of
giving them back the words took on wings. Stripping the text to
what seemed a primitive simplicity, he raised it up from the mere
two-dimensionality of the folk-voice and imparted to it an additional dimension of mind. Every tale gained something in the process.
The color and flavor of a modern story-teller was added to their
biblical clarity, and they became neo-biblical moral fables of a
newer form of Judaism—Hasidism. This great renderer of thought
into imagery infused rationality into the latter-day folk-Torah of
Hasidism. In the story "Between Two Mountains" one can see what
it was that Peretz sought artistically in Hasidism. Into the mouths
of the Rebbe of Brisk and the Bialer Rebbe he placed a dialogue
representing their two worlds, and in the process clearly demonstrated which of these worlds, or which of the "two mountains," he
would have preferred to climb:

> "Your Torah, rabbi, is pure justice without mercy, there's not a
> grain of pity in your Torah—and that is why it lacks joy, why
> a man can't breathe freely in it, why it even lacks the iron force
> of law. Tell me, rabbi, what do your teachings have for *all*
> Jews? For the woodcutter, for the butcher, for the artisan, for
> the humblest Jew? And, above all, for a sinful Jew? What do
> you have for the unlearned? Your Torah was hard indeed, hard
> and dry, because it is only the body and not the soul of the
> Torah."

In Judaism of the Hasidic type, Peretz found what Christianity
often claims for itself: pity for the lowest classes, for the silent and
the abject—the spirit of Dostoevsky and Tolstoy. He did not need to
read anything into Judaism, for he read it *out*, from the depths of our
own moral treasury. To the darkness of the Jewish towns and
villages that he visited in the course of a statistical expedition initiated by a Jewish apostate, he brought the artistic flame of Hasidism.

Since the world has not done us in completely, and since God
Himself has not found us guilty among the nations of the world,

we should not yield to the temptation to bend our shoulders sub-
missively, just because it is so easy to take on the aspect of a charming hunchback when one has grown weary of life. So, too, according
to the express warning of Peretz, must we under no circumstances
surrender to the blows of Jewish fate merely in order to sneak safely
through life. He never wanted to see us assuming an attitude of
complaisant submissiveness, so as to obtain an extra bit of life for
ourselves.

> Great, proud Jews
> Are we.
> We say to Him:
> We couldn't wait any longer.
> Fallen low—are we;
> We have been reduced to beggars' bread,
> But we do not beg.

So it is just as in "The Bridal Portion": why is it that Reb
Uzzer's God has so much power in his hands and yet we are power-
less? We come to Him as great, proud men even when we are poor
Jews, and we say to Him: we couldn't wait any longer. This is
Peretz's proud legacy. And it applies to Jewish literature as well as
to Jewish politics: we couldn't wait any longer.

And this was no mere hollow symbolism, something read into
the text by a critic. Peretz knew quite well what he was doing. One
need only read his articles about art to see this, and to see what he
demanded of Jewish art—since for him the word "art" was not
sufficient unto itself. What he demanded is that we Jews come to
the world with a spirit uniquely our own, to exchange and share
with the world, but never to be mere beggars. He demanded a
dynamic Judaism—in these two words you have the Jewish nineteenth century, "the Aristotle-principle" of Peretz's generation.

He came to our intelligentsia and warned them: "Look carefully
at what you are leaving behind. See what a treasure you are throwing away. See what you are renouncing, how many unrealized possibilities lie within you."

He knew how to approach the assimilationist and show him how
to understand his ancient people. "Bow your light heads low for our
immortal martyrs, for our ancient people"—light heads because
empty heads, because assimilation means, according to Peretz's
classic definition: renounce your heritage and do not count your
debts to it.

Well, we have now seen the failure of assimilation. Even those
who denied their heritage were counted as Jews like all the rest,

only they could not even derive the final satisfaction that remains in martyrdom, the knowledge of why they were suffering, for their minds had long been drained of Jewish content.

Through Peretz we were led, as proud Jews, into the nineteenth century, and so now we must proceed onward through him, as proud Jews, into the twentieth. He remained with us for fifteen years into our own bloody century, although he did not live to see the devastation that was to ensue; he did not even live to see the brief Jewish revival in Eastern Europe that turned out to be merely a prelude to the greatest slaughter of all time. We have now passed him by, watching him hold in his hands all the treasures of his own day, all our wholeness. We can only come as pilgrims to the ennobled language that he shaped for us with his Debussy-like style, his Cézanne-like sense of form, his Zolaesque social passion. We, his heirs, come each of us separately to embrace the wholeness of his legacy, remembering well what he told the young people about the death of the *Klezmurim* (musicians):

> Play on without me as though I were still there, and play well. Don't be like pranksters at a poor man's wedding.

That is Peretz's legacy. Just as he gave us a Jewish nineteenth century, so must we seek to render our own deadly portion of the twentieth—all its war-torn anguish, its slaughters and terrifying scourges, the graves of its six million nameless martyrs. Let us not shrink in fright before the long eulogy that must be chanted, and let us not prettify the tune with too easy an optimism. Hope? To be sure, but as an outcome of the maturity and insight that comes from experiencing tragedy. That is Peretz's legacy, and we will not renounce it.

1947

II

Eastern European Scene

The "old country"—life in the small Jewish town or shtetl, the rise of Jewish political movements such as socialism and Zionism, the growth of a Jewish proletariat in the cities of Poland, struggles against poverty and pogroms—has exerted a powerful hold over the Jewish imagination throughout the world. Whether seen as a sacred idyll, as in the view of Abraham Heschel, or examined with the dry objectivity of the sociologist, as in the manner of Abraham Ain, the life of the East European Jews has continued to stir the hearts of their sons and grandsons, sometimes to affection, sometimes to distaste. Here are several pieces which show something of the outer circumstances and inner vibration of East European Jewish life before it was destroyed by Hitler and Stalin.

The Eastern European Era in Jewish History

by Abraham Joshua Heschel

Translated by Abraham Joshua Heschel

In the last thousand years the spiritual hegemony in Jewish life was divided between Sephardic and Ashkenazic Jewry. Earlier in this period the primacy went to the Sephardic group; in the latter half the Sephardim were superseded by the Ashkenazic. All Ashkenazic Jews in the areas bounded by the Rhine and the Dnieper, the Baltic and the Black Seas, and in some neighboring states as well, comprised up to the nineteenth century a culturally uniform group. The beginnings of the cultural sphere go back to Rashi and Judah the Pious and his disciples. The zenith of its spiritual development was attained in eastern Europe, particularly in Hasidism.

The attempted appraisal of the Eastern European era is in the perspective of history; thus, events that loomed important only in recent years are considered in the aspect of their importance for the entire period, which extended over eight hundred years. Our task is to characterize those traits that, in our opinion, express the essence of the era; adventitious traits we must ignore. Neither shall we attempt to analyze the causes that led to the assumption of its particular physiognomy by the era under consideration. That problem requires a special study. Nor shall we describe the various accomplishments of the era, such as the development of the Yiddish language, the rise of the *Wissenschaft des Judentums,* the spread of Hasidism, Haskala, the revival of the Hebrew language, the modern Hebrew and Yiddish literatures, Zionism, Jewish socialism, the establishment of new centers, the rebuilding of Palestine, the various attempts to modernize Jewish life and to adapt it to changing conditions.

I

How do we appraise the historic value of an era? What standards do we use in measuring a culture? It is customary in the modern world to appraise an epoch on the basis of its cultural progress, the quality of its books, the number of academies, the artistic accomplishments, and the scientific discoveries. We Jews, the first nation in the world that began not only to mark but also to appraise and to judge the generations, evaluate eras on the basis of different criteria, namely, how much refinement is there in the life of a people, how much spiritual substance in its workaday existence, i.e., how much metaphysics in its material aspect? To us culture is the style of life of a people. Our gauge of culture is the extent to which the people, and not only individuals, live in accordance with the dictates of an eternal doctrine—the extent to which inwardness, mercy, beauty, and holiness are to be found in the daily life of a people.

The pattern of life of a people is more important than the pattern of its art. What counts most is not expression, but existence itself, the source of expression. The key to the source of creativity lies in the will to cling to spirituality, to be close to refinement, and not merely in the ability of expression. Creativity comes from responsive merging with infinite reality, not from an ambition to say something. To appraise properly the meaning of the Eastern European era in Jewish history, we must not merely dwell upon its contribution to literature, science and the arts, but upon its life-feeling and life-style. We shall then find that it was the era in which our people attained the highest degree of inwardness. From that point of view we are justified in saying that it was the golden period in Jewish history, in the history of the Jewish soul.

Jewish culture of the Hellenic and Sephardic eras is the product of a fusion, of a symbiosis of Jewish tradition with Greek or Islamic culture. Life is frequently oriented to the outer world. Literary forms, scientific methods, philosophical criteria, and even theological principles are adopted from others. The attempt is made to stress the elements Judaism has in common with the surrounding cultures, frequently overlooking its own specific, peculiar contributions. Often, the writing and thinking are in a foreign pattern, endeavoring to compromise with the theories of the great thinkers; at times even an apologetic note is sounded.

In the Ashkenazic era the spiritual life of the Jews is lived in solitude, among primitive Germanic and Slavic peoples. Spiritually above their neighbors, the Jews developed a unique collective life, based upon its own traditions, upon the cultivation of the indigenous and the personal, to the utter disregard of the outside world. They borrowed from other cultures neither substance nor form. Their literature was written by Jews and for Jews; no apologies were offered to philosopher or historian. No commendation was asked of either prince or penman. No comparisons with others were indulged in, no energy wasted in rebuttal of hostile prejudices.

Sephardic Jewry often lacked folk traits. Its culture was derived from above. Jewish men of learning of the Sephardic school were inspired by Arabs; Arab poetry and philosophical morality were frequently the prototype of their teachings. In the main, they devoted themselves to scholarship; their books being frequently designed for individuals or limited groups. Their Jewishness was aristocratic; their poetry was frequently written in a language intelligible only to the scholar. Many of the great among the Sephardim did not find complete self-fulfillment in their Jewish environment. Sephardic men of letters wrote many of their books in Arabic, including Responsa and commentaries on the Bible, the Mishna and the Gemara. The like is inconceivable in Poland, or even in Germany, among Ashkenazic Jewry. No one could imagine the *Toledot Yakov Yosef* (a Hasidic work of the 18th century) in Polish, or the Talmudic novellae of the "Pne Yehoshua" (Talmudic authority of the eighteenth century) in German.

A synthesis of Torah and people is attained by Ashkenazic Jewry. Eastern European Jews speak Yiddish, a language of their own. Hebrew, too, emancipates itself of its rhetorical artificialities, becoming simple and natural as in midrashic times. Because the collective life of the Jews is wholly pervaded by Jewishness, the relations among all the components of the Jewish community, between the saint and the untutored, the Yeshiva student and the farmer, are intimate, organic. The wholesome earthliness of villagers, the geniality of ordinary folk, and the ingenuousness of the *magid,* the popular preacher, penetrate the *Bet-midrash.*

In eastern Europe the Jewish people has come into its own. It does not live like a guest in somebody else's house who must constantly keep in mind the ways and customs of the host. The Jews live their own life without disguise, outside their homes no less than within them. The people itself becomes a source of Jewishness; it can truly say, "In my flesh I shall see God." The Jews begin to sing. Their fancy takes wings. The *pilpul* indulges in fictitious situations, the sermons of the preachers abound in parables. Everywhere one finds cryptic meaning and allusions. The author of *Megalleh Amukot,* in the 17th century, interprets the portion of the Bible *(Vaethanan),* in which Moses pleads with God for permission to enter the Holy Land, in 252 different ways. The manifest becomes occult; dialectic is joined with Kaballah, and in the *Hoshen Mishpat* (the part of the Shulhan Arukh dealing with civil and criminal law) one begins to discover profound mysteries. Even names of towns and countries contain allusions. The name Poland is allegedly derived from the two Hebrew words *Po-lin* ("here abide"), which was inscribed on a note descended from heaven and found by the refugees from Germany on their eastward journey at the time of the Black Death and the attendant massacres of Jews. On the leaves of the trees, the story goes, are inscribed sacred names and in the branches are hidden errant souls seeking deliverance through the intermediation of a pious Jew, who in passing would raise his voice in praise to the Creator.

Sephardic literature is distinguished by a strict, logical orderliness; it is written in accordance with a clear-cut scheme, in which every detail has its assigned place. Ashkenazic writers renounce clarity for the sake of profundity; the contours of their thoughts are not very clearly marked; the thoughts, however, are direct, moving, and natural. Sephardic literature is like classical architecture; Ashkenazic literature, like a painting by Rembrandt, profound and full of mystery. The former prefers the harmony of a system; the latter, the tension of dialectic. The former is sustained by a balanced solemnity; the latter, by impulsive inspiration. Frequently, in Ashkenazic literature, the form is shattered by the overflow of feeling, by passion of thought, and explosive ecstasy. Sephardic literature is like a cultivated park; Ashkenazic, like an ancient forest. The former is like a story with a beginning and an end; the latter has a beginning, but turns frequently into a tale without end.

The Sephardim, interested in preserving the spiritual heritage, classify and synthesize the material that has accumulated in the course of the centuries. The Ashkenazim are eager to discover the new, to probe deeper. The important thing with them is not to remember and to know, but to discover and to understand. Not the final decision is important, but the syllogisms whereby it was derived. The *Mishneh Torah* of Maimonides, the Sephardic Jew, classifies the laws according to logical concept, and reduces the stream of precepts and laws into an abstract system. The *Turim* ("Rows") of the Ashkenazic Jew (Rabbi Jacob, son of the R'o'sh, d. 1340), which forms the basis of the Shulhan Arukh, arranges the precepts in accordance with the daily program of the Jew, beginning with the rising in the morning and concluding with the night prayer of *Shema*. Maimonides' arrangement is logical; the *Turim* reflects the workaday life.

The Sephardim aspire to personal perfection, tranquility of soul, inner peace and contentment, attempting to express their ideal in rational concepts. Their ethic is frequently bourgeois, full of practical wisdom and prudence, advocating the golden mean as the best policy. The Ashkenazic ethic knows no perfection that is definable; its aims are: *seek higher than that*. The Ashkenazic moralist or Hasid is exalted. He yearns for the transcendental, the preternatural. Not for him the tranquil contemplation, the gradual ascent! Ecstasy without end, prayer, study without limit: these appeal to him. And although in effect one is engaged in a persistent struggle with the material, with the finite (one cannot escape one's self), one can at least aspire to self-abnegation.

II

A unique Jewish person has evolved, whose habits and taste are not in accordance with the classical canon of beauty, but who nevertheless, possess a specific charm. He is like a page in an open book, static in its own lines and in the proportion of text and margin. He is different. His soul is a book whose pages are constantly turning. He that dislikes being motionless, that has a quick grasp and is not seized with dizziness at the sight of constant change, will enjoy the beauty of genuine mobility. There are few artists that can both perceive and appraise this "Jewish nature." When this mobility takes shape in crystallized deeds and word, we find in these a certain "kink" for which there is no definition.

The charm of East European Jewry derives from their inner richness, from the polarity of reason and feeling, of joy and sorrow. Everything in their life is fixed according to a pattern; nothing is left to chance. But they have enough vitality to constantly modify the accepted pattern. New customs are continually added to, and a new "kink" introduced into, the old pattern. The deeds, the forms, are passed on from generation to generation, but their meaning and their motivation change. Thus, the source of perennial freshness never runs dry.

The pattern of life was not limited to religious activities. Not only what is to be done on the Sabbath, but also what is to be done in the course of the week, has a definite form. The pattern prescribes the kinds of food to be eaten on certain days, the manner of putting on and taking off shoes, deportment in the street. Every part of the liturgy, every prayer, every hymn, has its own tune. Every detail possesses its own physiognomy, each object bears its individual stamp. Even the landscape is Judaized. During the penitential season the fish in the streams tremble; on Lag b'Omer (scholars' festival

in spring) the trees rejoice. The spirit of a Jewish festival is felt even
by the domestic and wild animals. The nightingale sings with a
choir. And a magpie on a branch appears in the distance "as if
wrapped in a small white *tallis* . . . bowing in supplication."[1]

Eastern European Jewry was a people with a common will and
destiny. It was not merely a uniform group, a homogeneous tribe;
but a multiform society, uniform in its variety: one language, with
many dialects. Social existence was complex, frequently dominated
by centrifugal forces, but there was a common center and in most
cases also a common periphery. There was even a social dynamic
that created groupings in its own fashion. Hasidim, adherents of
one "Rebbe," regardless of the geographic and economic distance
separating them from one another, were a distinct group, with a
specific way of life, specific customs and interests, which were so
intensive that they affected their economic position. On the other
hand, economic divisions often imposed their stamp on religious institutions. Artisans of a class established their own places of worship,
making themselves independent of the community synagogue.

III

An important factor in the development of Ashkenazic Jewry was
the democratization of Talmudic study. In the first five centuries
following the redaction of the Talmud, the Babylonian Gaonate had
the hegemony over Jewish life. They explained equivocal passages
in the Talmud and rendered legal decisions. It was not until the
twelfth century that the Occident began to emancipate itself. By the
compilation of compendia of laws and commentaries to the Talmud,
the Jews in the distant parts gradually achieved independence from
Babylonia. The first commentaries, however, were merely to isolated
passages, and the first compendia were not sufficiently inclusive.
Only Maimonides' *Mishneh Torah* and Rashi's commentary on the
Talmud rendered the Jewish people independent of the *Gaonim;* no
longer was it necessary to refer questions to Babylonia.

Rashi and the *Tosafists* were particularly instrumental in making the people culturally self-sufficient. Without Rashi the Talmud
was an esoteric lore; through him, the paths to its understanding
were opened, for Rashi explained the meaning of words rather than
discoursed on methodology and dialectic. He democratized Jewish
education; he brought the Bible, the Gemara and the midrash (exe-
getical homilectical commentary on the Bible, 4th-12th centuries) to
the people, and made the Talmud a popular book, everyman's book.

[1] Mendele Mokher Sforim, *Fishke der krumer.*

In him was effected a fusion of the Palestinian and the Babylonian legacies. Scholarship ceased to be the monopoly of the few and became widely disseminated. In many communities, the untutored became the rare exception.

A Jewish township

is a place of learning of old standing, where practically all the inhabitants are scholars, where the House of Study is full of men and youths busily pursuing their studies . . . , where at dusk, between the *Minha* and the *Maariv* services, artisans and other simple folk gather around the table to listen to a discourse on the *Midrash,* the Bible, *Hobot Halebabot* ("Duties of the Heart," a moralistic book of the 11th century) and similar ethical and philosophical works . . . where on the Sabbath and on the holidays one hears fiery sermons kindling the hearts of the listeners with love of the Divine Glory, interspersed with words of comfort from the prophets, with wise parable and keen aphorism of the sages, in a voice and a tone that penetrate the entire being.[2]

Poor Jews sit like intellectual magnates. They possess a wealth of ideas and of knowledge, culled from little-known passages in the Talmud. One raises a question about a difficult passage in Maimonides; the other outdoes him in his answer, in the subtlety of his dialectic. The stomach is empty, the home overcrowded; but the heads are full of spiritual and cultural riches, and the Torah is free and ample.

For recreation one goes not to the tavern, but to the House of Study. Passions seek no outlet in gambling, drinking, and other dissipations, but in the desire to act as precentor in the synagogue.

What other nation has a lullaby to the effect that "study is the best of wares"? At the birth of a child, the school children come and chant the *Shema* in unison around the cradle. The child is taken to school for the first time wrapped in a *tallis.* School children are referred to as "sacred sheep," and a mother's pet name for her little boy is "mayn tsadikl" (my little saint). Hence, one is ready to sell all household belongings to pay tuition. Women work all their lives to enable their husbands to devote themselves to study. One shares his last morsel of food with a yeshiva *bokher.* And when the melancholy sweet tone of Talmudic study penetrates the poor alleys, exhausted Jews on their pallets are delighted, for they feel they have a share in that study. Unable to devote themselves to study because

[2] Idem, *Shloime Reb Khayims.*

of economic exigencies, they draw comfort from the thought of supporting the students. The ambition of every Jew is to have a son-
in-law a scholar. Nowadays we speak disparagingly of the institution
of *kest* (supporting a son-in-law). But what institution has done
more to promote the spiritual development of large numbers of
people?

Study was a song of longing, a pouring out of the heart before
the Merciful Father, a sort of prayer, a communion and an ardent
desire for a purified world. Inwardness has assumed super-real
forms. Jews immersed in a discussion of the laws pertaining to the
"merchant of Lydda" at the same time suffer the anguish of the
Divine Glory in Exile. They are endeavoring to unravel an obscure
passage in the MaHaRSha (Talmudic authority of the 16th-17th
centuries), and at the same time feel the affliction of the world.

Study was a technique of sublimating feeling and thought,
dream and syllogism, of expressing pain in a question and joy in a
solution found to a difficult problem in Maimonides. The tension of
the spirit found an outlet in the contrivance of subtle, practically
insolvable riddles, in yearnings and expectations, in the invention of
new logical devices. The greatest joy was to find an answer to gnawing doubts. A world of suppressed gayety and frolic lies in their
dialectic. The conscious aim, however, is not self-expression. One
does not want to exploit the Torah; one uses it as an ornament. The
people are enamored of study, therefore they put mind, heart and
soul into the Gemara. Borne up by the tune, one soars in the pure
spiritual realm of thought, far from the world and its objects, its
facts and aims, away from the boundaries of here and now, to the
place where the Divine Glory listens to what Jews recreate anew in
the study of the Torah. There was holiness in their acumen; the
psalmist's "my soul thirsteth for God" filled the entire being.

Every Jew felt himself a partner in the Torah. He struggled
over a difficult question and, because of his kinship with the Torah,
felt entitled to an opinion. He received the apparatus of study, consisting of various methods, and attempted to evolve a system of his
own, in addition to the acquisition of data. The result was that he
became a thinker, not merely a guardian of facts.

The Jews studied those parts of the Torah that had no rele-
vance to their daily life no less eagerly than those that had a direct
bearing on it. They busied themselves with studies that were not
actual, even far from the banal course of living. Their study was
non-utilitarian, free from pragmatic design; not practical but esthetic. He that studied for the purpose of becoming a rabbi was the
subject of ridicule. However, the weighing of subtle opinions and

the addition or subtraction of a nuance made the student feel as if he were the guardian of the treasures in the temple of the Torah. It was a kind of service that enchanted the spirit. Its priestly glory lay in the mere act of doing, not only in the results achieved. The Gaon of Vilna told his disciple, Reb Khayim Volozhiner, that at times "heavenly mentors" came to him, desiring to impart to him sacred mysteries, but he refused their offer. He would rather struggle over the Torah and attain the truth unaided.

The *pilpul* was a continuation of the disputation of the Gemara, a development and elaboration of the unending tradition. One could dispute with the authorities of the past. The boundaries between yesterday and today were obliterated. If there is a discrepancy between Reb Akiba Eger of the 19th century and Reb Isaac Alfasi of the 11th century, a Warsaw scholar of the 20th century reconciles it with a novel view on the issue in question. There is no desire to solve actual problems, merely to continue the study of the Tannaim and Amoraim, of the early and the later teachers. One is less interested in the solution of the problem than in its devising.

It is easy to belittle such a mentality and to dub it unworldliness. The soul is sustained by impracticality. The unpractical experiences are the heart of culture, the spring of energy of humaneness. A civilization that concentrates merely on the utilitarian is essentially not greatly different from barbarism.

The plain meaning of the Torah is too superficial for these Jews. They, therefore, delve into the words and find hidden thoughts in their depths. The simple idea of a principle, the straight line of a law, are too narrow and too confining to contain their glance. The storm of the soul held under control becomes a mighty impetus of the intellect. The inner restlessness finds expression in intellectual passion. Thinking becomes charged with strength. The mind breaks down the forms of the Talmudic thoughts and recasts them in fantastic molds, zigzags, in which the thought at first becomes snarled but finally succeeds in disentangling itself.

Just as acumen in thought is the favorite of those that study the "manifest teachings," so economy of expression is the forte of those that are absorbed in mystic lore. A style evolves that skips the hypothesis and at once reaches the conclusion. The aphorism aiming directly at a thought, instead of approaching it slowly and gradually, is the literary form most adequate to express the thought of Eastern European Jews. They speak briefly, precisely, concretely, almost in a hint.

Ideas are like precious stones. The thought animating them brings out a wealth of nuances and distinctions, as the ray of light passing through a prism produces the colors of the spectrum. Upon rotation, the multiform ideas emanate a light that changes in accordance with the direction in which they are placed against the light of reason. The alluring gracefulness, the variety of polished ideas, enlighten the intellect and dazzle the eye. The concepts become dynamic; they give forth colors and meanings that at first thought seem to have no connection with one another. Full of original devices, the joy of their discovery quickens the heart of the discoverer. This is no realistic thinking; but art, too, does not consist in imitating nature, nor is mathematics an imitation of something that already exists.

IV

We must understand the life-feeling that dominated Eastern European Jewry in order properly to appraise the fact that the majority of their best intellects were devoted to the study, the interpretation, and the development of the Law. To them the world was no treasure that the Creator had left ownerless. Life to them was not merely an opportunity for indulgence, but a mission that God entrusted to every individual. Life is at least as responsible an enterprise as, let us say, the management of a factory. Every man constantly produces thoughts, words, deeds. He supplies these products to the Powers of Holiness or to the Powers of Impurity. He is constantly engaged either in building or in destroying. It is incumbent upon man to restore to perfection that which has become impaired in the cosmos. Therefore, the Jews are engaged in the Service of God. They are rarely dominated by a desire for rigorism, or a tendency to irrational discipline. In the main, they are borne up by a sense of the importance of their mission. The world could not exist without the Law. This sense lends to their tone the magic of an artistic act, in which the material is not stone or bronze, but the mystic substance of the cosmos.

Scientists devote their lives to the study of the properties of plants or the life processes of insects. To science every trifle is significant, and its votaries inquire diligently into the most intricate properties of matter. The pious Ashkenazic scholars investigated with similar passion the laws that should govern the Jew's conduct. The devotion and honesty invested in their work have their parallel in scientific research. They wish to banish chaos out of human existence and to civilize the life of man on the basis of the Halacha. They tremble over every move, every breath; no detail can be treated lightly; everything is important. Hence, additional laws, new restrictions, are instituted. They are passionately striving to attain the maximum of piety. As the self-sacrificing devotion of the scientists seems torture to the debauchee, so the poetry of rigorism jars on the ears of the cynic. But, it may be, the question as to what benediction to pronounce upon a certain type of food, the problem of matching the material with the spiritual, is as important as the determination of the melting point of a certain metal.

V

As Rashi had democratized Jewish education, so, in the twelfth and thirteenth centuries, Judah the Pious and his disciples democratized the ideals of mystic piety. To attain to them, no high theoretical conceptions are necessary, the main requirements being faith, the heart, inwardness. Piety is more important than wisdom, naïveté ranks higher than speculation, the God-fearing man is above the scholar. By their apotheosis of simplicity, of warm faith, of humaneness and desirable moral qualities, they paved a way to God for the ordinary man.

Prayer, the outpouring of the heart before the Creator, is considered by them the basis of the Service of God. The Siddur, the folkbook of our literature, is dear and sacred to them; every word in it a precious jewel. They count the words, for in them are contained mysteries without end. Thence they attempt to uncover the old secrets that the prophets[3] transmitted to their disciples, which were later passed on orally and revealed only to the chosen few, the God-fearing.

In reality, however, the concentration upon the secrets is not the major aim. The heartfelt prayer of the simple untutored man frequently ranks higher than the prayer of the man of learning. A God-fearing Jew who does not understand Hebrew, but wants to pray with the proper devotion, may pray in the language with which he is conversant. A well-known legend tells of a simple Jew who, in the time of the persecutions, saved a community from imminent destruction through the merit of his recital of the Psalms.

The times are bad for the Jews; they are persecuted and hunted on all sides. Massacres are a daily occurrence; Jews are led to the slaughter like sheep; but all this is accepted willingly in submission to the Divine Will. With superhuman fervor they sacrifice themselves for their faith. The *Sefer Hasidim* ("Book of the Pious") finds it necessary to comfort those that "die on their beds" and have not merited death for the Sanctification of the Name. Life at its best is

[3] According to R. Eliezer of Worms, the author of *Rokeah* (13th century).

a battlefield. Man must constantly struggle with the Evil Inclination, "for Man is like unto a rope, one end of which is drawn by God and the other end by Satan." Hence one learns the tactics of this war, consisting, in the main, of eschewing all but the essentials of life, and in overcoming temptation. Lapses can be atoned for by fasts, which purge the soul of its stain.

The "Pious Men of Ashkenaz" attach great importance to the daily conduct of prominent Jews, or even ordinary Jews; to usages that are not the result of scholastic sophistication, but improvised instinctively; to customs that derive from the feelings, from the moods. They begin to commit to writing the various customs. Books appear aiming to teach the people tact, social refinement, proper religious practice. In this spirit books especially designed for the ordinary folk are written, poetic and tender in style, abounding in folk-tales and parables. They do not speak of high ideals in the abstract; they are didactic. There arises a literature in "Taytsch"— Yiddish, for women. For centuries they read the *Lev Tov* ("Good Heart") and the *Ts'eno Ur'eno* ("Go out and see") and pour out their hearts in the *Tehinot* (devotional prayers) written by women for women.

VI

In the 17th century, the mystic teachings of the Zohar and of Reb Isaac Luria began to penetrate Poland. These esoteric books were reprinted, and the people were seized with a desire to study the mystic teachings which had heretofore been known only to individuals but were by this time made available to all. The spread of mysticism had a profound influence upon the life-feeling of East European Jewry. The Kabbala breathed into them the consciousness of the importance of their actions for all worlds; all that takes place "above" in the upper spheres, depends upon man "below." It made every Jew somewhat of a Messiah. According to its teachings, redemption is not a thing that will take place all at once at the end of days; it is a continual process, taking place every minute. Man's good deeds are single acts in the long drama of redemption. Furthermore, redemption is not a process affecting merely the Jewish people; all the world is in need of redemption.

The sense of man's life lies in his perfecting the world. He has to distinguish, gather, and redeem the Sparks of Holiness scattered throughout the darkness of the world. This service is the motive of all precepts and good deeds. But the Jew, upon whom the deliverance of the world is incumbent, is in a position not merely to build but also to destroy. Endowed with gigantic powers, he can by means of the proper consecration ascend to the highest spheres. His spirit can create heavens. At the same time he must not forget, however, that his feet are upon the ground, close to the Powers of Darkness. It is quite conceivable that instead of ascending to the heavens, he may by Evil Inclination be cast down into the abyss. Hence, the Jews attempt to subdue the foe, matter, fasting every Monday and Thursday and undergoing other mortifications to purify the self. And the Evil Inclination pursues with a sharp ax; one wrong move, and the ax comes down. This feeling leads to both enthusiasm and sadness. One feels the infinite beauty of the heavens, the sacred mysteries of the precepts, but one is also aware of the gloom of the world. Man is so unworthy and sinful; the heavens are so exalted and far. What has man to do in order not to sink into the Nethermost Pit?

VII

Then came the Hasidim and brought down heaven upon the earth. They banished melancholy from the soul and uncovered the great fortune of being a Jew. Jewishness meant rebirth. Customs and quotations suddenly took on a breath like that of a new grain. A new prohibition was added: against being old. The spirit grew younger. One was enamored of God, one felt "the unbearable longing for God." One began to feel the infinite sweetness that comes from fulfilling the precept of hospitality, or from donning *tallis* and *tefillin*. What meaning is there to the life of a Jew, if not the acquisition of the ability to taste the joys of Paradise? He who does not taste Paradise in the performance of a precept in this world, will not feel Paradise in the world to come. No sooner has one come to feel life eternal in a sacred ritual, or in the Sabbath, than these and the world to come are identical.

The Jews became so refined that they ceased being afraid of the body. Commenting upon the passage, "Hide not thyself from thy own flesh" (Is. 58.7), the Baal Shem Tov said: "Do not mortify the flesh; pity it." One can worship God even with the body, even with the Evil Inclination; one merely has to be able to distinguish between dross and gold. For the significance of this world lies in the fact that a little of the other world is mingled with it. Without refinement, matter is full of darkness. The Hasidim have always maintained that the joys of this world are not the highest attainable; they, therefore, kindled in them the desire for spirituality, a longing for the world to come. Only its bliss, *Olam Haba*, was perfect.

The story is told of a *melamed* making a wintertime pilgrimage afoot to his "Rebbe." The town's rich man passed by in a sumptuous coach, drawn by four horses. Seeing the *melamed,* he asked him into the coach. The *melamed* consented, and was soon snugly tucked away in a corner, covered with heavy warm blankets. The rich man then offered him some brandy, cake, even some roast goose. Suddenly, the *melamed* turned to the rich man, saying: "Pray, tell me, what is your this-worldly joy, your *Olam Hazeh?*" The rich man was astonished: "Don't you see the luxurious coach and the expensive foods? Are they not enough of this-worldly joy?" "No," replied the *melamed,* "these are your other-worldly joys, the acme of your joys, your *Olam Haba,* but what is your *Olam Hazeh?*"

It was like the miracle that took place at the passage of the Red Sea, as told by our sages. An ordinary Jew frequently began to perceive what the scholars had so often failed to sense. And do not really a contrite sigh, a little inwardness, a little self-discipline and self-sacrifice, outweigh the merits of him that is full of both learning and pride? When study becomes an aim in itself, it may turn into a sort of idol worship. Excessive *pilpul* may dry up the spring of the soul. Hence the scholar who shuts his Gemara and sets out upon a self-imposed "exile," to live far from home, to bear humiliation, to taste the cup of privation.

The story is told of a scholar who once came to a "Rebbe." "What have you done all your life?" inquired the "Rebbe." "I have gone through the Talmud three times," replied the scholar. "But what of the Talmud has gone through you?" countered the "Rebbe."

From sheer piety one can forget the Creator. The main object is to feel the soul, in one's self, in the Torah, in the world. Man is no mere reflection; he is a spring. Divesting himself of the husks, he can illuminate the world. Hence the fate of his "dear people of Israel" is of such concern to God. He is the endless, no thought can conceive Him; yet in ecstatic contemplation of His infinity, the Jew exclaims, "Sweet Father!" It is incumbent upon the Jew to obey his heavenly father; He in turn is bound to take pity on His children. Everyone knows that God loves even the most wicked in Israel with a love surpassing our love for the most saintly in Israel. But when the suffering of exile is most severe and heavenly aid does not appear, Reb Levi Yitskhok of Berdichev summons God to stand trial, as it were.

In 1917–18, during the pogroms in the Ukraine, a friend of mine engaged in recording those events was struck by the fact that a certain town directly in the path of the passing hordes had in the various pogrom waves been persistently spared. My friend expressed his surprise to a resident of the town in question, who offered the following explanation: "We had been promised safety.

Centuries ago there lived in our town a great saint. It came to pass that on a certain Friday he had to go, for the sake of a *mitzva*, to a neighboring town. The saint hesitated for a while. How set out on a journey on the day preceding the Sabbath? But the distance was small, the trip urgent, and he departed. Unfortunately, the journey took much longer than he had expected. Finally, when he arrived in the town, the Sabbath candles were gleaming in Jewish homes. The saint was wroth with God, as it were, that He dealt thus with him. In his indignation he refused to recite the *Kiddush*—the blessing over the wine. The heavenly spheres were, of course, duly impressed with the saint's form of remonstrance. But the saint would not be placated easily, not until he was promised that there would never be a pogrom in his town. Only then he proceeded to usher in the Sabbath."[4]

The Jews had always known piety, the Sabbath, holiness. The new thing in eastern Europe was the introduction of a part of the Sabbath into the week-days. One could taste life eternal in the fleeting moment. In such environment it was not difficult to maintain the Additional Soul. No beautiful synagogues were erected; instead, bridges were built leading from the heart of God. There were no concerts or operas; instead, the third Sabbath meal was attended with such feelings that music was not sufficiently refined to express them.

The present overflowed its bounds. Life became more than life. One lived vertically, not horizontally, being with the great men of the past not only in narrating tales about them, but also in feeling and dream. Every Jew felt a kinship with Reb Akiba and Reb Simon b. Yohai. Jews studied the Talmud, and saw Abaye and Raba before their eyes. Elijah the Prophet attended their circumcision ceremonies, their *sukkas* were visited by the Holy Guests. History never ceases, in such vertical life. Among such Jews there live the thirty-six hidden saints. In that environment one is always ready to welcome the Redeemer. If Isaiah were to rise from his grave and were to enter the home of a Jew, the two would easily understand one another.

Korzec, Karlin, Bratzlav, Lubavich, "Ger," Lublin—hundreds of towns—are like holy books. Every place is a pattern, an aspect, a way in Jewishness. When a Jew utters the name of Mezhbuzh or Berdichev, it is as if he were to utter a holy name. A splendor emanates from ordinary acts. "Why do you make a pilgrimage to the 'Rebbe'?" an eminent scholar was asked. "In order to see how he

---

[4] Told by David Koigen.

laces his shoes." Hasidim tell how the "Rebbe" opened the door, how he tasted of the food: ordinary events yet full of mystery.

It is superfluous to speak of faith, for who does not feel the presence of God filling the entire universe? To preach to those Jews the necessity of observing the 613 precepts would be banal; to live according to the Shulhan Arukh became second nature. But the Jews wanted more. They wanted to be higher. The old Rabbi of Slobodka used to say: "If I knew that I should remain what I am, I would lay hands on myself. But if I did not hope to become like the Gaon of Vilna, I would not be even what I am." This longing for the higher spheres endowed them with almost superhuman powers. Everyone knows what beauty is and can conceive it with his senses. In eastern Europe holiness, the highest of all values, became so real and so concrete that it could almost be felt as one feels beauty.

Notwithstanding the life of poverty and humiliation that Jews lived, inwardly they bore the sorrow of the world and the vision of deliverance for all men and all creatures. There were Jews from whose spirit the suffering of the generations and of their times never departed. Yet, this did not interfere with their continuous festive mood. For there is no despair, says Reb Nakhman of Bratzlav. "Fear not, dear child, God is with you, in you, over you, around you. Even in the Nethermost Pit one can be close to His Blessed Name." The word "bad" does not come upon their lips. Trials do not terrify. For "all can be taken from me—my house, the pillow from underneath my head—but not God within my heart."

Miracles no longer startled the people, and it was believed that men endowed with the Holy Spirit were not uncommon. The later generations were no longer considered inferior to the earlier, no longer looked down upon as epigones. On the contrary, there were Hasidim who believed that it was easier to attain the Holy Spirit in their own day than in the days of the Tannaim. For there are two sources from which the Holy Spirit emanates: the Temple and the Complete Deliverance. And we are closer to the time of deliverance than the Tannaim had been to the time of the Temple. The splendor of the Messiah appears in advance. Pity Abraham Ibn Ezra! His period was far from both the Revelation at Sinai and the Messiah; hence his sober tone.

A discussion was being waged in the Middle Ages, whether man is higher than the angels. Saadiah Gaon maintained the affirmative; Abraham Ibn Ezra, the negative. In the Eastern European period there was unanimous agreement on man's superiority. The angel knows no self-sacrifice, he need not rise above obstacles, he has no choice in his course of action. Furthermore, an angel is stationary, remaining in the category in which he was created. Man, however, is a wayfarer, he goes forward or backward. He cannot remain in one place. More than that. Man is not merely the crown of creation, he can become a participant in the act of creation. Hasidim know the responsibility they bear, they know that entire worlds wait to be delivered from their imperfections. Not only are we in need of heaven, but heaven needs us as well.

VIII

No classical works were created in eastern Europe. The Gemara and the *Mishneh Torah*, the Zohar and the Shulhan Arukh, the Guide to the Perplexed and the Ez Hayim (of the mystic Hayim Vital, d. 1620), had their origin elsewhere. Eastern European Jewry had no ambition to create final forms of expressions. Their works are so unique and so rooted in a world apart that they are less accessible to the modern man than the works of the Sephardic scholars. The Ashkenazic Jews are but little interested in creating literature; their works are notes that they have made in the cause of their teaching. They are the product not of the writer's desk, but of the lecture hall, of the discourse delivered before the students. But their simplicity and humility conceal their great creative accomplishments. Their *obiter dicta* are like perfume. Their life was spirit; there arose in them an infinite world of inwardness, a Law within the Heart in addition to the Oral and Written Laws. They develop like artists that know how to fill the week-day hours with mystic beauty. They write no poetry. Their life is a poem. When Jews stand prepared to receive the Additional Soul, becoming enamored of God anew, and from their heart a song of rapture wells—what poetry can compare with this communion, this beauty?

The Jews did not disparage secular education without reason. They resisted the stream that sought to engulf the small province of Jewishness. They did not despise science. They believed, however, that the daily recitation of the prayer "Lord, guard my tongue from evil" was more important than the study of physics, that meditating upon the Psalms inspires a man with greater compassion than the study of botany. They had no confidence in the secular world. They believed that the existence of the world is conditioned not upon museums and libraries, but upon Yeshivas and Houses of Study. To them, the House of Study was not important because the world needed it; but, on the contrary, the world was important because the House of Study existed within it. To them, life without the Law and the precepts was chaos. A dweller in such a life was regarded with a sense of fear. Harassed and oppressed, they carried deep within their hearts a contempt of the "world" with its power and glory, its tumult and boasting. Jews that rose at midnight to devotions and spent the day peddling trinkets were not insulted by the scorn of the wicked, nor affected by his praises. They knew the world and did not turn it into an idol. Progress did not deceive them, and the magic of the twentieth century did not blind them. They knew that the Jews were in exile, that the world was unredeemed. Their life was oriented to the spirit; they could, therefore, ignore its external aspects. Externally, a Jew might have been a pauper; inwardly, he felt akin to royalty. The inner strength and freedom of a Jew wrapped in *tallis* and *tefillin* can be grasped only by him who has undergone that experience.

There are more attractive literatures and profounder philosophies than those that have arisen among the Eastern European Jews. In the pages of the latter, however, the light of the image of God was never extinguished. There were Jews who claimed that they could recall the time when their souls witnessed the Revelation at Sinai. Their will constantly resounded: "We will do and obey." Rarely was this affirmation uttered more fervently. Fiery young men would break into the streets and proclaim aloud: "There is none beside Him!"

When was there more light among the Jews in the last two thousand years? Could it have been more beautiful in Safed or in Worms, Cordoba or Pumbedita?

The story is told that once the Baal Shem with his disciples came to Berdichev to see the famous Reb Liber. The latter was not at home, for it was the day of the fair, and he had gone to the market. Arriving at the market place, they saw Reb Liber conversing with a peasant. "Do you know with whom Reb Liber is speaking?" the master queried. "It is Elijah," he said, and beholding the amazement of the disciples, he added: "It is not Reb Liber who is privileged to have a revelation of Elijah, but Elijah who is privileged to have a revelation of Reb Liber." This story perhaps best expresses what happened in that period. In the days of Moses the Jews had a revelation of God; in the days of the Baal Shem Tov God had a revelation of Israel. Suddenly there was revealed a holiness in Jewish life that had accumulated in the course of many generations. In the final analysis "We will do and obey" is as important as "I am the Lord thy God," and "Who is like unto Thy people, one nation" as important as "the Lord is one." Who would have believed our report: One looked at the Jews and beheld the Divine Glory!

IX

It is easier to appraise the beauty of the older Jewish life than the
revolutionary spirituality of the modern Jew, of the *maskil*, Zionist,
or socialist. The Jews of older days frequently overlooked this
world, because of the other world. Between man and world there
stood God. In the meantime, however, decrees and pogroms shattered the ground under the feet of the Jews. They had no peace, nor
the means to gain a livelihood. Then came young men with new
tidings. There arose the Haskala, the Jewish socialist movement,
Zionism, the *halutzim* movement. How much of self-sacrifice, of love
of Israel and of the Sanctification of the Name are to be found in
these modern Jews, in their will to suffer in order to help! The zeal
of pious Jews was transmitted to their emancipated sons and grandsons. The fervor and yearning of Hasidim, the ascetic obstinacy of
Kabbalists, the inexorable logic of Talmudists, found their reincarnation in the supporters of the modern Jewish movements. Of the
pair, Torah and Israel, they accepted Israel. Even those who have
abandoned tradition, even those whom the revolutionary impetus
has carried to the antithesis of tradition, have not separated themselves, like the sects of previous days, but have remained within the
fold. The powerful urge to redemption continued in them. The
Satan of assimilation is very seductive; but the Jews who have not
capitulated, who have not deserted Jewish poverty, who have re-
linquished careers, favor, and comfort in order to find a healing for
the hurt of their people: these have been like new wine in old
bottles.

The modern Jew in eastern Europe, with certain exceptions, of
course, has not only repudiated assimilation, but has developed a
militant attitude as well. Both religious and free-thinking Jews fight
for Jewish honor, for a dignified existence, striving to assure the
rights of the community, not merely those of the individual. They
manifest a collective will for a collective aim. With lightning rapid-
ity they straightened their backs, mastering the arts and the sciences; over three thousand years of history have not made them
weary. Their spirit is animated by a vitality that frequently leads
them into opposition to monumental traditions. They want to begin
anew, refusing to live on bequests. Not until recently have they begun to long for a union of the present with the past, a synthesis
which has not yet been realized.

In the dreadful anguish of these days, a bitter question sears
our lips: What will become of us, the surviving? Shall we, Heaven
forbid, be subject to the fate of Sephardic Jewry after the catastrophe of 1492: fragmentized groups in Turkey and Morocco, stray

individuals in Amsterdam, magnificent synagogues and fossilized
Jewishness? Shall we permit our people to be lost in the multitude?
Our Sabbath to be dissipated in the week-days?

Rich stores of potential energy, of intellectual resilience and
emotional depth, gathered in the course of generations of a disciplined mode of life, are now contained in us. Much wisdom and
much refinement are frittered away in intellectual trash, a good deal
of the soul is lost to Satan.

We must retain the Jewishness of our fathers and grandfathers.
Their Law within the Heart was not a matter of esthetics. Romantic
portraiture of Hasidism, nostalgia and piety, are merely ephemeral;
they disappear with the first generation. Solidarity with the past
must become an integral part of our existence. We are in need of
Jews whose life is a garden, not a hothouse. Only a living Judaism
can survive. Books are no more than seeds; we must be both the
soil and the atmosphere in which they grow.

The present generation is still in possession of the keys to the
treasure. If we do not uncover the treasures, the keys will go down
to the grave with us, and the storehouse of the generations will remain locked forever. The Eastern European era can become a source
of inspiration for all of us. It is incumbent upon us never to forget
the Jews that sanctified their lives by their proximity to heaven.

Mankind is now attracted by chaos. It has strayed into a desert
with but few oases. We might have to be sustained by drops of
manna.

When Nebuchadnezzar destroyed Jerusalem and set fire to the
Temple, our grandfathers did not forget the Revelation at Sinai and
the words of the Prophets. Today the world knows that what tran-
spired on the soil of Palestine was sacred history, from which the
nations draw their inspiration. A day will come in which the hidden
light of the Eastern European era will be revealed. This era was the
Song of Songs (which according to the rabbis is the holiest of Holy
Scripture) of Jewish history in the last two thousand years. If the
other eras were holy, this one is the holy of holies.

1946

Swislocz: Portrait of a Shtetl

by Abraham Ain

Translated by Shlomo Noble

I. GENERAL ASPECTS

Population and Appearance

Swislocz (Yiddish name: *Sislevich*) was considered one of the larger towns (*shtetl*) in the district of Grodno. According to the census of 1847, there were 997 Jews in Swislocz. Fifty years later, the town numbered 3,099 persons, of whom 2,086 were Jews. In the beginning of the present century the population again increased substantially. A leather industry of considerable size sprang up and a railway was built, linking the town with the industrial centers of Western Russia. Jews and non-Jews from surrounding villages flocked to the town. In 1906 it had some 600 families, of whom 400 were Jewish.

The town consisted of a market, five large and a dozen small streets and alleys, and a synagogue yard. The market covered an area of about two city blocks in the center of the town. It housed all the town's business places. All larger streets, which extended on the average to three or four city blocks, began in the market and terminated in the suburbs. These streets were known after the towns to which they led. Thus the Grodno Street led to the Grodno highway. Two of the larger streets, the market, and the synagogue yard were inhabited by Jews. The other large and most of the small streets were inhabited by both Jews and non-Jews. The non-Jews consisted of White Russians, Poles, a score of Russian civil servants and a dozen or so Moslem Tartars.

Reprinted with permission of YIVO Institute for Jewish Research, New York, from "Swislocz: Portrait of a Shtetl," by Abraham Ain.

At the end of every larger street, at the entrance to town, was a huge gate. Once upon a time the town had been surrounded by a deep moat. At the entrance to the large streets there was no moat, so that passage was only through the gates. In the daytime the gates were open; at night they were closed, and no one could then enter or leave town. In my days only three of the large streets had gates; the others were in ruins. Three of the large streets had cobblestone pavement; the other streets and the market were unpaved. On rainy days the mud was ankle-deep and crossing the market was no pleasant undertaking. In 1904, the chief of police ordered every property owner in the market to pave the street fronting his property to a depth of twelve feet. This was the sidewalk of the market.

At the eastern approach to the town were ruins of massive stone walls. These ruins were called the stores and represented the remains of a street, two city blocks in length, that had burned down. The stores had been erected by Polish noblemen, owners of the town, in order to encourage trade. Several times a year fairs had been held in town, each lasting four weeks. In the 1830's a conflagration destroyed the stores. The owners of the town, involved in the insurrection of 1831 against Russia, fled abroad, and there was no one to rebuild the ruins. Conflagrations were no rare events in the towns. In the course of the nineteenth century the town burned down to the ground twice. In 1910 half of the town was destroyed by fire again. Hence, the town was continually being rebuilt anew and its external aspect improved. Many of the houses were substantial two-story brick structures, adorned with balconies. Some of the newer houses had hardwood floors and papered walls.

In the center of the market was a square concrete pillar, some fifty feet high, twelve feet square at the base tapering off to two feet at the top. From the top of the post extended a brass bar, about a foot long, supporting a round brass ball some two feet in diameter. No one knew the age of the post. Tradition had it that the owners of the town had formerly erected the post. On the significance of the post there were several theories. One maintained that it was constructed as a lightning-rod. Another version claimed that the Russians had hanged on that spot several Polish noblemen for participation in anti-Russian activities, and their colleagues had erected the post as a monument to them. A third account had it that the brass ball contained ancient documents about the history of the town.

How Old Was the Town?

There were no records to indicate the age of the town, or the age of its Jewish community. The Holy Burial Association (*Khevre*

Kadishe) formerly had a *pinkes*, a minute-book, but it was destroyed in one of the periodical fires, and no other source for the history of the Jews in town was left.

The Jewish cemetery was divided into a new and an old burial ground. On the old cemetery, near the entrance, the tombstones had collapsed, so that it was difficult to tell that the place had once been a burial ground. Farther down, the tombstones protruded half-way from the ground, but the inscriptions on them were obliterated. On the new cemetery the graves and tombstones were in better condition. But even the new cemetery had probably been used for centuries, for in the first World War it was filled up and ground was broken for another cemetery.

In 1903, when a railway was being built through the town, a large number of human skeletons was unearthed. These skeletons were laid out in rows, close to one another, at a depth of about three feet. There were no clues for closer identification of the skeletons, nor was there any real interest in them. Apparently, the town had a long history, which was completely obliterated from the memory of the inhabitants.

The Vicinity

The immediate surroundings of the town were dotted with villages. Their inhabitants, chiefly White Russians, were, in the main, poor peasants who had to supplement their meager incomes by doing chores in town or laboring in the forests. Some of them worked in the leather factories in town; others were engaged in hauling timber from the forests to the railway depot. In the villages close to the forest skillful peasants carved all sorts of articles out of wood: pails, kneading troughs, felloes, yokes, and shingles. These articles they brought to town for sale, and with the money thus realized they purchased not only farm implements, but occasionally also flour and barley, for some peasants had so little land that they could not raise enough food for their families. There were also in the vicinity several large and small estates that belonged to Polish landlords.

Nearly every village and estate had a Jewish family, engaged as millers or lessees. On the eve of the first World War there were practically no more Jewish millers in the villages, for two Jews, former millers in a village, by installing two motor mills in town rendered the village miller superfluous.

Administrative Authorities

Administratively and juridically the town was linked with Wolkowysk, the county seat, which was at a distance of some twenty-eight versts. Economically, however, the town was closely bound up with Bialystok, some seventy versts away. In 1906, the railway through our town was completed, and a closer contact was established with Wolkowysk and other nearby towns.

To maintain order the town had a chief of police and a constable (*uryadnik*). In 1905 this force was augmented by eight policemen. The chief of police (*stanovoy pristav*) was the ruler of the town; his word was law. Frequently, this official would tyrannize over the town, but a way was always found to placate him. As a rule, he was not averse to a little gift. . . . In 1903, a new chief of police came to our town. Forthwith he launched a vigorous campaign against "subversive" elements, particularly among the young people. His zeal knew no bounds. Once, encountering on the outskirts of the town two young men reading a book, he had them arrested and questioned for two weeks. Subsequently, they were released. Another time, he raided a meeting of the clandestine Jewish Labor Organization "Bund" in the forest and arrested ten young men and three girls. The arrested maintained that their gathering was in the nature of a harmless outing and as no forbidden literature was found on them, they were released. The young bloods of the town decided to teach the chief of police a lesson. On a dark night they set fire to the woodshed of a school on the outskirts of the town. The regulations called for the chief of police to be present at a fire. A group of young people lay in wait for him and gave him a thrashing. This experience considerably diminished his zeal for discovering conspiracies. The constable, too, who began to peer into closed shutters, was given a beating, while in a somewhat intoxicated state.

The town had, moreover, a justice of the peace (*zemski nachalnik*), who adjudicated minor litigations of the rural population, and three excisemen, who supervised the manufacture and sale of alcoholic beverages.

Controversies in Town

The town, consisting exclusively of *misnagdim* (opponents of Hasidism), had a Synagogue and three Houses of Study, in which services were conducted three times a day. The Houses of Study possessed rich collections of books, and at dusk, between the *minkhe* (late afternoon) and the *mayriv* (evening) services, numerous groups could be seen busily pursuing their studies of the Scriptures, the Talmud, or some ethical text. The untutored had a teacher who instructed them in the weekly portion of the Bible on Friday evenings and Saturdays. The older folks were pious but tolerant toward the young generation, which was largely heterodox in its religious views. The young people, in turn, refrained from publicly offending the religious sensibilities of the orthodox.

On one occasion, however, a sharp conflict broke out between the young and the old generations. An itinerant preacher came to town. He was a man of eloquence and power and opposed to the "progressives," whom he attacked in his sermons. These sermons led to strained relations between some of the parents and their children. Once several young people entered the House of Study and interrupted one of the preacher's customary diatribes against them with catcalls. Some of the older people rose to the defense of the preacher and a fight ensued. During the altercation a butcher called out that the young people were justified in deriding the preacher because he was sowing discord in the community. The older folks avenged the slight to the preacher by prohibiting the butcher from selling kosher meat. The prohibition would have ruined the butcher, had not the Jewish Labor Organization or "Bund" sent an ultimatum to the trustees of the Houses of Study to repeal the prohibition, or it would adopt strong measures. The trustees were frightened and complied with the request.

There were also deep-seated and prolonged dissensions within the camp of the orthodox. They began toward the end of the past century, when the old rabbi of the town, Rabbi Meyer Yoyne, died, leaving a son, Rabbi Motye, who aspired to the position. Although he had been duly ordained and was qualified for the rabbinate, the old and prominent members of the community opposed his candidacy. The reasons for their opposition were that the deceased had not left a will designating his son as successor and that the aspirant because of his youth and familiarity would not command the respect due that office. They, therefore, selected one Rabbi Shneyer Zalman as rabbi. The artisans and small tradesmen, however, sided with Rabbi Motye and argued that since he was qualified for the position, the fact that he was a local man or that he was not well advanced in years should not be to his detriment. And so he, too, remained rabbi in our town. Rabbi Shneyer Zalman was a quiet and tactful person, and the tension between the two factions was kept at a minimum.

In 1903, Rabbi Shneyer Zalman died and Rabbi Joseph Rosen was chosen as his successor. The conflict flared up anew with increased bitterness. The young people remained largely outside of the struggle, although their passive sympathy was on the side of Rabbi Motye. Shortly before the first World War, Rabbi Motye died and his adherents chose no successor. After the war, Rabbi Joseph Rosen left for America, and the two factions were reconciled and agreed on one rabbi.

The Community Council
The Community Council administered all religious and community affairs. It gave financial aid to the various religious and charitable

associations, paid the salaries of the rabbi and other functionaries, and maintained the ritual bathhouse (*mikve*) and the poorhouse (*hekdesh*). The budget for these activities came from the tax on kosher meat known in our parts as *korobke*. The *korobke* was usually leased by one person, or by several partners, called the tax lessees. The *shokhtim* (ritual slaughterers) could not slaughter an animal or a fowl without a permit from the tax lessee. The permit for a chicken cost three kopeks; it was somewhat higher for a duck, goose, and turkey. The permit for a calf was sixty kopeks. For slaughtering a cow or an ox there was a certain tax, and an additional tax was levied on the meat, exclusive of the lungs, liver, head, and legs. To guard against the importation of meat from nearby towns, the rabbis prohibited the sale and consumption of such meat. In cases where this prohibition proved ineffective, recourse was had to the police.

Some twenty or twenty-five prominent members in the community, who were the trustees of the Houses of Study and the various associations, constituted the Community Council and ruled the community. They were the choosers and the chosen. The elections took place in the following way. By order of the rabbi a meeting was called, to which the Houses of Study sent delegates. The delegates were chosen in this manner. The trustee of the House of Study told the sexton to call out the name of the delegate. The sexton called out: "Rabbi Shmuel, son of Rabbi Mendel, first delegate! Will anybody second the motion?" The prominent members chorused, "Second." The sexton then called out: "Rabbi Mendel, son of Shmuel, second delegate! Will anybody second the motion?" The same members responded again, "Second." And so on, till the required number of delegates were "elected." The delegates met and elected the Community Council or passed upon matters of policy under discussion. Popular dissatisfaction with their decisions did not affect them.

Thus the Community Council ruled the town up to the first World War. During the German occupation of the town, the tax on meat was abolished. After the war, the Community Council was elected in a more democratic manner.

Associations

The Holy Burial Association (*Khevre Kadishe*) played a leading role among communal institutions in town. Its membership consisted of old and pious Jews. Membership in the Holy Burial Association was restricted. Admission took place in one of the following ways: first, members could enroll their children or grandchildren as minors and upon attaining maturity they became full-fledged members; or, second, an adult wishing to be admitted to the association had to serve for a year as a sexton, whose duties were the calling of the membership to meetings and attendance at funerals. The association purchased the site for the cemetery and took care of the surrounding moat (the cemetery had no fence). It obtained the necessary funds from the families of the deceased, in accordance with their financial abilities. To the credit of the association be it said that it never wronged these families. It was fair and reasonable in its demand and always conciliatory in its dealings.

The most popular of the organizations in town was the Nursing Association (*Khevra Line*). The function of this association was to provide nursing service for cases of prolonged illness. Constant attendance on the patient, in these instances, would leave the other members of the family exhausted, and this service would give them an opportunity for a brief rest. The association sent two members— to a male, two men, and to a female, one man and one woman—to attend the patient from ten o'clock in the evening to seven o'clock in the morning. The association had its medical supply department that lent thermometers, icebags, heating pads, and similar sick-room needs to poor patients. The very poor were also supplied with medicine and nourishing food. The association obtained its funds from weekly dues paid by practically every adult in town, from special pledges in the synagogue, from the collection on the eve of the Day of Atonement, and from grants of the Community Council.

Two types of visitors came to town frequently: poor Jews who went begging from door to door and itinerant preachers. The former were lodged in the poorhouse and the latter in a specially provided guest house (*hakhnoses orkhim*), consisting of a large room with several beds in it. The sexton would arrange for their meals in some household. The more distinguished preachers and the collectors for charitable organizations (*meshulokhim*) usually stayed at the inn.

The small merchants were always short of money and in need of a loan. Most of them had to resort to a private lender who charged usurious rates. For a loan of twenty-five rubles for a period of a half-year he charged four rubles interest, which he deducted initially. Repayments had to be made from the first week, at the rate of one ruble a week. There was in a town a traditional loan association, *Gmiles Khasodim*, granting loans up to twenty-five rubles without interest. But many people refused to apply to the *Gmiles Khasodim*, for they regarded such a loan as a form of charity.

In 1908–1909, a cooperative savings and loan association was established with the aid of the Jewish Colonization Association in St. Petersburg. The members of the association could borrow money at the rate of 8%. The state bank gave the association a loan of sev-

eral thousand rubles. People had confidence in the association and
instead of depositing their savings in the savings bank, they depos-
ited them in the association, which paid 6% interest. Even the non-
Jewish population did business with the association. In time the
private lender with his usurious rates was banished from the scene.

Sanitary and Hygienic Conditions

Sanitary conditions in town were far from satisfactory. Some inhabitants had to attend to their needs in the open. The wells were not
covered, and dust and dirt would find their way into them. Before
the war some wells were covered, and water was obtained by means
of a pump.

The Jewish community had a bathhouse, too small for the needs
of the population. On Fridays it was badly overcrowded, particularly in the winter. In the summer conditions in the bathhouse were
better, since a number of people bathed in the river. All types of
disease were prevalent in town, though they rarely attained epi-
demic proportions. Only during the German occupation in the first
World War and immediately thereafter, epidemics of dysentery and
typhus raged in town.

The economic situation of the town was fair; the people were
well-fed and well-dressed. As a rule, they had adequate medical attention. The town had a municipal hospital, with one physician, one
assistant (felcher), and a midwife. Hospital service was free to all,
and the non-Jewish population made use of it. The Jews, as a rule,
avoided the hospital, although they occasionally used the services of
the physician and the assistant in the capacity of private patients. In
addition there were two physicians (Poles, who had estates in the
vicinity), an assistant (a Jew), and two Jewish midwives in private
practice. The physicians enjoyed an excellent reputation in the entire district. One of them, a surgeon and gynecologist, attracted patients from points hundreds of miles away.

Education

At the age of five, a boy was sent to a school (kheyder) where he
was taught the alphabet and reading. In the kheyder the boy usually
spent a year or a year and a half, and was then promoted to a higher
grade, where he took up the study of the Pentateuch and the rest of
the Bible. The next step in his education was the study of the Talmud. Some teachers (melamdim) also instructed their pupils in
writing and in the elements of arithmetic. Thus, at the age of ten, a
Jewish boy knew a little of the Bible, could write Yiddish, had a
smattering of elementary arithmetic, and was studying the Talmud.

For the study of Russian there was a special teacher. Some boys studied in *kheyder* only part of the time and devoted several hours daily to the study of Russian, arithmetic, and writing.

Ordinarily the *kheyder* was in the home of the teacher. Study hours, except for beginners, were from nine in the morning to nine in the evening, with an hour for lunch.

For children whose parents could not afford the fee, there was a Talmud Torah, in which the fee was very low or tuition was altogether free. The Talmud Torah had three classes. In the first class instruction was given in reading, the Pentateuch, and the rest of the Bible; in the second class, in Bible, Talmud, and in writing Yiddish and Russian; in the third class, in Talmud, writing Yiddish and Russian, and in arithmetic. Instruction in the secular studies was given by two teachers who came for that purpose to the Talmud Torah for two hours daily, except Friday and Saturday. One teacher taught Yiddish writing and arithmetic and the other, Russian.

The years between twelve and fourteen were years of decision for the boys. Most of them entered at that age the leather factories, or were apprenticed to artisans. A small number of ambitious and promising boys left for the Yeshivas. Boys from the wealthier homes helped their parents in their factories or stores and simultaneously continued their education with a private tutor.

As for girls, their education was delayed to the age of seven or eight. It began with instruction in reading Hebrew and Yiddish, after which came instruction in writing Yiddish and Russian, and in the elements of arithmetic. At the age of thirteen or fourteen girls were usually apprenticed to seamstresses. The poorest became domestics. Some girls worked as saleswomen in their parents' stores part of the time and continued their education.

At the turn of the century a general public school, of four grades, and a modern Hebrew school were opened in town. These schools gave the foundation of a systematic education to a number of Jewish children. Moreover, some of the well-to-do parents began sending their children to secondary schools in the larger cities. At the time of the first World War, under German occupation, a secular Yiddish school was opened. After the war the old-fashioned type of *kheyder* became practically extinct. It was replaced by a net of Yiddish and Hebrew schools, which existed till the second World War.

Educational facilities for the non-Jewish population were provided by the Russian government. It maintained two elementary schools, one for boys and one for girls, and a seminary for the training of teachers for the elementary schools in the villages. The sem-

inary had some 300 students. These students came from the entire
district of Grodno and were provided with board and lodging by the
school. Together with the faculty and staff the seminary population
comprised some 350 people, who were a considerable economic factor in town.

Political Parties

The first political party in our town was the Zionist organization. On
a winter eve, some time in 1898 or 1899, the Jews were summoned
to the House of Study, where an out-of-town preacher and some
local men addressed them and Hebrew songs were sung. As far as I
recall, the speakers appealed to the audience to become members in
the Zionist organization, and the response was good. The work of
the organization consisted mainly in collecting money for the Jewish
National Fund. Before every Zionist congress there was some activity in town in connection with the election of delegates. The Zionist
organization also opened and maintained the Hebrew school in
town.

From 1905 to 1907 the town had an organization of Zionist Socialists, known by the abbreviated Russianized name of S.S. The
leadership of the group consisted of some temporary residents: a
teacher and several workmen. Upon their departure, the group dis-
solved. The town also had an anarchist club, with a leader who also
came from out of town. Upon his departure, the club closed its
doors.

The Jewish Labor Organization or "Bund" had its beginnings in
our town about 1900. By 1905 it had grown into a powerful organization. Its membership was drawn from all classes of the Jewish population. The organization conducted strikes in the leather factories
and in the shops. It helped elect to the first Duma a "Bund" representative, who received some 80% of the Jewish votes cast in our
town. But the years 1907 and 1908, the period of political reaction
in Russia, saw a decline of the organization in our town. Some active
members left town; others became disillusioned and gave up political activity. In 1909, the group was reorganized, concentrating
mainly on cultural activities: symposia, lectures, discussions.

The heroic period in the history of the "Bund" in Swislocz was
the year 1905. In the fall of that year a peculiar tension was felt in
town. People awaited eagerly the arrival of the mail to obtain the
latest news. Rumors of pogroms spread and there was talk of organizing a Jewish self-defense. Money was needed for the procure-
ment of arms; and the following way of obtaining the required sum

was decided upon, although the organization was in principle opposed to confiscation.

The town had two government stores for the sale of liquor. It was decided to stage an attack on one of these and to take its money. Once a month there was a fair in town, to which peasants and merchants from the neighboring villages and towns would come. During the fair the government stores took in considerable sums of money. The day of the fair was, therefore, deemed ideal for such an enterprise. Some time in October, 1905, in the evening following the day of the fair, as soon as the front door was closed, several of the most active members of the organization entered the store and, intimidating the salesgirls, departed with the money. Although the street was full of people and police (the chief of police summoned for the fair the police forces of the neighboring towns), no one noticed what had happened. When the salesgirls raised an alarm that they had been held up, no one believed them. Rumor had it that they embezzled the money and that the story of the burglary was an invention. It was only after the "Bund" published a proclamation taking responsibility for the act that suspicion of the salesgirls was allayed.

The attack was well organized, save for one serious slip. The participants entered the store undisguised, and the salesgirls identified two of them. One fled abroad; the other was arrested, and faced a long term at hard labor. After several months' imprisonment, he was freed on bail of five hundred rubles and likewise fled abroad. With the aid of the chief of police a false death certificate of the arrested was secured. The certificate was submitted to the district attorney and he released the bail. In the final analysis, the affair cost considerably more than it brought in.

Theatre

Formerly, Joseph and Esther plays were given in Yiddish during the Purim season. The actors, who were young men, took the parts of both men and women. Some time in 1905 or 1906 the first Yiddish play was given in which women, too, acted. This play was sponsored by the "Bund"; it was followed by several Yiddish plays given by the Zionist Socialist group.

Great difficulties were involved in these dramatic presentations, mainly in securing the requisite permission, which the chief of police was very reluctant to grant. Another difficulty was finding a suitable place. For a time a large barn was used, later on, a vacant factory loft. Under the German occupation and thereafter, dramatic presen-

tations in Yiddish were given more frequently, with the dramas of
Jacob Gordin enjoying great popularity.

Folkways

At the ceremony announcing the engagement of a couple to be married, plates were broken. After the engagement the bride and groom
were invited to the houses of their future in-laws for a holiday or a
weekend. On such occasions relatives and friends would send wine
to the house entertaining the guest, with a greeting, "Welcome to
your guest!" (*Mit lib aykh ayer gast.*)

Wedding festivities began on the Saturday night prior to the
wedding. The bride's girl friends would gather in her house for
dancing and merrymaking. This gathering was called the prelude
(*forshpil*). At dusk, the wedding proper commenced with a reception for the bridegroom, in which, as a rule, the older people par-
ticipated, and with the ceremony of "seating" the bride (*bazetsn*),
at which the young folks danced. After the reception, the bridegroom was led to the house in which the bride was "seated," where
he performed the ceremony of veiling the bride.

The wedding ceremony was usually performed in the synagogue courtyard. The bride and groom were led to the ceremony to
the accompaniment of music. First, the musicians led the bridegroom under the canopy and afterwards the bride was brought.
After the bridegroom pronounced the marriage formula and the
appropriate benedictions were recited, the young couple were taken
back to the house where the bride was "seated." At the entrance of
the house the couple were met by someone holding a tray with wine
and cake. Since both bride and groom fasted on their wedding day,
they were taken into a separate room, where they were given a light
repast.

After the ceremony the older folks sat down to the wedding
supper. Wedding gifts were announced by the sexton or the jester
(*badkhn*) in the traditional formula: "A gift from the bride's [or
groom's] relative!" When the elders finished their meal, the young
folks had theirs and afterwards continued dancing.

On the following morning, the bridegroom served brandy and
cake. On the Sabbath following the wedding, the traditional "seven
benedictions" were pronounced three times: Friday night, Saturday
morning, and Saturday afternoon. Saturday morning the bridegroom
was led by a group of men to the synagogue, with the bride similarly
led by a group of women. A bride and a lying-in woman were not
permitted to be alone in the house or on the street. After the bride
had been led to the synagogue and the lying-in woman had gone to

religious services, the restriction was lifted. On the walls of the room in which there was a lying-in woman, talismans, known as *shir hamaylesn,* after their opening words, were hung, containing psalm 121 and a number of incantations.

At the birth of a child, for the first seven days of confinement, the beginners in *kheyder* would come at sunset to the house of the lying-in woman and recite in unison several passages from the Bible, for which they were rewarded with sweets. If the newborn infant was a boy, a celebration called the *sholem zokher* was held on the Friday night following his birth, at which the guests were served boiled peas and broad beans. Some considered it particularly beneficial to have the child circumcised in the House of Study.

In case of death, the *Khevre Kadishe* was notified, and its representatives came and "lifted" the deceased, that is, strewed a little straw on the floor and placed him with his feet at the door. The grave digger was ordered to bring the coffin and dig the grave. Female members of the *Khevre Kadishe* sewed the shrouds. The sexton was sent to call out through the town, *"mes mitsve!"* implying that attendance at the funeral was requested. While these preparations were going on, a group of men would recite psalms in the house of the deceased. The *Khevre Kadishe* then washed the body, dressed it in a shroud, placed it in the coffin, covered it with a black cover, and carried it to the cemetery. One of the members of the *Khevre Kadishe* descended into the grave and put away the body, placed potsherds over the eyelids, two forked twigs in the hands, and boards over the body.

On the eve of Sabbath or holidays the people were summoned to the synagogue by the sexton. His summons served to indicate to the women that it was time to kindle the Sabbath candles. As soon as his powerful baritone voice was heard thundering, "To the synagogue!" the tradeswomen quickly closed their shops and rushed home to usher in the Sabbath. The people were also summoned to the synagogue when a preacher came to deliver a discourse.

The women believed in the evil eye, which they greatly feared. If a child was ill, particularly if it yawned, the mother immediately concluded that it had been given the evil eye. The only remedy was exorcism. For that purpose the women had several Yiddish incantations. One of them was in translation:

> There are three cracks
> In the ceiling wide.
> There the child's evil eye
> Will depart and hide.

Another incantation was:

> Three women sit on a stone.
> One says: "The child has the evil eye."
> The other says: "No!"
> The third says: "Whence it came
> Thither it shall go."

The incantation was followed by spitting three times.

Daily Fare

Like every other town, Swislocz, too, had a nickname: *sislevicher krupnik*. The town fully deserved that nickname. For there was not a day, except the Sabbath and the holidays, when *krupnik* was not on the menu of every Jewish home in town. What is *krupnik?* It is a thick soup of barley or groats mixed with potatoes. In the winter time, when meat was cheap, a slice of lamb or veal was added to the mixture. In the summer time, when meat was expensive, only the wealthy could afford to season their *krupnik* with meat. Most people had to be content with a little beef fat in their *krupnik,* to which onions were added as a preservative.

For the Friday breakfast the *krupnik* was prepared differently, as a rule with stuffed gut. It was eaten with fresh rolls, which nearly all Jewish women baked on Friday. Friday was also graced with potato pudding. Advantage was taken of the fact that the oven was kindled for the baking of Sabbath bread (*khale*). Some families had potato pudding twice on Friday.

Another popular dish was *lekshlekh bulve,* peeled potatoes, thinly sliced and boiled with meat. The dish was prepared in the morning, placed in the oven, and eaten for lunch or for supper. Likewise popular were potatoes boiled in their jackets (*sholekhts bulve*). The wealthy ate the potatoes with herring; the rest, with herring sauce. On the whole, potatoes were a staple in the diet of our district, both among Jews and non-Jews. It was not without a measure of justification that the district of Grodno was known in Russia as "the Grodno potato."

II. ECONOMIC ASPECTS

Occupationally, the Jews of the town were divided, in the main, into three categories: leather manufacturers and workers, merchants, and artisans.

The Leather Industry

Some 70% of the Jewish population were directly or indirectly connected with the leather industry. Its beginnings date from the 1870's, when Pinkhes Bereznitski opened a factory, in charge of a German master craftsman. Thereafter a number of other Jewish employers established factories. From 1900 to the German occupation (1915), the leather industry was the decisive factor in the general economic life of the town. At the beginning of this century the town numbered eight leather factories employing between forty and fifty workers each, and a dozen or so smaller shops employing from six to twelve workers.

The factories were divided into wet tanneries and dry shops. They produced leather from horse hides, which was used in the making of leggings and uppers for shoes and boots. The process of converting a raw hide into leather took about three months. The hide was taken into the wet tannery, soaked, scoured, and set out ready for the dry factory. These several steps took some ten weeks. In the wet tanneries the work was mainly unskilled, and most of the workingmen were non-Jews. In the dry factories it took another three weeks or so to curry, grain, wash, and otherwise make the leather ready for the use of the cobbler. Here the work was entirely skilled, and most of the workers were Jews. In both the wet tannery and the dry shop the work was done without machinery. It was hard work, the lighter tasks being performed by boys fourteen or fifteen years old. The big employers owned both wet tanneries and dry shops, with capital invested from twenty to forty thousand rubles. The business was conducted in a modern way. The raw hides were purchased in Bialystok with payments by drafts made out to a Bialystok bank. The leather was sent by freight to the leather merchants and the receipts for it were discounted in the Bialystok banks.

Practically all the manufacturers had to resort in part to borrowed capital. Some they obtained in the banks and some from private individuals on promissory notes. The interest private people charged on such loans ranged from eight to ten per cent. Every big employer went once a week to Bialystok to purchase raw hides and to settle his accounts with his banker. The smaller operators had no wet tanneries, but purchased half-finished hides in town or in nearby towns and finished them. The capital involved in such a business was between two and three thousand rubles.

Earnings of factory workers were good. From 1904 to 1908 earnings were the highest. An apprentice earned from two to four rubles a week; a semi-skilled worker, from eight to twelve rubles; skilled workers, from sixteen to twenty-five rubles. In 1908 and 1909 earnings declined about one-third. This lower level of earnings obtained up to the first World War. From 1904 to the first World War the working-day was eight hours: from eight o'clock to twelve o'clock and from one o'clock to five o'clock, with the exception of Friday, when the workers quit at three. Jewish workingmen did not work on Saturdays. Since the workers in the leather industry earned good wages, their standard of living was comparatively high. They were well-fed, well-clothed, and contributed freely to many a charitable cause. Frequently they extended loans of small amounts to hard-pressed merchants.

Merchants

There were some sixty stores in town, mostly small establishments, whose stock was worth fifty to a hundred rubles. A dozen or so were operated by women, with the husbands engaged in another occupation, such as tailoring or bricklaying. However, most of the merchants drew their entire sustenance from their stores. A few stores whose stock was valued at ten thousand rubles enjoyed the patronage of the landowners, officials, and leather manufacturers.

The big merchants took several business trips in the course of the year to Bialystok or Warsaw, where they purchased some of their stock. Otherwise, they purchased what they needed through a kind of commission merchant who did a two-way business. These commission merchants brought to town such farm products as butter, eggs, and mushrooms and shipped them to Bialystok on hired peasants' carts, usually on a Monday. Simultaneously, they took from the merchants in town orders for their immediate needs. On Tuesday mornings they would leave by train for Bialystok, attend to the orders given them, and sell the farm products that had in the meantime arrived in the city. On Thursday they would dispatch the carts back to town laden with merchandise and then go home the same evening by train. There, usually with the aid of wife and children, they delivered the merchandise to those who ordered it. Several of the more enterprising purchased some wares on their own account and sold them later on to the local business people.

Up to 1898 there were in town a dozen or so tavern keepers. After 1898, when the sale of liquor became a state monopoly, there were no more Jewish taverns. Several Jews obtained a license for a beer-hall (*raspivochno*), where bottled beer, tea, and a light bite were sold. Several Jews were grain dealers, buying from the landowners and the rich peasants. Part of the grain they ground to flour and sold to the bakers, and part they sold to wholesale merchants.

The district around the town abounded in forests; some were state owned and others the property of Polish landowners. (The Bialowiez forest, the property of the Czar, was a distance of fourteen verst from town.) A number of Jews were engaged in the timber business, some on a very large scale. The big timber merchants employed managers to supervise the work; the small merchants, who bought strips of forests (*otdelianka*), usually did all the work themselves. Occasionally, two or three small merchants formed a partnership. The better types of logs were floated down the Narew to the saw mills or to Germany. The others were used for railway ties. Defective logs were cut into fire-wood.

Artisans

There were two types of men's tailors in town: those that catered to the town's trade and those that worked for the peasants in the vicinity. The former were generally proficient in their trade and comparatively well-paid. Frequently, they employed two or three apprentices. The latter were less fortunate. In the summer time, when the peasants were busy in the fields, the tailors depending on them had a slack season. They had to resort to supplementary occupations, such as orchard-keeping and selling fruit. (The latter was usually the task of the wife.) Even in the winter time, when these tailors were fully employed, their earnings were meager. The materials they received from the peasants were home-made rough cloth, or sheepskins for coats. These materials could not be sewn by machine, but for the most part had to be stitched by hand.

The town had several women's tailors. Some employed one or two apprentice seamstresses. These tailors sewed bridal wardrobes, ladies' coats, or worked on orders for the wives of the landowners. They were proficient and well paid. There were, furthermore, a few seamstresses who sewed blouses and skirts for the town women. Other women sewed blouses or jackets (*kurtka*) for the peasant women. The remuneration for this work was very low: twenty or twenty-five kopeks per blouse. In addition, a few women were engaged in sewing underwear, pillowcases, and the like.

The shoemakers catered almost exclusively to the town population. Because the peasant went barefoot in the summer, a pair of boots lasted many years. The shoemakers made their wares to order. The uppers were cut according to measurement by the cutter (*zagotovshchik*). The soles, shanks, and heels were purchased in a store. The well-to-do shoemakers would purchase these supplies in larger quantities, and the poor, for each pair of shoes individually. A few wealthy shoemakers purchased leather for both uppers and soles in large quantities. These shoemakers employed several apprentices. During slack times, when orders were few, they kept on working, preparing a stock of shoes, and selling them later on, in the pre-holiday season. Before the first World War, when two merchants began to import shoes from Warsaw, the local shoemakers saw in this step a threat to their existence. They banded together and declared a boycott on the imported shoes: they refused to repair them. Some of the shoemakers were truly masters of their trade. They made a pair of shoes that vied in attractiveness with any displayed in the stores of the large cities.

The few blacksmiths in town catered, in the main, to the village population. They put rims on wheels, hammered out plows, and sharpened scythes. In the winter time, work fell off. It was practically limited to putting iron runners on sleds or shoeing horses. Some blacksmiths would purchase wheels in the winter time, put rims on them and sell the finished wheels in the summer, when there was great demand for them.

The town had eleven bakers. Two baked black bread, four baked both black and white bread, rolls, and *khale* for the Sabbath. Five baked cake, cracknels, and pastries.

The town also had a number of Jews without a definite occupation, shifting from one calling to another, or engaging simultaneously in two or more. Such a man would own one or two cows and sell milk, bake bread for sale, fatten geese, and bake matza for Passover. These tasks were carried out by the women. The men would go to the market, buy a measure or two of grain, and resell it to an export merchant. In the winter time, some of them would buy a calf or a lamb, have it slaughtered and sell the skin and the meat, retaining the head and the legs and other minor parts. Others would buy from the peasants skins of foxes and martens, wool, bristles, mushrooms, and berries, and resell them to export merchants.

These Jews without a definite calling were indirectly engaged in agriculture. The Jews who kept cows or horses had manure. The peasants in the vicinity were always short of manure. Those who owned fields near the town would sublet a strip of land for two years to a Jew who had manure. The Jew would hire laborers to strew the manure on the field and plant potatoes. The following year, he would plant barley, oats, or buckwheat. On the third year the field was returned to the peasant in a fertile state, ready for planting rye. The Jew, in turn, would have enough potatoes and barley, or any other cereal planted, for his use, and even a small quantity for sale. The straw, chaff, and very small potatoes served as food for the cattle.

Strikes and Lockouts
Until the turn of the century, working conditions in the leather industry were very bad. The working-day was fourteen or fifteen

hours and even more; wages were very low. Gradually, conditions improved. The number of factories increased and some of the smaller establishments expanded. More workers were needed, and wages rose. The higher wages attracted a number of young people from well-to-do homes, who deemed it below their dignity to become artisans. (These usually entered the more specialized branches of the trade, such as trimming and cutting, which were better paid.) Also young people from the vicinity came to work in the leather factories.

In 1900–1901 the "Bund" called the first strike in the leather factories. Members of the organization assembled a large number of workers and together formulated their demands: a raise of wages, and a twelve-hour working-day, from seven to seven, with one and a half hours for breakfast and one hour for lunch. Thereafter, a general assembly of the workers was called, at which these demands were discussed. A strike committee was appointed and a resolution adopted that no one should resume work until all demands were granted by the factory owners. This resolution was confirmed by an oath taken on a pair of phylacteries by each worker.

When the strike committee presented the demands to the factory owners, the latter remained unimpressed. They were inclined to regard the entire affair as a boyish prank. On the following day, however, when not a single worker reported for work, the factory owners began to take a serious view of the strike. They attempted to break the solidarity of the workers by promising higher wages to the older workers. Some of these workers remained unmoved by the tempting offers and in the case of others, the oath on the phylacteries acted as a powerful deterrent. The strike lasted only a short time and ended in complete victory of the workers.

A second strike in the leather factories took place in the summer of 1904. This was during the Russo-Japanese war, when the profits of the factory owners were high and the cost of living had gone up. By then the "Bund" was firmly entrenched in town, conducting systematic organizational and educational activities among the workers. The "Bund" called a general assembly of leather workers in a forest one verst and a half from town. To impress the assembly, a speaker from the neighboring town of Wolkowysk was invited. The speaker presented the demands formulated by the "Bund": 1) a raise of about 35% in wages; 2) a working-day of nine hours, from eight to five; 3) job tenure, no worker to be discharged without sufficient cause; 4) medical aid, the employer to pay the medical bills of the ill employee.

That evening the demands were presented to the factory owners. They were ready to negotiate a reduction in working hours and a raise of wages, but would not consider the other two demands. They were particularly incensed by the demand for job tenure, which to them appeared highly arbitrary. The strike committee refused to negotiate their demands piecemeal, and a strike was called. It lasted three weeks and again ended in a victory for the workers. The newly acquired working conditions were in effect till the end of 1907.

The political reaction, which set in after 1905, began to show its effects in the economic sphere. In November, 1907, the factory owners called a general assembly of their workers and put before them the following conditions: 1) a reduction of 35–40% in wages; 2) discontinuance of medical aid; 3) abolition of tenure. Refusal to accept these conditions, they threatened, would be answered with the closure of all factories. The workers rejected these conditions and countered with a strike. Although the "Bund" was then considerably weakened, it took over the direction of the strike.

In the first weeks of the strike it became evident that the developments had more than a local character. The leather factory owners of the entire dictrict were anxious for a victory of their fellows, in which instance they would follow suit and put before their workers similar conditions. On the other hand, the workers of the entire region were hoping for the success of the strikers in Swislocz. The Tanners Union of the district sent a professional organizer to advise and guide the strikers. He was an energetic young man and an eloquent orator, who inspired confidence. He also traveled throughout the district to collect funds for the strikers. The Tanners Union also enlisted the interests of the union in the district of Vilna and there, too, collections were made for the benefit of the Swislocz strikers.

Most of the strikers did not require aid. Before the strike, they had earned decent wages and had managed to accumulate some savings. The few less skilled workers whose earnings were in need of aid, were given one and a half rubles per week, if single, and three, if married. To keep up the spirit of the strikers, daily meetings were called. Since it was the winter and assemblies in the open were impossible, the strikers met daily, with the exception of Saturday, in the House of Study. The trustees of the House of Study raised no objection, for the majority of the Jewish population was in sympathy with the strikers.

At first there were no difficulties with the police. At the time of the strike the chief of police was a quiet and liberal man who gave assurances that as long as the strike was conducted peacefully, he would not interfere. It was difficult, however, to conduct the strike peacefully, and a clash between the strikers and the police occurred.

The strikers had pinned their hope on the factory owners' need for money to cover their outstanding notes. When these notes became due, the factory owners decided to raise cash through the sale of half-finished leather. This transaction led to the clash. In the seventh or eighth week of the strike, the strikers were told that a factory was shipping half-finished leather to other towns. A group of strikers left for the factory to prevent the loading of the leather. At the entrance to the factory yard several policemen denied entry to the strikers. When they attempted to force their way into the yard, the police fired a salvo in the air. The strikers retired and marched to the homes of the factory owners, demanding that the police be withdrawn from the factories. In the altercation that ensued, a factory owner was beaten up. The chief of police took a grave view of the situation and called for soldiers to patrol the streets. Tension mounted steadily.

Fortunately, the strike committee kept cool heads. An ultimatum was presented to the factory owners to withdraw the police and the military from the factories and the streets, or they would bear responsibility for the consequences. The police and military were soon recalled, and the strike again assumed a peaceful character.

The strike continued into the ninth and tenth week. Some strikers began to feel discouraged. At the meetings of the strikers in the House of Study demands were made for opening negotiations with the owners. The strike committee decided to call a conference of the Tanners Union of the Bialystok and Vilna districts. The conference met in Swislocz in the twelfth week of the strike. (The chief of police might have known of the conference, for it met in the neighborhood of his office.) It lasted two or three days and was attended by delegates from a number of towns. After prolonged discussions, it was decided to continue the strike. Following the conference, a general meeting of the strikers was called at the House of Study. Several delegates addressed the strikers, moving the audience to tears.

When the strike entered its fifteenth week, the spirits of the workers flagged. Aid from the neighboring towns came irregularly. The Passover festival was approaching, and the needs of the strikers were great. The demands for a settlement became more urgent, and the factory owners, too, were in a conciliatory mood. A week later the strike was settled with a compromise on wages. The workers won on the other points.

The Leather Industry from 1908 to 1919

A few weeks after the strike, the factory owners renewed their demands for the abolition of tenure of job under the threat of a new lockout. When the workers refused their demands, they carried out their threat. The "Bund" was then weak and the workers were exhausted by the previous strike. After three weeks of lockout, the workers capitulated and accepted all the demands of the owners.

The workers were quite demoralized. Since several factories had closed, a number of them were unemployed. Furthermore, the large factories began selling their product in half-finished form, which meant that the workers in the dry factories were left without work. Dry factories that had previously employed forty and fifty workers reduced the number to fifteen or ten. In these factories the percentage of Jewish employees was very high, and the growing unemployment affected chiefly the Jewish workers.

Some of the unemployed workers opened their own shops. Two workers would usually go into business in partnership. For about two thousand rubles they could rent a shop, hire a couple of workers, buy a quantity of half-finished leather and finish it. The small shops paid lower wages than the factories. Thus, a worker who had received before the strike some sixteen rubles a week in the factory, was paid for the same work in the small shop ten or nine rubles. Even at their best these small shops could give employment to only a small fraction of those who were out of work. A large number of workers then decided on immigration to the United States and Canada.

Emigration

Up to the turn of the century few Jews emigrated from our town. In 1896, several families left for Argentina to settle in the colonies of Baron de Hirsch. In the beginning of the present century there was a slight rise in emigration. After the depression resulting from the strike in 1908, the tempo of emigration quickened, with England, the United States, and Canada as destinations. In 1916, under the German occupation, several groups of women went to America. Emigration assumed mass proportions after the first World War, chiefly to the United States. There was also considerable emigration to Canada, Palestine, and Argentina.

1949

Three Generations

by Shlomo Bickel

Translated by Joseph Leftwich

Three generations: in each three brothers, one of them a rebel. In the first and third generation he was named Eliezer; in the second, he had missed that name by the space of a day. Each went his own way, following a personal vision, and each died before his time.

My great-grandfather, Reb Shlomo Halfon, once said of his three sons: "My Mordecai is a devout man, and walks in God's way; my Leizer has a sharp mind and soars high in the heavens; and my Moshe, the baby, is growing up to be a Gaon." From the start the drama of the family took place around Leizer. At the *bris* of his son, Reb Shlomo Halfon surprised everyone by not giving to the Mohel the name of a dead member of the family; instead, in a moment of distraction or rebellion he cried out, "The Lord is my God and my help—Eliezer!"

Leizer grew up to be a tall, fair man with dark eyes and a flaming red beard. His resistance to the traditional values of the family and his quest for freedom and transcendence took two different courses. The first was the pursuit of wealth. Coming from a family that piously distrusted the world of commercial goods and sharp dealing, Leizer stubbornly put his mind to work inventing a series of business enterprises. With his Menachem Mendel dreams of get-rich-quick, he invented wonderful schemes for distilling alcohol or for exporting beans to distant places. On money he borrowed from the family, or that the family borrowed from others, he climbed toward his desire of becoming a figure of commanding wealth. The truth was that Leizer was no more a man of affairs than was Sholom Aleichem's hero; his different enterprises all failed, leaving himself and the family with vast debts.

Once on the heights Leizer was reluctant to leave them. He did not come down to earth; he merely transferred his passion from worldly to other-worldly interests, from unconventional activities to unconventional ideas. His family had held for the most part to the traditional orthodoxy of the Mitnagdim. Careful and clear-minded scholars, they had also ventured into forbidden territory of free thought that lay even beyond the ideas of Ibn Ezra and those of Maimonides. However, Leizer became the first member who consorted with the world-estranged Hasidic Cabbala students. Together with them, and eventually as their leader, he worked on through the heavily mysterious nights in the Aziepol Bet Hamedrash—calculating the coming of the last days and striving to bring the Messiah before his time.

He was only in his middle thirties when, in 1892, he fell mortally ill. His brother's wife was expecting at the time, and by a tremendous effort of the will Leizer struggled to die before his nephew was born and so secure the preservation of his name. For weeks the family and even the community were drawn to this last act in the drama of Leizer's life. His struggle was unavailing, the infant was named Jacob on the day before Leizer's death.

Leizer's name was not perpetuated until ten years later, in the third successive generation of three brothers. It was given to the second of my father's sons.

"Leizer" of the second generation, my father's brother Jacob or "Yankel," was only a few years older than I. We both grew up and were educated in the congregation of Reb Itzik's Bet Hamedrash, where my pious grandfather Mordecai—to whom had been given the endearing name of Mordecai the Man—occupied his father's seat with all its privileges.

Yankel was a slender, sallow-faced youth, his expressive eyes flashing with laughter or abruptly clouded with sadness. He was a quick, natural scholar, but one whose temperament led him to take pleasure in putting barbed questions to his mentors—first to the Gemara teacher, then to the instructors in the Synagogue, and eventually even to the Dayan, Reb Joshua Heshel. Yankel was content to ask questions without pressing for an answer. During the years we were growing up together, he was never insolent in matters of faith, but it was not hard to see the portent in his thinly veiled skepticism and his air of observing the commandments mainly out of respect for his father. These were clear signs that he, like most children of his kind, though coming from good orthodox Jewish homes in our town, was already traveling the road that led to Haskalah and Zionism.

Yet we were wrong in our predictions. While his father was still alive, he was to exceed him in his piety and strictness of observance. Keeping the commandments, in fact, became Yankel's obsession. No one knew how this radical change in him had come about. Yankel was never to tell anyone. We became separated during the flight of the Jews from Kolomea during World War I, and his abrupt return to Jewish tradition and orthodoxy remained for many years a mystery to me.

Meanwhile, there was Leizer of the third generation. A few years ago my father and I spent a sunny Sabbath afternoon in his home at Givat Shmuel, in Israel, reminiscing about my brother's youth and the quarrels that the three of us had had, usually before breakfast, in the village of Sotevitz and in the city of Czernowitz.

"Of all the madcaps," my father mused, beginning to weave again his memories, "from my uncle Leizer to grandfather Shlomo Halfon and great-grandfather Moshe Nahum, and back to Shlomo Satanover, who was the first to come down from Russia to Galicia, it seems that my Leizer was the maddest." My father was not in the habit of praising his children, but having said this, he went on to recall with obvious pride and pleasure Leizer's incredible feats as a schoolboy. When we had fled to Moravia at the start of the First World War, Leizer was twelve. His religious education had already been interrupted by the closing of the *heder* and he received no tutoring through the years of our flight, first to Maehrisch-Weisskirchen in Moravia and then, after three years, to Czernowitz. Yet Leizer had managed to absorb enough Hebrew to later support himself as a tutor and to retain whole sections of the Bible in his memory.

He was no less a prodigy, my father recalled, in triumphing over the difficulties of being educated during the course of our emigration.

"He entered class five of the Czech-German high school in Maehrisch-Weisskirchen and with no previous knowledge of Czech and little acquaintance with German he was by the end of the school year not only the top pupil in his class, but (as the principal announced, more astonished than pleased), the top pupil in the whole school." My father's face was lit with the strange, unexpected force of his pride as he continued on, recounting Leizer's next success at Czernowitz high school where he had again been publicly congratulated for the knowledge of Rumanian and Rumanian history he had acquired within a single year of study. At the same time he had be-

gun his daily siege of reading Spinoza's *Ethics* in Latin, having got
caught up in Czernowitz with a circle of Constantine Brunner's
disciples.

My own memories during that afternoon of reminiscences with
my father came mainly from the period that followed, particularly
the summer vacations we would spend with father in the Bukovina
village where he then lived. I would be home from Bucharest, Leizer
at first from Bucharest and then from Berlin, and the youngest,
Meshulem, from high school in Czernowitz. I joked with my father
about the arguments that had inevitably ensued between him and
his older two sons. I did not wish to disturb the pleasures he was
taking in his memories and so recalled certain scenes as humorouly
and agreeably as I could. But in fact there had been little humorous
or agreeable in those quarrels. They had been tense and dramatic
clashes, especially between father and Eliezer, often ending in angry words and even a feeling of bad blood.

During those vacations father would be up at dawn to begin his
studies. Seated at the breakfast table he would pore over some volume of Jewish learning, but now and then he liked to look into the
books that we had brought home with us. One of the first of our passionate arguments flared up on the morning that father had come
upon Brunner's *Die Lehre von den Geistigen und vom Volk,* possibly
the most important work in our generation on the development of
Spinozism. It begins with Brunner's statement about the radical difference between the thinking of the intellectual and that of the people, and about the hostility on both sides that "has grown more acute
and must perforce lead also to outer separation."

Eliezer tried to prove to father that Brunner's position had nothing
to do with elitism. It concerned two different kinds of "I" and the
God-cognition and way of life that followed from them.

"What new discovery has he made?" father exclaimed, going to
his bookcase and taking down Maimonides's first book of *Mishneh
Torah.*

"Maimonides spoke centuries before your Brunner of the intellectual. He described him as holy and separated and a guide for the
whole people, and he singled him out as one for whom he had prepared the privilege of being filled with the Holy Spirit, and of 'becoming a different man, exalted above the height of all the sages.'

"Yet Maimonides with all his theories of holiness and separation
and being a guide for all," father went on passionately, "was considerably under the influence of Christianity. To the Nazarenes sanctity
is acquired by separation from the world. To Jews a holy man is no

self-segregated hermit. In this respect Hasidism has understood
Judaism beautifully and profoundly. The sanctity of the Hasidic
Rabbi was in effect that of a King among his people."

A few days later father took from Eliezer's bookcase Brunner's
Der Judenhass und die Juden ("Jew-Hatred and the Jews") and
read the chapter "Speech to the Jews: We Want Him Back."

These pages are Brunner's greatest literary achievement, written with a terse, stormy eloquence that shakes and moves the reader.
Father was no exception, but what was stirred up in him by Brunner
was his anger and revulsion against Christianity.

"What do we want him back for, the Nazarene?" father stormed.
"What good will he do us? Hasn't he cost us enough blood? They've
been hunting and murdering us for two thousand years in his name,
and suddenly we are now to want him back!"

"How is Jesus to blame for the things done in his name?" Eliezer
replied, calm but challenging. "In whose name have people not
committed the most atrocious crimes? Haven't they done so in the
name of God Himself?

"If we recall," Eliezer went on, while father struggled to keep
from interrupting him, "if we recall the barbarities and the infamies
committed in Jesus' name, we must not forget the brave and beautiful things that people have done in his name. Not only Christian
hypocrites invoke Jesus' name; so do those who, by the power of the
Christ figure, have conquered evil temptations and have gone the
road of self-purification, the road of sanctity and seeing God."

"Every time I hear these saintly people boast of their conquest
of temptation," my father said, "I fail to understand what they have
achieved. Maybe one who conquers temptation is a hero—but what
makes him a saint too?

"Do you know who is a saint?" he then asked. "The poor woman
who has more trouble than she can bear, and curses everything
round her, even her own children, even herself—she is nearer to
God than all the saints and self-purifiers who have conquered all
their temptations. Job is nearer to God in Chapter 3, when shattered
by the blows upon his body and mind, he opens his mouth and
curses the day he was born, than in the last chapters when he has
conquered himself and subdued his just complaints. Not for nothing
did the Psalmist say, 'The Lord is nigh unto them that are of a
broken heart.' And God stands at the right hand of the poor."

Yet an argument as heated as this could still end with a joke.
One of us recalled the story of Mechel, the *shokhet* of Kolomea, who
prayed to God that He should for once stand at the right hand of
the rich, at the side of Hersh Rammler or Mendel Brettler, not to let

them earn enough for the Sabbath. We laughed over it, or at least we smiled, and then father called to mother in the next room:

"Beile, please give me a pill for my headache, and let the boys have their breakfast. We've talked our belly full!"

The most violent argument we three had those mornings in the village was again over one of Brunner's books. This time it was *The Duties of the Jew and the Duties of the State,* one of his weakest efforts. Brunner attacks here the whole idea of a Jewish people, inveighs against Zionism, and calls for a radical program of assimilation. Brunner argues his case with little knowledge of Jewish life or culture. Speaking of the many literary figures of the Diaspora, for example, he asserts, "They have nothing to say in their jargon, and therefore they have no literature."

Eliezer, who knew and loved the Hebrew and Yiddish classics, didn't attempt to defend such gross errors. He merely argued that these statements did not alter the truth: that we Jews had been declining and disintegrating as a people for generations, and that by assimilation we could achieve more for our peace and security, for the benefit of mankind, and for our spiritual mission among the nations.

Father's response was to call Eliezer "the volunteer Jonah," who flees to Nineveh to carry out his spiritual mission and thinks that he will be received there with open arms.

"I want you to know," father said to him, "that as soon as the ship of the nations feels the slightest contrary wind, the people on board will start at once to investigate whose fault it is. They soon find out by casting lots (they are great ones at casting lots) that the Jews are to blame, and they ask—Whence come you? What is your country, and of what people are you? No matter how ardent the Jew is in his desire for assimilation and for his spiritual mission, the others will throw him into the sea, and will persuade themselves that the sea has ceased raging because they got rid of the Jew."

Eliezer took up father's interpretation of Jonah's fate, and in his quiet but emphatic way, he continued the story:

"True, Jonah was cast into the sea, and he endured the bitter experience of being in the belly of the whale for three days and three nights. But when he escaped by a miracle, God again commanded him to go to Nineveh, and 'make unto it the proclamation that I bid you.' And in the end 'the people of Nineveh believed God.' After all his troubles God did not release Jonah from his mission—and Nineveh did repent.

"If that is so," Eliezer continued in a tone touched by sarcasm as well as deep conviction, "perhaps it is true that for God's mission we must be prepared to suffer no less than for the existence of the nation."

The argument grew fiercer. What impressed me most of all was the point at which father, speaking in a whisper, which sounded louder than a shout, declared: "If one of you, my three sons, ever speaks publicly against the existence of our people, I shall—" and he placed his hand on his breast, then quickly took it away.

During these discussions I would sometimes wonder what the position of my uncle and friend, Jacob, would now be on these decisive issues of Jewish life. We knew that he had settled in the little Carpathian town of Bolechov where he continued to practice his austere and rigorous religious faith. As the years passed, and Meshulem pursued his studies at Czernowitz University and Eliezer completed his medical courses and became a member of the medical faculty in Berlin, Jacob remained apart from us and from the modern world we had entered. For ten years we didn't see each other at all, but shortly before Hitler's war I happened to be traveling from Bucharest to Vienna and stopped off to surprise him in his little town of Bolechov.

It was a day late in summer and as I approached the house in which Jacob lived, I chanced to see in the light of the sun upon the window the figure of a Jew in *tallis and t'fillin* shining out at me. It was Jacob. Still slim as a boy, his face was shadowed now by a thick dark beard and earlocks—the face of my grandfather Mordecai, of blessed memory.

Standing there at his devotions he must have heard me enter and speak to his wife; but if he recognized my voice, not for an instant did he open his eyes to look at me till he had finished his prayers. His soft, warm voice, whistling when it rose to a high note, went on from the point of "Blessed, who in mercy givest light to the earth and them that dwell on it. . . ."

As had been the practice in our family, Jacob lingered earnestly over this prayer, which speaks of God's great love for the Jews. When he reached the phrase *"Ahavo rabo"* ("with abounding love") and *"chemlo gedolo"* ("with great compassion") his body seemed driven by a strong inward force that carried him from one end of the room to the other. When the prayer was over Jacob stood motionless. Then, in a whisper, he recited the rest of the morning prayers. His voice rose only twice—at the words *"Shema Yisroel"* and "That you may remember and do all my commandments and be holy unto your God." They were words of grief and anguish, and by a sudden movement of his body, he twisted himself, as it were, within them. He took hold of both ends of the *tallis,* and stamped his feet, as though emphasizing to himself the exhortation of God in the Book of Numbers to remember that one must keep all, absolutely all of the commandments.

I sat there for perhaps a whole hour, pretending to be reading the Polish newspaper I had bought at the station. But I didn't for a moment take my eyes off Jacob. Observing his stubbornly closed eyes and his thinly drawn lips enunciating with painful sharpness each word of the prayer, I no longer wondered why Jacob did not pause in his prayer to greet me, after ten long years, nor even to open his eyes to look at me.

The question of Jacob's unnatural absorption in his manner of observing Judaism, would probably not have been raised were it not for Jacob's wife. Afterward, as we sat at the table talking about family affairs, she listened intently while she tried to quiet their impatient little seven-year-old daughter. But when Jacob asked me about my father, she suddenly broke into the conversation as if she had been waiting anxiously for an opportunity to declare what she felt.

"I'm sure your father, may he have a long life," she turned to me with a laugh that was more of a sigh, "doesn't spend three quarters of the day saying his prayers, as his youngest brother does."

"My brother Itze," Jacob answered for me, "is no great sayer of prayers. He's a fine, gentle sort of man, a scholar, one always poring over books, and not only the Siddur and the Mahzor.

"But I, Itze's youngest brother Yankel, I know"—his expressive eyes fixed on my face to watch my reaction—"I know that the most important books of all are the Siddur and the Mahzor. For, my dear Gittel, prayer is to a Jewish soul the same as—in a different, lesser way—salt is to a piece of meat on the salting board. The prayer, like the salt, draws out the unclean in the blood and makes it kosher—clean and pure.

"Do you know," Jacob said to me, when his wife and little girl had left the room, "the meaning of *'Vehiyisem kedoshim leilohei-chem'*—Be holy unto your God? It means that each Jew must break his own way through to holiness for himself, to the 'Light that is sown for the righteous.' No one can make that journey for you. You must tread the road yourself. And the road goes through prayer, through the hard, the very hardest burden of commandments—'that you may remember'—by wearing the heavy yoke of all the commandments."

I tried to catch him on the point of the Fifth Commandment.

"Do you mean to say that you are more scrupulous in the observance of the commandments than your father, my grandfather Mordecai?"

Jacob gave me a troubled glance, but he went on in a patient way.

"My father, of blessed memory, was a pious Jew indeed. But like your father he was also somewhat of a Hasid—a pious Hasid, to be sure, not like your father who was a heretic going on pilgrimages to the Rebbe."

I was astounded.

"Quite simply," said Jacob, "your father's Rabbi is Zionism, Herzl, Ahad Ha'am; and my father, of blessed memory, also went on pilgrimages to a sort of Wonder Rabbi. Of course he prayed, all his life, with all his heart and with all his mind, but more than his own prayer, more than his own chapter of the Psalms, more than his own Tractate of the Mishna, he leaned on the merit of his fathers, on the learning of Joshua Heshel the Dayan, and on the body of the congregation, together with Reb Itzik's synagogue."

Then, wagging his finger at me, he forestalled what I was going to say.

"If you think I am copying my grandfather, Shlomo Halfon, going his road, you are very much mistaken. Grandfather Shlomo did not believe in observing 'all My commandments.' He wanted to get there through reasoning, and found himself entangled in doubts. . . ."

At this point Jacob's brother-in-law arrived. About ten years older than Yankel, he was a typical, stout, prosperous scholar, complete with pince-nez and an air of self-importance. He was the leader of the "Mizrachi" in the town.

The first words he addressed to me were: "Don't worry about eating in your uncle's house. He's the most observant Jew in town. He has never eaten a crumb in my house, just a glass of tea with sugar." He spoke in a bantering tone, but I could sense an undertone of grievance much like his sister's. I felt increasingly hostile toward Jacob's way of life, and even more toward his attitude of being certain that his road alone was the right one. I said to Jacob as quietly and as soberly as I could:

"As I understand you, then, your aim is to bring the light of Paradise to earth for yourself alone by strict observance of all the commandments. Congregation, community, the Jewish people, all lead you away from holiness, from dwelling with God in your own lifetime."

But then, almost involuntarily, I spoke the harsher words that had been forming in my mind. "So you are, as the saying goes, a saint in armor, thinking constantly only of yourself, only of your own soul's salvation!"

Jacob merely smiled as though gratified by my remark.

"No, it isn't that," Jacob's brother-in-law said, obviously wishing to intervene. "No one in this town has any complaint against your uncle, nobody says that he doesn't do his duty, God forbid, as a good neighbor. There is nobody like him in the concern and help he gives to the poor and the sick. Yet there is something. I am myself an observant Jew, living among observant Jews. But that the name Herzl is impure and mustn't be mentioned on the Sabbath is something I heard for the first time from your uncle."

"What is there so surprising about it?" declared Jacob. "The Sabbath is holy to a Jew, the day when he divests himself of all that is material. Therefore he can give himself up fully to his sensibility and approach closer to God's holiness. If he allows himself to be distracted in the midst of his Sabbath state by Herzl, by community, by meetings, and by other outside affairs, it would be absolutely wrong not to remind him that he is squandering a holy day, on which he could do much for himself."

"For himself, for himself," his brother-in-law repeated, his voice no longer evasive but scornful. "Among Jews it is sacred, not this or the other man is holy. It is Israel that is a holy people."

"That's it! That's just my point!" cried Jacob. He took hold of his brother-in-law's hand, as if wanting to ask his forgiveness in advance for what he was going to say:

"You think, Moshe, that if a people lives in the Land of Israel, and speaks Hebrew, to say nothing of going to synagogue on the Sabbath, it is a holy people. You're quite wrong! We can be a holy people only if each Jew, for himself, develops his holiness by his own force and strength. A holy people must consist of people who are holy. There is no other way. Each Jew must work for himself."

Again, I was repelled by the tranquil assurance in his words, and still more by their similarity to Christian monasticism. No doubt I was moved by this echo of the controversies in which we, my father and I, had been engaged for some years with my brother Eliezer. It was the same theme, the same problem of being holy, though now in the domain of Torah, not of Spinoza and Brunner.

"I hope you realize, Yankel," I said to him (the smart-aleck way in which I said it is still a humiliating memory to this day), "that your road to holiness is not Jewish but Nazarene. The Nazarenes don't recognize the intervening link—people—between God and

man. They have no religious 'we.' And the individual who seeks to
come closer to God than the rest must segregate himself from the
community, must renounce wife and child, must become a Nazarite,
or as they call it, a monk. Jews come closer to God, praise Him,
through prayer in common, through studying Torah in common. It
seems to me, Yankel, that you are a Nazarene in *tallis* and *t'fillin.*"

This time Yankel's face went white. His fine eyes looked tortured and he almost screamed:

"How can you compare me to the Nazarenes! They worship
idols. For them God Almighty has a son, and all their holiness is
directed toward being near to the son, not to God, praise His Name.
How can you mention them in the same breath?"

I had already regretted my words. His brother-in-law looked at
me reproachfully.

The atmosphere was only broken by Jacob's wife coming in to
ask us for dinner. The brother-in-law excused himself and left. At
the table we spoke only of family matters.

I told Yankel that my brother Eliezer, who was now a doctor,
had published a book in Berlin called *The Renaissance of Philosophy.* "It's the same seeking for holiness," I said, laughingly, "only
while your road is prayer, his is speculative thought. You are both
trying to soar. You both take after Uncle Eliezer whom you were
very nearly named after."

Jacob looked grave. But from his sallow face and dark beard
there rose a gleam of satisfaction. He asked me to convey his greet-
ings to Leizer and to tell him in his name that the road of thought
led to doubts and pitfalls, and the surest road could only be the road
of prayer.

I traveled back that same evening to Stanislav, and then on to
Vienna. I never saw Jacob again. He perished ten years later, for
the Sanctification of the Name. He reached his passionately desired
state of holiness together with all the other Jews of Bolechov without any special effort of prayer or thought.

It was in the spring of 1933, only a few months after my encounter
with Jacob, that Eliezer came back from Berlin to make his home in
Bucharest. He had given up his hopes for a lectureship at the Medical Faculty of Berlin University. On April 1, 1933, the day of the
official boycott against the Jews, the jackboots of the SS had also
sounded for the first time in the university corridors. Eliezer's superior, Professor Wagner, asked him to his room where he begged
him to return to Rumania. There was no question now of getting him

a lectureship: this powerful figure in Berlin medical circles would
not even be able to protect his assistant against physical attack from
the Nazi students in the lecture hall.

So we two brothers, Eliezer and I, sat in my room a few days
after his arrival in Bucharest, discussing practical matters like getting him a house, arranging a surgery, securing an appointment in
the City Hospital or the Jewish Hospital, and translating some of his
medical writings from German into Rumanian. However, I had told
him of my afternoon with Jacob and soon the pattern of argument
in which we two brothers and our father had been engaged over the
last ten years began to weave itself again.

"Your uncle Yankel, who was nearly named Eliezer," I said,
"doesn't believe in the people of Israel, any more than you do. The
difference between Yankel and you," I went on, "is only this—that
for him there must be a free psychic area where every Jew can
achieve holiness, so that the Jews may afterward become a true nation, a holy people. And according to you we must be as free as possible from the 'superstition' of Jewish nationhood to wage unhampered the war of personal liberation, and to prophesy more effec-
tively and with more success in Nineveh."

As I spoke, Eliezer shifted from one hand to the other the heavy
gold ring with the Greek inscription "*Kalos Kagathos*" (good and
beautiful) that his colleagues in the Constantine Brunner Society
had given him a year before for his thirtieth birthday. His deep blue
eyes sparkled with that magical intense light of truth revealed and
found, and of absolute conviction, that I had seen only six months
before in another face. "You've forgotten," he said in a playful voice,
"that among other differences between Yankel and me, I'm not so
frightened of Jesus as he. On the contrary, I believe, as you know,
that it was only by means of Jesus' original personality (the fact that
he based himself on the Jewish Massorah and spoke its tongue did
not in any way diminish his originality) that the miracle occurred
of Judaism influencing other nations outside the Jews. It was only
through Jesus and his apostle Paul that Judaism became a matter of
world-historic significance. Brunner is right when he says that no
one but Jesus could have done this, not Rabbi Akiba, nor Rabbi
Huna, nor Rabbi Ashi. It is also true that it was only through this
world-historic Judaism that the wall between peoples and races,
between God and man was destroyed."

Eliezer continued in the measured magisterial way that must
have contributed to the rebbe-hasid relationship he enjoyed in the
Brunner Society.

"Jacob certainly is not a Christian, not even in the remotest

way. He is as far from the Christian church and from the Christian
religion as you and I. But his own God-seeking, his own desire for
moral purification has led him beyond questions of the community
and nation, and brought him back to himself.

"You know me, Shlomo," he went on, bending toward me to
emphasize his words, "and you surely won't mistake my religionless-
ness for godlessness. My heart certainly recognizes no King in
Heaven, yet I do know something about the happiness of piety. My
God, Spinoza's *Deus Sive Natura*, is like the mystical God of the
soul itself. Yankel's God Almighty stands like the God of all religions outside the human soul, outside nature; that is why our pious
uncle believes He can be reached only through prayer."

I broke in: "I am more concerned to know what you think, in so
many words, about the meaning of the concept of the Jewish people.
The fact is that in telling you about my argument with Jacob I em-
phasized the point of Jewish peoplehood, because I am keeping to
our agreement—remember?—when we had our talks two years ago
in Berlin, in your room in the Charité, and then over lunch in the
little restaurant near the hospital. We decided then to end the ten-
year-old quarrel between us, we two brothers and our father, and to
regard ourselves like the two brothers in the story, who went out
each on his own road to conquer the world, and discover the supreme value in life—and only from time to time, when necessary,
would we exchange the experiences of our struggle and achievement.

"It seems to me," I went on, "that you must now have something to tell me about your experiences during the past year and
particularly in recent months in the German Nineveh. As you can
realize, Hitler Germany has strengthened my Jewish nationalism,
has made my dreams of Jewish national redemption more urgent.
But I imagine that your dream of assimilation confronted with the
reign of evil in Berlin has taken a serious beating, if it has survived
at all."

Eliezer said, with a nostalgic smile, "They were fine, those ten
years of bitter conflict, and the finest and the most fiery fighter
among us was father. He raged like a storm, because it seemed to
him that his son Eliezer had ceased or was ceasing to be a Jew. I
am far, very far from that."

Then he went on. "I can never drain away the stream of Jewishness that my inherited way of life and my upbringing and education
have left in me. But I must confess to you that if I have a son I shall
bring him up free from all religion, and do all I can to give him the

chance of assimilating to the surrounding people, particularly to the dominant people of the state."

"Doesn't that mean an education in insignificance and, to a certain extent, in hypocrisy?" I asked, aiming at his disclosed wound.

"There will be no hide-and-seek between me and my son," Eliezer cried out, deeply pained. My deliberate shot had struck home. "My son will know, will see over and over again in me, who have neither the strength nor the desire to be anything else—I will also teach him—that he comes from the great Jewish people. And if he isn't a clod he will be proud of his honorable descent."

"And his honorable descent," I continued remorselessly, "is to assimilate to the surrounding peoples, who have now shown in the ugliest way how dishonorable they are."

Eliezer struggled to get control of himself. "You asked me about my experience in Nineveh," he said with quiet gravity. "I give you my answer—now, more than ever, when our trust in the civilized nations is shaken, we need a radical assimilation to the surrounding world, in order—"

"In order—" I yelled impatiently, "in order that one should be able to work out one's own inner liberation, and prophesy successfully in the sinful city of Nineveh. So we are back at our old discussions. Every Jew is a Messiah for himself and a Prophet to the nations. That is our mission, for which we must pay with the death of our people."

"Not 'we must pay' but 'we pay.' With and against our own will," Eliezer amended my words. "And the mission, you must admit, is a great one. Nothing to be ashamed of."

Within two or three years after his return from Berlin, Eliezer had become one of the leading Jewish gynecologists in Bucharest. He also did a lot of work in philosophy. He taught Spinoza's *Ethics* to a group of Brunnerists. He finished his book *Problems and Aims of Thinking*, which was brought out by a Zurich publisher just before the war. And from the summer of 1937, when he was entrusted in Brunner's will with the publication of his posthumous works, he was busy preparing some of them for the press.

I left Bucharest with my family early in 1939 for America. Eliezer remained in Rumania, and lived through the bitter years of the Antonescu regime and the Rumanian-Soviet war. He narrowly escaped death in the January pogrom in Bucharest, and then in a tremendous effort of devotion, he succeeded—almost by a miracle—in saving our parents from deportation to Transnistria.

For nearly five years all contact between us was broken. It was only at the end of 1945 that we were able to correspond again. I sent him my books which had been published in Yiddish in New York, *A Town of Jews,* and *Details and Conclusions,* and he sent me the manuscripts of a six-volume philosophic work.

I saw from this manuscript that Eliezer's philosophic thought had grown, deepened, and broadened. I also sensed that he had taken a great step forward during the war years, in his ethical life. Like his two predecessors in the family, he was still struggling toward self-transcendence along his Spinozist path of ethical perfection set forth in one of the last pages of *Wirklichkeit und Wahrheit des Denkens:*

"One who thinks *sub specie aeternitatis* cannot morally judge and condemn, because he knows that to do so according to the criterion of good and evil has only a practical justification and is entirely anthropomorphic. The struggle must therefore be waged not against people but against our own feelings and the dismal thoughts of reason, that deprive us of the capacity of spiritual vision and rob us and obscure from us the fulfillment of our eternity. Whoever has known the joy of the spirit must perforce demonstrate in his life that he is worthy to be and to act in such a way that he should not be cut off again from the sources of his changed existence. He must do so because that is for him the only way, and vice-versa."

My feeling that these words expressed not merely another stage in Eliezer's philosophy but a deep change in his moral being was confirmed when I saw him in Canada, where he had come to live in 1950 and where he died only a year later. His experience in the hell of Bucharest had made him a stern master of himself, but he was also endowed now with a new gentleness of understanding, with an enthusiasm for noble acts wherever he found them, and with a forgiving smile for the individual's "moral judgments."

As I go now once again through his letters, I can see that our family argument never really ended. He wrote to me in February 1946 in answer to a letter in which I must have been recounting my Jewish experiences in the war years:

"The enthusiasm into which your letter plunged our parents and my parents-in-law is as alarming as it is true. They applauded you with all their hearts; you were their spokesman and advocate. It seemed to them that my ideas and my arguments were shattered, broken to bits, and they hoped from minute to minute that I would reveal myself to them as a true penitent."

Then he came to the point:

"I did not read your words coldly, and I did not dismiss them with an easy no. I put into them all the force and intention you

wanted. What drives you to feel as you do is your love for our mar-
tyred Jewish dead. But believe me, I haven't purchased my point of
view from dry logic either, nor fashioned it at my writing desk.

"The Jewish people and the Jewish religion have been for a long
time now in a ceaseless process of dissolution. Not because of ill-
will nor because of national disloyalty. It is the demand of life, the
natural direction of history. Emancipation isn't an idea invented by
a few 'traitors.' These 'traitors' saw where life was leading them, and
they wanted to hasten the natural process. They had more love for
the individual Jew than for the Jewish people. The conscience of a
thinker instructs us to turn away from ideas which are contrary to
life. We mustn't allow ourselves to be misled because we are bound
to them by a thousand invisible threads of emotion and desire. Tradition and subconscious feeling have often proved to be the enemy
of life and truth."

This is the concluding paragraph of Eliezer's letter:

"Emancipation has proved impossible? But hasn't the road to
national independence proved more than once 'impossible'? The
road to the Land of Israel is no smooth and comfortable return home
either. The road of assimilation is likewise not easy for those who
for various reasons can't do what Zionism requires. . . ."

Even in the choking atmosphere of early Nazi Germany and
then in the nightmare of Iron-Guardist Rumania, Eliezer had held
with his stubborn Jewish feelings to the idea of assimilation. It was
only when he came for the first time into the freedom of emancipation in France and then Canada, and observed Nineveh and its great
Christian civilization, that his faith in assimilation was shaken.

After a few months in Toronto, he wrote to me:

"What attracted me so much to the West (though I would probably have very quickly got rid of my material worries in Israel) was
the prospect of slipping out of the narrow circle and entering the
large world of spiritual aspirations and spiritual trends. But here?
Besides the cult of money there are only sports and religious activities, and they are merely social entertainment. If I had no heart for
the nationalist hot-house mood in Israel, how should I be pleased
here? In Israel everything—accepted or not—is sound and *genuine*,
because it is the expression of an organically emerging nation. But
here many things are false, just phrases, mere empty pretense. . . .
And there is little hope of coming into contact with other, freer circles, who are *really* interested in higher matters, because the religious communities are severely exclusive one from the other."

In the end, then, experiences in the free "Nineveh" finally altered Eliezer's assimilationist convictions and brought him spiritu-

ally nearer to the State of Israel. Above all he came to admire its cultural distinctiveness, that genuine character which is "the expression of an organically emerging nation."

I sent to my father Eliezer's letters to me and a copy that I had made of his last foreword to Brunner's books—in which he welcomed the new State in Brunner's name. Father answered me in expressions of faith and conviction, that please God, he would meet Eliezer very soon, and would finally reach an agreement with him. Still, "in this world Eliezer's last words are certainly a consolation."

About four months later, my father died. He had grown increasingly religious in his last years in Israel. The Siddur and the Mahzor were his constant companions. He never spoke of it himself, and if anyone else did, he took an ironic attitude toward his piety. He had always been very good at that.

The day before I left Israel to return to America I spent several hours with my parents in Givat Shmuel. While I was there one of his rare communications arrived from my youngest brother, Meshulem, who had remained in Rumania. Father passed the card to me:

"The baby is a Prophet, as well. A captive of Amalek, he teaches French in a high school, and keeps chastising himself, seeking out his sins. Read it—'I tell myself and I don't stop repeating it: Errors upon errors. You should have done differently and better with your life.'

"As for my older sons," Father went on, "they are both of course prophets. One prophesies in the streets of Jerusalem, and the other in Nineveh. But there isn't a single one to say Kaddish."

In the Kaddish year for my father that followed I often thought of these words of his. "The Prophet to Nineveh" is no more. The captive of Amalek is still a captive; and I don't even know if the news of Father's death got through to him. I alone am alive and free. But what security can there be for one like me, who had in common with my generation cast off the burden of mitzvas, and had not realized in time that this burden alone can give a Jew a little Jewish freedom in the freedom of the Emancipation?

1956

The Jewish Factor in My Socialism

by Hayim Zhitlowsky

Translated by Lucy S. Dawidowicz

From my friends I learned about socialism, which in their proud conviction was the last word in scientific knowledge. New horizons opened up for me with new methods of measuring and evaluating phenomena, foremost among them socialist science, the last arbiter in all matters of human concern. I learned much of this, not systematically but from my socialist friends. These ideas deeply affected me. Their conclusion that Jews were, in the main, parasites filled me with sorrow and shame. It was not easy to submit to the judgment issued by socialist science. But still, think of it: science, socialism!

This new socialist ideology did not vindicate antisemitism, but if I would then have asked "Are you for us or against us," the answer definitely could not have been "for you." Socialism was a stream of ideas containing elements inimical to Jewish existence in the Diaspora. (I could not even conceive of another kind of Jewish life. It was still before the pogroms and before the Palestinian movement.) Years later Bebel referred to the relation between socialism and antisemitism—in his famous saying that "antisemitism is the socialism of fools." That would not have applied to Russian antisemitism, which was pure evil on the part of evil men, without the barest trace of a socialist idea. But between my Judeophilia and this socialism which regarded the whole Jewish people as a multitude of parasites yawned a chasm which I had to vault. It was not pleasant to think that Moses Montefiore was a louse, that your father and mother, your relatives and friends whom you loved and respected were these same repulsive creatures.

For me personally, the idea of cosmopolitanism was for a time like healing balm for the pain I had felt ever since it had been explained to me that we Jews lived a parasitic existence. Jews were parasites, but not Jews alone. Even Heine did not treat the stock-exchange Jews of his day with kid gloves. No one had any *special* responsibility to maintain a *special* Jewish existence. The messiah would soon come, and then differences among nationalities would vanish. So we became cosmopolitans—intellectually. But feeling is not so rational. Having lost our national Jewish orientation, our feelings nevertheless demanded a people to belong to, to unite with, to serve. And so we became Russians.

Many of that generation, having shed their tears over Nekrasov's poetry, made a binding covenant of tears with the Russian people. Why not with the Jewish people? Pondering the assimilatory effect that Russian literature with its Turgenevs and Nekrasovs had on us, I find it was because we had no such Jewish literature. That was before Sholem Aleichem and Peretz; there were only individual works in Yiddish that had not yet converged in one stream of literary development. These individual works presented descriptions of Jewish life that could not evoke love or even feeble sympathy for their Jewish characters and situations. They described a world decrepit and moldy, rotting away and fouling the air with its stench of corpses. Those literary works were the product of the Haskala, with a totally negative attitude toward prevailing Judaism and to all the institutions it had shaped. It was enough to compare descriptions of childhood in Yiddish literature with those in Russian literature, and you could understand the differences between our life and "theirs."

Later, when I had again become Jewish conscious, I realized that had we had a progressive cultural Jewish environment in Yiddish and a Yiddish literature which would have depicted Jewish life as the Russian or Polish literatures depicted theirs—then our radical youth would not have made such an assimilationist break. But the fact remains that both the Russian language and Russian literature made us Russians. From untold sources, Russian life, Russian ideas, Russian hopes and aspirations streamed into our inner consciousness.

It was to take some time until I was truly an adult and able to follow an independent course in my life. Yet one thing was then sure: I knew definitely *that I was not a Jew*. From this I concluded that I must change my Jewish name to a Russian name. I still remember how I chose a name. When I had first enrolled in gymnasium, as an ardent Jewish patriot, I had not been ashamed of my name Chaim; on the contrary, I bore it with pride. Now it was different. Since "Chaim" meant life, the logical name would have been

"Vitali," which sounded quite elegant. But I thought it was too elegant, suggesting an upstart. Yefim, the usual Russian equivalent for Chaim, was more natural. Besides, I remembered I knew a coachman called Yefim, which meant it was truly a democratic name. That was how an aspiring Russian revolutionary came to be called Yefim Osipovich.

I finally decided that the best thing for me was to prepare myself earnestly and systematically as a socialist propagandist, to go to the people, either village peasants or factory workers. It occurred to my friend Ansky that I should go to Tula, where he had an uncle. In that way it would be easier for me to leave home and extricate myself from the bourgeois atmosphere which caused conflicts between my parents and me.

Though our family life had its spiritual side—rabbinic learning, Hasidic fervor, and a smattering of newfangled Haskala, there was also another side, much less spiritual. Among almost all the wealthier members of our extensive family, a true cult of materialist pleasure prevailed. My father, who was very learned in Talmud and qualified as a rabbi, tended to be a lenient interpreter of Jewish law, permitting some things toward which other authorities might be stricter, like the length of time required to soak herring to make it permissible for use during Passover. At table they often spoke of culinary delights, like mushrooms marinated with little cucumbers. Corpulence was considered God's gift, a sign of grace.

These respectable and pious people were not ashamed to tell unseemly stories and jokes, even with the children at the table. What could children understand? They did not notice how the children blushed and that their minds were captured by these sweet, enigmatic secrets which they could not yet understand intellectually, but which stirred their blood. Once there was some talk about my parents' early married life, when they lived with my mother's family and I was a year-old infant. My mother was saying I had made it a habit to beg myself into her bed at night, screaming at the top of my lungs. "Then," she related, "Papa took a thin strap and lightly whipped his fingers. Little Chaim really wailed then." My mother had told this story so melodramatically that the tears welled up in my eyes—I was then six or seven and felt terribly sorry for that baby.

"What else?" My father defended himself, with an ironic grimace. "I needed him in our bed like a hole in the head."

At that time our family lived well and had a good income. Each year the desire for worldly pleasures grew. When we moved from the wooden house at the end of town to a large brick house in the very center of town, quite a new life began—in which more liberal ideas lightened the former strict piety. My mother uncovered her hair and my father began to wear his coat shorter. In place of the old spiritual ideals came the thirst for luscious living and luscious earnings. Material wealth became their idol. The old values of religious learning, piety, and family were replaced by the cult of money.

From this bourgeois atmosphere I had to escape. I was then only about sixteen, bound with innumerable ties to my home and my mother, whom I loved dearly and who loved me, and to my father for whom I had the greatest respect from earliest childhood. There were, however, no tragedies and no conflicts at my leaving. At first, my mother tried to dissuade me, but then both parents gave their consent and, of course, their financial support.

I had gone to Tula as a Russian to work for the Russian people, among whom I counted the Jews who would become just as Russian as I. But I had accomplished nothing. In the summer of 1883 I returned to my birthplace, the little Jewish village of Ushach, where all my youthful fantasies of living as a Russian among Russians faded. In the foreground emerged the Jewish question, confronting me like a Sphinx: Solve my riddle or I will devour you.

The philosemitic solution of the Russian-Jewish press, demanding equal rights and justifying Jewish merchantry and its achievements for Russia, could not impress me. In fact, it revolted me. I sensed it as an absolute contradiction to my socialist ideas and ideals, which had a pronounced Russian populist, agrarian-socialist character.

Samuel Solomonovich Poliakov built railroads for Russia. Those railroads were, according to Nekrasov's famous poem, built on the skeletons of the Russian peasantry. My uncle Michal in Ushach distilled vodka for the Russian people and made a fortune on the liquor tax. My cousin sold the vodka to the peasants. The whole town lived off the Russian peasants. My father hired them to cut down Russian woods which he bought from the greatest exploiter of the Russian peasant, the Russian landowner. The lumber was shipped abroad, while the Russian villages were full of rotting, dilapidated huts, covered with rotting straw-thatched roofs. They could have used my father's merchandise. Wherever I turned my eyes to ordinary, day-to day Jewish life, I saw only one thing, that which the antisemites were agitating about: the injurious effect of Jewish merchantry on Russian peasantry. No matter how I felt, from a socialist point of view, I had to pass a death sentence not only on individual Jews but on the entire *Jewish* existence of individual Jews.

Assimilation, the complete disappearance of the Jews and their merging with the Russian people so that the Jewish abscess would not be distinguished from the Russian one, was the most logical and consistent solution to the Jewish question. The most logical, yet for me psychologically impossible. For why fool myself? I felt myself a Jew. I was happy and comfortable in my Jewish world. Jews were closer to me, more my own kind, than many Russians with whom I was good friends and closely associated because of our common views. Why fool myself? After all, I was a Jew.

What then? Must we Jews disappear? What an insult to me and those I love and cherish! Were the Jewish nationalists right with their Palestinism, which had its logic and consistency? So, the balance rose and fell, with assimilation on one scale and Palestinism on the other, until an experience in February, 1884, when assimilation was hurled off the balance.

All my doubts were removed by a purely literary experience. One of Shchedrin's fables, "The Old Wolf," hit me like hammer blows. I interpreted the old wolf as the personification of Jews in Russia. The wolf attacks the bear. At the end, the bear says to him: "You are a most unfortunate beast. I cannot judge you, but I will tell you: I, in your place, would consider death as your good fortune. Ponder on these words."

As I read this story, I thought—so, we are wolves, are we? Must we die? Must we assimilate? Cease to exist as a people? I trembled with rage and fury. I cannot say that my ideas flowed in any logical order. These were rather aroused feelings of national pride. I felt deeply insulted. The idea of assimilation disappeared like smoke.

The collapse of assimilation as an ideal and the upsurge of my Jewish nationalism was not a result of a theoretically based and logically thought-through mental process. Now I know it was intuition, like a waking from a light sleep in which fantastic elements are mingled with real ones. Upon waking, the fantastic disappears and one sees clearly what is real.

It became clear to me that the subject of nationalism, Jewish nationalism, particularly in relation to both progress and reaction, was a troublesome matter which had first to be researched and theoretically clarified. I began to gulp every serious book and discussion that offered a theoretical analysis of our progressive outlook. The intellectual world of the sixties, with its Chernyshevskys, Pisarevs, Zaitsevs, Dobroliubovs gradually faded. Other names, other intellectual worlds—more profound and more fundamental—replaced them.

I read Ferdinand Lassalle in German. Then Karl Marx—the first volume of *Das Kapital* in Russian and *Poverty of Philosophy,* his polemic against Proudhon, in German. How many hours of strained concentration it cost me till I mastered "value" and "surplus value."

As the old radical authorities faded away, two new intellectual leaders grew in stature: N. K. Mikhailovsky and Peter Lavrov. Mikhailovsky made the greater impression on me, though I did not yet understand the originality and significance of his new approach to theoretical problems. Mikhailovsky's ideas massaged the rigid muscles of my dogmatic and self-satisfied logic, making them more flexible, so they could move freely in different ideational worlds. Both Lavrov and Mikhailovsky, though they represented different philosophies, sounded the same basic theme that neither logic nor common sense was the source of true knowledge, but only scientific investigation, which is inimical to every form of metaphysics. Positivism, whose foundations were laid by August Comte, replaced materialism. This completely new approach to philosophical problems opened up for me a new intellectual horizon with stars of the first magnitude, each revolving around the central sun—August Comte. Thereafter, the order of reading was Spencer, Mill, Buckle (in Arnold Ruge's German translation), Lewes. All this had only an indirect effect on the development of my Jewish program. It gave me a wider perspective, richer knowledge and, most important, total liberation from those intellectual chains with which the radical outlook of the sixties had fettered our thoughts.

In those days there were not yet any socialist Jews, but only Jewish socialists, who did not care to be identified as Jews. I never heard of any socialist theories that harmoniously united socialist ideals with the problems of Jewish life. That formulation was one of the most important goals which engaged me a great part of my life. I think I am justified in saying that my theories about national socialism played a role, one way or another, in the development of Jewish socialist movements. These theories, too, it can be proven, had a great effect on the formulation of the nationalities program of the Socialists-Revolutionaries, a movement which emerged in the nineties, and one of whose first flag-bearers I was.

My position on the nationalities problem was also given serious consideration by the Austrian Social Democrats, even before Otto Bauer's and Karl Renner's splendid theoretical studies appeared. But all this came later. The prehistory of how I came to view these matters is what I am now describing.

All during this period when I was thinking of my Jewishness, my emotional state was poor. I was suffering from acute neurasthenia which at times reached a stage near hysteria. It was impos-

sible for me to remain at home in the kind of atmosphere which I
described before. I told my mother I was going to live by myself.
She was very upset and, as a compromise, I agreed to come home
every day for dinner.

I had a few hours of tutoring to cover my small expenses, and I
rented a small room from a Polish widow. There I moved my library
of semilegal publications which young people, Jewish and non-
Jewish, used to borrow. The library kept expanding, thanks to my
older brother's purchases of classical radical literature. He worked
in my father's lumber business and always had some ready money.

I did not conduct any propaganda. I merely advised the young
people what and how to read so they could become "intellectually
developed." I used to show them where they could find explanations
for one or another problem that interested them. Such tiny intellectual centers like my library were then coming into existence all over
Russia. The more reactionary the government became, the tighter
the censorship of the printed word, the more backward the trends in
official educational institutions, the more the young people needed
sources from which they could draw free ideas. But this work among
the youth did not satisfy me very much. I was busy reading and
writing poetry.

Without any conscious Yiddishist forethought, my poetic muse
expressed itself in Yiddish. One poem I wrote was so descriptive of
my mood at that time, I will set it down in prose, for it may not even
have deserved poetic form:

"I myself know not why my heart grieves; why I am bathed in
tears; why I have no peace and nothing can subdue my wild ideas. I
know not what drives me hence and uproots me; what attracts me
elsewhere? A feeling grows within me I cannot understand and wild
thoughts sans words."

"Bathed in tears" was not pure rhetoric. I often used to weep,
sometimes hysterically. Several such attacks occurred in the summer
of 1884. That was when I first read Goethe's *Faust* in Russian translation. It had an extraordinary effect on me. Its ending stirred my
soul to its depths. I had to exert my utmost control to restrain the
hysterical lament that arose in me, for it was obvious that the final
scene had a deeply symbolic significance for me.

For me then, Gretchen was our Jewish people. Our people is
sitting in a dark prison, its mind unhinged, clutching to its breast a
bundle of rags instead of a living child. Faust the liberator arrives,
but the people do not understand his words. But when they comprehend what the liberating intelligentsia demands of them, they choose

instead the dark prison, the doll and certain death, instead of freedom and life. The intelligentsia is then forced to abandon the people to their fate.

Need I explain the symbol of the doll which the people embraced? I was then still hostile to every religion, and especially Judaism. I then still had not the faintest idea that for us religion was the only source of life which gave us the spirit to exist as a people.

On a hot, quiet afternoon that summer, I rowed downstream on the Dvina. I pulled up near the hilly, overgrown shore, resting in the shade. Everything about me was frozen in silence. Suddenly, from above, as from the heavens, I heard a lamenting singsong feminine voice: "To whom have you abandoned me?" Above, on the hill, a young woman was weeping at a grave in the Jewish cemetery.

That single lament tore through the air, and then again the motionless silence. I felt hysteria coming over me and hastily I began to row upstream, back home.

The long-drawn-out despairing lament reechoed within me like a symbolic reproof. It evoked from me the pledge I had given to myself—always to remain faithful to the Jewish people, never to abandon them, to solidarize myself with their historic fate, whatever befell them.

Thereafter I never had any doubts or hesitations in thought or feeling about my moral responsibility. That was the central axis around which all my efforts revolved, in communal work, and in large part in my theoretical studies.

At this point the practical question emerged: What should I do?

Among the various plans I had in mind was one to which my thoughts kept returning. That was an idea to publish a legal monthly journal in Yiddish, an organ of enlightenment and struggle for those universal foundations of human progress which could be advocated even under Russian censorship. The decision to issue the journal in Yiddish did not originate from any conscious Yiddishism. The theoretical works on nationality, with which I was familiar, gave no particular importance to language, which was merely one of the characteristics of national existence. My later studies were to introduce considerable revision in this outlook, but at that time I shared the view that language was no more than a means of expressing and communicating ideas. My reasoning then went something like this: One must talk to a people in its own language. But our people use two languages: Hebrew and Yiddish. In the world in which I grew up, both languages had the same prestige. None of my pious relatives looked down upon Yiddish. After all, Torah was studied and interpreted in Yiddish. Hebrew, the sacred tongue, was valued more, but only religiously. As a secular language, in which one read the paper or a Haskala book, it may have outranked Yiddish slightly, not for any inherent reason, but because of its association with education.

The question facing me was to decide in which language to appeal to Jews, not just the ignorant masses, but the whole people, to train an avant-garde to fight for the ideals of universal progress and for their realization in Jewish life. I decided on Yiddish. This was my calculation: We, the carriers of ideas of universal human progress, had to appeal to the people with our message about quite a new world, the world of modern, progressive West European culture. Vis-à-vis this world the whole Jewish people were like the ignorant masses. My father, greatly learned in rabbinic literature, a sharp mind and a thorough one, was just as ignorant as the shoemaker or tailor of Western culture. One could make no distinctions between classes and levels of education. One had to use the language that everyone understood. That was Yiddish, the vernacular of every Jew. I did not go into this matter any further, but it was easy to see what this first step meant and in what direction it would take me.

1935

III

A Few Central Themes and Figures

Even in the most wretched and demoralized intervals of their history, Jews have cherished the sense of a unique past, stretching back to the very beginnings of history itself. The following essays provide a sampling of the range of subject matter and methods of approach in Yiddish historical writing: from J. I. Trunk's half-playful speculations on the meaning of Biblical characters to Israel Zinberg's careful study of a segment of the Jewish enlightenment in Germany. Seldom allowed the advantages of institutional support, scholars writing in Yiddish have had to work under precarious conditions. There has nevertheless grown up a body of significant historical work composed in Yiddish, which deserves to be known far better than it is.

Jacob and Esau

by Jehiel Isaiah Trunk

Translated by Lucy S. Dawidowicz

I

When great historians recount the events of the past they always have in view some future destiny. Through historical deeds they wish to delineate the nature of the persons who performed them. Every character soon reveals his destiny—that is, the line of history that has been ordained for him. Destiny will complete and perfect the qualities that inhere in the active character.

In this sense the Biblical story about Jacob and Esau is one of the most remarkable of historical documents. In what are ostensibly family records about the earliest ancestors of the Jews, an author succeeded in disclosing the complete psychic picture of Jewish history in its future course and also the relations between Jews and gentiles in the history to come. The author of the Biblical tale about Jacob and Esau is a meticulous craftsman. He is also an out-and-out historical-minded writer. We will see this later, both in the themes on which the story was constructed and in the sophisticated manner of its composition. It could be supposed that we are dealing here with an author of a later period who had already seen and experienced the nearly complete and structured pattern of Jewish history —an author, let us say, living somewhat before or after the destruction of the Second Temple. Such a conjecture would be rash and absolutely incorrect. The author is without doubt a Jew of antiquity who lived back in the first beginnings of Jewish history. You see that in his style, in his diction, and in the whole Canaanite way of life which he describes. It is obvious: in his time Jews had not yet become settled. They were tribes of shepherds and nomads. His motifs

137

are nomad motifs. He composes from the folklore, tales, jokes, and pranks of shepherds and hunters. This story is too maturely and cleverly composed for anyone to say that the author's historical-philosophical standpoint just happened to leak out. No, he wrote this with the clearest intent and the most profound insight into the essence of his Jewish origin. He wants to foresee—both by understanding and intuition—Jewish destiny, that is, the lifeline of later Jewish history.

II

Most likely, the Joseph story, which is really a continuation of the story of Jacob and Esau, was written by the same hand, with the same historical-philosophical standpoint. The narrative motifs in the wonderful epic novel of Joseph are nothing more than a sequel. Thomas Mann has already remarked that the mystery of Jewish history is reflected in the Joseph story. In constructing his four-volume epic on this story, Mann was strongly influenced by Freud's depth psychology, as well as by the dark mysterious land of Egypt. In his novel Mann used the Jacob and Esau story only as the background to Jewish historical subconsciousness. Being a non-Jew, Mann blended into this subconscious a reconstruction of Freud's myth about totem. That is to say, human history began with a bloody conflict between the father of the primeval human flock and his sons. The sons killed the father and devoured him. This original sin, still lying in mankind's conscience as unextinguished memory and guilt feeling, is the basis of our morality and religion. It is the eternal conflict in our conscience. Thomas Mann set the stage for this conflict with all the gods and cultural images of the ancient Egyptians and he introduced Joseph the Jew as a new motif of destiny for mankind, that is to say, the destiny-motif of the Jews in their course among the nations. I disagree entirely with Thomas Mann that the Jacob story is merely a Freudian background of the Joseph story, serving only to heighten the sense of a mystical destiny around the figure of Joseph. No. The story of Jacob was treated by the author with the same realistic technique, perhaps even with more realism. The life of herdsmen and hunters in Canaan was more familiar to the author than the courtly ceremonies of the high nobility in Egypt, though all Egyptologists admire the author's expertness in this regard. If we wish to look for Jewish destiny and character descriptions by our farseeing genial author, we will find them much clearer and more evident in the psychological interplay between Jacob and Esau than in the poetry of Joseph. In the Joseph story we have more fantasy and wishful imagination (especially in the motifs of Joseph's dreams) and in the Jacob story, more reality and representation of life. There more poetry, and here more character. In the Jacob story the destiny which the author wishes to extract from the events is inextricable from deeds and patterns of character.

III

A modern novelist would have constructed a multivolume epic from the Jacob motifs. The ancient Jewish author's pen lacked the breadth of great narrative and he limited himself to the barest necessities. He is stingy with words. He wants to present the most important scene in just a few words. Yet despite the scantiness of space, the author undertook to write a work of the scope, let us say, of Romain Rolland's *Jean-Christophe*. He wants to give the history of his heroes starting in their mother's womb. He wants to pattern the whole picture of their characters in the womb. The two brothers Jacob and Esau are twins ("Two nations are in your womb"), but they are also much more. They are two paths in human history, two directions, two world views. The great and eternal struggle between the two has already begun, a struggle which is both the beginning and the finale of man's route in cosmic existence. Later Jewish legends and the midrashim underscored even more deeply and more explicitly the historical meaning of this struggle between the two brothers in their mother's womb: namely, as the outlooks of two cultures. "But the children struggled in her womb." When Rebecca passed a synagogue, Jacob struggled to emerge. In the proximity of idolatry, Esau detected the element of his universe and he struggled to emerge. The author takes pains also at their birth to describe the struggle to be out first in the world. When it comes to physical strength, Esau wins and Jacob remains the *shlimazl* and has to hold on to his stronger brother's heel. Jacob must win his birthright in the world by quite other means, by means of intelligence and spirit. The author does not scruple at all to describe Jacob's spirit through motifs of frequent and pointed cunning.

IV

The author's sympathy for Jacob is clear. In this composition Jacob, despite all his helplessness, nevertheless remains—how much historical foresight—the final victor. Yet the author wants also to maintain the coolest objectivity. Toward this great struggle between gentiles and Jews, the objective view is profoundly right. The author is concerned to show how the destiny of history depends absolutely on the character of the participants in the historical process. He therefore wants to present his heroes in the amplest light of actual historical events, but also through an imaginative psychological portrait of the heroes' characters. He does not want to dress them up in romanticism or sentiment. Nothing hinders him from presenting Jacob, the primeval father of the Jews, in the light in which Jews actually appear in history. Still more, in his objectivity, he presents the Jewish physiognomy as even opponents of Jews imagine it to be. Jacob is a quiet, wily, little Jew, somewhat like a shopkeeper, with little physical courage and vitality. So he thinks up tricks for how to stay on top. We say, a Jew is smarter than a non-Jew. The author tells us that in contrast to his ruddy and hairy brother Esau, the quiet smooth-skinned Jacob was "a quiet man, dwelling in tents." The Jewish legends and midrashim, which always try to underscore the historical-philosophical view of the ancient Biblical author, explain that "in tents" means that, sitting all day in the prayerhouse, Jacob was a studious type who had diligently studied Gemara in the yeshiva of Shem and Eber.[1] But our author did not know of this later Jewish way of life. With "in tents" he means simply just that: Jacob sat in the herdsmen's tents and watched Isaac's lambs. Isaac was a wealthy man (may no evil eye harm him) and burdened with sheep and cattle. In the ancient Biblical world in which our author lived, the calling of a shepherd probably did not require any great prowess. For all his lambs, Jacob could have remained the shrewd shopkeeping little Jew that the author makes him out to be.

Esau, by contrast, is a huntsman, a man of bow and arrow. He makes his living by the sword. He does not watch placid sheep, but sustains himself among the wild beasts in the field, killing what comes to hand, and has his sustenance from spilled blood. Jacob in the tents is a tranquil man, habituated to the warmth of the sheep and the fields. His ears are accustomed only to the rustling of the wind in the grass and to the bleating of the lambs. When he is hungry, he cooks a pot of lentils to eat. Esau returns flushed from the hunt. His hands and his garments are stained with blood. According to *Sefer ha-Yashar*,[2] Esau in this particular scene had just about

---

[1] According to the legends of the rabbis, Shem, the youngest son of Noah and ancestor of Abraham, Isaac, and Jacob, founded an academy in which the Torah was studied and where Jacob was a pupil. Eber, Shem's great-grandson, later joined him and the academy was named after both.—Transl.

[2] One of the late works of midrashic Haggada, written in Hebrew probably in the twelfth or thirteenth century in southern France or Italy. It deals with the history of the Jews from Adam to the Judges, interweaving imaginary narrative, interpretations, and moralistic teachings with Biblical passages. It was first published in Naples in 1552. Translated into Yiddish (as early as 1674), it was widely read in Eastern Europe until the Holocaust.—Transl.

killed Nimrod and returned from the bloody slaughter all worked
up and ravenous. He sees the lentils cooking in Jacob's tent and he
craves them. When gluttony overcomes him, Esau is apt to surrender
a world. For the pottage the smooth-skinned, quiet man, Jacob of
the tents, demands just a trifle, no more than a trifle—an abstract
concept: the birthright.

Good. Abstraction is a dense idea for Esau and he sells his
birthright for a pottage of lentils. Esau does not wash before eating,
according to the midrashim. He recites no blessing; he makes no
benediction. He gorges himself like the beasts that he hunts in the
field to shed their blood. The smooth Jacob, dweller in tents, who
wears out the seat in the yeshiva of Shem and Eber, knows from
the Gemara that in a concept, in a word, in an abstraction, man has
hidden the riches and the blessings of all worlds. And he tricks Esau
out of his birthright.

v

To build tension in the struggle between the two brothers, a struggle
which—according to our author's view—should exemplify the eternal dramatic conflict in human history, our clever and exceedingly
sophisticated author has introduced supporting characters. The first
we see are the two brothers' parents—Isaac and Rebecca. The author has no reverence when he needs to create characters and introduce supporting players. He needs a comic character here for his
composition. No matter that Isaac is the middle Patriarch, the author forgets every respect for tradition and as long as he needs
Isaac for his comic figure, he goes ahead with complete literary
freedom and disregards authority. Why deny that in this composition Isaac emerges as a true nincompoop? He is not at all a wily
Jew, our great-grandfather Isaac. Rather he is quite witless. He
likes to fondle his wife at the window for all to see and for people
to laugh and gossip about at the market in the daytime and under
the blankets at night. When he has to concoct a lie in Gerar, he does
so ostensibly with the same technique as his father Abraham. But a
liar must have brains and not just mechanically imitate someone
else. The lie in Gerar comes out lefthanded. Moreover, Isaac has no
cause to complain, heaven forbid, of a bad appetite. He sits, blind in
his tent, and thinks only about a tasty morsel. We see this clearly in
all his commissions and omissions. He is a sort of Jewish Falstaff, but
much more awkward and more of an old dodderer. The author does
not want to spare him in the least. He introduces Isaac in all his
comicality—when he has need of him to plot the dramatic hap-
penings.

Isaac, then, is no great intellect. He knows that Esau, with his bow and arrow, can bring the choicest fare from the field. Isaac thinks about delicacies and barbecued kids. His appetites run wild with all the lusts of this-worldliness. How comic! When Isaac senses that these are his last days and that he has a great blessing to bestow, he thinks all over again about good food. In that connection, wondering who will bring him a good dinner, he reminds himself of Esau.

Rebecca, like any curious woman, listens at the door to Isaac's conversation with Esau. It is her wish that Jacob should receive the auspicious blessing. The author does not try very hard to explain why Rebecca chooses to sympathize with Jacob. He is essentially concerned with the bearers of two world views, Jacob and Esau, and the great dramatic play of their destinies. He does indeed apportion the roles, but he treats the supporting characters with a lighter hand. Perhaps Rebecca's love comes from the fact that the tranquil idylls of sheep appeal more to the womanly being than the hunter's heated chase and the whistling of arrows through the air.

VI

Once again the scene shifts, and with the greatest consistency on the part of the characters.

Esau goes out hunting to bring Isaac the kill. Jacob, all over again, uses mental wiliness to trick from his father the mastery of the universe. The author must surely have drawn upon the folklore of the ancient Canaanite shepherds for the description of how Jacob disguises himself and puts the skins of kids on his hands. In any case, that is also the opinion of practically all Bible scholars. The motifs are too extreme and original to have occurred even to the greatest poet. The common folk has more imagination than the most imaginative person. No individual has yet equaled the marvels of myth. Such fantastic stories and jests about clever shepherds were probably recounted in the cold nights around the fire. The sheep were already asleep within the fold. In the dark heavens the stars twinkled. The earth was damp with dew—it is the best time to tell tales. Incidentally, in these tales the clever ones were probably always the shepherds while the duped fools turned out to be the hunters. That is occupational loyalty. Similarly, the later story of how Jacob tricks Laban and takes the newborn lambs from him is likely also to come from familiar folklore. It shows that the author was a contemporary and knew Canaanite folkways well. Precisely with this material of simple folktales and folk jests, he undertakes to construct the greatest and most profound dramatic spectacle in mankind's history.

But let us not outrun the events.

Rebecca prepares a kid for Isaac and puts the kid skins on Jacob's hands. Jacob goes in an Esau-skin to trick the blessing out of Isaac. Yet we must admit that Jacob—we know him heretofore as a wily shepherd who has tricked the birthright from the hunter and struggled to emerge first from his mother's womb into the luminous world—Jacob, I suggest, does not feel quite comfortable in the role of a disguised Esau. We have the impression that he is afraid and begins to play his role very uncertainly. He enters Isaac's tent. Isaac is waiting for Esau's delicacies and asks who it is. "I am Esau, your first-born," Jacob replies, not in high spirits. Isaac wonders that Esau has returned so speedily from the hunt. Here the cat slips out of the bag and Jacob out of his role. He cites God, as all later Jews do, and says that with the help of God, blessed be He, he caught his prey without toil and trouble. Faith. A cleverer man than Isaac would have caught on right away that he is being taken. But Isaac is not much of a judge of people. Besides, the roast from Jacob's plate smells delicious and the hungry blind man probably began to drool. To him, Isaac, the voice seemed quite suspicious. Here the midrashim comment that the name of God which slipped so naturally from Jacob's mouth roused Isaac's suspicion. This is, somehow, not Esau's diction and Isaac touches Jacob's hands: Esau's hands, hairy, animal hands. He smells him. The blind man wants to smell the field in which Esau hunts the beasts. Here also Jacob tricks him. From Jacob too comes the smell of the field, another field: "The smell of field that the Lord has blessed," a sort of heavenly field. Isaac senses the presence of destiny, but he does not know what to make of it. He eats Jacob's delicacies and makes him master of the world.

VII

It is not the intent of this essay to tell about the terrible fuss that Esau made when he learned that Jacob had once again tricked him, and forced his way into the future course of history as the superior one. The reader can look this up in the Torah. Esau is brooding over the idea of killing Jacob. Jacob must flee.

The midrashim, which always want to complement the historical-philosophical trend of the Bible, tell a story here, and quite a characteristic one:

Esau's son, Eliphaz, a big leaseholder and a warlike horseman, undertakes to pursue Jacob and destroy him with the blade of the sword. Jacob, meanwhile, is wandering around and has hidden himself in the prayerhouse of Shem and Eber and, while there, browses a little among the religious books. He has now become even more smooth-skinned and paler, more Jewish and thinner. Later, an utter pauper with only his beggar's staff, he starts out on the road to Paddan-aram. Here Eliphaz catches up with him. Eliphaz and his men are armed from head to foot. Eliphaz looks at this pauper with a beggar's staff and rubs his eyes: This is the master of the world? The adversary? It is against his knightly honor even to touch such a wretched antagonist with his sword. Jacob makes himself look even more wretched and helpless, humbles himself before Eliphaz and, standing before him with his torn cap in hand, shows him his ragged and dusty garments and calls him master and honored lord. Behold, why do you fear a poor Jew? Can the master of the world look like this?

Looking at this scraping Jewish pauper, Eliphaz is repelled, spits in disgust and rides off—the gentile knight with his armed force. Jacob takes staff in hand and goes on. In Luz night catches up with him and he goes to sleep with a stone under his head. The poor homeless Jew on the bare stone has a dream that he is lying under the gate of heaven. A ladder is lowered and angels bring down the tidings that God will never forsake him and that in all the heavens mastery over the world of spirit has been prepared for him.

VIII

To intensify the dramatic climax, the author uses a technique of all great storytellers: at the most powerful moment of fateful tragedy he turns our attention to lighter motifs, idyllic or comical. Our author now presents us with both an idyll and high comedy. In both motifs he reaches the heights of artistry. We step into a pastorale. Jacob arrives at Paddan-aram. He encounters flocks of sheep at the well and converses with the shepherds. Rachel arrives with her flock. The first thrill of love between the shepherdess and the alien wanderer. Despite the spareness of the narrative, it captures the mind with a magical charm. It is surely among the most beautiful pastoral scenes in world literature. We see, incidentally, that the author is familiar with contemporary shepherd life. Surely it is absolutely wrong to place him in a later time, as some Bible critics do.

In this sunny and romantic pastorale a new antagonist to Jacob comes on stage. He, too, is a wily, shrewd shepherd—Laban the Aramean. We know this fellow from an earlier Bible story. We met him at the well where Eliezer was standing with Patriarch Abraham's camels. From that story we know of Laban's greediness and his lust for gold. In the scenes between Jacob and Laban the author uses, as it seems, his rich knowledge of Canaanite folklore. From this store of knowledge he constructs the most comical and absurd scenes. It is a continuous chain of deceits and trickeries which both shepherds play upon one another. Laban believes that he has found a pushover and tries all his tricks on Jacob. He exploits Jacob for his flocks. As for his daughter, Laban performs a real switch. He exchanges one woman for the other and makes Jacob a laughing stock. Jacob keeps quiet, but Laban has mistaken his adversary. Here it also turns out finally that the Jew is cleverer. At the end, Jacob has taken from Laban the youngest and best flocks, he has taken from him his daughters, the maid servants, the camels and the kids. When this supposed *shlimazl* Jacob has assembled a tidy fortune, he thumbs his nose at the shrewd Aramean Laban and sets out without a fare-ye-well.

IX

The author once more picks up the thread of his historical drama.

Jacob goes to a new encounter with Esau. Esau hears that his smooth-skinned brother is again approaching his boundaries. Esau gathers his forces and goes to meet Jacob. The worldly account between these two brothers is open for reckoning.

Jacob here employs two strategies which Jews would later—even until today—make use of in their history with considerable effectiveness. Jacob knows Esau well—he remembers him still from that pottage of lentils—and knows that Esau has a terrific weakness for bribery. Put something in the palm of his hand, and you can still his rage. Jacob selects she-goats and he-goats from his flocks and sends them ahead as a gift to his brother Esau. "If I propitiate him with presents in advance, and then face him, perhaps he will show me favor." Secondly, Jacob divides his forces. With a brilliant strategic plan deriving from a stiff-necked insistence on survival, Jacob divides his forces. He has made a very clever and keen calculation: "If Esau comes to one camp and attacks it, the other camp may yet escape." Forces must be divided, carefully, one at a time. In this world-contest with Esau he dare not risk everything on one gamble.

It is clear as day that this strategy of Jewish survival—whose originator was Jacob—was the feat of a historical leader. Many times we tried gifts, but mainly we have divided ourselves and, divided, have managed to survive on all the world's surfaces. Had we, during our struggle with the Roman powers and during all the thousands of years of our history, been concentrated in a single ter-

ritory, ah, with one blow and at one time Esau would have succeeded in destroying us. He would have encountered us rooted in a
land. That is all he needs. Esau has a terrific sense of earthly reality.
When in our struggle for Jewish survival—which is really an ideological world struggle—we confront him with a territorial reality of
a kind he understands, we can be sure in advance of our total defeat.
What could the frail Jacob with his wives and lambs have done
against his brother Esau's four hundred armed warriors? A lost
struggle. Only in the abstractness of world spaces can Esau fail to
capture us.

To show us Jewish history's clever logic of survival, the Biblical
storyteller tries here to describe the full state of Jacob's powerlessness. He is a weak cowardly Jew, Jacob, on the day when he must
meet the powerful master of the sword—his brother Esau.

X

When the reader starts to become worried and to think that now
Jacob's end is really at hand, for the swords of Esau and his warriors
can already be heard, our author suddenly takes us to another dimension of this universal spectacle. Jacob is alone at the river Jab-
bok and night falls. Night is the universal time of dreams and visions.
A new antagonist approaches him, not Esau but a divine being.
Here Jacob is in his historical element. Jacob, whom we have just
seen powerless and trembling before Esau, suddenly transforms
himself, on the planes of vision, into a fighting hero. He engages in
struggle with the divine being and wins. He wrestles all night until
the morning star begins to rise. The divine being pleads with him,
"Let me go, for dawn is breaking." Jacob says, "I will not let you
go, unless you give me earthly mastery over spirit." And the divine
being called him Israel and bestowed upon him earthly mastery over
spirit.

XI

The Pentateuch itself and the midrashim try to explain why
Esau's heart suddenly softened at the sight of his weak, powerless
brother and, instead of killing him, Esau became quite friendly.
Some see great insincerity in this and others an uncanny fear of
weak Jacob. Let us not forget: Jacob is once more playing the role
of the wretched little Jew and bows and scrapes before the hairy
master of Seir. Here Esau has subconsciously sensed that this little
Jew Jacob is indeed a mythical hero who has just emerged victorious
from a struggle with a divine being. No need here to go into details.
Suffice it to say that Esau shows generosity, suddenly turns into a

good brother, and proposes that Jacob return with him to Seir. Jacob exhibits even more wretchedness and bemoans his weakness, the weakness of his household, and even the weakness of his flocks. Jacob, he does not rush to go along with Esau. Jacob, he has time. Slowly, slowly, dear lord, will I follow you, I, the weak Jewish man. In deepest humility will I follow your footsteps—and I will catch up with you for the reckoning on the last day of the world.

1946

Sabbatai Zevi—The Messiah as Apostate

by Hayim Greenberg

Translated by Shlomo Katz

I

Why did Sabbatai Zevi[1] become an apostate? How did it come about that the man who considered himself the redeemer of his people, the Messiah, the messenger of God announcing the salvation of the world, bowed his head before the Sultan's court Mufti, donned a Turkish turban and adopted the Moslem name Mohammed?

For many years his followers and disciples sought an answer to this riddle. The opponents of the False Messiah assiduously exploited Sabbatai Zevi's conversion to the Moslem faith to prove to the aroused and messianically exalted public that their hero, upon whom they had pinned such high hopes, was a mere charlatan, a "destroyer of Israel" and an apostate. But Sabbatai Zevi also had many followers who found it difficult, or altogether impossible, to renounce their messianic dream, and who therefore spared no effort to defend Sabbatai Zevi's good name to themselves and before the Jewish people as a whole. The ordinary, unsophisticated public which had for so long adored Sabbatai Zevi and literally counted the minutes until he would display his divine power, almost at once created a legend to account for what happened and to refute all doubts. According to this legend, Sabbatai Zevi did not become an apostate at all. One of the greatest miracles occurred in the Sultan's palace— a kind of emanation, a ghostly reflection separated itself from Sabbatai Zevi and it was this image that adopted the Mohammedan faith.

[1] Sabbatai Zevi (1626–1676), a false messiah who for a time won an enormous following among east European Jews. He ended as a convert to Islam.

148

Sabbatai Zevi himself vanished from the palace unnoticed and an angel bore him on his wings to heaven. There was also no lack of rationalists among the people who did not deny the fact of Sabbatai Zevi's apostasy, but interpreted it in their own fashion. Since Sabbatai Zevi would soon become the king of a free Eretz Israel, they said, he intentionally, though only superficially, adopted the Moslem faith in order to become a welcome visitor in the Sultan's palace and thus have an opportunity to observe at leisure the ways of royalty and to study the art of war.

But among Sabbatai Zevi's disciples there were also some who knew and believed that it was the real Sabbatai Zevi who had adopted Mohammedanism, and who could not stomach the rationalist and all too prosaic and earthly explanation that he betrayed his God in a make-believe gesture only in order to worm his way into the Sultan's palace. It is precisely the ones who were closest to him who had to reject such a realistic political interpretation, because for them Sabbatai Zevi was not a politician, nor a national hero in the secular-political sense of the term, but, above all, he was the great prophet, the Messiah annointed by God who came into the world to uproot evil and to liberate all mankind from its contradictions. Sabbatai Zevi's closest disciples and associates were deeply imbued with the visions and moods of the "applied Kabbala" of Ari and Chaim Vital, and they had perforce to seek mystical interpretations for Sabbatai Zevi's act which appears to have come as a surprise also for them. This led to a series of sophist, paradoxical interpretations which, in their unique form, reflected the moods of that mysticism-ridden time—the tragic conflicts of those passionately messiah-anticipating times.

Sabbatai Zevi's closest "armor bearer," Nathan of Gaza, did not lose heart even when he realized that his "King of Judah" was now called Mohammed. So far as he was concerned, Sabbatai Zevi remained the same "Our Lord the Messiah" that he had been before. He sent letters to all the communities which had accepted Sabbatai Zevi, in which he explained that Sabbatai Zevi's act was the fulfillment of the ancient prophecy that the Messiah would appear in the world as "a poor man riding on an ass." The term 'ani, a poor man, Nathan explained, should be understood allegorically and not literally: the Messiah must for a time be in a state of spiritual poverty and deprivation. He cannot fulfill his mission until he will have been tormented by impurity for a time. He cannot display his true messianic power until he will, for a time, deprive himself of the fulfillment of the commandments and deny himself good deeds. This,

Nathan believed, explained Sabbatai Zevi's adoption of Moham-medanism. The Messiah must suffer, and through his suffering be purified and strengthened; and now that he was in the bosom of the ruling church, he experienced the greatest possible suffering. More-over, the greater his grief and the more profound his spiritual "pov-erty," the nearer we will be to redemption.

Nathan of Gaza also cited the Zohar according to which the Messiah must have his hours of being "internal" rather than "ex-ternal," and this prophecy of the Zohar, he maintained, was fulfilled now that Sabbatai Zevi's external being was most unattractive as a result of his having become an official "Ishmaelite" wearing a Turk-ish turban on his head. Sabbatai Zevi, Nathan of Gaza explained, was at the moment experiencing what Queen Esther had experienced once before him. She merited becoming the savior of her people only after undergoing the degradations of Ahasuerus' harem. And somewhat later Nathan of Gaza declared that Sabbatai Zevi entered the Moslem world in order to "redeem" the sparks of holiness that lie hidden within the depths of impurity, since the elements of good and evil, of sanctity and profanity are not sharply dissociated and redemption can come to the world only after they are totally sepa-rated one from the other. The Messiah must therefore descend to the lowest depths of depravity in order to elevate from its abysses the individual sparks of sanctity which suffer there and plead to be redeemed from their "exile." Looked at in this light, Sabbatai Zevi did not at all capitulate before a ruler of flesh and blood by becom-ing a Moslem. On the contrary, his apostasy was one of the greatest works which the Messiah must perform on earth, and his entry into Mohammedanism was really a declaration of war against evil, and a glad tiding for the scattered sparks of holiness lost in the deserts of uncleanness and yearning for liberation. The Patriarch Abraham took Hagar for a wife. Jacob married the daughters of Laban the Aramite. Moses descended to the uncleanness of an idolatrous priest and took his daughter for a wife. And now "Our Lord the Messiah" descended into the murky abysses of the Moslem world. But the aim of all of them was to rescue the "sparks". . . .

Among Sabbatai Zevi's followers there were also some who felt no need to resort to the sanction of quotations from sacred books or to rationalizations of a historical nature. For these it was obvious and understandable that it was Providence that led Sabbatai Zevi on the road to apostasy in order that the cup of his suffering be filled and that he be made ready for his great mission. During the seven-teenth century many *anusim*—forced converts—from Spain, Portu-gal, and from the Italian districts ruled by the Vatican, wandered about. Many of these had already been brought up on the dogmas and images of the Catholic Church, and considerable numbers had already been born Catholics. It was therefore natural that even after they shook off their enforced Catholicism and returned to Judaism they should retain elements of Christian mysticism. These forced converts, who were brought up in the Christian dogma of the mystery of the "Suffering God," felt less doubts than anyone else at the sight of the fall of the Messiah. Sabbatai Zevi was being mocked. Jews and non-Jews insulted and humiliated him. They taunted him and jeered: "Messiah, where is your divine power?" But the same was done by Jews and Romans to Jesus before his crucifixion. His mockers placed a crown of thorns on Jesus' head, and Sabbatai Zevi permitted to be placed on his head a Turkish turban which was a still greater humiliation for him and pained him even more than thorns might. In the minds of these former Catholics, the Christian Passion of the Lord and the Jewish Agonies of the Messiah (*hevlei mashiach*) became so inextricably interwined that to some of them it seemed that had the misfortune of Sabbatai Zevi's apostasy not have taken place, this would have been the most convincing proof that he was indeed a false messiah. The Kabbalist Abraham Michael Cordoza, who had himself been a forced convert to Catholicism and had returned to Judaism, suggested in his famous letter on Sabbatai Zevi's apostasy that "final redemption" would not come until all Jews first became victims of apostasy, and from the depth of their degradation—like the lost sparks of sanctity embedded in evil—they cried out to God to send them their redeemer.

Such were the lines along which Sabbatai Zevi's devotees tried to rehabilitate their messiah. It is not inconceivable that among them some were not entirely sincere, and repeated these excuses not because they truly believed them, but in order to sustain the messianic movement with which they did not want to break for one reason or another. What is clear is that in an environment that was intoxicated with kabbalistic concepts and images, in a community which regarded the Zohar, and even lesser mystical works, as more holy than the Bible or the Talmud, the interpretations described above appeared so natural, understandable and obvious, that no effort was required to accept them.

Naturally, Sabbatai Zevi's enemies, and also those of his former disciples who in time succeeded in ridding themselves of the fumes of their former messianic intoxication, reacted altogether differently and began to abuse their deceiver who had first inflamed within them such high hopes and then so cruelly and bitterly disappointed them. To these it was clear proof that by adopting Mohammedanism

Sabbatai Zevi demonstrated that he had been no more than a "scoundrelly swindler" all along. Their most common accusation was that Sabbatai Zevi had from the very start had no other aim than to seduce Jews from the path of righteousness and that he intentionally misused the trust of the people for his power ambitions, and at the first moment that real danger threatened him from the Turkish power, he saved his own skin by embracing Mohammedanism without giving the matter a second thought. But even some of these opponents found some justification for Sabbatai Zevi and tried to be impartial in this situation. These pointed to Maimonides and cited his famous *Letter to Yemen* in which Maimonides declared that it was the duty of a Jew to practice *Kiddush Hashem*, to sacrifice his life for the sanctification of God, when compelled to worship idols, but that this commandment did not apply in the case of forced conversion to Mohammedanism, because the pure monotheistic concepts of Islam brought it close to Judaism.

In this connection it is interesting to point out that Rabbi Jacob Emden, who had devoted much energy and passion to eradicating all organizational and psychological traces of the Sabbatai Zevi movement, was nevertheless inclined to find some justification for the false messiah. In his famous work *Torath Hakana'ut* (The Study of Zealotry) he subtly suggests that Sabbatai Zevi resolved to convert to Mohammedanism only after the Sultan's personal physician, Guidon, himself an apostate, called his attention to the danger that threatened all the Jews in the Turkish empire should he, Sabbatai Zevi, as the chief culprit, refuse to pass to the dominant Moslem faith. But Jacob Emden hinted at this thought so subtly (perhaps because of his extreme caution about everything he said on this subject, considering that he was the chief opponent of all the aftereffects of the Sabbatai Zevi movement) that recent Jewish students of that period who depended so heavily on *Torath Hakana'ut* hardly noticed Emden's hint. Graetz, too, felt no need to examine carefully the chief motives that dominated the life and career of Sabbatai Zevi. Graetz maintained with almost unquestioned certainty that Sabbatai Zevi accepted the Moslem faith just as soon as Guidon informed him that if he remained stubborn, "burning torches would be tied to his body, he would be dragged through the streets and flogged with rods." Graetz even doubted whether "Sabbatai Zevi experienced an inner struggle before he decided to accept the advice of the apostate doctor." In Dubnow, too, we find a similar approach to the subject. "Guidon," Dubnow says, "frightened him so with threats of torture, with the humiliation and degradation of the death penalty, that he [Sabbatai Zevi] lost his head altogether. The instinct of self-preservation suggested to the false messiah that he must decide to adopt the Moslem faith."[2]

Even modern Jewish historians were not sufficiently unhampered in their researches to probe the tragic and conflict-ridden world of Sabbatai Zevi's inner life with original methods or with intuition. Unconsciously, perhaps, they painted the portrait of Sabbatai Zevi using the same harsh colors employed long ago by Sabbatai Zevi's rabbinical opponents. They oversimplified his personality and refused to note the complex and dramatic elements in his character.

II

No psychologically convincing explanation of Sabbatai Zevi's abandonment of Judaism was thus provided either by his disciples or by his opponents. The former introduced too much mystical speculation in their apologies; the latter resorted to oversimplified rationalizations.

We will naturally disregard Sabbatai Zevi's unsophisticated followers from among the common people who resorted to the easiest way out: they simply refused to believe the entire story; they denied the facts; it was not Sabbatai Zevi who embraced Islam, only his apparition, and thus he made fools of the Sultan, his courtiers and his clerics.

But we must seriously consider the more earnest explanations offered by Sabbatai Zevi's more refined and mystically minded disciples and associates. Their interpretations are characteristic of an environment that was saturated with kabbalistic mysticism which endowed them with a capacity for unique thought and imagination. But from the documents they left us, it is evident that all their interpretations cannot explain the objective nor even the subjective causes of Sabbatai Zevi's apostasy.

It is no accident that all during his life, until the moment when he stepped over the borderline into Islam, Sabbatai Zevi never so much as hinted of such a possible eventuality—assuming another faith in order to "redeem" the "sparks of sanctity" that lead an existence of enslavement within the realm of "uncleanness." It is also suspicious that neither Nathan of Gaza nor Cordoza, in all their letters defending Sabbatai Zevi, even hinted that he had ever suggested the possibility of such an intentional "descent" as a pre-condition for a subsequent "rise," despite the fact that such a statement—even a

[2] Heinrich Graetz (1817–1891) and Simon Dubnow (1860–1941) were distinguished historians of the Jews.

forged one—would have served the purpose of their letters: to save the public from melancholy, disappointment and despair.

Sabbatai Zevi's action appears to have come as a total surprise also to his closest followers, even to his Judas Iscariot (the Polish kabbalist Rabbi Nehemiah Cohen) with whom Sabbatai Zevi maintained a relationship of the closest confidence till the last moment. Had Sabbatai Zevi confided his intended apostasy to the Polish kabbalist, who first made a pilgrimage to him in Turkey and only later lost faith in him, one of two results would have followed: either Rabbi Nehemiah Cohen would have truly believed that the impending apostasy was planned for kabbalistic reasons and his faith in Sabbatai Zevi's messianic mission would have been strengthened. (Such an explanation would have readily appealed to Nehemiah Cohen, for he, too, temporarily embraced Mohammedanism for the sake of general Jewish interests.) Or, having decided to expose Sabbatai Zevi as a swindler, he would have widely publicised his plan of "redeeming the sparks of sanctity" and warned the Jews not to trust in the integrity of the false prophet's statements. The fact that some time *after* his apostasy Sabbatai Zevi hinted at his mission of redeeming the sacred from among the unclean, proves nothing. The defeated hypnotist might himself have become a "medium" for the hypnosis which he induced in his disciples.

On the other hand, there are no grounds for doubting that had Sabbatai Zevi harbored the idea of embracing Mohammedanism for mystical reasons—the same kind of reasons that his disciples later advanced in his justification—he would have done so earlier and not under duress; he would not have postponed such a crucial act to a time of such unfavorable circumstances that his apostasy could be interpreted as a result of cowardice and incapacity for *Kiddush Hashem*. All his preparations for his encounter with the Sultan, his dividing the earth into twenty-six kingdoms corresponding to the number of his nearest associates, his conversations with his visitors when he was already imprisoned in the Gallipoli fortress—from all the details that are known to us regarding the last days preceding his apostasy, it is evident that he regarded his impending audience with the Sultan as the great moment that would reveal to the entire world his divine mission and supernatural might, and that he did not at that time foresee that his visit to the royal palace would merely mark the beginning of a difficult and painful stage on the road of his mission.

It is still more difficult to agree with the oversimplified explanations of his opponents. It is impossible to conceive that a mere "swindler," a dishonest and conscienceless careerist, could successfully become the leader and psychological focus of such a grandiose and overwhelming movement which seized upon a large part of the Jews in all the countries of the Jewish dispersion of that time—from Gaza and Jerusalem to Amsterdam and Venice. Suffice it to recall the effect Sabbatai Zevi produced on the Jews of Eretz Israel when he was annointed in the Gaza synagogue as Messiah in a ceremony of exalted veneration, or the enthusiasm of the entire Jewish community in Smyrna when he was there proclaimed as Messiah. Special prayers and hymns were composed and sung in his honor in many European and Asian synagogues and houses of prayer. A veritable tide of pilgrims streamed with irresistible impetus from remote countries to the Turkish fortress where he was imprisoned. The diplomatic reports of the English ambassador in Turkey to his government, told of Sabbatai Zevi's great influence on Balkan Jewry. And even such a sober and disciplined mind as Baruch Spinoza's was impressed by the Sabbatai Zevi movement. Taking into consideration all these factors, it becomes evident why the rationalizations and all too smug simplifications of Sabbatai Zevi's opponents have such an unconvincing ring.

Sabbatai Zevi possessed one great talent—the talent of sincere and profound faith in the reality of his mission and the actuality of his dreams. When scores of thousands of Jews obeyed him when he ordered them to transform ancient and historically sanctified fast days into occasions of orgiastic celebration; when in the synagogues of hundreds of cities prayers on behalf of "our Lord the Messiah" were intoned; when many Jews decided to abandon all their earthly possessions, to leave their old established homes and go to Eretz Israel; when hundreds of the most pious rabbis, scholars, kabbalists and community leaders expressed their enthusiasm for Sabbatai Zevi and his mission, we must naturally explain this, first of all, as a result of the fevered moods and mystical yearnings of that tragic time. But there also can be no doubt that Sabbatai Zevi's personality was largely instrumental in uncovering these secret yearnings for a messiah and transforming them from a potential to a real force. In this regard he could become effective only as a result of his special talent —his sincere and profound faith in himself, in his vision and in his hallucinations. The mass man of that time needed a hero, a focal personality that would reflect and crystallize his yearnings and challenges, and this hero had to possess, above all, sincerity and faith. Had Sabbatai Zevi lacked these qualifications, the "mob" of that time would have been compelled and able to produce for itself a "genuine messiah" instead of the false one. In times like those, when the mass rises above itself, when it transcends its daily routine rhythms, when its senses react with passionate intensity, it becomes productive and gifted and capable of "producing" an additional couple of prophets and messiahs. It is therefore instructive that in Sabbatai Zevi's day it never even occurred to anyone to compete against him. No one felt able to satisfy better and more intensively the messianic thirst of the time than Sabbatai Zevi. In such times one "swindler" gives rise to a competing one; one pretender evokes another. But the fact that Sabbatai Zevi had no competitors within the messianic movement is perhaps the most convincing proof that he was *subjectively* the true messiah, and that his mission was one inspired "by God."

III

How then are we to explain Sabbatai Zevi's abandonment of Judaism?

We have no choice but to assume that this was an instance of one of those sudden crises that are characteristic of the lives of particularly exalted natures whose passionate feelings and experiences lead them to states of extreme hysteria. Sabbatai Zevi's adoption of the Moslem faith was no doubt completely unexpected by himself as well as by his followers. It is quite possible that even half an hour before his appearance before the Sultan, or before his talk with the court physician, Guidon, he would have regarded the fatal step which he made with such terrifyingly silent determination as absolutely out of the question.

At that moment there seemed to have occurred in Sabbatai Zevi's life one of those "accidents" which lie dormant in a kind of embryonic state below the level of consciousness and await, in a manner of speaking, a suitable occasion when they break through with catastrophic force. They are "accidents" only in relation to the conscious awareness of the person; but for the subconscious, for the underground existence of the personality, such "excesses" are thoroughly motivated, well prepared and "illegally" nurtured. Spontaneous decisions, such as Sabbatai Zevi's, occur either in moments of highest elation, when the individual is especially confirmed in the strength of his ego, or in moments of deepest depression, when all one's hopes and dreams suddenly disintegrate within one. In either case we are confronted with illogical decisions which feed on deep, internal, "unconscious logic."

Such logic characterized Sabbatai Zevi's fatal decision. His mystically-heroic striving to bring about an absolute transformation in Jewish life was from the very start pregnant (if one may use such a simile) with a determination to depart from Judaism. His messianic mission which was fundamentally a mighty affirmation of Judaism, was, on its reverse side, a striving for the total negation of Judaism and its future existence. His messianism was an expression of a despairing will not to be reconciled to the ordinary, prevailing mode of Jewish existence, which admitted of only two alternatives: the supreme summits of courage and strength, or the lowest depths with their demonic fascination of extinction and death. The absolute negation of the *galut* and all its manifestations, the revulsion against continued passive waiting for redemption, the stubborn refusal to be reconciled to the hobbled reality of Jewish life—these were fundamentally the psychological factors which at that time gave rise to messianic yearnings and that, more than anything else, determined the life pattern of Sabbatai Zevi. To *galut* he declared in no uncertain terms: "I reject you." He challenged Jewish destiny to combat, and this declaration of war contained the logical conclusion never to revert to existing conditions. He must either rise above this fate, or descend below it, but under no circumstances would he remain face to face with it. *Galut* must be destroyed either by means of the complete liberation of Jewry, or as a result of its total extinction. This was the unconscious but deeply rooted "logic" of Sabbatai Zevi's messianic career.

The Sabbatai Zevi movement was one of the mightiest protests in Jewish history against the traditional Jewish submission, against the accepted sense of duty to tolerate patiently and to wait passively, against the necessity to suppress vital needs and always to adjust to alien conditions of life. When we also consider the great and hitherto unappreciated role which the forced converts played in this movement, it becomes clearly understandable why this explicitly negative attitude toward *galut* inevitably led to excesses such as Sabbatai Zevi's apostasy, which served as a signal for an extensive wave of apostasy among many of his followers.

The *anusim*, the forced converts, introduced into the movement a particularly potent drive. Their yearning for the liberation of the Jewish people was naturally much more intense and profound than among the rest of Jewry, not only because they had suffered more than other Jews, but also on account of other no less compelling psychological reasons. Their life as forced converts who led a secret Jewish existence developed within them a morbid yearning after publicly professed Jewishness on one hand, and on the other hand it sharpened their striving for a more normal and free existence in general. Though their professed Christianity was insincere and had been foisted upon them by force, we must bear in mind that as official Christians they had for some time lived in close relationship

with more normal and happier peoples, and it was natural that in
the course of these relations there should awaken within them long
suppressed human urges. When many of these forced converts to
Catholicism flocked to Turkey, where they could resume their Judaism openly, they nevertheless, in a certain sense, continued to regard
the Jewish ghetto and its mode of life from the viewpoint of their
erstwhile Christian coreligionists. The Jewish *galut* revealed itself
to them as something loathsome and deformed. Uriel Acosta, who
broke the chains of the Catholic Inquisition and returned to Judaism, also felt impelled to break the bonds of *galut,* of the ghetto, of
the confining rabbinical discipline, after he had lived in the Amsterdam ghetto for a time. This revulsion against the ghetto explains the
phenomenon which at first glance appears incomprehensible, that
many former forced converts to Christianity who returned to Judaism after much suffering and effort, later returned to Christianity,
and this time of their own free will. And it was precisely among such
forced converts that Sabbatai Zevi found his most exalted devotees
who, on their part, strengthened in their leader a negative attitude
toward *galut* which he already felt strongly. Characteristic in this
regard was the prophecy of the Kabbalist A. M. Cordoza that the
final redemption would come only after all the Jews adopted another
faith. This prophecy reflected extreme anti-*galut* sentiments which
filled the hearts of the *anusim* and which communicated themselves
to other Jewish circles and strengthened in the "hero" of that time,
in Sabbatai Zevi, the determination to put an end to the *galut,* if not
by means of total redemption, then at least by means of an act of
desperation which would lead to the extinction of Jewry in general.

For years Sabbatai Zevi prepared himself for an "exodus from
galut." He believed that there existed a supernatural exit from *galut,*
and all his mystical preparations tended toward a single aim: finding the keys to this exit. But when it became absolutely clear to him
that the supernatural exit was irrevocably sealed and that all his
preparatory steps had been in vain, that the keys could not be found,
he turned to the subterranean exit, to the redeeming abyss of national self-destruction. At the moment when Sabbatai Zevi donned
the Turkish turban on his head, he fiercely "attacked" the *galut* just
as he had stormed it before when he underwent the rites of practical
kabbala which he believed would place upon his head the crown of
The King of Judah.

Only a total despairing in his own strength, only a profound
conviction of the full inner bankruptcy of his spiritual existence
could have made Sabbatai Zevi put on the Turkish turban. And
when Rabbi Jacob Emden suggested that Sabbatai Zevi decided

to adopt Mohammedanism in order to save the Jews of Turkey from the danger which loomed over them on his account, this too is an indication that when Sabbatai Zevi stood before the Sultan he had already lost his faith in his messianic mission. Had he at that moment still retained his messianic exaltation, had he continued to believe that he was still the bearer of supernatural powers that would enable him to open for Jewry a supernatural exit from *galut,* he would not have felt humbled also when the Turkish authorities threatened him and when Guidon warned him. His exalted imagination would have come to his aid at that moment and suggested some way out of the danger, and he would not have surrendered.

Why and how he lost his faith in himself and in his mission and in the power of "practical kabbala" is a psychological riddle to which the meager documents and information about the Sabbatai Zevi movement do not provide a convincing answer. It is quite possible that Rabbi Nehemiah Cohen, who was himself an informed practitioner of practical kabbala, had feverishly and daily awaited the coming of the Messiah, and had undertaken the arduous journey from Poland to Turkey in order to meet Sabbatai Zevi, and later declared that he did not believe in Sabbatai Zevi's mission, served to undermine Sabbatai Zevi's confidence in himself. We do not know the substance of the long conversation which Nehemiah Cohen had with Sabbatai Zevi when the latter was already imprisoned in the fortress some days before his appearance in the Sultan's palace. We know but one thing of this conversation which was supposed to have lasted three days and three nights—that Nehemiah Cohen offered Sabbatai Zevi numerous proofs that he was not the messiah and thus caused him unheard-of anguish. It is possible that this conversation aroused grave doubts in Sabbatai Zevi and finally altogether destroyed his faith in his mission. Sabbatai Zevi had awaited Nehemiah Cohen's arrival from Poland with great impatience. He had pinned great hopes on this kabbalist, and to his close disciples he said that Nehemiah Cohen had been sent by Providence itself to precede him and to clear the way for his great triumph. And then this Nehemiah Cohen turned out to be the one to declare courageously—in an environment which was literally aflame with faith and enthusiasm for Sabbatai Zevi—that he did not believe at all in Sabbatai Zevi's mission.

There are thus grounds for assuming that Nehemiah Cohen played an important role in the bankruptcy of Sabbatai Zevi's faith in his mission. But whether for this or for other reasons, it is clear that Sabbatai Zevi experienced a critical moment before his abandonment of his Judaism—a moment when he suddenly awoke from the intoxication of the dreams and visions which had held him in their power for many years. He experienced a moment of sobering and he suddenly beheld the grey expanse of the tedious reality of the world, with its merciless physical and material laws which formerly he was neither able nor willing to see. Instead of his own private reality, he suddenly became aware of the actual reality. He looked into the face of this reality which now confronted him and at once sensed his total powerlessness and the complete impossibility of transcending this reality for which he had striven all his life. He saw before himself two alternatives: the dreary, sad and endless road of the *galut,* and the other road which led directly to the yawning mouth of the abyss. Which of the two could he choose? Which did he have to choose? Long ago he had vowed, silently, never to return to the way of the *galut*—he now chose the other way.

There is a possible element of truth in one detail of a popular legend of that time. According to this legend the Turks in the palace did not see what actually happened. The Turkish courtiers in Adrianople merely saw a frightened and broken man who bowed his head before the Sultan and his learned Mufti. They were not aware that what was taking place before their eyes was the tragic act of revenge of a fallen hero. Sabbatai Zevi may have thought of Rabbi Joseph della Reina, and he donned the Turkish turban and accepted the name Mohammed not out of fear of the Ottoman king of flesh and blood, but as a protest against the "King of Kings," against the merciless God of Israel. . . .

1926

The Jewish Enlightenment in Germany

by Israel Zinberg

Translated by Bess and Herbert H. Paper

The following vignette is taken from a much larger historical work in which the author tries to deal with the Haskala, or Jewish Enlightenment in eighteenth-century Germany, in a tone more objective and even sympathetic than was customary among historians composing in Yiddish in eastern Europe. The Haskala had come under severe polemical attack as laying the basis for assimilation by Jews into the surrounding alien culture; but Zinberg treats it, instead, as a movement arising from and in response to needs felt within the Jewish community.—Eds.

In the post-Enlightenment period, after the Haskala ideals had so tragically lost their glamour and many of their former advocates had repented, a hostile warring tone began to appear in Hebrew literature with regard to the "Berlin Haskala" and its standard bearers. It is enough to recall the struggle Peretz Smolenskin waged against Moses Mendelssohn's enlightening activity, in which there is such bitter discussion of the creators and carriers of the Enlightenment among Prussian Jews. Several decades—an era of enormous social and spiritual upheavals—separate us from these feelings of repentance which the unexpected collapse of the Enlightenment's ideals called forth. It is now possible therefore to give a more objective and a historically more correct evaluation of the Berlin Haskala at the end of the eighteenth century.

At the outset, we must consider the extraordinarily difficult circumstances under which the "philosopher and freethinker" Frederick II held the throne. Frederick had actually declared with pride

that everyone in his realm could follow his faith freely and undis-
turbed. This, however, did not at all hinder him in behaving toward
Jews with the most poisonous enmity. In his hostility toward them,
notes the historian Ludwig Geiger, Frederick II even surpassed his
predecessors. Like all the German philistines of the time, this
crowned "thinker" was firmly convinced that Jews, as a harmful element, should have their civil rights restricted and that the one
benefit to be derived from them is the extortion of taxes. The civil
condition of Prussian Jews therefore became to a certain extent more
difficult under his dominion than under his predecessors. According
to the edict Frederick William I had issued in 1714, every "protected
Jew" had the right to transmit his "privileges" to his three oldest
children. Frederick II, however, found this to be too generous, and
according to the "General Privileges" of 1750 a "protected Jew"
could favor only his oldest son with his rights of residence and commerce. Frederick himself had given the reason for this a year earlier
when he pointed out that if every protected Jew were allowed to
hand over his rights not to one but to two of his heirs, then the specific objective of the Prussian law—to reduce the number of Jewish
inhabitants—would not be achieved. In accord with this goal, the
younger children of a privileged Jew who could not benefit from
their father's "rights" did not have the right to marry; the so-called
"extraordinary" protected Jews also did not have the right to be
heads of families in Frederick II's capital city. In addition to the
"extraordinary" protected Jews, the "General Privileges" also specify
the so-called "tolerated Jews"—all of this with one specific objective: to restrict the Jews in their rights.

Frederick II was more sensible and practical than the Russian
Empress Elisabeth who in her hatred of Jews had reached the point
of declaring that she wanted to have no benefit whatever from
Christ's enemies. Frederick regarded his Jews as cows to be milked
and as long as this "philosopher" held sway over Prussia, the number of special Jewish taxes increased enormously.

When Moses Mendelssohn, already renowned as an esthetic
and philosophical writer, requested the grant of residence right of
a "protected Jew," he did not even receive a reply. It was only
through the intervention of the Marquis d'Argens, who was very
much in favor at the royal court, that Mendelssohn finally obtained
(1763) the restricted right of an "extraordinary protected Jew."
Neither did Frederick find it possible to grant Mendelssohn's request that he be allowed to bestow his restricted residence right on
his children. Mendelssohn was after all only an employee of a silk
factory at the time, not the owner of one.

In the Berlin Jewish colony, spiritual growth began to be noticed along with economic power. Jewish merchants and bankers, satin and silk manufacturers, had close ties with foreign countries and frequent contact with the highest German nobility, which was especially noteworthy in those days for its self-disparagement before what was "foreign," particularly all that originated in France. German literature of the seventeenth and eighteenth centuries imitated French models in every detail, and Frederick II, eager to gain a reputation with his French poems, looked with scorn at everything that was created in the language of his own land. Wealthy Berlin Jewish houses came into friendly contact with their close neighbors, the large local French colony, which was the mainstay at that time of the industrial-entrepreneurial progressive-intellectual circles in Berlin. Bourgeois Jewish youth thus had the possibility of becoming acquainted with the new waves of ideas that had begun to appear on the other side of the Rhine under the influence of the encyclopedists and enlighteners. Henriette Herz gives us an interesting picture, in her memoirs, of how these encounters came about: "The first who began to study French were the daughters of the wealthy Jewish circles. The parents were not opposed, because of purely utilitarian motives—after all, it was possible to communicate with the entire civilized world by means of the French language. At first, Jewish girls used their French fluency to carry on gallant conversations with officers and court cavaliers who used to visit their parents on money matters. But later they began to use their French for more important matters—to become acquainted in the original with the French classics and the newer writers."

Solomon Maimon describes in his *Autobiography* how Jewish young men, who used to come to Berlin to work as teachers, devoted themselves primarily to studying French. The numerous Yiddish letters which the young Moses Mendelssohn wrote from Berlin to his fiancée in 1762 are quite typical in this regard. These letters are studded with French expressions that were apparently current in everyday speech. Mendelssohn writes, for example: *vi ambrasirt ikh bin, zikh mokiren, komoditet, distinktsye, pretekst, deranzhirt, rezultirt*, etc. He never tires of reminding his "beloved Fromet" each time that she should, for the sake of Heaven, diligently study the French language "which can almost become the mother tongue."

Bursting forth with their fresh strength, the youthful idea-bearers must have made a powerful impression with their fiery preaching on the disenfranchised dwellers of the ghetto. In these sermons, they heard the message of liberation and equality of all "citizens of the world," of the destruction of all caste privileges. . . .

Is it any wonder that the ideas of the French "enlighteners" found a clear response in certain Jewish circles?

Old-fashioned rabbinic Jewry, frozen in its practices, was incapable of stemming these ideological currents. True, the rabbis were on their guard, trying to fence off their community from foreign notions, everything that might arouse the merest taint of heresy. In the 1740's, a founder of the Bleichröder family, then a poor yeshiva student, was driven out of Berlin because a community charity collector caught him with a German book under his arm. Yet twenty or thirty years later there already existed a bridge of European culture for the growing number of young people, children of Jewish bankers, manufacturers, and city notables. For these youth, the freethinker Voltaire served as the ultimate authority, his sharp epigrams passing from mouth to mouth. Bleichröder's companion, also a poor rabbinical student, on whose behalf the young Bleichröder had been carrying the "defilement"—the German book—he it was who occupied one of the central positions in the German literature of the day and had become the recognized standard-bearer of the Enlightenment era of German Jewry. The yeshiva student bore the name Moshe, son of Menahem Mandel of Dessau. . . .

For generations Mendelssohn passed as the "father of the Haskala," founder of the Enlightenment. During his lifetime he was enthusiastically proclaimed as the "third Moses, who raised us from the deepest mire to praise and renown," the emancipator who "freed the people of Israel from spiritual bondage and led it forth on the bright path of culture and education."

Right after Mendelssohn's death, the journal *Meassef* declared that "the truth and the correct interpretation of the Torah were wrapped in darkness for generations until God commanded—let Moses appear!—and it suddenly became light!"

One of these "Haskala forerunners," Israel Zamosz, was the person who first acquainted the still quite young Mendelssohn with Maimonides's *Guide for the Perplexed* and awakened in him the notion of critical research. Zamosz was also the teacher of that extraordinary personality who had so great an influence on Mendelssohn's spiritual development—the physician Aaron Emmerich Gumperz. Gumperz was six years older than Mendelssohn; and Zamosz had aroused in him an interest in mathematics, philosophy, and the natural sciences. In 1751, Gumperz passed his examinations as a doctor of medicine, but being a person of means who did not have to worry about a livelihood, he never practiced. A friend of Frederick II, the Marquis d'Argens (author of *Lettres juives*), had a strong influence on the young Gumperz (he served as the Marquis's secretary for a time). Thanks to him Gumperz became acquainted with literary-scientific circles, a member of the "learned coffee house" in Berlin, a regular guest of the "Monday Club" which had developed into the assembly point of the Berlin "enlighteners." There Gumperz met Lessing, Nikolai, and others. Under the influence of these groups, Gumperz also decided to busy himself with "enlightenment" work in his own immediate sphere. He set out to write a large work in Hebrew that would encompass all the sciences. He lacked, however, the requisite creative ability and his intended book was never completed. He only published the preface (1765) in which he gives a general overview of all branches of learning in a clear, easily understood form, and endeavors to convince his reader of the great value of general worldly knowledge. At the same time he underscores that in such knowledge only foolish, ignorant persons can see a danger to faith. The learned doctor strives to have his reader understand the great significance of the experimental scientific method —a reader brought up in the tradition of *pilpul* and scholasticism. There is need, Gumperz asserts, to follow the road laid down by such great figures in Israel as Maimonides, Ibn Ezra, Gersonides, and Joseph Solomon Delmedigo—all of whom were armed with general knowledge and tirelessly struggled against the ignorant fools who persecuted the carriers of learning and science.

It is to Gumperz's credit that he was the first who revealed to the young Mendelssohn the wide world of European culture. He diligently taught him the European culture-languages, French and English, and acquainted him with Lessing, who had so decisive an influence on Mendelssohn's literary development. "It can be justifiably asserted," declares Mendelssohn's biographer, Kayserling, "that without Gumperz, Mendelssohn would not have become Mendelssohn." In one of his letters to his fiancée Fromet, Mendelssohn himself writes, "I have to thank him alone (Dr. Aaron Gumperz) for all that I have gained in the sciences." Aaron Gumperz demonstrates very clearly how exaggerated is the view held by many that Mendelssohn was the first among German Jews to attain the higher reaches of European education. Of course, Mendelssohn was certainly the first Jew who appeared as a significant and generally recognized German writer and who, as a master of literary style and language, carved his name into the history of German literature. It was he, the son of the Torah scribe Menahem Mendel of Dessau, the "extraordinary protected Jew," who was the first German author to treat the deepest philosophical problems in so fine and clear a style. It was he, the son of the disenfranchised ghetto, who was crowned with the honored title "Socrates of Berlin," and with whom royalty and the most significant researchers and thinkers of the day eagerly sought to make acquaintance. It was he who in 1743, a penniless fourteen-year-old yeshiva student, timorously knocked at the Rosenthal Gate (the only gate through which a Jew could enter Berlin)—only to be awarded twenty years later the first prize by the Prussian Academy for his philosophical work "Uber die Evidenz der Metaphysischen Wissenschaften."

We must also take into account Mendelssohn's gentle character, the special charm of his warm personality—all of this illuminated Mendelssohn's name with so much renown and extraordinary glory, created the "Mendelssohn legend," the pathetic myth of the "third Moses who led the Jewish people out of the night of spiritual bondage."

The truth is, however, that Mendelssohn, according to his temperament and world-view, was little fitted to become the standard-bearer of a reform movement. He himself confesses in a letter to Lessing that the very term "free spirit" arouses dread in him; that he actually trembled at the news that his longtime friend, the author of *Nathan the Wise,* had in his last years leaned to the atheistic view that denies the existence of a first cause ruling the world. With his whole heart Mendelssohn was tied to the old Jewish way of life and was faithful to the traditions of religious practice. His rationalist adherents, who consider themselves Mendelssohn's disciples, try to prove that all of this was only superficial; but this contention is refuted not only by his work *Jerusalem,* but also by many of Mendelssohn's personal letters. Thanks to them we learn, for example, that when Mendelssohn was on a trip in Brunswick he did not utilize the occasion to visit his friend, Lessing, only because there was a possibility of desecrating the Sabbath. He abruptly interrupts his letter to Abbt because "the Sabbath is at hand"—another time he writes to the same Abbt "the Sabbath is near and I must finish"; he refuses the glass of wine that Lessing offers him because it is "forbidden wine." "I am happy," Mendelssohn candidly confesses, "with every religious custom that does not lead to intolerance and misanthropy; I am happy, as are my children, with every ceremony that has something true and good as its basis." The book of Psalms was particularly dear to him not merely as a literary monument, but as prayers in which he pours out his religious feelings. "They (the Psalms) sweeten my burdened disposition," writes Mendelssohn to Sophia Becker a week before his death, "and I recite and sing them, as often as I feel the need to pray and sing."

All the while that Mendelssohn was famed as a brilliant writer and esthetic critic in the German literary world, he continued to be

the traditional learned scholar in Jewish surroundings, carefully observant of all the commandments, and behaving with the utmost
respect to the rabbis of the time, even asking the greatest of them to
bestow on him the honorary title "khaver" (companion). There can
really be no question at all of hypocrisy stemming from fear of persecution on the part of the rabbis—he himself points out in his well-
known reply to Lavater, "What can restrain me? Fear of my coreligionists? Their worldly power is too small for them to be able to
inspire me with dread."

Mendelssohn's personal world and his entire world-view are revealed most clearly in the work which made him so renowned in
wide intellectual circles: *Phädon or On the Immortality of the Soul*.
This German essay, so closely bound in outer form and style to Plato,
is yet a typically Jewish work in theme and content and is directly
related to the most important problems which occupied so prominent a place in Hebraic religious-philosophical literature. Not in
vain did Mendelssohn indicate in his preface that he had originally
intended to write it in Hebrew. "Many important reasons," Mendelssohn points out, "did not permit me to carry this out and forced me
to write my planned book in a language of the gentile nations, just
as in their day those greater and more important than I composed
their works in Arabic."

Mendelssohn repeats this almost with the very same words in a
personal letter (dated 25 May 1779) to Avigdor Levi of Glogau.
Nevertheless it seems beyond doubt that the prudent Mendelssohn
does not reveal the whole truth. He suggests more clearly and definitely what the intention of his publication was, in a second letter,
written also in 1779, to his Christian friend August von Hennings:
"After much thought I have come to the decision that with the re-
mainder of the energy still left to me I can be of service to my children and also to a significant portion of my people, if I should give
them a good Bible translation with an appropriate commentary. *This
will be the first step on the road to enlightenment from which my
people are, unfortunately, still so remote that actual doubt arises
about the future of the Jewish people*."

It is beyond question that Mendelssohn set himself a double
goal with his literary project: 1) to make it easy for German Jews to
become acquainted with the German literary language by means of
a Bible translation printed in Hebrew letters; 2) through his accu-
rate translation and the clear, systematic commentary to give the
new generation the possibility of getting to know the classic poetic
beauty of the Biblical text and the grammatical characteristics of
the Hebrew language, so as to arouse in Jewish youth the desire to

turn away from intricate *pilpul* and dry scholasticism and back to
the Bible and Biblical style. It was for this reason that Mendelssohn
was deeply immersed in translating the Psalms at the same time that
he was translating the Pentateuch. These prayers preserved from
ancient times had a strong influence on Mendelssohn's religious
sense; but he also valued them highly as first-class examples of
lyrical poetry. And in his letters to various friends he stresses that
with his translation he intends to accustom the reader to see in the
Psalm-prayers an example of the classical "lyrical poetry of the
Hebrews . . . without looking for the prophetic and mystical which
both Christian and Jewish commentators have found in the Psalms
only because they were searching for them; and they searched for
them only because they were neither worldly-wise nor judges of art."

Mendelssohn intended one thing more with his Bible translation: to erase from Jewish life "the Jewish-German dialect". . . . In
Mendelssohn's eyes, the Yiddish *zhargon* was only a straightforward
mixture of "Hebrew with German." And "I hope," he writes in August 1782 to his friend, Ernst Klein, "that the fact that recently my
brothers have begun to use the pure German language will have a
very good effect. . . . *Simply no mixing of languages!*" So Mendelssohn concludes his letter.

1936

Moses Hess—Socialist, Philosopher, Jew

by Hayim Zhitlowsky

Translated by Moshe Spiegel

By the early seventies of the last century Moses Hess had been almost entirely forgotten. It was only on the occasion of his death in 1875 that the world was reminded of this lonely thinker and fighter. The writers of obituaries, particularly in the Socialist press of Germany, bestowed on him a title he truly deserved, *Der Alt-Vater des deutschen Kommunismus*. But those obituaries were no more than a flicker, dispelling only for a moment the darkness that obscured his name.

As interest mounted in the earlier history of the German Socialist movement, the significance of Moses Hess became clearer. The "scientific socialism" of Karl Marx, we came to see, had its theoretical roots in the spiritual movement launched by Moses Hess; the youthful Marx had become interested in the social problems of his time as a direct result of Hess's socialistic dispatches from Paris, and until trying his own wings, Marx had continued to be his disciple. To this day the Marxist system has retained certain ideas which Moses Hess had been the first to introduce into the socialist outlook. Hess (or "Rabbi Moses," as Arnold Ruge used to call him) had already expressed the salient Marxist contention that capitalism and its factories constituted the cradle in which socialism must of necessity be nurtured—and that the proletariat, as it emerged in the capitalist system, was bound to be its victim. This view Hess set forth in 1843, just before Marx shifted from political radicalism to socialist theories and began eagerly listening to voices that until then had been alien to him. Still other forms of "scientific socialism" now associated with Marx stem from the so-called "true socialism" of which Moses Hess was the spiritual founder.

The characteristic traits of Hess as thinker and philosopher have begun to unfold still more sharply than those of Hess the socialist. Historical research has not yet arrived at a final verdict on this point either; some aspects of his world outlook, however, justify awarding him a place of honor even as philosopher.

I do not mean to imply that Moses Hess discovered a new trail in the philosophical wilderness. By no means. The direction he pursued, and exhorted us all to follow, had long been known to philosophy: it had been opened up by Baruch Spinoza. This is a synthetic monism opposed both to idealism and to materialism; it views with disfavor a spirit devoid of body, or a body devoid of spirit, and it also discountenances both a God without a world and a world without divinity. The independence and courage of Hess's thinking is shown in the fact that where the entire generation of radical thinkers to which he belonged had become intoxicated with Hegelian idealism, Hess alone remained sober, with the search for a course of his own bringing him to Spinoza. Later, when materialism had been enthroned in place of spirit, even so revolutionary an upheaval failed to shake Hess: he had long been aware that materialism is merely the *sitra achra* of idealism (or, as Hess preferred to put it, of spiritualism), and that both are no more than abstract shadows of a unique, everywhere rationalizing, everywhere divine and, at the same time, everywhere material reality. To be able to withstand the magnetic attraction of the Hegelian philosophy that was captivating the minds and hearts of his close associates, was a mark of spiritual fortitude.

Nor was it in this alone that Hess showed his philosophical independence. He was ready to abandon the system of Spinoza where it lagged behind the new requirements of philosophical thought. Spinoza's world is the best of all possible worlds—handed down once and for all, it endures forever as it is, because divine reason is eternal and unalterable. Spinoza left no room for *development,* for a striving toward higher goals, because a goal is something outside of the God-world—and for him that was inconceivable. But in the time of Hess, philosophical thought demanded first of all an answer, a solution to the problem of development, something that had already been glimpsed by Leibnitz and was paramount in the philosophies of Kant, Fichte, Schelling, and Hegel.

Does everything in this world develop? Yes, Hess emphatically stated. But does everything in the world develop infinitely, without a goal to which it aspires? Not so, replied Hess. Everything that is subject to development in the world is also bound to have a final goal toward which development aspires. That goal is perfection, and it is attained only after a long process of internal frictions and struggles. That which has to develop commences with a chaotic state in which all of its elements strive to come out of the chaos: they fashion their individuality and contend with one another for existence. Only in that struggle can the conditions of peace and mutual harmony be formulated. This harmony of contending elements—"the Kingdom of the Messiah"—constitutes the destination of all development.

"From chaos through struggle to harmony"—this, in brief, is the theory of development proposed by Moses Hess.

In the spiritual life of mankind, Hess again finds the general law of development to be from chaos through struggle toward harmony. Thus, for example, spiritual development begins with chaos in which elements of science, philosophy and religion are intermingled. In the course of struggle, each of the elements emerges with its own aims and attributes. They contend with one another, and each one denies the right of others to exist. But this competition must likewise terminate in harmony, in an everlasting peace when each of the spiritual spheres will safeguard its own frontiers and will not impede the growth of the other—whereupon they will join in a higher unity.

This, in brief, is the basis of Hess's philosophical outlook. There remains another aspect of his thought that assures a place of honor for Moses Hess. We refer to his internationalism.

If we are not mistaken, Hess was indeed the theoretical father of *international* socialism; at any rate, in German socialist literature he was the first to treat internationalism as a new principle, one opposed to both of its predecessors: cosmopolitanism, the principle of international turmoil, and nationalism, the principle of contention and rivalry. Anyone who studies the theories advanced within the International Workingmen's Association, which arose during the lifetime of Karl Marx, and compares them with the theories Hess had set forth a few years earlier, must admit that the early Marxists assimilated the ideas of Moses Hess almost word for word into their own system.

Mankind aspires toward a state of affairs in which the nations are to become amalgamated into a living organism. Equality among nations is to be contingent not upon the creation of identical values but upon the enjoyment of equal rights. But just as each part of an organism contributes its share to the activity of the whole, so must each nation, maintaining its individuality, make a contribution which no other can make as well. The organic harmony of nations is a task that must be accomplished before there can be social harmony among individuals; the abolition of war must precede the abolition of class differences in society.

Hess's theory of race can obviously also be seen in terms of

"Historical Materialism," since he saw the forms of subjective consciousness as deriving from objective material existence, namely race and social institutions. Nonetheless, the early theoreticians of internationalism were correct in not following Hess on this matter. For regardless of how engaging his ideas are, the race theory as set forth by Gobineau, and as expanded by Chamberlain and Dühring, is, after all, merely a hypothesis or a paramount question which we put to historical philosophy, and which historical study has unfortunately thus far failed to clarify. The great importance of the racial aspect is now felt everywhere, yet no one seems able to establish its fundamental character, the nature of its influence, or the limits of its power.

But for Hess, the theory of race was an absolute, just as the theory of economics was for Marx. He assumed that the theory of race was the sole foundation on which the structure of socialist internationalism could be built, just as the Marxists speak of their "economic basis." Both are in error. The race theory as Hess perceived it can be just as easily disavowed as the economic theory formulated by Marx, without any damage to the structure of international socialism.

At first glance, it might be assumed that Hess's attitude toward Jewish nationalism is inherent in his philosophical and socialist beliefs. After all, the Jews do constitute a nation, and thus may not be excluded from the brotherhood of nations or from the right to an independent development. But that is merely a first impression. Karl Marx likewise rationalized internationalism; he was not an adherent of cosmopolitanism either, yet how remote he was from Jewish national thought! That Moses Hess had also been a fervent Jewish patriot, the first socialist Zionist, came to light only at the beginning of the 1890's.

The fact that Hess became known so late was a detriment to our generation, the generation which in the 1880's was racking its brains over the basic problem of Jewish socialism: how to combine socialist principles with the idea of a Jewish renaissance. An acquaintance with Hess's Rome and Jerusalem would have spared us a great deal of theoretical spadework. This is not to imply that the Jewish theories of Moses Hess constitute a Mosaic Law; but his formulation of the problem, the way he went about his search for a solution, was a new approach to the whole of Jewish history.

There is tragedy in the fate of Moses Hess: his ideas were set forth in 1862, when they were not understood; they were not to be seen on the horizon during all those years that we yearned for them, and only came to light when the major task had been completed without them. This in no way diminishes the theoretical stature of Hess, but it does considerably lessen his historical importance in the development of Jewish socialism.

The whole attitude of Moses Hess toward the suffering of the Jews was similarly tragic. His childhood had been spent in an atmosphere imbued with Jewish piety and patriotism. On his mother's side he was descended from a Polish rabbi who had had to flee from Germany. Hess's grandmother never let him forget his ancestors and hoped that Moses, too, would prove an avid student of the Torah. His grandfather had been both a merchant and a Talmudic scholar who devoted his leisure to poring over the Gemara. So steadfast was his faith in the coming of the Messiah that in his commercial dealings he never planned for the distant future—always bearing in mind that the Messiah might suddenly appear at any time.

All the influences of Hess's youth faded, however, once he came into contact with German culture and the progressive tendencies of his age. Hess became aware of his Jewishness only in 1840, "in the midst of zealous efforts in behalf of Socialism," when the ritual murder case known as the "Damascus Affair" aroused the European world. "In the midst of my Socialist aspirations," he tells us, "it occurred to me for the first time and with great anguish that I belonged to an unlucky people, condemned and isolated, scattered throughout all countries but continuing to survive. I was far removed from Judaism even then. Nonetheless, I yearned to express both my grief and my patriotic feelings as a Jew. However, that outcry was soon stifled within my breast by the overwhelming anguish that had been awakened in me by the European proletariat."

Shortly after the February Revolution, Hess migrated to France. Following the suppression of the revolution by Napoleon III, he withdrew from politics and turned to the study of natural science. Through his studies be became convinced that a new era had begun in which nations would be reborn.

"I was particularly drawn to my Jewish people," he writes at the beginning of his *Rome and Jerusalem*. "A thought I believed had been stifled in my breast forever now rose before me, once again imbued with life. The thought of my nationality, which could not be uprooted from the heritage bequeathed to me by the patriarchs, by the Holy Land and the Holy City—the site where the belief in a divine unity of life and a future brotherhood of all men had been born.

"The images of my ill-fated forefathers that had hovered about me in my youth now manifested themselves again, and long suppressed feelings could no longer be stifled. The anguish that had

been a transient thing at the time of the Damascus Affair now became a dominant and enduring part of my spirit. I no longer tried
to stifle the voice of my Jewish consciousness. If anything I delved
even deeper in order to discover its roots."

He now unearthed from his files the manuscript he had written
at the time of the Damascus Affair, in which we already find the
beginnings of his later attitude toward the Jewish problem. We offer
a few excerpts typifying Hess's ideas at the time:

So long as the Jews submitted to humiliation and persecution,
they regarded both as a visitation from God and they hoped that
His nation would some day be regenerated. His only concern
was to hold Himself and His people in reserve until the time
came to reward His nation for all the sufferings it had endured
—a time when God would take revenge against the enemies of
Israel. However, our enlightened Jews no longer possess such
faith and hope. At the same time they consider each false accusation an affront to their honor and civic status. What good is
emancipation to them? Of what avail is it that here and there
a Jew may be elected to high office, if the term *Jew* carries a
stigma any arrogant scoundrel and second-rate hack can turn to
account? . . .

So long as the Jew denies his nationality, because he lacks the
necessary self-esteem to admit solidarity with a persecuted and
ridiculed minority, his false attitude is bound to become more
insufferable with each passing day. Why delude oneself? The
nations of Europe have always regarded the existence of Jews
in their midst simply as an anomaly. We shall always be aliens,
even among the nations that may emancipate us because of
humanitarianism and righteousness but will never respect us so
long as we set forth as the cornerstone of our faith the principle
of *Ubi bene ibi patria* ("Wherever I dwell, there is my country"), and discard our own national memories. Not the old-
fashioned Orthodox Jew, who would rather have his tongue cut
out than use it to deny his own nationality, deserves contempt,
but the modern Jew who denies his nationality because the
hand of destiny weighs so heavily upon that nationality. The
eloquent appeals to humanitarianism and enlightenment he so
glibly mouths, in order to conceal his betrayal and his fear of
being identified with his less fortunate fellow Jews, will not protect him from the harsh verdict of public opinion. In vain does
the enlightened Jew offer as evidence his geographic and philosophical alibi; he wears a thousand masks, he changes his name,

his religion, his customs and manners, in order to camouflage his identity. Nonetheless, each indignity inflicted upon a Jewish name will hurt him more than it does the upright person who confesses solidarity with his brethren and champions their honor.

With these words Hess in 1840 poured out his heart's bitterness in the privacy of his study, chastising himself and his generation—only to forget it all again for two decades more.

Hess was stirred anew by Jewish national feeling only at the end of the 1850's and the beginning of the 1860's—the period of the Italian upheaval. But it was not the renewed persecutions of Jews that ignited his feelings. The new voices of the time that called the subjugated nations to freedom, also stirred in Hess an awareness of the national aspirations of the Jews.

For him it was not enough to feel that Jews were a subjugated people and consequently must fight for their freedom. He did not base his Jewish nationalism on the fundamental right of every nation—however small and insignificant—to independent existence. Such a position, at that time, would still have been premature. The potential champions of Jewish freedom were then even more widely scattered in alien camps than now. They had first of all to be brought back into the fold, and Moses Hess believed that by offering no more than an abstract theory of the rights of peoples he would not be able to win them over. Hess himself had not yet fully developed the feeling of those who, rather than seeking the authority of this or that theory, choose to live out of a simple *desire to live*. The flickering life-instinct of the assimilated Jewish intelligentsia had first to be brought to life with a strong stimulant.

Hess did his best to prove that the Jews were no ordinary people. Their right to a free and independent existence, he felt, was based on their enormous importance to the entire history of mankind. With this theory, Hess became one of those spokesmen of the Diaspora who would champion the spiritual struggle for Jewish existence, one of a long line of Jewish thinkers that extends from Philo to Ahad Ha-Am. By vocation they are all to some degree religious philosophers and advocates of Judaism—individuals who have replaced the life of the senses with a simple "unorthodox" existence in this world, and who recognize that existence only when it has been sanctified by some kind of ideal.

All nations, according to Hess, are organic parts of humanity, although not all are equally creative. The Jewish people belong to the most creative part, because of their skill in creating "the holy singular love" that derives from their religious devotion to the idea of God. "Jews have always been the teachers of the knowledge of God," as he observes elsewhere. "Our nation originated the noblest religion of antiquity, which became a treasure house for all of the civilized world. . . . And this mission will remain with the Jews until the 'end of days'—I mean the time when the world is filled with the knowledge of God, even as our prophets have foretold."

The characteristic trait of Judaism, Hess continues, is that it is not individual but social and even cosmic. There is nothing so alien to Judaism as that redemption of the soul of the separate individual toward which the Christian religion aspires. Judaism has never alienated the individual from the family, the family from the nation, the nation from mankind, mankind from the organic and cosmic creation, or creation from the creator. Rabbi Johanaan's concept of the ultimate goal of creation is the Messiah, and the Messianic kingdom is a concept that contains the entire essence of Judaism. The Jewish people, mankind, the world and God are all one. In the Jewish religion, properly perceived, it becomes evident that there is no place for belief in a hereafter, or in a personal immortality in a world to come. Only the people are immortal. According to Hess, our "immortality of the soul" extends into the past to embrace the patriarchs and into the future to the Messianic kingdom. Egoistic personal immortality could not be tolerated by Judaism, because Jewish reasoning had never divorced the soul from the body. The synthetic monism of Spinoza is essentially an ancient Jewish concept. Only after Christianity drifted away from Judaism did a dualism of spirit and body emerge. Jewish life was never spiritualistic. Even the Essenes and the early Christians—who grew out of the Essenes— were not really spiritualistic sects. And Jewish thinking is equally hostile to total materialism. Jewish life is monistic, as is its idea of God.

A second basic trait of Judaism is its dominant concern for the future, manifested in the love shown by Jews for children. The children, "implying the future," are the pivot about which all of Jewish life revolves. Sacred prophets could emerge among the Jews because Jewish love takes a long-range view of the future. Judaism is a historical religion, its chief tenet being a development looking toward the achievement of a historical goal, the Messianic kingdom of social and international justice. Modern socialistic theories and tendencies are the offshoot of concepts inherent in the Jewish historical process. If modern Jews had been aware of this, they would not have allowed the currents of modern thought to carry them away from the consciousness of belonging to a Jewish nation.

Thanks to Judaism, declares Hess, the history of mankind became a sacred history—a unique process of development that begins with the love of the family and that is unlikely to be completed until the whole of humanity has become a single family whose members are as closely linked, thanks to the creative genius of history, as the various organs of a living body are united, thanks to the same creative force in nature. Until the French Revolution, only the Jews had been the bearers of sacred history. Since the Revolution, France and other nations have applied themselves to the same task.

All these views about the progressive, quasi-socialist, and Spinozan substance of Judaism have, in our opinion, little significance when it comes to implementing a progressive Jewish nationalism. For one thing, they are subjective views. It is not difficult to prove that Moses Hess had to some extent infused his own philosophical system into Judaism—and had left out nearly all the dubious aspects.

Primarily, however, progressive Jewish nationalism has no need to glorify either Judaism or the Jewish people as a race. The normal development of human culture demands that every nation should have the possibility of an independent cultural life. True, contemporary culture is the product of a relatively few nations, one of those few being the Jews. This is not to imply, however, that the less progressive nations are to be absorbed by peoples who are more creative culturally. Mankind is only at the beginning of its historical road. Which of the currently "passive" nations are to flourish, what wonderful products of human culture they are to contribute—this cannot be foreseen. Accordingly, every people has potentialities for cultural creativity, perhaps within a millenium or twenty millenia from now. This fact alone makes it incumbent on us not to let any people perish, and to ensure that each enjoys all the necessary conditions for a free and independent life. Moreover, each would be entitled to those conditions even if it were to remain "passive" forever—just as every human being has a right to an independent life whether or not he is a genius. Of course, one can take pride in belonging to a flourishing creative people. And when such a people is being trampled and harassed, one has not only the right but the duty to raise one's head and assert its qualifications to all mankind. But to justify the demand for an independent national life on that score alone—this is no more than a logical fallacy.

Of greater substance are Moses Hess's views on the destiny of the Jewish people in the Diaspora, and especially his attitude toward the Orthodox and the Reform branches of Judaism.

His theory of a Jewry that transforms the Jewish religion into a pantheistic world outlook and a socialist idea, Hess made into a weapon in the struggle against the Jewish intelligentsia which had completely abandoned the Jewish people. The philosophical socialism that Hess injects into Judaism was intended to serve as a magnet that would draw the hearts of the intelligentsia.

But the defecting intelligentsia were not the only Jewish group with whom Hess had to cope. "On the home front there was also a spiritual life" in need of criticism. In the days of Moses Hess, the spiritual life "on the home front" consisted of two branches: the Orthodox and the Reformed—both of which Moses Hess challenged in his *Rome and Jerusalem*. It is remarkable, however, that in the spiritual opposition to both tendencies his pantheistic socialism played only a minor role. A totally new criterion was being applied here—a criterion which, although it did not run counter to his social philosophy, nonetheless had little in common with it. Here, for the first time, we come upon his truly revolutionary thought, in which he was ahead of his time by several generations, and to which even Karl Marx did not attain: the idea that the quintessence of Jewish existence is not in any way dependent on the economic or social situation of the people (as Karl Marx maintained), and that there is only the fact from which the separate existence of the Jewish people issues—the fact that Jews are a nation apart.

This thought is clear in Hess's evaluation of Reform Judaism. He is of course somewhat critical of the general spiritual poverty in the ostensibly progressive trend of Jewish religious thought. He ridicules the superficial "heresy" and "enlightenment" (as he would express it) that had prevailed since the time of Moses Mendelssohn, and sharply criticized the "Mission Theory" of Reform Judaism which still discerned in Jewish monotheism an ideal to be preached to Christian nations. "For their religious dogmas alone," he quite correctly observes, "both the Jewish and the Christian religions ought to have vanished long ago." But Hess saw as the principal fallacy in Reform Judaism a false view concerning Jewish existence. They assumed that Jews were solely a religious sect, and that the Jewish problem could be solved by the advancement of religious belief. In reality, the Jews also constitute a nation, and their misfortune is rooted in the loss of their homeland and having to wander throughout the world.

According to Hess, the foundation of the Jewish people consisted of the original Jewish stock, "which perpetuates itself despite climatic influences," and whose national traits have not been obliterated over thousands of years. Contemporary Jews have the same facial features as the Semitic faces depicted on the murals inside the pyramids. Such a race cannot be exterminated by mere apostasy.

Even in mixed marriages, Jewish features re-emerge in the third or fourth generation. Race gave rise to the Jewish national conscience, and the ancient Jewish religion is merely the manifestation of that same ineradicable conscience. Jewish religion comes to be seen by Hess as first and foremost Jewish patriotism. The sense of the Talmud and the Shulhan Arukh—that is, of all the laws and customs of the Jewish faith—rests not in their religious significance but in their national role and their value for the existence of the Jewish people. All the feast and fast days, the devotion to the Jewish traditions, the glorification of the Hebrew tongue, the entire Jewish cult and its dominating influence on daily life—all of these are based on the patriotism of the Jewish people. "Even Spinoza," Hess observes, "regards the Jews as a nationality and conjectures that the rebirth of a Jewish sovereign state is contingent upon the courage of the Jewish people."

The ancient Jewish faith served as an armor for the Jewish people in their struggle for national existence. Thanks to the Talmud and Rabbinical legislation, the Jews as a people were preserved in the Diaspora; and the more we revere and cherish the historical meaning of Jewish Orthodoxy, the more we ought to cherish its sanctities. Hess is especially indignant because the Reformers dispensed with the most important Jewish prayers in their worship services. Hess cherishes those prayers: "for me they are an echo of a thousand generations that chanted them to heaven out of the anguish of their hearts." And their national character is their most stirring element, since a pious Jew is first of all a Jewish patriot.

In the Jewish religion, even in the form it had taken in the Diaspora, Hess discerns a great and sacred thought: the individual lives not for his own sake alone but also for the sake of his people. Hess refers to this as the *historical cult,* and he suggests that not only the Jewish people but every other nation in the world ought to have such a cult, in which the most hallowed element for each individual would be the nation to which he belonged—and the role that nation had played or ought to play in the development of mankind.

This sacred nucleus of the Jewish historical cult is still prevalent in the Jewish religion. But now the nucleus is covered with a hard shell of law and custom; and Hess thinks it would be erroneous to believe that this shell can be shattered from without by way of enlightenment and criticism. It is only when the people have been regenerated nationally that the Jewish religion can be reformed. It is only when the ice of Orthodox Jewry has melted that the national spark within it can blaze into a great conflagration. Hess states elsewhere that the static forms of Orthodoxy are fully justified until the

national rebirth erupts by a natural process, thanks to the force of
growth inherent in Jewish nationality. Until that time, all reforms
will be in vain. No one—not even Mendelssohn—has succeeded in
breaking open the hard shell with which Rabbinism has encased
Judaism as in a suit of armor, unless to destroy its essence or extinguish its sacred life.

Contemporary Orthodoxy will disappear when the Jewish people have created a new Torah; and the new Torah will go forward
when the Jewish national question has been resolved. Just as deliverance from Egypt brought forth the Mosaic Law, and release from
the Babylonian exile produced the oral law, so the Jewish religious
genius will create a third Torah when it has been set free from the
third Diaspora. Therefore it can make no sense to desert the Jewish
religious community or even to introduce any reforms into it. The
one thing that Hess called for was an improved esthetic sense in the
interpretation of the liturgy so that every Jew may be able to appreciate it.

Hess adopted toward the Jews in Eastern Europe a totally different attitude from that of the enlightened Reformers, who regarded
them only as obscurantists and fanatics. He praised the east European Jews precisely because they remained loyal to the ancient faith
and thus sustained the Jewish nationality. "I would like to go to
those millions of loyal brethren," he writes, "and to exhort them:
'Carry your banner high, my people! You have preserved the living
nucleus which, like the seeds found in the sarcophagi of the Egyptian
mummies, slumbered for thousands of years without losing their
ability to take root and grow. It is bound to grow, once the hard shell
in which it was encased has been cracked; then, as soon as it is
planted in cultivated soil, it will spring into life drawn from the
light of day and from the dew of night.'"

From his arguments it is obvious that it was not Orthodoxy in
itself that Hess cherished but rather the nationalist nucleus it contained. The question that arises is of great interest to the present
generation. What if that nationalist nucleus were associated with
some religion other than Judaism? Would a person of such persuasion still be regarded as a Jew—and what should our attitude be
toward him?

To this question Hess gave a reply both radical and consistent.
Comparatively few of our enlightened radicals today could answer
so well.

Hess teaches us that the religion of the Jews demands a study
of the knowledge of God rather than mere faith. According to Hess,
the natural foundation of religion is the Jewish nation—to which

every Jew belongs, *including the apostate,* or one whose parents have embraced Christianity. Hess maintained that "the apostate Jew also remains a Jew, despite all his protests. In our time it is difficult to find a difference between the enlightened and the convert. My friend, Armand L., whose grandparents embraced the Christian faith, shows a greater interest in the joys and sorrows of the Jews than many a circumcised Jew, and has clung much more loyally to the Jewish nationality than our enlightened rabbis."

From this standpoint it makes no difference whether one is an apostate or not, whether one is a follower of Christ or of Moses. The principal issue is whether one is a nationalist or an assimilationist. According to Hess, we should cherish a Christian Jew who is whole-heartedly nationalist more than one who has remained loyal to Judaism but for whom the national faith and the rebirth of his people either has been rooted up out of his heart as a matter of principle (as in the case of Reformers) or is simply dead (as in the majority of Orthodox Jews).

Hess's attitude toward Christianity is particularly interesting. The first centuries of Christianity, until the Christians broke loose from the Jewish people, he regards as one of the most progressive periods for the Jewish spirit. The Christian "Pater Noster" is for him a purely Jewish prayer expressing Messianic hope. And even later, after Christianity had lost touch with its Jewish origin, it still constituted a great stride toward the goal the prophets had set forth in their visions of the Messianic age. Christianity, however, was merely one step that had its justification only until the time came for the advent of the Messiah.

According to Hess, the Messianic era began with the philosophy of Spinoza—but only in the realm of human consciousness. In the social sphere the first clear step was taken with the French Revolution; the second and still more important step came in the 1880's, when the subjugated peoples were reawakened to an independent historical life. That, for Hess, was the true time of Resurgence.

"We should not longer be astonished by Resurgence," he wrote, "at a time when Greece and Rome are reawakening, when Hungary is arming itself for the last battle, and when one sees about to dawn an uprising of all the enslaved peoples who have been for so long oppressed and despoiled by Asiatic barbarism. . . . In the name of a higher good they will wage war against the arbitrary dominion to which the ruling peoples have resorted, whether in a barbaric or a civilized fashion."

The most important sign of the Messianic era and of the Resurgence that stirred the Jewish people with hope of redemption was the "regeneration of the Italian people above the ruins of Rome. For as long as the Austrians held sway in Italy, and the Turks in the Holy Land of our forefathers, the Italian and the Jewish people were incapable of awakening into life. But the French, the soldiers of modern civilization, shattered the dominion of the barbarians, and with their Herculean power they took away the stone from the tomb, and the people once again came to life."

Hess also discerned signs of the Messianic era in the internal life of the Jewish people, in the flowering of Jewish science in Germany, in the founding in Paris of the *Kol Israel Haverim* organization, and in the rebirth of Hebrew literature. True, all of these were meager signs, not to be compared with those turbulent eruptions of Jewish national energy which three of four generations later were to produce the Zionist movement and the Jewish socialist and revolutionary trends, as well as Yiddish literature. But for Moses Hess they sufficed to bolster his Jewish aspirations.

Hess could not have perceived still another sign of Jewish regeneration, perhaps the most important in his own time—the emergence of Moses Hess himself. A dead nation could not have given birth to such a man, one whose spiritual force was allied with so ardent a love for the people and so profound a belief in their future. It was only because of so impassioned a love and so profound a faith that, on the basis of a few unspectacular political developments, Hess could foresee that "with the liberation of the Eternal City on Mount Moriah, and with the rebirth of Italy, will come the Resurgence of the land of Judea."

During the time of Moses Hess there could be for a Jewish nationalist no national ideal other than Zionism, nor could there be any idea of Zionism other than that currently referred to as the "general" one. There were as yet no Jewish wage-earners and practically no Jewish democracy; there had still been no attempt at the testing of national powers against the Diaspora, at buffeting the waves of assimilation, much less any effort to carry out all this without the help of the Jewish religion, relying only upon a progressive national energy. Hess was thus spared the pain and effort of bringing into accord the ultimate Zionist goals, which up until then had been shielded from Jewish religion, with the radical nationalist aspirations of the Diaspora that undermined the foundations of the ancient faith—a painful effort from which no serious modern Zionist can be free.

The emancipation of the Jewish people was for Hess an event of universal history, and one of no less interest for mankind as a whole than for the Jewish people itself. The development of mankind thus became, as it were, an essential part of his Zionism, because the ultimate goal, as he saw it, could only be attained with the concurrence and support of all nations. "What one man could not gain from his brother, or one person from another person, one nation will gain from another nation," he declares at the beginning of his *Rome and Jerusalem*.

No wonder, then, that his Jewish nationalism did not, as he assures us, interfere in any way with his participation in the socialist movement of his time. A few years after the publication of his *Rome and Jerusalem*, we see Lassalle urging Hess to write a socialist tract for German workers—and Hess accepting the suggestion. From the time Hess adopted the national Jewish position, there was no conflict between his devotion to the Jewish people and his love for the "alien" people among whom he lived and worked. For a socialist there simply are no alien peoples. There are only those other than his own whom he must treat as his brothers. I and my "brothers"—this is the formula which, for the socialist, supplants the old chauvinistic formula of "my own" and "alien." The entire fault of the purportedly international (but in fact assimilative) socialism that had thus far prevailed among Jewish intellectuals lay in the fact that for the sake of the "brothers" they became oblivious of the "I." Incidentally, Hess believed that the merging of Jewish nationalism with love for the homeland during the Diaspora was nothing new in Jewish history or for the Jewish conscience. As he saw it, the culture of the Jews in Spain demonstrated how it was possible to be a pious Jew and at the same time love a second fatherland and take part in developing its culture.

"A socialist to the gentiles, a Zionist to the Jews"—is an approximation of Hess's formula for the practical blending of nationalism and socialism. The shortcomings of this formula have long been apparent in the theory and practice of the Jewish socialist movement. But Hess may be forgiven these weaknesses, since during his lifetime it was truly impossible to unite nationalism and socialism in the *practical* task of Jewish regeneration. In his own time Hess was entitled to believe that in the Diaspora "Jews are condemned to pursue the life of parasites"—and that only after being set free from the Diaspora would the Jewish people be able to participate in the progressive movements of mankind.

What, then, was to be done at home? How was the ultimate goal of Jewish hopes to be fulfilled? Were we to establish Jewish organizations for agriculture, industry and commerce in Eretz Israel according to some "Mosaic Law"—that is, according to basic socialist tenets—or build colonies in Eretz Israel and wait, nursing the

hope of a political rebirth? Some historical opportunity would present itself, and the nations would give us back our homeland. Moses
Hess could offer no other program for Zionism; and—who knows?—
perhaps there is no other program.

Hess put little faith in elderly Jews for the implementation of
the program, "because the darkness of Egypt still prevails" among
them. That is why he believed that the Jewish youth in Eastern
countries, "which sacrifices its life for everything noble and holy,"
would soon flare up with love for the national Jewish ideal.

This prophecy, among others made by Hess, has now been
realized: the Jewish youth in Eastern Europe are fervently in love
with the ideal of the Jewish nation. But the effect of this prelude has
been to uncover many new problems for radical nationalist thought,
of which Moses Hess could have had no inkling.

Moses Hess—philosopher, socialist, and Jew—is the most important precursor of modern Jewish socialist thought. That modern
Jewish socialism was formulated without any direct influence from
the theories of Moses Hess, is proof that those principles are not the
subjective illusions of some genius but rather a logical consequence
of national-socialistic thought proper. Whoever should apply it is
bound to arrive at the same conclusions as Moses Hess; and the entire history of the Jewish people must then appear in very much the
same light as it appeared to him.

To the title of *Alt-Vater des deutschen Kommunismus* one more
might be added. It is that of Worthy Disciple of Our Holy Prophets,
one who put before humanity its highest ideal: the fellowship of
nations, the union of mankind.

1912

Josephus and Simon

by Abraham Koralnik

Translated by Marion Magid

In the early years of the Zionist movement in Vienna no other name
was mentioned so frequently—or with such loathing—around the
office of the Zionist weekly *Die Welt* as the name of Josephus Flavius. It was a kind of generic term for anti-Zionists and assimilationists of all varieties, as well as Jewish Council presidents and
journalists of Liberal-German-Nationalist leanings.

Josephus's chief opponent on the paper was a certain Czech
Jew, a big clumsy bear of a fellow who was an ardent Zionist
though a complete ignoramus—a first-class boor—in Jewish matters.
He couldn't so much as read the Hebrew alphabet, not knowing the
first thing about either the Jews or Judaism and having no interest
whatever in the subject. He also detested Jewish scholars with a
primordial passion and would gladly, given the chance, have made
mincemeat of them all. But how good he was at taking on the anti-
Semitic students at Vienna's university! Every Saturday morning he
would put on his cap, his shiny patent leather boots, and his blue-
and-white chestband, and with the help of the other Jewish National
Party students, he would fight like a lion—or a bear—against the
German Nationalists. It was a real pleasure to watch.

After the battle, radiant, happy, occasionally with a bandaged
head, he would go straight to the office to write his article for *Die
Welt* (he was a contributor of long standing)—an unfailing diatribe
against Josephus Flavius.

A few years later, I met another Jewish writer—not a Czech this
time, not the least bit bearlike, and anything but an ignoramus. On

the contrary, this short, puny individual, all skin and bones, who
looked like some proverbial ascetic out of Jewish folklore, was a
true scholar in the old sense of the term, and a rabbi's son. His
father, an old-fashioned, small-town type representing a strain of
orthodoxy almost extinct in our day, was the rabbi of Dubovo, an
utterly unworldly man who really had no idea that there were other
cities in the world besides Dubovo and Jerusalem, a Jew who for all
practical purposes lived not in the district of Uman in the province
of Kiev, but somewhere in ancient Babylon, or perhaps even in
Jerusalem itself among the true sages.

And this rabbi's son became enamored of Josephus Flavius, fell
so much in love that he even became Josephus's namesake and
adopted as a pseudonym that same historic appellation—Ben Gurion
—which the Jewish folk tradition has always erroneously identified
with Josephus Flavius.

Nor was his choice surprising. For M. J. Berdichevski,[1] that
rabbi's son and Josephus disciple I have been describing, was perhaps himself the Josephus of modern Jewry, one of the few who
never gave up the dream of a form of Judaism free of all earthly
bonds—free of materialism, free of the state, free of the world—a
spiritual force and nothing more.

From the town of Dubovo, Berdichevski's path led to Weimar,
and from the House of Study to Friedrich Nietzsche. And he came
to despise the "Zealots" of the present day, all our contemporary
versions of the Zealot leader Simon Bar Giora—all those converts or
sons of converts who are little better than half-Jews, all those Jews
who are so cut off from Jewish culture and Jewish tradition that they
are not even critical of Judaism, not even involved enough to take a
stand against it, not even desirous of seeing its renewal. For Berdichevski there was a bridge between Nietzsche and the Torah of the
sages; but from that ancient brand of Judaism exemplified by Simon
Bar Giora, the path led nowhere.

So Berdichevski dreamed of a time when Josephus would be
restored to the spiritual treasure-house of Jewish culture, when he
would be taken back by the Jews and redeemed from his Greek
captivity. Until now we have known Josephus, of course, only in his
Greek disguise; yet the Jerusalem aristocrat and priest who was the
author of *The Antiquities* and *The Jewish War* wrote these books,
according to his own words, "in the language of his people"—i.e., in
Hebrew or Aramaic. But the originals, like nearly all the other ancient books about the life and history of the Jewish people, have

[1] Micah Joseph Berdichevski, 1865–1921, Hebrew writer.

been lost. The Jews, it seems, have always hated history. They above all, the people epitomized by its extraordinary history, *the* world-historical people, have never taken the slightest trouble to safeguard their own historic documents. History is, after all, action; and from the moment the Temple was destroyed—that moment when the physical Jewish entity was superseded by a Judaism of pure spirit—the Jewish intellect renounced action. The past, yes, but only so long as it was God-centered, so long as it was a parable which could be explicated. And the same for the future, that "Messianic Era" which was once again God's, and once again a parable. But the present—the living, vital, everyday present—held no interest for the Jews. As a result, all that remains to us of our ancient history—traditionally acknowledged as such—is either midrash or lamentation, either poetry or mourning.

Yet there once existed a rich body of literature about the Jews and Jewish life during the remarkably turbulent and energetic period of the Second Temple. Josephus himself mentions several works, including the Book of Nicholas of Damascus and the Book of Julian, among others, which were written in the Jewish vernacular as well as in Greek. But of all the books written at that time, in Jerusalem, in Antioch, in Alexandria, only one has survived—the monumental work of Josephus Flavius.

It really is high time that the Jews made an effort to repossess their past, for each new document that comes to light gives us a new perspective on Jewish life and the Jewish spirit. And it is time too that we became acquainted with the historical literature which did survive.

I have no intention here of attempting to assess the real character of Josephus Flavius. Was he a traitor, an assimilationist, a sycophant, and a hack, or was he a political genius with a transcendent intuition about Jewish history, a kind of prophet who foresaw the ultimate course of world events?

Any attempt to justify historical acts and the men who perpetrated them is worthless, for history is not a matter of morality, but of critical evaluation. And moralizing after the event when it is in any case too late is particularly pointless. Instead we must try to place historical facts and historical personages in their proper context and evaluate them accordingly.

Still, in the course of rereading the story of the destruction of the Temple and the end of Jerusalem, I found myself asking a different question: Have we any reason to regret the outcome of the story? If history had taken a different turn, if Titus had been a lesser strategist than Josephus makes him out to be, or if a miracle had taken place, as happened, for instance, in the case of Vespasian, who was forced to cut short his Jewish war by sudden uprisings elsewhere in the Empire, or if Jerusalem had heeded the counsel of Joseph Ben Matthias and submitted temporarily to Roman rule in order to preserve the Temple and the established order—would it have been better for the Jews, would Judaism have ultimately benefited?

And who was vindicated before the bar of history—Josephus the Priest and the aristocratic man of letters from Jerusalem, or Simon Bar Giora, the rough-hewn half-Jew from across the Jordan who stood up for the common man and for democratic freedom?

With the limited historical means at our disposal it is difficult for us to understand what the Zealots (or "the Robbers," as Josephus calls them), incited by Simon Bar Giora and John of Gischala, hoped to accomplish. What enraged them so? Why did they slaughter so many people, singling out priests and members of the aristocracy in particular? Were not the Zealots as aware as everyone else that tiny Judea could not possibly withstand the Roman colossus, that the battle was hopeless? Josephus provides no explanation; yet from his narrative, and from the curses he heaps on the heads of the Zealots, it becomes clear that the battle in progress was not only a political battle against Rome, but also an internal social struggle against the old ruling caste, and a struggle for the authenticity of Judaism.

In one of the last and most tragic chapters of Josephus's history there occurs, almost as an afterthought, the following wonderful vignette. Josephus and several companions who had fled the city and found refuge with Titus are walking back and forth outside the walls of Jerusalem and pleading with their brethren inside the beleaguered city: "Lay down your arms and surrender. You sacrifice the Holy City in vain. You bring destruction on the Temple!"

The city is in flames, its towers about to topple. Within the Temple, where they have barricaded themselves, the warriors are in despair. Even they know by now that all is lost, yet they will not surrender. They shout back in reply: "Why all this talk of the Temple? Whose house is this if not God's? And does not God have another house, and have we not another Temple? Our Temple is *the whole world!* Let the Temple burn if it must. If we survive and remain free, we shall build a new one; and if not, if we are destroyed, then what good is the Temple to us?"

Josephus recounts this episode only in passing, for he considers his own words and the lengthy speeches of Chanan, the High Priest, far more significant. For us, though, who have the benefit of hindsight, and who still bear the scars of that historical catastrophe, the words have quite a different ring. They offer us a key to Jewish history and illuminate the meaning of our lives.

Which is it to be—Judaism as an ossified institution, or Judaism as a vibrant, living force? The Jew who lives for the Temple (in whatever form)—or a Temple which is destroyed only to be rebuilt, which is burnt down only to be called forth again, a Temple broader than any house, a Temple which encompasses the whole world? The Jewish soul is rent by these opposing alternatives until the present day.

Joseph Ben Matthias and Simon Bar Giora—the two sides of the Jewish coin, the two aspects of the Jewish universe.

Josephus remained Titus's captive and went on to write books, while Simon was taken prisoner and dragged off to Rome where the executioners caused his head to be smashed to bits against the Tarpeian Rock by the Capitol. Josephus, the defender of establishmentarian Judaism, remains a literary figure and nothing more. Simon the ignoramus, the half-Jew who longed to be wholly Jewish and who believed with all the force of his naïveté and pathos that Judaism could possess the whole world as its temple, outlived Rome and its Capitol and its Tarpeian Rock. From Jerusalem's burning tower he leapt into the profoundest depths of the Jewish soul, and he lives there still.

All of us today relive the life of Simon Bar Giora and reenact his battle with Joseph Ben Matthias—willingly or unwillingly, knowingly or not.

1940

IV

Jewishness in America: Beginnings

We turn to a major locale of Yiddish cultural life—the United States in which for at least half a century Yiddish literature, Yiddish theater, and the Yiddish press reached a peak of influence. There is an enormous literature, both published and in manuscript, of immigrant memoirs describing the trauma of arrival in a strange and not always hospitable land; few of these memoirs are more vivid than that of I. Kopeloff, who came here during the first great wave of immigration in the early 1880's and whose experiences seem to form a kind of paradigm of much that would follow. The development of the Jewish trade unions as agencies of struggle and acculturation for the immigrant masses; the internal conflicts concerning self-definition and identity which followed the first years of settlement—these are among the themes that one finds in the following essays.

First Days in America

by I. Kopeloff

Translated by Leonard Wolf

Castle Garden, a large circular rotunda-shaped building, had the appearance, to my eyes, of the arsenal in the castle of Boberisk, or of its tower, and struck me with gloom. All the immigrants, particularly those in third class, had to pass through the building. For many newcomers, Castle Garden served as their first hotel in America. For those who had no other place to stay, it served as a refuge for a certain time. The main hall was huge and barren, and gave off an uncanny coldness which produced in its inhabitants an involuntary oppression. One after another sighed and sighed.

At two sides of this "barn" there stood cheaply painted red benches. On the other two, there were tables, counters and desks used by all sorts of philanthropic organizations whose officials busied themselves with the needs of the immigrants. For one, they sought out a relative or a guarantor and telegraphed to say that his guest had arrived; for another, they purchased a cheap railway ticket and directed him somewhere in the country. For still another, who might be a skilled workman, a job was found. At the very least, something to eat was generally provided for the newest arrivals. The philanthropic work was done in the American style: methodically, mechanically, and smoothly, but one sensed that the officials were not deeply concerned with the misfortunes of the immigrants.

Since, at landing time, there were no special difficulties put in the way of the immigrants (all comers were welcome), Castle Garden was often so crowded, so jammed, that there was simply nowhere to sit by day, or any place to lie down at night—not even on the bare floor.

The filth was unendurable, so many packages, pillows, feather beds and foul clothing (often just plain rags) that each immigrant had dragged with him over the seas and clung to as if they were precious—all of this provided great opportunity for vermin, those filthy little beasts, that crawled about freely and openly over the clutter and made life disagreeable. The constant scratching and the distress of the little children touched one to the quick and drove one out of Castle Garden.

Only the bitter need of the poor forlorn immigrants kept them there, as if chained until they found work that they could do.

As it turned out, my Baltic friend and I stayed a full four weeks in this "hotel," and it seems to me that as a result, we will someday be excused from purgatory. We had not one friend in the new land; we knew no one from the old country and had not a penny to our names. We had no choice but to wait around in the filth of Castle Garden and eat whatever chance might throw our way.

Only a few steps from Castle Garden—as if deliberately to tease us immigrants—there was a park that was so beautiful, so fresh and lovely that, compared with our "poorhouse," it seemed like paradise compared with hell. The park had stately trees and green grass and charming secret paths that wound here and there and benches on which to rest and just nearby a broad body of water over which all sorts of ocean ships passed, piping and whistling. Almost always, there played over it a mild, caressing and endearing breeze.

But only by day could one enjoy the lovely outdoors. After eight or nine o'clock, the greenhorns of Castle Garden were not permitted out of its confines—not for anything in the world. That freedom might have eased their hearts too much.

I spent my days following up the advertisements of the *Staats-Zeitung* looking for work. I went to factories, stores, employment agencies, but one look at me was enough to bring the dry reply, "No help wanted."

On the fifth day, luck suddenly shone on us. A Castle Garden official himself went around among the immigrants crying, "Night workers wanted." We grasped at this opportunity as if it were a precious jewel. Some sixty of us were led to a ship and after a good hour's travel we arrived at a freight depot. The foreman of the depot examined us, selecting out workmen. Of our whole group, he chose some fifteen people. The others he drove away unceremoniously.

It was already evening, one of those New York summer evenings when the heat is so oppressive that one's very shirt feels like a weight against the flesh. No matter how much you gasped, there was not so much as a whiff of air with which to catch one's breath, particularly since we were dressed in heavy old country suits and linen shirts that rasped the skin.

We were in some vague corner of Brooklyn. Just as we left the freight depot, we ran into a volley of stones from all sides. Boys, girls, and grown young men were hailing rocks, hunks of wood and iron at us. Taking to our heels, we ran like the devil, but the crowd pursued us, yelling, screaming, hurling whatever came to hand. Finally we wore them out and they turned back. The incident unsettled me terribly. I was deeply hurt. Just think! Just think! It wasn't enough that we had been bitterly deceived—taken to jobs and then given no work; that we had been carried the devil only knows where and had now to drag ourselves back a long distance—that wasn't enough. Now they were beating us, throwing rocks at us. How could this be . . . why did we deserve it? *What is my sin and what my transgression?* Was this justice? Equity? Was this the land of the free? The fat land where ducats roll about in the streets? I couldn't absorb the outrage.

It was a good couple of hours before we dragged ourselves back to the ferry, where we had to pay two blood-stained cents to get across to the other side.

We arrived in Castle Garden worn out, whipped, humiliated, and hungry. My Baltic friend who was a strapping youth wept like a child. I didn't feel any better but I plucked up courage and preached to him, amusing and consoling him; not so much for his sake as for my own. "Well," I said. "So what. Things will be better yet." Then I flung myself to the bare earth and slept like a clubbed man.

In the morning, around six o'clock, the same official woke us once more and asked if we wanted to go to work. Again we grasped at the chance, but this time with the proviso that if we were not put to work we would be brought back here. The fellow promised that today we would be luckier and would be put to work.

We were arranged in rows, as if on parade. A couple of policemen led the column and two others followed. We hadn't gone but a few blocks when we arrived at the job. Again, a freight depot.

My friend and I were chosen to work. Hurrah for our elusive luck! We set to work at seven in the morning—*and we worked.* Some of us inside, in the depot, others outside, on the ships. My friend and I were assigned to a place outside. After an hour or so, I was so overheated that my head ached and I had such pains over my heart I nearly fainted. Evidently the foreman noticed me because he led me to the pump where he poured cold water over my head. I felt much better and when I had rested half an hour, he put me to work inside where I was protected from the searing sun.

Out of gratitude to the foreman for his good treatment, I worked with great eagerness until noon.

My job was to roll huge, heavy barrels from the door at the entryway where they were unloaded to the other end of the depot. From there, I rolled other barrels back to the door. All the while, I had to work bent over. At noon when the foreman signaled that we should quit work, I found I couldn't straighten out at all. I tried to stand up several times—it was impossible. Without meaning to, I cried out and my Baltic friend together with some other greenhorns laid me down. They tried to comfort me by telling me that I hurt because I was unused to the work, but that did not make me feel any better. I didn't eat lunch but lay still for several hours. Then, though my back still hurt, I concluded that to lie still this way served no useful purpose (after all, I'd come to work) and got up. The foreman came by, noted down the time I'd lost, slapped me genially on the shoulder and said, "All right."

Again I started to work. The Germans watched and thought I was funny, the Italians smiled at me, the Jews looked on with great sympathy. "A pity, poor fellow. Guess he's never worked like this before. Damn Columbus and his Golden Nation—wearing out our decent kids this way."

I worked three days in the freight depot and made five dollars and twenty-five cents. My first money—earned by my very own sweat and toil. I was enchanted, full of self-esteem. As for the lost time—it was not deducted.

On the evening of the third day, there came to us at Castle Garden a delegation of "The People's Committee" and explained to us that a strike was going on—and that we were scabs who were taking the bread out of the mouths of the strikers' families!

One of them, a student from Kiev, spoke in Russian—so warmly and passionately that we had tears in our eyes, though to tell the truth the situation did not become much clearer. I couldn't understand what I was doing wrong or what my sin was. Why should I not be permitted to earn my bit of bread? And what was this thing, this union, or why were those who were for it *kosher,* and those who were against it *tref?* At home, in the old country, were things any different? There also everyone grabbed whatever he could without regard for others. Still, I decided not to work any more. It seemed better that I should do without.

Many of us, in fact, did not go back, though some of the Germans, Italians, Slovaks and Jews acted as if they didn't know what it was all about. Their response was, "What: Union? Scab? Did we come here to harvest good deeds?"

My Baltic friend was one of them. No matter how much I tried to tell him that it wasn't right to come from another country and take bread away from the workers who were already here, who had worked all those years, nothing helped. He did not want to know or hear. "Well, let them take us into the union," he said. "Do they worry about me? Why should I worry about them? Whoever heard that a man should not be allowed to work? No matter where I go, I'd be taking somebody's place. What difference does it make whether it's here or there or you or someone else? It's all the same. Somebody's bread is taken, so what's the difference? Should I die of hunger or go steal from a church?" I could not change his mind.

One fine day, however, the strikers caught several of the greenhorn scabs and beat them up. Moreover, they were shown revolvers and promised that if they didn't stop scabbing, they would be shot down like dogs—someone would creep into Castle Garden by night and they would all be slaughtered.

This threat worked. It worked like magic. The desire to work disappeared as if someone had snapped his fingers, and no persuasion on the part of the Castle Garden functionaries would help. Not even an undertaking by the company to pay twenty-five cents a day more; not even the promise that the greenhorns would be protected from the strikers. The pickets had thoroughly frightened the greenhorns.

In a couple of weeks the strike proper ended and we were without a stitch of work. The whole story began once more. *And the people said, "What shall we eat?"* Again, we ran about looking for work. I even tried going to the Committee on State Street, but at the door was a gray-clad policeman who stood around like a king, though with a stick instead of a scepter in his hand. Under no circumstances would he let anyone in. Not only that, but the entryway was so besieged by old people, women, and children that I lost any hope I would ever get in. Incidentally, my Baltic friend who had plucked up his courage and sneaked in through the cellar once, had been well beaten by the policeman and thrown out. I learned enough from his experience and gave up expecting help from the Committee. Meanwhile, we still had a couple of those miserably earned dollars and we lived high. There were no bounds to our generosity. Having eaten an entire loaf of bread with a hunk of sausage and drunk it down with a glass of soda water, we would go for a walk in Battery Park, delighting in our youth. We slept well, too, that is in those happy times when there was room enough to stretch one's feet at Castle Garden.

Finally, our last pennies were gone. We were very much against begging for a free meal at the "philanthropic" tables where one had always to give a report—how long one had been here, why one was here, why one was unemployed. All of this filled us with revulsion and we preferred to stay hungry. But what is it the Russians say? *Golod ny tyotka*. Hunger is nobody's aunt. And things got very difficult for us. Once again we had to put our noses to the grindstone. In an effort to earn at least something for our miserable livelihood, the two of us separated but with no better luck. No matter where we went, we always found a large crowd of unemployed natives and greenhorns, healthy and experienced, ahead of us. It was bad and embittering, enough to dismay the soul. Every evening we came back to our "poorhouse" tired, hungry, filthy.

Finally, I discovered an agency which sent people to work at a brick factory in a town somewhere near New York. The pay was twelve dollars a month all told. We had to be ready to go at ten o'clock in the morning. Of course we grasped at the chance as if at a treasure.

We were a happy group—six Jews, several Germans, Italians, and Slovaks—who went off on a Tuesday morning with our bags and chests and packages to board a car on a train in the direction of our sudden luck.

The marvelous, almost first-class carriages with their soft plush seats enchanted us. We made various conjectures—some of us suggested that our employers must be very upperclass people who had ordered these fine carriages on our account. No doubt they would deal with us in the finest way. Soon, we would lack for nothing.

We felt considerably better. The train passed through green fields and shady forests toward which we yearned. The cool air came in through the open window and did much to refresh us. After a couple of hours journey, we arrived at our station where a large wagon harnessed to a couple of good horses was waiting for us. At first we thought that the wagon was there to take us all to the palace, but it turned out that it could just about hold the baggage with which we were all so richly encumbered. Each of us had dragged along a variety of treasures. I, for instance, had with me a couple of bound volumes of *Russky Yevrei* and *Razsvet*, Antonov's *Grammar*, Lipshitz's *Yiddish-Russian Dictionary*, several pairs of wool socks, a woolen jacket and other such necessities for America. The others had no less important articles. One of the Italians had with him a huge picture in a heavy frame of the Virgin Mary. A Slovak had some scruffy boots from which he could not bring himself to part. In short, there was no place for us in the wagon and we had to go on foot. The wagon was sandy and crusted over with dry clay.

The sun shone pitilessly and though the horses did not hurry, they
went before us at a pace considerably faster than our own, and we
had to take quick steps to keep from losing sight of the wagon on
which were piled all of our worldly goods. After some hours, we
arrived, sweating and breathless.

The wide-windowed palace we had looked forward to turned
out to be a huge tent along whose sides triple-tiered beds were set.
We put our bags and packages under the beds. Nearby, there was
a large washroom where from a peg there hung a single long towel.

In the middle of the main room there were long, oil-cloth-
covered tables knocked together out of boards. Near the tables were
long, hard benches.

We were told to eat and there was a tumultuous rush to grab
places. People moved with such speed as if God only knew what
good things waited for them: two thin slices of bread, two boiled,
unpeeled potatoes, some bits of ham and in a dish for general use,
a sort of *haroset*,[1] otherwise known as molasses.

Of course we Jews did not even stir in the direction of the ham,
and I did not eat the molasses either. The two pieces of bread and
the potatoes merely teased the appetite, without satisfying it.

Immediately after the meal, we were put to work. The foreman
asked me to take a wheelbarrow, fill it with sand, and push it along
narrow boards laid out as a track across deep holes to a place where
the sand was to be mixed with clay to make bricks.

I was very industrious and filled my wheelbarrow with as much
sand as it could hold, but when I tried to budge it, it didn't move.
Too bad. I look up to see the foreman watching me, smiling. At my
despairing look, he indicates with his hand that I should pour off
some sand. I pour some off and try to move the wheelbarrow—still
too heavy. I pour off some more; and some more, until finally there
remains only enough to cover the bottom of the barrow. I am embarrassed to pour off still more, on my own account as well as the
foreman's. Gathering all my strength together, I give the barrow a
tremendous shove across the boards and—first the barrow, then I,
willy nilly, fall into the deep hole.

I lay there. The foreman, my Baltic friend, and a couple of
other workers with difficulty dragged me out of the hole bruised and
beaten, and carried me to the tent and put me on a cot. A doctor was
sent for who prescribed ice packs, bandaged my right hand and
right foot, gave me some medicine, and forbade me to eat anything

[1] A brown paste of nuts, apples, spices and wine, eaten at the Passover
feast.

—though he allowed me to drink a bit of milk. I lay there for four days, in great pain.

My working career was ended. And there were also others who could not endure the pace: my Baltic friend and another Jew, as well as a German and an Italian. Twelve hours a day under the hot sun, with insufficient food added to the general unpleasantness, played havoc with them. The five of us agreed to leave the place.

However, we were so afraid that we did not ask to be paid for the little work we had done; nor could we bring ourselves to let the foreman know of our decision. After all, we had contracted to stay for a month, and the company had paid for our transportation. Who could tell what they might do to us? Perhaps they would keep our belongings, God forbid.

And so we decided to sneak away at three in the morning. And did, though the way back to the station with our heavy baggage was by no means an easy one. We had to stop to rest so frequently that it took us a good four hours to get to the depot where it turned out that none of us had the money for so much as a single ticket. What then had been the sense in all that helter-skelter running to the station? None of us had given the matter any thought, each supposing that the others had money that they would certainly share. We were overwhelmed by a single idea—escape—and no one thought much past that event. It was only after we had sat for several hours in the depot and were beginning to feel faint with hunger that we noticed that not one of us made any move to buy food. Then the general error became clear to us all: we were there without a cent.

It was a hot day and we drank water endlessly. Our situation was beginning to perplex the stationmaster who saw five people with their baggage sitting in his station for more than half a day. Trains came and went all the while, but the five did not budge from their places. He tried engaging us in conversation, but we couldn't understand what he said. Finally, he brought over a German to whom we told our whole story.

Around one o'clock, some rolls were sent to us from the village as well as a couple of cans of sardines, some cheese and crackers. We did not wait for an extended invitation. . . .

We ate the snacks and resumed our anxious waiting. Another hour passed. More people came and went. The depot master talked with everyone about our strange situation. People stared curiously or sympathetically at us, shrugged their shoulders and went on. We sat and waited, though for what none of us knew. The hands of the clock pointed to five P.M.

Then a man in an expensive rig drove up to meet a friend and the depot master interested him in our problem. They talked for a while. After a bit, the man came over and handed each of us a train ticket to New York as well as fifty cents in cash. His unexpected generosity, and the sudden arrival of the New York train so confused us that we didn't manage to thank our ministering angel. We plunged into the train in a wild panic, as if frightened lest our benefactor should change his mind. We had time for a quick wave through the window that was meant as "Thanks" and "Farewell" at once.

On the way back, I was very depressed, my optimism of a few days ago entirely dissipated. Ominous Castle Garden waited for us once again and the prospect of the daily runaround looking for work. I wondered anxiously, sadly, about where such a life could lead.

We got back to Castle Garden late at night. As it turned out, the place was a little roomier than usual and we flung ourselves down and slept. In the morning I woke well rested and refreshed, but nagged by the painful question: "What next?" I was too weak to go looking for work—I could still feel the pain of my fall in every bone. But aside from that, I had entirely lost all desire for further heavy manual labor. Clearly, it wasn't for me, though my friend, the Balt, still went about looking for work, with the usual result.

The fifty cents the stranger had given us lasted a few days, then I was down to my last couple of pennies. To run about like a dog snatching at a mouthful of food felt disgraceful—a bitter shame. It was bad, bad. Yet what else was there to do?

I had no other choice, finally, than to present myself before the Committee, but how to get past that bandit policeman who never lets anyone pass the threshold? I put my mind—all my ingenuity— to work on this problem and finally hit on a device: I would write the Committee a letter.

I wrote it in my best Hebrew, pouring out my heart's store of bitterness in the most flowery language. I sealed the letter and gave it to the policeman who gave it at once to the Committee. When it was delivered, I walked slowly away, speculating meanwhile on the results it would produce. In my mind's eye, I was already a foreman.

Suddenly, the policeman is chasing me. Panting he catches at my sleeve and drags me back. I couldn't understand what this devil out of hell wanted from me, but he has brought me before the Committee and, pointing a finger triumphantly at me, he cries, "That's him. There he is," as if he thinks God knows what kind of crime I have committed with my letter.

1928

The East Side and the Jewish Labor Movement

by Abraham Menes

When the Jewish immigrants from Eastern Europe began settling in great numbers in New York's East Side in the early eighteen eighties, they little dreamt that they were opening a new chapter in the history of Jewish life in America, let alone in the history of the Jewish people throughout the world. The East Side ghetto came into being without plan. Indeed, the seething and frenetic life that filled the narrow streets and crowded tenements of the East Side more nearly resembled a symbol of chaos and planlessness. But despite this external impression, there was profound historic sense in this mass concentration of Jewish immigrants within the narrow confines of an old part of the city of New York. Here, under grueling sweatshop conditions, a generation of tailors and cloakmakers set the path of Jewish history for our generation and for others still to come.

The importance of this immigrant Jewish community on the East Side becomes apparent when we recall some figures. A bit more than a century ago there were about five million Jews in the entire world. Eighty-five percent of this number lived in Europe. Only slightly more than one percent lived in America, and the remaining thirteen percent were scattered throughout Asia and Africa. The number of Jews in Palestine was insignificant. Ninety years later, at the time of the outbreak of World War II, the number of Jews in the world exceeded sixteen million. In the course of not more than four generations the Jewish population in the world more than tripled its numbers. The distribution of the Jewish population shifted radically. America and Palestine became important centers. But the bulk of the

Jewish people remained in Europe, primarily in the eastern part of the continent.

It is generally assumed that the mass Jewish emigration from Europe was caused by external factors, and that the emigrants themselves performed only a passive role. It is undeniable that economic pressure within the Jewish communities in Eastern Europe, and the wave of anti-Semitism and pogroms that swept Southern Russia in the early eighties, were potent factors. Nevertheless it would be a grievous error to overlook the fact that the Jewish emigrants themselves were the chief factor in the exodus from Eastern Europe. It was not the weak elements, ready to resign themselves to fate, who began to trek. Even under the conditions of disenfranchisement which prevailed in Russia it required courage to resolve to leave home and family and native town. Effort, determination, and pioneering initiative were required to embark on the long, and then unfamiliar, journey. Though many rumors were current regarding opportunities in America, it remained a remote and strange country. It was the poorest elements, who in most cases even lacked the fare to a port city, who were the ones to go. So far as paying the ocean passage was concerned, the majority did not even dream of possessing the requisite one hundred rubles ($50)—a sum that was considered a veritable fortune in the impoverished Jewish towns of Poland and Russia.

How, then, did they reach America? Some of the emigrant pioneers made the trip in stages. The first stage of the journey brought them across the Russian border. At the time of the pogroms in Russia in 1881–82, the commercial city of Brody on the Austrian side of the Russian border, was the main first stopover. In 1881 alone, about four thousand emigrants received assistance in Brody from the large Jewish philanthropic organizations which gradually provided them with the means to continue their journey to America. Others settled temporarily in Germany, France, or England. If luck was with them, they obtained employment here and saved enough to resume their trip. The number of emigrants who left home with sufficient means to pay for the entire trip was infinitesimal.

But this trickle did not by itself account for the mass emigration of hundreds of thousands. The path of these pioneers was not an easy one even after they reached America, yet despite their hardships it was they who made possible the subsequent flood from Eastern Europe in the later eighties. The decisive factor stimulating the mass Jewish emigration to America from 1885 to 1890 was the assistance from relatives already in America who were themselves still strangers in the country. "Everyone who came here," writes B.

Weinstein, one of the pioneers of the Jewish labor movement in America, "constantly cherished one hope—to save enough money to bring other members of the family."

The growth of the East Side becomes comprehensible from Jewish writing in America five and six decades ago. Here we find a host of touching descriptions of how poor immigrant laborers, burdened with a sense of guilt, worked far beyond their strength, denied themselves necessities, and went into debt in order to provide passage for some member of the family still in the Old Country.

They were obsessed by one idea: to work as hard as possible and spend as little as possible in order to save passage for the family. *The accusation leveled against the Jewish immigrants of that time that they were themselves to blame for the intolerable working conditions in the sweatshops was not entirely unfounded.* A theory was then propounded that it was in the "nature" of Jews to work endless hours and to drive themselves at their tasks, in disregard of the fact that Jews were the historical pioneers of the idea of definite periods of rest (Sabbath and holidays) and just as firmly defined hours for prayer and study during week days. Also overlooked was the fact that the sweatshop system already had a long tradition in America. It is undeniable, nevertheless, that the sweatshop system became especially acute in the needle trades at the time when Jews became prominent in this industry as workers and contractors. It is equally an established fact that the manufacturers and contractors met with but little resistance from their workers when they tried to extend the work day. *The workers themselves wished to work longer hours and thus to earn a little more, so as to hasten the day when they could bring their families to America.* It was this intense devotion to family and friends in the old home that made possible the mass influx of Jewish immigrants in the late eighties.

The aid extended by the new immigrants to their relatives still overseas, merits our attention as *an example of the decisive role that can be played by purely moral factors in the life of a people.* Had the concern of the Jewish arrivals in America at that time not been directed so intensely to their native towns, they would have sent less material assistance and the number of immigrants would have been much smaller.

The distinctive nature of the Jewish immigrant is readily confirmed by statistical analysis of the immigration trends, as a whole, to America at that time. Our attention is at once drawn to the fact that the Jewish immigrants came to America to stay. As a general rule about one third of all immigrants left the United States; Jewish re-emigration, however, amounted to somewhat less than five percent. The figures also show that the percentage of women and children was considerably higher among Jewish immigrants than among others. This fact imposed a greater burden of duties on the family heads and compelled them to work harder and longer hours.

The pressers and operators of the East Side provided their kin with more than mere passage money: they also secured for them opportunities to earn their livelihood. As long as Jewish immigration was limited in scope, the problem of employment was virtually nonexistent. As late as the seventies of the last century, the majority of Jewish immigrants found their livelihood in peddling and trade. These callings were especially characteristic of the Jewish immigrants from Austria and Germany. It should be noted in passing that peddling was a grueling occupation, and that the immigrant peddler of the frontier performed a difficult and responsible task.

But such middlemen's occupations could absorb only a small number of immigrants, and many opportunities in commercial life were not available to the newcomers because of language difficulties. This hardship was not a major problem for the Jewish immigrants from Germany, because they came as part of a tidal wave of general German immigration which, during the five decades 1841–1890, comprised fully one third of the total immigration to the United States and exceeded even the immigration from Ireland. Knowledge of the German language thus opened to many the doors of opportunity in commerce, and developments among German Jewish immigrants largely paralleled those of the general German immigrant community.

The mass immigration of Jews from Eastern Europe had to confront an entirely different situation. Their arrival occurred at a time when the industrial revolution in America was in full swing. The frontier era was virtually ended, and the rapid growth of large cities and huge empires of capital overshadowed all else. Industry was the sole area of the economy which could, at this time, absorb the hundreds of thousands of immigrants who annually streamed into the country. Jewish immigration had to adapt itself to this economic fact.

Industry did not everywhere welcome the immigrants. A number of trades excluded them altogether. The skilled and organized workers looked at the newcomers as competitors who served as instruments in the hands of capital to depress the wage scale. Nor were these suspicions entirely unfounded. Religious factors added to the difficulty of economic integration. Most of the Jewish immigrants of that time tried to observe the Sabbath and *kashrut* as far as possible, and many avoided employment in factories and businesses where the majority of workers were non-Jewish. Not knowing the language, they felt themselves strangers in such shops and factories, and even when need compelled them to take such employment they did not give up their search for work in traditional Jewish vocations.

Since the characteristic Jewish trades were not yet in existence in America, these had to be created. The garment industry was still in its infancy in the eighteen nineties, as is demonstrated by the following table:

Production of Women's Clothing

Year	Number of Enterprises	Number of Workers
1879	562	25,192
1899	2,701	83,739
1914	5,564	168,907

Thus the opportunities in this field, for workers as well as for manufacturers, were considerable, and it was not necessary to storm an already-occupied economic position. The opportunities were still further enhanced by the fact that as far back as the seventies Jews, largely from Germany and Hungary, were already prominent in the garment industry both as workers and as employers. The dominant role of the Jews in the garment industries of Eastern Europe, from which most of the immigrants now came, was still another factor contributing to the ease with which they entered this field.

Concentration in specific trades was a distinctive feature of the Jewish communities in Eastern Europe. In America this concentration assumed extreme forms. More than half of all Jewish workers (wage workers and self-employed) were engaged in garment manufacturing. Of the wage workers, two-thirds were employed in the needle trades. Since the eighties the needle trades increasingly passed into Jewish hands.

The sweatshop system may have contributed to the predominance of Jews in the needle trades, but it was not the sole or even most important factor. There is no doubt that Jewish skill in these trades, as well as Jewish initiative, played the chief role in the development of the garment industry. Thus it came about that the pioneering labors of the Jewish tailors and cloakmakers during the eighteen eighties and nineties paved the way for "the great migration" early in the twentieth century, when nearly one and one-half million Jews entered the United States in the course of fifteen years.

As might have been expected, the growth of the East Side was also marked by negative aspects which at one time were quite prominent. The sweatshops may have performed a necessary function in the development of the garment industry, then in the period of primitive exploitation characteristic of pioneering capitalism. But the methods it employed could not but retard the emergence of a sound and normal community.

The dangers of primitive capitalist exploitation were still further enhanced by the rootlessness of an immigrant community. The industrial revolution, the growth of cities, and the influx of immigration upset the equilibrium even of the long-settled population which for generations had lived serenely in their small communities:

> The influx of alien tides to whom our precious heirlooms are as nothing, the growth of cities and the inextricable perplexities of their government, the vast inequality of condition between man and man—what room is there for the little primary council of freemen, homogeneous in stock, holding the same faith, on the same level as to faith and station?[1]

The Jewish immigrant coming to America from his small native town was even more profoundly shaken by this transition. For though there had been no social equality in the East European town, the Jewish community nonetheless felt united by family bonds:

> In my town everything was done in common. The town was like one large family . . . Jews clung together, like children abandoned in a desert. . . . The Jew felt more secure when he was with others. . . . Should anything happen to a small town Jew, the entire community would share his joy or his sorrow.[2]

Upon coming to America the immigrants clustered together and tried to recreate the *shtetl* in the guise of the *landsmanshaft*. The Jewish immigrants from Russia felt little sympathy for the czarist empire whose victims they were, but they cherished a powerful nostalgia for their families and native towns.

The cultural and historical role of the *landsmanshaft* has been beautifully described by Professor Morris Raphael Cohen in his autobiographical work, *A Dreamer's Journey*. Though Cohen became integrated in American culture, he displayed a profound understanding for the generation of pioneers. He did not break

---

[1] Samuel Adams, *The Man of the Town Meeting*, quot. by Edward M. Saveth, *American Historians and European Immigrants*, p. 24.

[2] M. Olgin, *Medyn shtetl in ukrayne*, p. 54.

completely with the old home, though spiritually he had become
an integral part of the culture of the new home. His *landslayt* from
the town of Nieswiez remained close to him. On November 5, 1936,
two days after his mother's death, he wrote:

> My last two years with her made me appreciate her qualities
> more than I did in the years when I saw little of her. If I had to
> make a speech, I would have spoken of the spiritual importance
> of the Neshvieser Verein—how it enabled the hardy pioneers to
> adjust themselves to the new land, to keep people in self-
> respect and to make a home for the new generation; how the
> tradition of learning was a light—not like the modern electric
> but like the ancient candle or torch—which enabled people to
> interpret the new life.

Yet, the *landsmanshaft* could not take the place of the *shtetl*,
because the immigrant now lived in the turmoil of New York where
he frequently felt isolated, with that peculiar sense of alienation of
one who has been uprooted from his old home but has not yet struck
new roots. Economic adaptation was the easiest aspect of the problem, and here the process of Americanization proceeded rapidly;
but cultural and social integration went on at a much more laborious
pace. And during his first years in America the immigrant had no
time for anything except material survival.

It is therefore not surprising that economic success became the
center of the immigrant's ambitions, and that its attainment also
paved the way to social recognition. Material success became the
yardstick with which values were to be measured, and this, in turn,
engendered an attitude of contempt for spiritual values and the cultural traditions of the old home in particular. The successful "all-
rightnick" was not content with his place in economic life, he also
felt the need to assert his claim to position of spiritual leader. This
accounts for the defeatist moods that seized some of the Jewish
intellectuals. America was lampooned in the pun *Ama reka* (hollow
people) which recurs in a large number of articles and critical essays
both in the Yiddish and Hebrew press of the past century. The situation of the intellectuals was indeed difficult, and especially so in the
case of the older ones. They could no longer hope to adapt themselves to a regimen of manual labor, and their intellectual attain-
ments were not in demand. The great upheaval which the migration
caused created many weird situations. Former *melamdim* who were
sufficiently aggressive assumed posts as rabbis, whereas modest and
gentle scholars, unable even to attain positions as teachers, turned in

desperation to hard physical labor. The following is a touching description of this phenomenon:

> There are few more pathetic sights than an old man with a long beard, a little black cap on his head and a venerable face—a man who had been perhaps a Hebraic or Talmudic scholar in the old country, carrying or pressing piles of coats in the melancholy sweatshop; or standing for sixteen hours a day by his push-cart in one of the dozen crowded streets of the ghetto.[3]

Since material success seemed to make up for all shortcomings, there appeared to be no need to ascribe importance to moral principles. The danger of moral degeneration became still greater, because the success of the self-made man brought out in greater relief the want and loneliness of the immigrant mass. Concentration in the most neglected sections of the big cities, overcrowding, dirty streets and equally dirty tenements, combined to undermine the moral discipline of the older generation, and were a poor backdrop for the moral education of the young. The insecurity of the immigrant went hand in hand with uncertainty regarding moral values. He lived in two cultural realms and was estranged from both. Hillel Rogoff, an authority on the East Side, gives the following description of the spiritual instability prevailing at the turn of the century:

> Physical exhaustion was aggravated by moral and spiritual anguish. The old-fashioned religious Jew saw his traditions discarded and even ridiculed. He saw his children drift away from him to pick up strange new ways. The safe old moorings of Jewish family life loosened, the privacy of the home was invaded and its sanctity frequently profaned by boarders, the minds of the children were often poisoned against their parents by the ridicule of the gutter and by the ill-digested enlightenment of the school.[4]

Many immigrants held financial success to be synonymous with the ideal of Americanization—a fallacious conception yet also a partial truth. The American philosophy of rugged individualism, in part a heritage of Puritan theology, was vulgarized. Furthermore, the dominant strata in American society had little understanding and still less respect for the culture of the later arrivals, even though they were themselves children or grandchildren of immigrants.

America was built by pioneers confident of their strength and

[3] Hutchins Hapgood, *The Spirit of the Ghetto*, pp. 11–12.
[4] *An East Side Epic*, p. 5.

luck. This gave rise to a tradition of stubborn individualism and un-
quenchable optimism. In a land of unlimited opportunities, consistent effort nearly always paid off in the end. Nearly everyone in
America had started out with his bare hands. The cult of the self-
made man is therefore quite comprehensible. The development of
spiritual life in this country extended its sanction to this cult, and
thus helped the ideology of individualism to strike deep roots.

Max Weber tried to demonstrate the immense influence of the
Puritan ethic on economic developments in England and America in
his epoch-making work, *The Protestant Ethic and the Spirit of Capitalism.* Weber's theory aroused widespread debate, and it appears
certain that he had overextended himself on some points. Yet the
basic premises of his theory are well established.

For the purpose of this essay we are primarily concerned with
the Puritan attitude toward economic activities in general, and
toward the problem of individual success. The Calvinist ethic elevated man's economic activities to the level of a religious commandment: God can and should be served through labor. It is therefore
the duty of every man to guard his position in economic life and to
respect his calling:

> God doth call every man and woman . . . to serve in some
> peculiar employment in this world, both for their own and the
> common good. . . . The great Governour of the world hath ap-
> pointed to every man his proper post and province, and let him
> be never so active out of his sphere, he will be at a great loss, if
> he does not keep his own vineyard and mind his own business.[5]

The dividing line between religion and economic life was thus
obliterated. Work, trade, and even banking are part of God's plan,
and it is our duty to endow our every day labors with religious emotion. If it is a religious duty to conduct business sensibly, then it
follows that the ambition to make profits and to expand business is
likewise in agreement with God's plan. The Puritans endowed the
establishing, organizing and conducting of business with endless
devotion; and capitalist drive for profits acquired supreme moral
sanction.

Equally important in the theology of the Puritans were the principles of predestination and election. Though all men were created
equal, not all had the good fortune to enjoy divine favor in equal
measure. Calvinist theology teaches that there exists a class of the

[5] Richard Steele, *The Tradesman's Calling,* quot. by R. H. Tawney,
Religion and the Rise of Capitalism. Mentor ed., p. 200.

elect upon whom the Creator bestows His favor both here and in the
hereafter, while He withholds it from others who, incidentally, constitute the vast majority. Why this is so we do not know, for the ways
of God are inscrutable. According to Puritan theology, material success is therefore the best indication of God's blessing, and it is only
natural that those who are successful should feel secure and satisfied
with themselves. From this it follows, as a matter of principle, that
radical social reform is intolerable. Since God chose to create the
poor, we must not interfere with His plan.

The theory of election seemed to be made to order for the pioneers of capitalism. It spared them many sleepless nights and re-
lieved their conscience of the nagging doubt: Why do I deserve so
much fortune, and what sin has my brother committed that he
should be destined to live in need and an outcast? The philosophy of
success left no room for the problem of a Job.

A small group of liberal intellectuals in America realized as far
back as the eighties and the nineties of the past century that the profound changes engendered by the industrial revolution in America
necessitated also a new approach to the problem of poverty. This
group included such settlement workers as Jane Addams, Lillian
Wald, Florence Kelly, and others. The workers of the East Side encountered these idealistic representatives of American humanism
during the early days of the Jewish Socialist movement. There was
a measure of rapport between these two elements, though, as a general rule, the Jewish Labor movement followed a different path—
one that had been determined by the specific historical experiences
of the Jewish people.

The Jewish immigrants from Eastern Europe brought an entirely different approach to the questions of happiness and misery in
life. Jews found it hard to become reconciled to the idea that material success is an outstanding indication of God's favor. The Puritan theology was well suited for the courageous pioneers who
achieved their goals by means of stubborn diligence. But the Jewish
historical experience was of a different kind, and scholarly thought
was preoccupied with those who failed despite all efforts. Jewish
thinking propounded the election of the injured and the suffering.
Job's tragedy consisted not so much in his physical suffering as in
his painful recognition that not even his friends believed in his innocence. "You have sinned," they repeatedly said to him, "and God
has punished you for it." Job protested with all his strength against
being abandoned by God and deprived of consolation and encouragement even from his closest friends.

The Job problem and the Jewish problem were basically alike, and to the question posed by the existence of suffering in the world, the Jews counterposed the old answer of faith in the coming of a new world at the end of time. This old, yet ever-new, Jewish solution to the problem of suffering was now propounded by the tailors and cloakmakers of the East Side.

It is impossible to account for the unique response of the East Side to socialist propaganda without taking into consideration the Messianic tradition. To the Jewish masses, socialism was incomparably more than the program of a political party. It was more than a dream of a beautiful future. For the workers of the East Side socialism was a new faith which helped them endure the hardships and disappointments of everyday life. Socialism bolstered their faith in themselves: it saved them from despair and from the loss of respect for both themselves and their fellows in need.

The problem of human dignity was no less important than that of material want. In the *shtetl* even the poorest Jew was a personality in his own right. "In my *shtetl* every Jew was a secret prince; every pauper concealed within himself the spark of secret aristocracy," wrote M. Olgin. The individual was not easily lost in a small town, and everyone had his recognized status, even if on the lower rungs of the social ladder. In the capitalist metropolis, on the other hand, it was much easier to lose one's individuality. Of what account is an individual among millions of his fellows? True, there were some among the immigrants who had left the old home with the express desire to "disappear," to shed their past and become "new" people. But only seldom was it possible genuinely to become a new person with a distinct individuality.

Work in the sweatshops could not provide moral satisfaction. The attitude of the bosses and subcontractors, themselves mostly former workers, was galling. It was an everyday occurrence for workers to be abused and fired without cause, and there were even instances of bosses beating their workers. Some of the early strikes were called because of such mistreatment. The workers also lacked permanent homes. The bachelors lived as boarders, three or four to a room, which was merely a place to spend the night. Even married workers with families seldom had homes to themselves. The sense of forlornness was great even when there was employment; if a worker lost his job, his situation became intolerable.

There has been a tendency to overlook the moral factors influencing the social and political conflicts of our time. It is very easy to see the material needs of the masses. Yet the unrest which agitates so many is often the product of the mounting depersonalization characteristic of modern society. This unrest is the protest of the *mass man* who refuses to become reconciled to his fate. He resents having to remain a *mass man* all his life. He wants recognition as an individual. The class conflict between rich and poor is becoming overshadowed by another social conflict—the struggle between those who have status in social life, the class of *somebodies,* and the great and nameless mass lost in the turmoil of modern life, the class of the *nobodies.* The East Side fought with especial vigor against this trend toward depersonalization. The entire labor movement in the country fought the same battle, but there was one distinction between the general and the Jewish labor movement. Until the time of the New Deal, the American labor movement, as represented by the American Federation of Labor, had been strongly influenced by the Puritan philosophy. This was apparent in the structure of the union movement. The principle of industrial unionism would without a doubt have been more practical in many instances, yet the unions stubbornly clung to the principle of craft unionism. The Puritan philosophy of "calling" was effective here. The skilled and better-paid workers proudly guarded their superior status and their privileged position as skilled labor. They did not care to mingle with the unskilled and thus lose their separateness.

The Jewish workers lacked this attitude toward a "calling" that was so characteristic of the Anglo-American tradition. For one thing, the conditions of work were very different here from what they were in the old home. The skilled Jewish workman, in particular, was frequently depressed because his craftsmanship was superfluous here. Most of the workers were what was then known as "Columbus' tailors," people who had learned the work after coming to America. As a result of an increasing division of labor, few truly skilled workers were needed. This was one reason the needle trades largely escaped the conflict between craft and industrial unionism. The ideology of "unionism pure and simple" as classically formulated by Samuel Gompers likewise found little response here. Even trade unionism as such appealed but little to the workers of the East Side.

For what the East Side yearned for was a reevaluation of values. It needed a philosophy that would give the worker comfort and status. In the course of generations of trials, the Jew had found consolation in his faith in his chosenness. This faith was now shattered, and the spiritual crisis of modern times further undermined the authority of religion. Moreover, the old-fashioned religious leaders were themselves at a loss in America; they did not comprehend the new reality and had no answers to the problems it posed. As for the philosophy of Reform Judaism, it was altogether alien to the workers of the East Side.

The socialists introduced a new scale of values. Today we can scarcely grasp what the teachings of the socialist propagandists, who stressed the unimportance of individual success and the insignificance of money as a yardstick for social values, meant for the Jewish workers of the East Side. If the poor were indeed the righteous and if the workers were the true creators of wealth, then they need not be ashamed of their social status. Socialism restored to them their human worth and aroused their sense of individual pride.

Socialism lent added prestige to spiritual values. While a segment of the Jewish intellectual class found it especially hard to adapt to the new conditions, this was not the case for those within the socialist camp. Socialist intellectuals enjoyed a sense of historic mission, as well as the balm of enthusiastic audiences, and since they were in the forefront of the struggle against the cult of success, they found it easy to stress the importance of spiritual values. Enlightenment and social justice were the two main themes of socialist propaganda. Young workers, boys and girls, enthusiastically undertook their self-education. They read, studied, discussed problems after their hard labor in the shops. The ancient Jewish tradition of individual and group study was revived in a new form. How important these intellectual pursuits were, can be judged from the fact that the majority of Jewish immigrants came to this country with but scanty education—many were, in fact, almost illiterate. Intensive educational work was therefore required in order to prepare a reading public for the socialist newspapers, books, and Yiddish literature in general.

Socialist educational work on the East Side was integrated into the broad framework of the social and political problems of the world. These were extensively reflected in the Yiddish socialist press as far as the nineties. Morris R. Cohen remembers:

As I look back on the Yiddish and English press in the last decade of the nineteenth century I cannot help feeling that the former did more for the education of its readers than the latter. Having no army of reporters to dig up sensational news, the Yiddish press necessarily paid more attention to things of permanent interest. It tried to give its readers something of enduring and substantial value. . . . The Yiddish press has prepared millions of Jewish people to take a worthy part in American civilization while also promoting the natural self-respect to which Jews are entitled because of their character and history.[6]

[6] *A Dreamer's Journey*, p. 220.

The pioneers of the Jewish labor movement gave the Jewish worker a sense of his own dignity. First they won for the Jewish worker the respect of the American labor movement. Working conditions in the sweatshops of the East Side were not of a kind to win the sympathy of organized labor. But this attitude changed almost overnight when a series of bitter strikes in the garment industry aroused public opinion, and the world became aware that the Jewish workers knew how to defend their rights.

The Jewish labor leaders were keenly aware of the importance of winning public opinion, perhaps because Jewish labor was still weak and urgently needed the moral support of the native American workers. The Jewish workers gained a reputation as good strikers but poor union people. This reputation was not unfounded, though their shortcomings as union people were not the result of a lack of understanding of the importance of organization.

How account for the fact that Jewish workers so frequently resorted to strikes when their unions were so weak? For there were even instances when they struck before formulating their demands.

The workers of the East Side often went on strike for reasons other than formulated economic demands. For them the strike was frequently a way of expressing their protest against a form of society that tried to transform the laborer into a robot. In an article published in the *Forward* (July 27, 1910) concerning the historic cloakmakers' strike, the poet A. Liessin characterized the mood of the workers as follows: "*The seventy thousand zeros now became seventy thousand fighters.*" The worker refused to maintain his passive role in the shop or in social life, and struck for his rights as citizen and man.

The great cloakmakers' strike in 1910 marked a turning point in the history of the Jewish labor movement. It may even be maintained that it was a turning point in the history of the American Jewish community. The embittered fight of the workers aroused the entire Jewish community, with prominent persons like Jacob Schiff, Louis Marshall, Louis D. Brandeis, and others becoming involved as intermediaries. Agreement was reached after long negotiations, and both parties signed a Protocol of Peace which became a milestone in the history of industrial relations in America.

The authors of the Protocol of Peace did not regard it as a temporary agreement, but as a kind of constitution for labor that should make possible peaceful resolution of conflicts. For this purpose a Board of Arbitration was set up, consisting of three members: "One nominee of the manufacturers, one nominee of the unions, and one representative of the public." In this manner the right of labor to bargain about working conditions even when no strike was in progress, and the right of the public to intervene in industrial disputes, were officially sanctioned.

The pacific philosophy underlying the Protocol clashed sharply with the ideology of a number of socialist union leaders. In time, however, it became obvious that the system of impartial arbitration had many advantages and helped strengthen the position of the unions in the shops. Furthermore, the system of arbitration was familiar to the Jewish workers from the old country. It also appealed to a number of employers and to the liberal elements in the Jewish community at large. The harsh working conditions in the needle trades had lowered the prestige of the Jewish community, and leaders like Marshall, Brandeis, and Schiff understood that the workers were also fighting for the good name of the Jewish people. Even some of the employers understood this. "I do not want my children to feel ashamed," one employer said, "when they say their father is a clothing manufacturer."

As the unions gained strength and influence, they could increasingly protect the interests of the workers without resorting to strikes. In recent decades it has been the pride of the needle trades unions that they have solved most conflicts through negotiation, and we are confronted with the remarkable phenomenon that the unions which had been influenced most by socialist ideology became the pioneers of cooperation between employers and workers. It should also be observed that this cooperation between unions and manufacturers extends far beyond the mere settlement of conflicts.

From the start, the Jewish labor movement was distinguished by the fact that it did not confine itself to a narrow sphere of activities. Parallel with the unions there arose a variety of organizations and institutions—political groups, the *Forward*, Workmen's Circle, Jewish National Workers' Alliance, and others. Some feared that this variegation might diffuse the strength of the labor movement, but these fears proved unfounded. In times of trial these organizations aided one another loyally, the entire movement becoming as one family and the struggles of one organization always evoking sympathy from the others.

The Jewish labor organizations often had to devote much time and energy to a variety of relief activities at home as well as on behalf of numerous Jewish and non-Jewish labor organizations overseas. In this area, too, the Jewish labor movement distinguished itself. At the time of the great cloakmakers' strike in 1910, the *Forward* collected the sum of $70,000—a substantial amount for that time.

Some years later the cloakmakers contributed tens of thousands of dollars to the strike funds of the furriers and men's clothing workers. During the great steel strike in 1919, the Jewish needle trades contributed $175,000—half of what was contributed by all the other unions in the country. Moreover, this was accomplished at a time when Jewish workers were engaged in a great relief campaign for the Jews in Europe.

The general labor movement in America has not succeeded in attracting the intellectuals for its purposes. In part this was an intentional estrangement. Samuel Gompers had no confidence in the socialist intellectuals, and his distrust was well founded. The ideological conflicts between the various political trends in the eighties and nineties caused no little harm to the labor movement. The political wrangling and the bitter polemics that engaged the various party groups were also not without effect on the East Side. But with us, labor and the intellectuals never parted ways, nor was the dividing line between workers and intellectuals sharply drawn on the East Side. Nearly all Jewish immigrant intellectuals began by working in shops. On the other hand, by the twentieth century, numerous workers came to America possessed of some education. Moreover, the two groups needed each other too urgently. The intellectuals needed the workers of the East Side as an audience, while in turn the labor movement was a powerful influence in Jewish cultural life. Gradually spheres of influence were marked out. The unions and the Workmen's Circle were dominated by workers— more correctly, by a group of leaders who came from the shops. The Jewish labor movement created a mighty press where the intellectuals dominated and exerted their influence on the entire movement. It should be noted that the Jewish workers were the only labor group in America who created a press of their own possessing high standards and a mass circulation that exceeded by far the circulation of the nonlabor papers in Yiddish.

Until 1903, cosmopolitanism was the dominant trend in the Jewish labor movement. The pogrom in Kishineff in the spring of 1903, which aroused Jews everywhere, did not fail to leave its impress on Jewish labor. The remarkable growth of Yiddish literature raised the prestige of Yiddish as a cultural language (and contributed its share to the new sense of national self-consciousness). Jewish workers were increasingly drawn into the sphere of Jewish interests and problems, at the same time that they were becoming more integrated into the life of America, and established closer relations with the general labor movement in the country. Americanization and

Jewish self-consciousness went hand in hand. Its very prominence made the Jewish labor movement feel responsible for the fate of the Jewish community as a whole.

The foregoing traces the general contours of the development of the Jewish labor movement in America up to the twenties of this century. The radical changes introduced in the immigration laws after World War I, gave rise to an entirely new situation in the "Jewish trades" and brought about far-reaching modifications in the social and economic structure of the entire Jewish community in America.

Much light came from the East Side. The historians must note it and record it. Coming generations ought to remember it.

1970

Nationalism, Secularism and Religion in the Jewish Labor Movement

by C. Bezalel Sherman

Translated by C. Bezalel Sherman

I

Secularism as a *Weltanschauung* is a much older phenomenon among American Jews than secularism as a Jewish philosophy. Which is to say that American Jews were dedicated to the proposition that church must be separated from the state long before the notion that Jewish survival was not inextricably bound up with the survival of the Jewish faith had made any kind of a dent in their thinking.

For half of the three hundred years that Jews have lived in this country there was no Jewish community life outside the synagogue. The first congregation has celebrated its three hundredth anniversary, but the oldest Jewish charitable agency in the country cannot claim to be more than one hundred and fifty years of age. B'nai B'rith, the first national Jewish membership organization, was founded in 1843, while Jewish institutions that were completely divorced from Jewish religion did not appear on the American scene before the end of the nineteenth century. Prior to that time, all non-congregational Jewish social welfare and cultural agencies recognized the primacy of the synagogue in Jewish collective life. It is no accident that immigration from Germany, which supplied American Jewry with the most effective builders of its institutional edifice, also provided the mass base for classical Reform which, while considering Jews a religious fellowship, rejected the concept of Jewish peoplehood. At the very moment that the German Jews were blanketing the United States with a network of Jewish hospitals, orphanages, homes for the aged and similar institutions, they also produced the Pittsburgh Platform which, among others, contained the following statement:

> The modern era heralds the approach of Israel's great messianic hope for the establishment of the Kingdom of Truth, Justice and Peace among all men. We consider ourselves no longer a nation, but a religious community, and therefore expect neither a return to Palestine, nor a restoration of the sacrificial worship under the sons of Aaron, or of any of the laws concerning the Jewish State.

Traveling a different road and moved by a totally different motivation, the founders of the Jewish labor movement arrived in practice at the same conclusion as the authors of the Pittsburgh Platform, namely that mankind was on the threshold of Utopia and that Jews did not constitute a people. In a declaration adopted at the first conference of Jewish workers' organizations in the United States and Canada, held in New York in 1890, the view that the Jewish question had ceased to be a national problem found the following formulation:

> We have no Jewish question in America. The only question we recognize is the question of how to prevent the emergence of "Jewish questions" here.

The motto of classical Reform, coined by Gustavus Poznanski at Charleston, South Carolina, in 1840, that "America is our Zion and Washington our Jerusalem" found its proletarian paraphrase at the workers' conference, fifty years later, in the slogan: "The world is our fatherland, socialism our religion."

The common ground upon which the two social extremes in American Jewish life—the rising Jewish bourgeoisie as represented by the Reform movement and the rising Jewish labor movement as represented by the socialist groups—met was the denial to Jews of a secular identity. Both hoped to hasten the arrival of human brotherhood by tearing themselves away from their own national roots.

At this point it becomes necessary to delimit the territory we intend to cover in the present essay. A line should be drawn between secularism and secularist ideology. As defined here, secularism is merely an extension of the principle of the separation of Church and State and, hence, not incompatible with the profoundest religious feeling. It marches alongside, rather than in opposition to, religion, and concedes to the latter priority in the sphere of influence which democratic society assigns to faith. Secularist ideology, on the other hand, seeks to eliminate religion from a voice in social relationships.

Secularism's quarrel is with the overreaching ambitions of the Church; secularist ideology, in addition to distrusting the Church, is also suspicious of religion itself. This explains why irreligion and atheism flourish in the orbit of secularist ideology.

Both secularism and secularist ideology gave rise to Jewish mass-movements at the end of the nineteenth century. Riding the crest of the surging waves of immigration from Eastern Europe, these mass-movements found programmatic expression in large organizations, with secularism, as we have defined it, receiving its fullest crystallization in Zionism and secularist ideology in Jewish socialism.

American Zionism, although nonreligious as a movement, except of course for the Mizrachi groups, has always worked closely with the synagogue and has manifested a great loyalty for the tenets of the Jewish faith. Zionism has thus been able to cut across denominational divisions and to enlist the rabbinate as its most effective propagandist, while secularist ideology was sectarian in its very nature. It gained adherents only among certain sections of Jewish labor and, although fairly successful during the formative stages of the Jewish trade unions, proved to be, as will be seen below, no more than a one-generation phenomenon in American Jewish life. It is the main purpose of this article to point out the reasons why secularist ideology failed despite a rather auspicious beginning.

II

To understand why cosmopolitanism was the dominating strain in the ideological fabric of the Jewish labor movement during the first two decades of its existence, it is necessary to remember that that movement was recruited almost exclusively from immigration from Eastern Europe—a part of the world where the Jewish communities constituted states within states, as it were. On one end was the political state which held its entire populace in subjugation and denied Jews the few restricted rights other subjects enjoyed; and there was, on the other end, the "State" of the Jewish settlement which regulated every move of its members in matters concerning Jewish belongingness. Organized religion was a factor in each one of the states. The church was one of the pillars which supported the despotic governments of the political state; and the synagogue was the central institution of the Jewish "State" which, resting on religious authority, was not infrequently also bolstered by certain legal prerogatives. The Jewish immigrant, who became a worker for the first time in his life upon arrival in the United States or Canada, thus brought with him the image of government and religion as anti-labor factors.

This is the reason why the founders of the Jewish labor movement, whose social conceptions were fashioned in the school of non-Jewish, primarily German, socialist thought, were able to instill an assimilationist philosophy into the young Jewish trade unions. They won by default because there was no one else at the time to guide the inexperienced Jewish workers on the untrodden path of proletarianization; and because, too, the sudden transplantation of the Jewish immigrant from a ghetto life in a tyrannical, semifeudal empire to the clear air of an industrial civilization in a political democracy left him in a state of confusion and bewilderment. This was not a gradual transformation, not a planned or systematic growing into new conditions, but a political socioeconomic and psychological upheaval, one in which there was lacking a transitory period. The young Jewish worker had, as yet, had no time to break out of the cobweb of old prejudices and erase the bitter memories that obscured his vision. At the time he first became acquainted with political activity, the image of government and religion he had brought over from abroad still colored his relationships with society. He was mistrustful of all authority, religious or secular.

Lack of a period of transition also marked the religious and communal transformation the new Jewish workers had experienced. Never before had they seen a state or community that was not wedded to organized religion; and there was no bridge to span the gulf that opened up between the total identification of Jewishness with Jewish religion that they had known in their native lands and the system of religious freedom they had found in this country. They had to jump from an all-embracing rigid orthodoxy which regulated all phases of Jewish life for thousands of years to a secular society that made religion a matter of individual conscience. To many this represented a leap into unfaith.

It is this neck-breaking leap that holds the key to some peculiar features in the development of the Jewish labor movement—features that would remain unsolved riddles and inexplicable contradictions but for the use of this key. Uprooted people who never saw a friendly government or a beneficial law would naturally embrace, before finding new moorings, radical programs which called for the complete revamping of the social system. It should, therefore, cause no surprise to find so many of the new Jewish recruits to the industrial working classes accepting, despite their want of a proletariat tradition, the ideology of a militant socialism which advocated the abolition of class society, or of an anarchism which urged the dissolution of the state. Nor should the fact that so many turned irreligious or atheistic despite recent emergence from a purely religious way of life cause any wonderment.

This is not to say that all, or even a majority, of the early Jewish workers were radicals or antagonistic to religion. Quite the contrary. Most of them remained steadfast in their religious loyalty, joined Orthodox congregations in large numbers and went to incredible lengths to safeguard their spiritual heritage. Countless thousands of Jewish workers were willing to endure the misery and degradation of the sweatshop merely because it allowed them to observe the Sabbath; and they also resisted the efforts of the early union leaders to hoist upon their personal lives the flag of national nihilism. They resisted in the only way that was open to them—by dropping out of the labor organizations as soon as strikes were over. The instability of the early Jewish unions was noted by all students of organized labor; so much so that John R. Commons, historian of American trade unionism, was certain in 1906 that Jewish workers, ready for the greatest sacrifices during economic struggles, were innately incapable of remaining organized in times of industrial peace. Commons, who subsequently changed his views, and others failed to detect in the loss of union interests the reaction on the part of the rank and file to the irreligious policies of their leaders. A comparison between those policies and the activities of the synagogues and *landsmanshaften*, whose membership was to a very large extent also made up of working immigrants, would reveal how wide the gap was that existed between the social philosophies of the trade unions and the mores of their members.

The average Jewish workers were too raw, too inexperienced, too bewildered, and too immature politically to challenge the ideologies of the leadership openly. They could only resort to the passive resistance of abstaining from union activity which did not relate to matters of immediate economic concern. As for the leaders, they were united in the conviction that socialism required the obliteration of national division as well as of class differentiation. Cosmopolitanism, merely another name for assimilationism, was their answer to the Jewish question. As regards religion, there was agreement among them that it tended to blunt the class consciousness of the Jewish worker. They did not all see eye to eye, however, when choosing methods to "enlighten" those of their followers who clung to time-worn "superstitions."

The anarchists, anti-Marxian in their approach to social issues, accepted as gospel truth the Marxian injunction that religion was the opiate of the working people, and made aggressive atheism an integral part of their program of action. They sent their shock troops to storm the gates of heaven by putting on antireligious spectacles in the heart of religious neighborhoods. It was the era of the Yom Kippur Ball and the atheistic *Haggadah*—an era not to recur until a generation later when the Jewish communists produced antireligious performances which put the early anarchists to shame.

The socialists, the most powerful and more enduring wing of Jewish radicalism, as a rule frowned upon the antireligious antics of the anarchists. Nevertheless, there were some among them who, like Benjamin Feigenbaum, used whatever Jewish learning they had picked up in the Lithuanian or Polish yeshivas to point up inconsistencies in the Bible or to dig up passages in the Talmud that could be given an antilabor twist. The Feigenbaums were decidedly in the minority, however. Most of the socialist leaders favored an attitude of respect and tolerance in dealings with professing Jews.

Outstanding among the leaders was Abraham Cahan whose influence on the Jewish labor movement in America is unequaled by any one individual in history. He was the first among the founders of the Jewish Socialist movement to respond to the realities of American life and to be affected by the attitudes toward religion that prevailed in the general community. As early as the 1880's he realized the folly of trying to win over Jewish workers to trade unionism by addressing them in Russian, German and, to a lesser degree, in English. He was the first to employ the Yiddish language in socialist propaganda, and the first to insist on the proposition that relationships between Jewish workers and international labor were not a one-way street. He unfolded the banner of labor solidarity among Jewish workers, but he also missed no opportunity to remind international socialism that it owed something to the Jewish people.

Illustrative of Cahan's attitude toward antireligious anarchists and socialists is an article, not his first on the subject, which appeared in two installments in the *Forward* on April 22 and 23, 1911. The following lines are worth quoting:

> The most comical, and at the same time, saddest thing is to see an atheist turn his irreligion into a cold, dry, unfeeling, heartless religion—and this is something most of our unbelievers used to do. One must not sit at a Seder; one must extend no sympathy to the honest, ignorant mother who sheds tears over her prayerbook; one must deeply wound traditional Jews by eating and smoking on Yom Kippur in front of the synagogue. Verily, the former unbelievers were, in their way, just as fanatical, just as narrowminded, just as intolerant as the religious fanatic on whom they warred.

Cahan did not manifest any sympathy for the Zionist cause until late in his very long life. To the end he had very little, if any, faith in the future of the American Jewish community. He never assigned an independent social role to Jewish labor, considering the latter a mere stepping-stone to the American labor movement. Yiddish was to him not an end but a means, one to be employed until such time as the Jewish workers learned to get along in English. First to carry the message of socialism in terms of Jewish conditions, he never had a clear conception of how he wanted those conditions changed.

III

From its inception the Jewish labor movement, as mentioned before, rested on ideological and organizational foundations that were largely borrowed from non-Jewish sources. With no body of experience of their own to draw upon, the Jewish trade unions and socialist groups considered themselves mere props on the stage of international socialism and conceived of their tasks as merely ancillary to those of general labor. Efforts to set up an autonomous Jewish federation in the American Socialist Party were successfully balked until the eve of the Frst World War. A Yiddish propaganda bureau in the apparatus of the Socialist Party was all that the Jewish workers were entitled to, even though the Jewish districts were at the time the most important strongholds of the socialist movement. The above-mentioned conference in 1890 made it clear that it was setting up a Jewish workers' organization in this country not as a permanent institution but only as a stopgap body. It was a matter of expediency rather than principle, as the following statement contained in the declaration adopted by that conference explained:

> Because only we, Yiddish-speaking citizens, can be effective among Jewish immigrants; because only we speak their language and are acquainted with their way of life—solely because of this fact do we form this special Jewish body. The Yiddish language is our weapon; to obliterate all lines dividing Jew and non-Jew in the world of labor is one of our goals.

The first protests against the tendency to relegate Jewish workers to an auxiliary position in the general labor movement were raised after 1905 when, following the unsuccessful revolution against the Czar in Russia, there came to this country many thousands of Jewish workers who had been trained in the labor movements of their native lands and had received political schooling in the Jewish socialist parties which had become significant factors in Eastern European life at the turn of the century. Although the first and largest of those parties, the Bund, founded in 1897, still vacillated at the time of the 1905 revolution between neutralism as regards Jewish national continuity and localism as regards Jewish culture, it had

nonetheless implanted in its members a loyalty to modern Jewish
spiritual values which they were not willing to abandon when they
reached American shores. The members of the Labor Zionist and
Socialist-Territorialist parties were even more outspoken in their
opposition to the policies pertaining to Jewish issues that the official
labor leadership was pursuing here. Despite violent conflicts between
Bundists and Poale Zionists regarding problems of Jewish national
existence, they had a common denominator in the affirmative evaluation of the part secular Jewish culture played in contemporary Jewish life.

That evaluation found its classical exposition in the works of
the late Dr. Hayim Zhitlowsky, the outstanding theoretician of Jewish
nationalism in the camp of socialism. Ideologically close to some
Jewish socialist parties and at one time or another a member of
others, he was never really fully identified with any one of them,
although he influenced all. Long before the Bund came into being,
he insisted that it was incumbent upon a Jewish socialist to participate energetically in endeavors to rejuvenate Jewish national life.
Unlike the Bundists, however, who discarded their theories of Jewish
cultural autonomy the minute they struck roots in American soil,
Zhitlowsky tried hard for nearly a half century to translate his theories into a program which he hoped would strengthen Jewish group
life in this country. The fact that that program in no real sense
differed from the original platform he proposed for Russian Jewry
as early as 1887 is eloquent testimony of his failure to come to grips
with the new elements America introduced into Jewish historical
experience.

Zhitlowsky's great contribution to the Jewish renaissance—a
contribution that has won for him a prominent place in modern
Jewish history—was his relentless struggle against the assimilatory
policies and practices which distorted the class conceptions of the
early Jewish socialists and made them oblivious of their responsibili-
ties as members of the Jewish community. Mankind, he stressed,
was divided into nations as well as into classes. Class interests and
national interests intertwined and crossed each other like the black
and red squares of a checkerboard. One set of interests could not be
ignored without injury being inflicted on the other. Nations were
not created artificially; they were the result of immutable social and
cultural processes. These processes cannot be halted, but they can
be diverted to either progressive or reactionary channels. Hence,
there was nothing intrinsically bad in nationalism. On the contrary,
if harnessed to serve liberal causes, nationalism was a creative and
constructive force which made for the spiritual and cultural eleva-

tion of the human spirit; utilized for reactionary purposes, nationalism inclined to turn into chauvinism and become a menace. It was
the mission of the socialist movement to guide nationalism along
progressive lines.

With this general theory of the relationships between socialism
and nationalism as his point of departure, Zhitlowsky proceeded to
spell out a program designed to normalize Jewish national life. He
declared war on all ideologies, bourgeois or proletarian, which ne-
gated Jewish peoplehood and devoted himself from the first day he
settled in the United States, in 1909, exclusively to the Jewish scene.
This brought him into head-on collision with the recognized leaders
of the Jewish labor movement who by that time had become firmly
entrenched in their organizational prestige and ideological influence.

As against the policy of cosmopolitanism, theoretically envisag-
ing a society in which all national differentiation was obliterated and
concretely fostering assimilationism, Zhitlowsky propounded the
principle of internationalism which conceived of mankind as a family
of independent nations with each free to develop to the fullest extent
the individuality of its national genius. The Jews of the world were
entitled to a dignified place at the table of this family of nations.

The creativeness of modern nationalism, Zhitlowsky argued, re-
sided in the cultural values of a people rather than in its religious
traditions. The Jewish religion which sustained the Jewish people for
thousands of years has lost its cementing power. It has even become
a disintegrating force, in that it tended to divide Jews into denominational sects and into professing and nonprofessing groups. Zhitlowsky summed it all up in the following words:

> We reject all religious teaching as a basis for our national exis-
> tence and productivity, because religious teaching, if it is to be
> truly religious, cannot be national in character; because it fetters
> free thought; because it tends to sunder the bonds that tie par-
> ents to children and integrate members of a people into one
> folk; because it tends to isolate a nation and doom it to stagna-
> tion; because constricted religious teaching is a contradiction in
> terms; because national religious teaching is no safeguard
> against language assimilation, the most dangerous foe of our
> normal existence and of our free development as a progressive
> people among modern nations.

The fallacy of Zhitlowsky's reasoning consisted in his persistent
employment, vis-a-vis the Jewish people, of criteria that may have
been applicable—though even that was questionable—to normal nations living in certain lands and at certain times. He was schematic

in his thinking, inclined to over-simplification, and he overlooked the characteristics that distinguished Jews from other peoples. He insisted that it was theoretically possible, although inconceivable from a practical point of view, for one to be a Christian by faith and a Jew by nationality, even as it was possible for one to be a Frenchman by nationality and Muslim by religion. Should a democratic Jewish community ever be organized in the United States, it would have to provide for the religious requirements of its Christian members out of community funds, as well as for its Jewish religious members. As a matter of principle, such a community would not only have to supply its needy members with matzos for Passover but would have to see to it that none of its Christian members went without pork on Easter.

For it is not religion that weaves Jews from all over the globe into the spiritual pattern of nationhood. Modern Jewish culture, centered about the Yiddish language, is the power that holds Jews together and makes for their creative continuity as a people. The cultivation and spread of Yiddish is therefore the cornerstone of Jewish survival. Yiddish is not a tool that is losing its usefulness as the union leaders contend, but a vital instrument for Jewish self-expression and national salvation. Backed by survivalists of all sorts in the ranks of labor, Zhitlowsky initiated a campaign for the establishment of Jewish secularist schools with Yiddish as the language of instruction.

Labor Zionists were the first to embark upon a program of Jewish secular education. They were a small minority in the Jewish labor movement at the time they founded their first school in 1910. That they were able to surmount all difficulties and overcome the opposition of the official trade union and socialist leadership was a tribute to the persuasiveness of Zhitlowsky, Joel Entin, and other intellectuals in survivalist Jewish socialism, as well as to the determination of the newly arrived Jewish workers who dedicated themselves to the creation of a base of operations for modern Jewish culture in America.

But things were also stirring in the Workmen's Circle, the fraternal order which with the Forward Association and the United Hebrew Trades constituted the trinity that guided the Jewish labor movement in this country. Bundists and non-Zionist or anti-Zionist nationalists joined the Workmen's Circle en masse and bored from within in the direction of a more positive attitude toward Jewish cultural effort. Zhitlowsky also became a member of the Workmen's Circle and attacked that bastion of cosmopolitanism both from within and without. Pivotal in that attack was the demand that the Workmen's Circle enter the field of Jewish education by opening schools of its own. The "Old Guard" fiercely resisted the demand on grounds of practical considerations and ideational consistency. On the practical level the proposition was advanced that the Workmen's Circle, although one hundred percent Jewish in its membership, was officially not a Jewish organization. On the ideational level there was the old argument that socialists must not engage in undertakings of a religio-nationalist character. Neither position, however, could be maintained at the time of the First World War with that degree of certainty and finality with which the leadership of the Jewish labor movement brushed aside survivalist demands in previous years. Under pressure by Yiddishist groups inside the Workmen's Circle and the Labor Zionist groups outside it, the "Old Guard" was forced to give ground. It was routed in 1916 when a national convention of the order decided to promote the establishment of Workmen's Circle schools based on the Yiddish language and socialist aspiration.

There was for some years still enough opposition to the new venture to dampen the enthusiasm of its proponents and to give the Workmen's Circle schools a somewhat negative motivation. As formulated in the report submitted by the Educational Committee of the National Executive Committee to the 1916 convention, Workmen's Circle schools were necessary because:

> . . . the Talmud Torah cultivates only religion and, more often than not, also fanaticism of which we would like our children to be free. And the Labor Zionist schools give the children an ultra-nationalist and, for the most part, even openly Zionist education. . . .
>
> We do not want our children to receive either a religious or a Zionist education, but a free Jewish education.

What that "free Jewish education" was to represent was not stated. That it had very little Jewish substance, judged by present standards, is evidenced by the fact that as late as 1920 a national convention formulated the program of the Workmen's Circle schools in the following terms:

> 1. To tie the Jewish working child to the Jewish working class . . .
>
> 2. To inculcate in the Jewish child a sense of justice, love for freedom and reverence for the fighters for liberty . . .
>
> 3. To develop in the child an appreciation of beauty . . .
>
> 4. To stimulate in the child a lofty idealism and a striving for great deeds . . .

Not a word here about strengthening Jewish group life or about creating conditions for meaningful Jewish survival.

There was still another trend in the secularist school movement, the one known as the Sholem Aleichem Shulen which have combined into the Sholem Aleichem Folk Institute in 1918. The leadership of these schools—the first was founded in 1913—came from the camp of non-Zionist Jewish nationalism. It was strongly Yiddishist but not nearly as antireligious as most of the leaders of the Workmen's Circle. The Sholem Aleichem Schools crystallized their views on Jewish survival in a program adopted in 1927, point three of which read:

> The language of our environment is Yiddish; its culture is the modern Yiddish culture. It does not regard religion as the cornerstone of our spiritual life. It sees in the Jewish religious customs only a partial product of our age-long creativeness. Hebrew and those parts of Jewish creativity which are tied up with Hebrew (Aramaic) belong to our national cultural treasure which we evaluate from an objective historical point of view.

The three types of schools which constitute the secularist trend in American Jewish education kept matters of faith out of their curriculum. There were differences of opinion, however, in their assessment of the value of religion to Jewish survival. The divergencies have remained although all schools have since changed their theories and practices and came closer to a consensus on Jewish education than existed at the time they were organized.

IV

The Labor Zionist schools, now known as Folk Shulen and sponsored by the Farband-Labor Zionist Order, Poale Zion Organization, and Pioneer Women, were the first to realize that Jewish education could not be totally severed from Jewish religious tradition. As early as 1914 Hayim Lieberman read a paper at the first national conference of the Labor Zionist Schools in which he insisted that for the schools "to play hide-and-seek with religion was impossible." How, he asked, could we explain to our children Jewish otherness if we do not initiate them into an understanding of Jewish religion? Although roundly scolded by Zhitlowsky, who accused him of introducing reaction into progressive Jewish education, he was not without success in bringing about reforms in the Labor Zionist schools. The 1914 conference passed a resolution which stated in part:

> National radical education must instill in the children a sound view on Jewish religion which should be approached from a

cultural historical standpoint. The teachers should endeavor to present to the children the national-ethical and poetic aspect of Jewish religion.

Today, Labor Zionist schools do not apologize for their affirmative approach to religion. They consider the teaching of the Bible in the original and the observance of certain Jewish religious practices an indispensable requisite in Jewish education. The Sholem Aleichem Folk Schools do not go so far, but they too have veered away from their former neutralism and now include a number of Jewish rituals in their curriculum.

Even the Workmen's Circle schools have changed with the times. Alongside the Folk Shulen and the Sholem Aleichem schools, they give tangible recognition to Bar Mitzvah and celebrate Jewish holidays both in classroom and in adult education programs.

Thus we see the three school systems arriving at a program of Jewish secularism that has practically abandoned the old secularist ideology which was based on varying degrees of irreligion. Since these schools, more than any other institution, reflect the position of the secularist movement as a whole, it is necessary to examine the reasons which have brought them around to their present conception of Jewish values. These reasons can be grouped under three main headings: (1) sociological factors that have changed the structure of the Jewish community in this country; (2) the growing Americanization of the Jewish population; (3) the bankruptcy of secularist ideology as a philosophy of Jewish living.

V

Technological advancement in this country has wrought havoc with the Marxian prediction, accepted by practically all Jewish socialist groups at the time of their formation, that the middle classes would in time disappear and leave the working class in the majority of the population. In the country as a whole and much more so among American Jewry the exact opposite is taking place. The Jewish community is becoming more middle class and less proletarian every day, and a program based on the slogan "the Jewish working child to the Jewish working class" would be an anachronism—the more so in view of the fact that individual Jewish workers in the United States, of whom there are still hundreds of thousands, no longer form a Jewish labor movement. It would, therefore, be impossible for Jewish schools to continue on a narrow class basis. If they are to exist at all, they must fit into the new socioeconomic framework of the Jewish population and flow as a tributary to the general

Jewish educational system which has as its aim the perpetuation of the Jewish community. This truth has by this time been recognized by all those who are actively engaged in promoting modern Jewish culture.

One factor should be singled out from among the many that have altered the complexion of the Jewish community, and that is the growing Americanization of the Jewish population. The word "Americanization" is used here in its most literal sense—in the sense that some seventy-five percent of American Jewry is today of native birth. The American-born Jew simply cannot conceive of a Jewish identification in which Jewish religion is completely missing. It is incomprehensible to him first because he cannot separate his Jewishness from some rootedness in the Jewish faith, and second because he sees all other Americans placed in some religious frame of reference. The introduction of various religious rituals into the secular Jewish schools proceeds at a rate that stands in direct proportion to the enrollment of children from native American homes.

It would be wrong, however, to attribute the changed attitudes in the secularist schools solely to considerations of expediency. The fact is that the leaders of Jewish secularism have come to realize that they cannot carry on without the use of some sustaining values from the residue of Jewish religious tradition. Even Zhitlowsky sensed it in his less argumentative moments. In a work titled *The National Poetic Rebirth of Jewish Religion*, published in 1911, he extolled the virtue and beauty of a number of religious institutions which he felt had meaning not alone to the Jew but to others as well. He wrote in that work:

> If the branch called "religion" should ever wither away and fall off the cultural tree of mankind—something I cannot possibly conceive—there will still be left in the possession of man the noblest heritage in the form of the finest and most exalted feelings . . . even the darkest religion has its bright side, to which should be credited the fact that it has taught the human soul to sense holiness and the infinite.

The above lines were written at a time when the ideological struggles between Zionist and anti-Zionist socialists revolved around Palestine and problems of Jewish life in the Diaspora. In relation to America they were practically all Galut-nationalists in that they all ascribed a nationality status to the Jewish community after the fashion of the relationships that existed in Eastern Europe. Again we must turn to Zhitlowsky for elucidation of this view. America, he maintained, was not a melting pot but a chaotic entanglement of various cultural strands of which only one, the Anglo-Saxon, had unrestricted opportunity for normal development and expansion. The principles of democracy required that the other strands, rather than losing their identity or getting into each other's way, also be given *lebensraum*. Jews were entitled to a spot in this arrangement, and it was up to them to equip themselves economically and culturally to occupy and hold the spot. While Zhitlowsky could not gain general acceptance of his autonomist economic notions, he persuaded most nationalist Jewish socialists to follow him in matters pertaining to Jewish culture.

The view that Jews could or would constitute a nationality in the United States with Yiddish as its vernacular and secular Jewish culture as the basis of its group cohesiveness could be maintained only so long as the Jewish immigrant community represented an enclave, as it were, in American society. When this view became shaky, the theory of cultural pluralism was seized as a crutch to support it. But to no avail: the whole ideological super-structure erected by Zhitlowsky and others collapsed beyond repairs after the First War, pulling down with it the last remnants of secularist ideology. The survivalist elements within the Jewish labor movement have been compelled to come around to a position regarding the relationships between Jewish religion and Jewish peoplehood that approximated the secularism of American democracy. The latter, it should be pointed out again, was based on cooperation with religion in clearly defined areas.

VI

Viewed historically, secularist ideology as defined in this essay proved to be a culturally sterile episode in Jewish labor history. Neither atheism nor irreligion has produced a single literary work of enduring significance despite the success they enjoyed from time to time during the early stages of the Jewish socialist movement. One cannot find an important Jewish poet or novelist who has ever been inspired by the irreligious notions entertained by the proponents of secularist ideology in this country. The great Yiddish literature, probably the most important achievement of immigration from Eastern Europe, has from the beginning been secular in spirit, not secularistic. Insofar as secularism did not represent a complete break with Jewish religious tradition, it has created values that will forever enrich Jewish culture here, in the State of Israel, and in other lands.

1961

Notes on the Melting Pot

by Hayim Greenberg

Translated by Marie Syrkin

Karl Kautsky, the great exponent of Marxism, once took up the cudgels on behalf of the Jews, to answer certain uncomplimentary assertions made by Werner Sombart, in his famous work *Jews and Modern Capitalism*. In an article entitled "Race and Judaism" published in 1915 in *Die Neue Zeit*, Kautsky, paying us many compliments, assured us that our historic martyrdom was bound to come to an end as soon as mankind progressed toward a better future. That end, as he saw it, was Nirvana. Israel would find its salvation by dissolving like sugar in a cup of tea.

"Once lawlessness and persecution of the Jews have ended," the Marxist prophet comforted our people, "they will then of themselves cease to exist as an entity. . . . We shall not be able to say that we have passed out of the Middle Ages as long as Judaism exists in our midst. To the extent that Judaism begins to disappear, both the world and the Jews will be better off. The result will be the rise of a higher type of human being. Ahasuerus, the wandering Jew, will at last have found his paradise of rest. He will live on in the memory of humanity as the greatest martyr of history, as one whose reward at the hands of mankind for all the blessings he bestowed upon it had been brutality."

Kautsky was incomparably kinder to the Jews than Karl Marx, for whom Judaism was synonymous with social corruption and evil. And yet the only solace that he could offer us was the promise of extinction, and in later generations, encomiums in history-books. Banish all your cares about the future, oh, poor, suffering men; rest assured that you shall some day have an elaborate funeral—or at least a monument with a poetic epitaph inscribed in gold.

234

Kautsky's "philosemitic" treatise came to my mind, when I read a review by Pearl Buck of a two-volume book on the Jews of China published by the University of Toronto. In the paragraphs she wrote on the work in a monthly magazine, Miss Buck, though disclaiming any special knowledge in that field, does arrive at certain general conclusions about the Jews and sees a lesson in the fact that China today has no Jews and no Jewish problem. The large Jewish community which once lived in China is now almost completely extinct, not because it has been physically exterminated in the European fashion, but because China has been more humane and more tolerant than the Christian nations of the West. The Chinese did not persecute the Jews; so the Jews, of their own free will, became submerged, not only culturally, but also socially and biologically.

Pearl Buck, a great admirer of Chinese civilization, believes that America ought to learn from that experiment with the Jews in the great country of the Mongols. Let Americans desist from discriminating against Jews, and the Jews will of themselves dissolve as an ethnic group, leaving no traces behind them.

The greatest ideal which a certain type of liberalism holds out for us is still one of painless death.

These days, there are even some Zionists among my acquaintances who object to the inclusion of America in the *Galut*. They are shocked to hear that term, which means exile, applied to American Jewry. To put God's country on the map of Jewish homelessness, they argue, is an insult to America and a misrepresentation of the position of American Jewry. It is true that Polish Jews live (or rather *lived*) in Galut, and the same is true of Hungarian, Rumanian, German, and other Jews; and when no one is around, they will even admit that Soviet Russia lies in the *Galut* zone, but not the United States. Latterly they have been using a special term to designate the socio-political character of America in relation to the Jews. By the grace of God and George Washington, we, the Jews of America, are said to be living not in *Galut*, but in *Tefutza*. This Hebrew term, denoting dispersion, is pronounced in such accents as to carry overtones of meaning like expansion, growth, and prosperity.

The Italian who sells newspapers in my neighborhood is naturally uninformed about this disputation among Jewish intellectuals. He may or may not look upon himself as an exile from Italy, and nostalgia for his Sicilian village may or may not be strong; but he lives in America and knows that his Jewish customers ought to be treated with proper "delicacy." When a man buys an English

and a Jewish newspaper from him, the vendor, scrupulously observing the ethics of his profession, quickly wraps the Jewish paper
inside the English, making the former invisible, and so inoffensive
to the eye.

The other day his thirteen-year-old boy sold me my bundle of
papers. But he arranged them so that the *Times* and the *Herald
Tribune* were hidden inside the Yiddish *Forward* and the *Morning
Journal*. The father quickly noticed the offense and, furiously
snatching the papers away from the boy, rearranged them in the
proper way for the "convenience" of his customer. At the same time
he explained to the lad that such a one as he, the offspring of a female canine, far from being of any benefit to the business, was
merely an affliction on one's anatomy. Clearly the Italian who sells
newspapers in my neighborhood operates on the theory that American Jews live in *Galut*.

Some time ago a well-known United States judge tried to ex-
pound to me the theory of *Tefutza*, or Felicitous Dispersion. I did
not argue the matter. Congenital inertia prevented me from engaging in polemics on an over-discussed subject. But if one could
debate by proxy, I should gladly delegate the newsman in my neighborhood to dispute with the judge. He does not see well when it
comes to the printed page (even in his native Italian), but in other
respects he is not blind at all. In fact, he is quite perspicacious.

The Greek restaurant-owner in Atlantic City sat at my table, watching with hospitable pleasure while I drank the small cup of Turkish
coffee and nibbled my *rahat-lukum*. The bridge between us was a
gastronomic one. In America, he said, he seldom meets real con-
noisseurs. When he heard that I was ready at any time for a dish of
Greek *tuffteli*, he beamed even more: he sensed in me a man after
his own heart. *Tuffteli* was not a small matter. . . . His mother was
once a cook for Venizelos, who could not find enough words to
praise her art in making *tuffteli*. If I only should come to visit at his
home, he said, he would show me a picture of Venizelos with an
inscription, a present his mother had once received from her great
master. . . .

I thought of the large placards I saw three years ago, "Get
Americanized—Drink Coca-Cola." I asked my host whether he had
not in all these years accustomed himself to American foods. No, he
said, he could not get used to them at all. "Their" dishes have no
taste and "their" drinks make one sick. He added that even his
children could not take "their" stuff.

I asked him what he meant when he said his children were

"Americanized"; don't they feel any longer that they are Greek? My host thought for a moment, looking far away into invisible distances and heaved a quiet, deep sigh:

"My children, dear friend, are *chulemos.*"

That was farther than my erudition in modern Greek went. I asked him the meaning of the word *chulemos.* It turned out that in the mountainous region of Greece from which he hailed, the peasants use such as expression for ducklings hatched by hens from ducks' eggs. They are your own, it would seem, yet they are strangers to you and sometimes they are downright distasteful.

"What is going to become of them I don't know. Many times I get such a gnawing feeling at my heart, so that I would readily leave everything here and run away with my wife and children back to Greece or to Macedonia. Let them grow up to be shepherds or swineherds and go around in rags, as long as they are merry and there is some fun in their life. All week, things are not so bad. I am busy, they are busy at school, and the time passes. But when Sunday comes, they don't know what to do with themselves. Especially the oldest son; he is sixteen years old. The younger ones we take along to church every Sunday morning. We have a place of worship of our own here. It's a small building, but neat and pretty, with a few beautiful icons that were once brought from Constantinople. We beg our eldest boy to come along with us, but it's years now since we have been able to induce him to come. He says he is bored, why should he sit there and yawn? You see, our prayers are all in Greek and the priest insists on preaching in Greek, and my Theodoros has forgotten how to speak his mother tongue, and he can't read the prayer-book either. It hurts me. So while we are at church he loafs on the boardwalk all by himself. . . . My mind is not at ease: what's going to happen to him when he grows up? And what's going to become of the younger ones? Without God, without religion, without a *basilica*—you know how many gangsters have grown up in America on account of that? . . . So one day I took heart and said to my Theodoros: 'I'll tell you what, my son. Here, only two or three blocks away from us there is another church, a Presbyterian one. I don't know what that means, but, after all, they too are Christians, they believe in God and pray to Him and read out of the Scriptures. Go over there,' I said, 'everything there is in English, you won't be bored.' Next Sunday he went to the Presbyterians. He came back in high spirits; he even brought home a tune from there—some old English hymn I think it was. So I think to myself—all right, let it be that way, even if it is not our own, as long as he does not grow up without a faith and a church, like a wild nettle in the field. But the

Sunday after, he came back home upset and irritated. . . . He would not eat, and lay down to sleep in the middle of the day. No matter how much we kept asking him, it did no good; he was as mute as the wall. Not till evening did we manage to get a few words out of him, which I can't make out to this day: *I don't belong*. . . The devil knows what that means. No mater how many times we ask him to tell us what happened to him in church, all we get out of him is, 'I don't belong, that's all'."

The two of use were silent for a few minutes. The restaurant owner, after one of those coughs which help to overcome hesitation, quickly asked me: "And how is it with you, the Jews?"

It is of little importance what I replied. It was commonplace.

On the way to my hotel I though of only one thing: "What would be the Jewish equivalent of *chulemos?*"

1944

V

The Holocaust

Like an absolute shadow of darkness, the holocaust has loomed over contemporary Jewish life in the United States, in Israel, wherever Jews still live. The victims of Hitler managed somehow to leave behind them voluminous accounts of their martyrdom, though none is more authoritative and stirring than the diary kept by Emmanuel Ringelblum, a Jewish communal leader in Warsaw who died during the heroic ghetto uprising. From this remarkable document we have excerpted some pages in which Ringelblum, shortly before his death, tries to come to terms with the horror of the ghetto experience. Complementing Ringelblum's diary is another record by Michael Zylberberg. Zylberberg wrote his diary in 1943-44, but it was only twenty years later that friends of his discovered it in a Warsaw ruin and sent it to him in London, where he has lived since the war.

In the Warsaw Ghetto

by Emmanuel Ringelblum

Translated by Jacob Sloan

26/JULY–DECEMBER, 1942

They Escaped from the Wagons!
Those who had experience.
Young men.
One [young man] escaped two times—organized eight "spring-ers"—people who escaped extermination in Oswiecim by springing out of the railroad wagons taking them there.

Resistance
The Jew from the Small Ghetto—who grabbed a German by the throat. The Other was shot—went bersek and shot thirteen Jews in the courtyard (Panska or Twarda Street).—The Jew from Na-lewki Street who tore a rifle out of a Ukrainian guard's hand, and fled.

The role the youth played—the only ones who remained on the battlefield [were the] romantic phantasiasts—Samuel—couldn't survive the tragedy of the Ghetto—the decisions by the [various] factions involved in the resistance—the attempt at [setting the Ghetto on] fire—the [resisters'] appeals of the 6th of September for the populace to resist deportation regarded [in the Ghetto] as [Nazi] provocation. Attempt to assassinate Szerynski.[1]

The groups of porters who had lost their families and dreamed of revenge—[the people who] offered money to avoid deportation

[1] Head of the Jewish police in the Ghetto.

—the idea of using coal gas in defense against the Jewish police—
partisans—diversionary acts.

Oct. 15

Why?
Why didn't we resist when they began to resettle 300,000 Jews from
Warsaw? Why did we allow ourselves to be led like sheep to the
slaughter? Why did everything come so easy to the enemy? Why
didn't the hangmen suffer a single casualty? Why could 50 S.S. men
(some people say even fewer), with the help of a division of some
200 Ukrainian guards and an equal number of Letts, carry the
operation out so smoothly?

The shops as traps—They took the best specialists away—"a
couple of porters" laughed—they were taken away—the professionals were taken away. They looked at their hands, *clean palms.*
Office employees taken away . . . only wearing work clothes—wearing slippers. Accompanied on the way [to the Umschlagplatz] by
Ukrainians—they kept shooting.

Selection for deportation in the street among whole blocks—at
first, on the basis of working papers, later on the basis of appearance
(people dyed their gray hair).

They shaved off all the beards—tore off all the frock coats, ear
locks. The street dead all day, except for after the barricade[2] and
from five in the morning to seven—the movement from one street
to another, where there had already been a barricade. But the
Others kept barricading the same neighborhood day after day.—The
Jewish agents informed the Others about the populace's mood,
about the hideout methods.

The role the shop owners played in the barricades—their cooperation with the S.S.—how they fooled people, for example, [the
shop owner] Toebbens at 65 Niska Street. He said he wanted to
avoid a barricade, so he took away all the workers' laundry.

Jewish [work] directors helped catch the illegals,[3] for example
at Hallman's shop.

The Umschlagplatz—What It Looked Like
The heroic nurses—the only ones who saved people from deportation without [asking for] money. Szmerling[4]—the hangman with
the whip.

[2] Streets were barricaded to prevent any Jew from escaping the selection for deportation.
[3] Those who had no work permits.
[4] Commanding the Jewish police at the Umschlagplatz.

The scenes when the wagons were loaded—the industriousness of the Jewish police—the tearing of parents from their children, wives from their husbands, Rabbi Kanal, Lubliner.

The shooting on the spot of those who tried to escape through holes in the Wall at night—the exemption of people who pretended to be doctors. Nurses' headkerchiefs saved hundreds of professionals, employees of the Jewish Council.

The Great Pursuit—Szmerling currying the Others' favor.

More than once he tore the badges off policemen who had saved Jews from the Umschlag.

Faithful executor of Their orders—introduced a check of the nurses because they allowed people to escape without paying money.

Great grafter—took more than 100 zlotys per head. Most of those who were exempted—bought off the watch at the gate.—The police made enormous sums.

["The Thirteen"] Special Service made a lot of money exempting people too; com. [munity] institutions set up a fund to save the professionals.

The tragedy of those seized two, three, and five times—the mother who wouldn't go without her child—the husband who wouldn't go without his wife, etc.—and afterward they all went in the same wagon—hundreds of families went to the Umschlag together because of the children.

Because the quota wasn't met, the Germans seized people on the street, drove them directly into wagons, not to the Umschlag but straight into the wagons—12,000 killed during the resettlement.

The Pot on Niska Street
The 6th of September—the cruelty. In the middle of the night Lejkin was instructed to have all the Jews in the quadrangle bounded on one side by Gesia, on another by Smocza, on a third by Niska, and on the fourth by Zamenhofa to select [deportees] and round up illegals—Massacre of 25,000 people, perhaps even more. Of the barracks that were emptied out (everyone ordered out of the barracks) two or three houses set aside for each shop, most of them in the country—some shops' [workers] got back into their apartments that day—others not till the next day, or the day after.

"Ah, but we had a fine pot!" said Witasek, who directed the resettlement operation.

The tens of thousands who remained on Niska Street—the continual slaughtering—seventy people killed in one apartment on Wolynska Street—in two days, 1,000 people killed, taken to the graveyard—hundreds killed in the street during the selections, all forced to kneel on the pavement [to be killed].

Hundreds and thousands of people lay in their hiding places all week, without water (a water main burst), without food.

Hoffman's shop consists of two industries. One is reworking old things collected in Germany. The things are washed, mended, and then sent back.

Illegals. "Illegals" are those people who do not have [work card] numbers, people who, according to the law, should have been on the Umschlagplatz, and yet are still alive. How many there are of this kind nobody knows. There are various estimates. Many people place the number of illegals at 7,000, others estimate 10,000 and even 15,000. The fact is, they *are!*

Who are they? A large number are members of the family of "legal persons"—mostly the police, Jewish Council officials, etc.

The illegals also consist of officials of the Council, or of the YYGA, who were let go, but did not go to the Umschlagplatz; instead they went into hiding, and now they huddle close to their former colleagues for protection.

And then there is a third category—"everyday Jews," who simply hid out and are still in hiding. They pay off the Work Guard and live at home. Many of the illegals are people who worked in shops that were given up, who managed to save themselves from the Umschlagplatz. Shops of this kind were Hans Miller's, where many Jewish artists, actors, and others perished. There are houses, such as 35, 37, 41, etc., Nalewki Street, which are entirely occupied by hundreds of illegals.

The problem of offering relief to the illegals is becoming daily more pressing. The ex-officials among them receive a ration of soup and bread.

How the Selection Took Place
In the Jewish Council, around 3,000 employees,[5] elsewhere [in other community institutions] entire departments were sent to the Umschlag.—At Hallmans' [shop] 700 were numbered off and [exempted] on the spot; the remaining thirty carpenters with their wives and children were taken away.—At the brush factory, 1,200 were numbered off [and exempted], the rest sent away, mechanically, including the shop where the *chalutzim* worked, valuable human material, the young.

[5] At one time, the Jewish Council had as many as 5,000 employees.

Thousands of people who had managed to save their lives all the time by staying in their hiding places went to the Niska [quadrangle], because they believed they would be leaving the Ghetto for good.

The goal [of the Niska Pot]: to get the secret Jews—the ones in hiding—to come out.[It] succeeded. Tens of thousands taken in the Niska Pot.

Prehistory of the Resettlement
Letter from Lublin [warning about]—Szamek Grayer[6]—about 60,000 Jews [to be left] in Warsaw, about a work Ghetto [to be set up in Warsaw]—letter from Wlodawa about the [sacrificial] "altar" being set up in the Warsaw neighborhood—the rumor about Pelcowizne—Kohn and Heller's warnings—the S.S. threat to stifle bloodily those who spread these rumors. . . .

The arrival of [Oscar] Lotisz[7]—the readying of special wagons to Treblinki.

How the Blocks Were Set Up
The slaughter at Schultz's [shop]—Nowolipie Street [the site of] the first German barricade—They took thousands of people—gave them half a day to move—the same true at Toebbens'. The activities of the "Jew boys," who proposed such plans, Hallman's humane behavior—negotiated with the House Committees for the gradual yielding of apartments.

The Blocks as Special Ghettos
[With their] own bakeries, drug stores, grocery stores, shoe stores, barbers, even synagogues—separate towns, even to the point of local patriotism—when it came to fund raising.

The hyenas of the shops—workers had to pay money to get into a shop—money for every registration [of the shop's workers].

The work the shops were supposed to do during the barricades —[shops] sprang up quickly, had no orders, had no raw material, [workers] left the factories, except when the Germans came—the same true of the brush factories.

The shops as a means of looking after the workers' families—at first the families were taken to the shops to spend the night there [and avoid being picked up for deportation at home]—hence the

---

[6] Jewish Gestapo agent from Lublin sent to Warsaw to help in the extermination.

[7] The Lett collaborator, to help in the extermination.

idea of blocks—self-contained living and working areas—the slaughter on Nowolipie Street.

Shameful document cited by the Jewish Council about the rumors that there would be a resettlement [of Jews from the Warsaw Ghetto] to the East.

[At the same time] the Council's work office knew the resettlement meant death.

The suicide of Czerniakow[8]—too late, a sign of weakness—should have called for resistance—a weak man.

Insecurity, Unclarity of the Situation
Deadline. The Damocles sword of extermination hangs constantly over the heads of the Warsaw Jews. Their fate is tied to that of the shops. So long as the shops have orders, the Jews have the right to live. But it so happens that not all of the shops have long-term orders. Not long ago (mid-October), Schultz's received orders and raw material [sufficient to last] until April—there was universal rejoicing. People drank toasts, threw parties, and the like. But an early deadline hangs over some of the shops. Included in this category is a shop that is one of the most valuable, socially speaking, the O.B.W. shops, whose deadline ended the 20th of October. Eventually, the deadline was extended another thirty days. Put yourself through an effort of the imagination in the minds of those people whose fate is linked with that of the shops. If the shops go out of existence, *they* lose the right to live. They become people without [work card] numbers, without homes, without food-supply cards.

The Signs of Modern Slaves
    1. Numbered and stamped.
    2. Live in barracks—without their wives.
    3. Wives and children removed, because slaves don't require families.
    4. Walk in crowds, not individually.
    5. Beaten and terrorized at work.
    6. Inhuman exploitation (agreement at Schultz's [?]) like coolies.
    7. Ban on organization of any kind.
    8. Ban on any form of protest or sign of dissatisfaction.

[8] The head of the Jewish Council committed suicide on July 24, 1942, after a visit from two S.S. officers, who demanded that the daily quota of those resettled be raised from 5,000 to 7,000 and eventually to 10,000.

9. Every slave dependent for his life on his master and the [master's] Jewish assistant. At any moment a man can be sent to the Umschlagplatz.

10. The murderous discipline, and the sending of workers to forced [labor] camps because of lateness as happened at Schultz's.

11. Compulsion to work, even [when worker is sick] with temperature.

12. Worse off than slaves, because *they* must look after their own food.

13. Confiscation of property from a dead worker's family, because the right of inheritance has been abolished.

14. Locked inside the residential block.

15. Ban on leaving your apartment and walking in the street after work hours.

16. Limitation of personal freedom, of movement.

17. *Worse than slaves,* because the latter knew they would remain alive, had some hope to be set free. The Jews are *morituri*—sentenced to death—whose death sentence [has been] postoned indefinitely, or has been passed.

18. The sick and the weak are not needed, so ambulatory clinics, hospitals, and the like have been liquidated.

Communication

Every shop is a unit in itself; by the decree of [the 29th of] October, one may not leave the shop's bounds. This is true of the Ghetto, too. Persons caught in the street without a pass are sent to the Umschlagplatz. After work hours (seven in the morning until six or five in the evening in some shops), one can move about somewhat more freely—by attaching oneself to a group that is going from work to its residence block, or to an outside work detail on its way home—but such a group is usually under close supervision, particularly if it is a small one. Individual Jews may not move about the streets.

A second way of being out in the street during the workday hours is to ride in a carriage. They are not bothered, and this is held to be a safe method of passage.

Treblinka—The news about the gravediggers (Rabinowicz, Jacob),[9] the Jews from Stok who escaped from the wagons . . . loaded with gold and foreign currency—the unanimous description of the "bath," the Jewish gravediggers with yellow patches on their knees.—The method of killing: gas, steam, electricity.

[9] An escapee from Treblinka, who was the informant.

The news about Treblinka brought back by the investigators sent out by the families of those deported there.[10]—The story about the tractors: According to one version, tractors plow under the ashes of the burned Jews. According to another version, the tractors plow the earth and bury the corpses there [by covering them over].

Treblinka as the Jewish populace sees it—they become aware of the recent extermination.

The Jews from Western Europe have no idea what Treblinka is. They believe it to be a work colony, and on the train ask how far it is to the "industrial factory" of Treblinka. If they knew that they were going to their death, they would certainly put up some resistance. They arrive carrying brand-new valises.

Women, children—Shops without women—the breaking up of families—children, whole families annihilated—[parents who] refused to leave their children; husbands who refused [to leave] their wives—the father who wraps his child in a coat to conceal his presence and takes him along to the resettlement. The little criminals who must hide in a room for months on end—the face of a child grimacing with fear at a blockade.

The tragedy of families: thousands of men without wives, men who have remained alive and don't know what they are living for—in general, the tragedy of persons who have lost some thirty members of their family—left all alone in the world—without a purpose in life.

Unhappy the women who had [work card] numbers—depended on them [to be exempted from deportation], and stood in line—those without numbers remained [behind, but] hurried to register their children as errand boys, handwagon pullers—they were all taken away—*men* protected their wives and children.

The heroism of Dr. Korcszak, Koninski, Janowski, refused to leave the children from their home. Korcszak built up the attitude that everyone [including directors of the home] should go to the Umschlag together. There were directors of homes who knew what awaited them at the Umschlagplatz, but held that at a difficult time such as this they could not let the children go alone and must go to their death with them.

The tragedy of parents—the problem of old people—some people poisoned [their elderly] parents—others went to the Umschlagplatz with parents; the home for the aged liquidated—[its

---

[10] In July, 1942, Zygmunt (Frydryck) had been delegated to verify the news about Treblinka. He reached Malkinia, where he met Esrael Wallach, an escaped prisoner from Treblinka, who confirmed the worst reports.

inmates] carried in rickshas to the Umschlag with their valises—
children sacrificed themselves to save their parents, most of the
older generation done away with—many saved in hiding places—
children who didn't [?] protect their parents—in the YYGA—Jewish
Self-Aid Society—there were scores of eighty-year-old cleaning
women.

Most of the old people were lost at the Niska [Street Pot]—
[or when their children were] moving into the new residential
blocks—or are lying in hiding to this day.

Polish organizations combatted and did away with blackmail. Guard
the streetcars.—Pol.[ish] professionals frightened, refuse to accept
any Jew.[ish] friends [for protection] outside of the Jewish elements [belonging to their own profession].

As of the end of October, 150 Jews have been seized [who escaped to] the Other Side. Polish streetcar people's attitude to the
Jews very good. Police assigned to work at the streetcar platforms
allowed them [Jews] to work without permits, received Jews cor-
dially, good relations. The same true of other outside work details
where Jews happened to work alongside Poles.

[Polish] professional colleagues took care of their Jewish associates: Prof. Hirszfeld, Bruno Winawer, etc. [taken care of].

Commerce—Economy. The resettlement produced a great revolution in the economy both of the Ghetto and of the Aryan side of
Warsaw. Certain items became cheap. Clothing, and particularly
linen, was sold at four or five times less than before the resettlement.
. . . Bedding was valueless. Pillow cases were removed, and the red
[comforter] covers and feather stuffing let out. Bedding lies around
in every street, in every courtyard. In some courtyards they set fire
to it. Nor have dishes any value—they're thrown into garbage cans.
This is true of glass and porcelain dishes, as well as tin ones. Beds,
and furniture in general, are worthless. They chop up furniture to
heat apartments with the wood. Linen has value only if it is brand
new. Second-hand or mended linen is worthless and cannot be sold.
A man's suit can be sold for some 300–400 zlotys, i.e., the cost of
2 kilos of ham or butter (1 kilo of butter costs more than 200 zlotys).

The graveyard is an important business center, Christian smugglers coming there. Prices are a little higher there, too. The chief
middlemen between the Ghetto and the Aryan Side of Warsaw
are the workers in the outside details, who take things with them to
[sell on] the Other Side. But commerce with the Other Side has become more difficult lately, because every single work detail is

checked, and they are not permitted to take either money or things with them. There was the case of a gendarme shooting a man in a work detail because he was wearing two pairs of pants—one of which he was going to sell on the Other Side.

Street selling is vigorously combatted by the Germans and their assistants—the Jewish police and the Work Guard. Until a short time ago, the remaining 10 per cent of Warsaw Jews were selling what they had left on Smocza and other streets; now all the selling is going on in the blocks, in homes, and the like. People are busy selling [their last possessions] after work hours.

The Polish police are the most active buyers of Jewish things. The police stations are really commercial agencies where business is transacted all day long. They also purchase gold (35 zlotys a gram as of the end of October), diamonds, foreign currency (a paper dollar is worth 40 zlotys, a gold one 200 zlotys).

Why Were 10 Per Cent of the Jews of Warsaw Allowed to Remain?
Many people have attempted to answer this question, because the answer to a series of fundamental questions hangs on it. How long shall we remain in the Ghetto? How long shall we live? How long shall we survive? When shall we be done away with? The opinion of a large group of perceptive persons is that the motive behind Their allowing 10 per cent of the Jews to remain in Warsaw is not economic but political. It matters little to Them that the Jews are producing, even for the Wehrmacht. Germany, which dominates all Europe, can easily make up the [economic] loss sustained by a deportation of Jews. If They took the economic factor into account at all, They would not so casually have sent thousands of first-class craftsmen to the Umschlagplatz (incidentally, the S.S. are literally searching high and low for Jewish craftsmen now—carpenters, apprentices, and [offering] good work conditions). The same was true in the provinces, where complete cities were cleaned out of Jews, although the entire Jewish population was engaged in working for the Wehrmacht—as for example in Zamoszcz.

The fact remains that, insofar as Jews are concerned, economic criteria do not apply—only political criteria, propaganda. This being so, the question poses itself even more strongly: Why, then, has a "saving remnant" been allowed to remain in Warsaw? The answer is political. If all the Jews were to be cleared out of Warsaw and out of the Government General [of Poland] as a whole, They would lose the Jewish argument. It would be hard for Them then to attribute all their difficulties and failures to the Jews. The Jews have to remain, in keeping with the proverb: "God grant that all your teeth fall out, except one to give you a toothache!"

There is another factor that influences the Germans to allow a handful of Jews to remain in Warsaw for a while. It is world public opinion. They have not publicly acknowledged the massacre of millions of Jews. When 40,000 Lublin Jews were liquidated,[11] the Warsaw newspaper published a news item describing how well off the Jews were in Majdan,[12] how wonderfully They have turned smugglers and fences into "productive elements," living respectable lives in Majdan.

The same is true of Warsaw. They don't want to admit to the world that they have murdered all the Jews of Warsaw, so they leave a handful behind, to be liquidated when the hour strikes twelve— not just for the toothache, but also for the world to see. Hitler will use every means in his power to "free" Europe of all the Jews. Only a miracle can save us from complete extermination; only a speedy and sudden downfall can bring us salvation.

Hence the bitter pessimism dominating the Jewish populace. *Morituri*, that is the best description of our mood. Most of the populace is set on resistance. It seems to me that people will no longer go to the slaughter like lambs. They want the enemy to pay dearly for their lives. They'll fling themselves at Them with knives, staves, coal gas. They'll permit no more blockades. They'll not allow themselves to be seized in the street, for they know that work camp means death these days. And they want to die at home, not in a strange place. Naturally, there will only be a resistance if it is organized, and if the enemy does not move like lightning, as [They did] in Cracow, where, at the end of October, 5,500 Jews were packed into wagons in seven hours one night. We have seen the confirmation of the psychological law that the slave who is completely repressed cannot resist. The Jews appear to have recovered somewhat from the heavy blows they have received; they have shaken off the effects of their experiences to some extent, and they calculate now that going to the slaughter peaceably has not diminished the misfortune, but increased it. Whomever you talk to, you hear the same cry: The resettlement should never have been permitted. We should have run out into the street, have set fire to everything in sight, have torn down the walls, and escaped to the Other Side. The Germans would have

[11] In March and April, 1942.

[12] The camp at Majdanek, where the Jews from Lublin province were sent for extermination.

taken their revenge. It would have cost tens of thousands of lives, but not 300,000. Now we are ashamed of ourselves, disgraced in our own eyes, and in the eyes of the world, where our docility earned us nothing. This must not be repeated now. We must put up a resistance, defend ourselves against the enemy, man and child.

Police

The Jewish police had a very bad name even before the resettlement. The Polish police didn't take part in the forced-work press gangs, but the Jewish police engaged in that ugly business. Jewish policemen also distinguished themselves with their fearful corruption and immorality. But they reached the height of viciousness during the resettlement. They said not a single word of protest against this revolting assignment to lead their own brothers to the slaughter. The police were psychologically prepared for the dirty work and executed it thoroughly. And now people are wracking their brains to understand how Jews, most of them men of culture, former lawyers (most of the police officers were lawyers before the war), could have done away with their brothers with their own hands. How could Jews have dragged women and children, the old and the sick, to the wagons—knowing they were all being driven to the slaughter? There are people who hold that every society has the police it deserves, that the disease—cooperation with the Occupying Power in the slaughter of 300,000 Jews—is a contagion affecting the whole of our society and is not limited to the police, who are merely an expression of our society. Other people argue that the police is the haven of morally weak psychological types, who do everything in their power to survive the difficult times, who believe that the end determines all means, and the end is to survive the war—even if survival is bound up with the taking of other people's lives.

In the presence of such nihilism, apparent in the whole gamut of our society, from the highest to the lowest, it is no surprise that the Jewish police executed the German resettlement orders with the greatest of zeal. And yet the fact remains that most of the time during the resettlement operation the Jewish police exceeded their daily quotas. That meant they were preparing a reserve for the next day. No sign of sorrow or pain appeared on the faces of the policemen. On the contrary, one saw satisfied and happy individuals, well-fed, loaded with the loot they carried off in company with the Ukrainian guards.

Very often, the cruelty of the Jewish police exceeded that of the Germans, Ukrainians, and Letts. They uncovered more than one hiding place, aiming to be *plus catholique que le pape* and so curry favor with the Occupying Power. Victims who succeeded in escaping the German eye were picked up by the Jewish police. I watched the procession to the wagons on the Umschlagplatz for several hours and noted that many Jews who were fortunate enough to work their way toward the spot where the exempted people were standing were forcibly dragged back to the wagons by the Jewish police. Scores, and perhaps hundreds, of Jews were doomed by the Jewish police during those two hours. The same thing happened during the blockades. Those who didn't have the money to pay off the police were dragged to the wagons, or put on the lines going to the Umschlagplatz.

A scene I witnessed at 3 Dzszika Street, opposite the Umschlagplatz, one day when every policeman had to meet a quota of four "heads" (this was several days before the end of the "operation") will remain in my mind *the* symbol for the Jewish police in Warsaw. I saw a Jewish policeman pulling an old woman by the arm to the Umschlagplatz. He had a hatchet on his shoulder. He used the hatchet to break down locked apartment doors. As he approached the Umschlagplatz where the watch was stationed, the policeman shamefacedly took the hatchet off his shoulder and transferred it to his hand. It was the general rule those days to see individual policemen dragging men, women, and children to the Umschlag. They took the sick there in rickshas.

For the most part, the Jewish police showed an incomprehensible brutality. Where did Jews get such murderous violence? When in our history did we ever before raise so many hundreds of killers, capable of snatching children off the street, throwing them on the wagons, dragging them to the Umschlag? It was literally the rule for the scoundrels to fling women on to the Kohn-Heller streetcars, or on to ordinary trucks, by grabbing them by the arms and legs and heaving. Merciless and violent, they beat those who tried to resist. They weren't content simply to overcome the resistance, but with the utmost severity punished the "criminals" who refused to go to their death voluntarily. Every Warsaw Jew, every woman and child, can cite thousands of cases of the inhuman cruelty and violence of the Jewish police. Those cases will never be forgotten by the survivors, and they must and shall be paid for.

Dec. 12

Hatred of the Police

So long as the "operation" was in progress (that was the name for the massacre of the Warsaw Jews), the populace was silent. They allowed themselves to be led to the slaughter like sheep. I know

254   Voices from the Yiddish

that porters from the CENTOS (Children's Aid Society) ware-
houses, who had many a time displayed courage in the face of
danger, allowed themselves to be led off like lambs during the
"operation." The same can be said of most of the men and women
taken to the Umschlag at the time. This will be an eternal mystery—
this passivity of the Jewish populace even toward its own police.
Now that the populace has calmed down somewhat, and they are
reviewing what took place, they are becoming ashamed of having
put up no resistance at all. People remember who was responsible
for the mass slaughter, and conclude that it was the Jewish police
who were the chief culprits; some people go so far as to lay the whole
guilt on the police's shoulders. Now people are taking their revenge.
They pass up no opportunity to remind the Jewish police of their
crime. Every policeman you talk to nowadays acts as innocent as a
newborn babe. *He* never took part in the operation. He was assigned to this or that institution. Or else, if he *was* there, he saved
people from the Umschlag. Others did the seizing, not he. From
these protestations, one would gather that those who seized people
for the Umschlag were themselves deported to various labor camps
or to Treblinka—since none of them are around; we know the truth
is exactly the opposite. It is the hoodlum and criminal element in
the police that has remained among the 300 policemen who are now
on guard duty in the Ghetto, while, on the contrary, the less diligent,
who didn't have enough money for "protection," have gone either to
Treblinka or to camps like those at Lublin.

So the time for soul-searching has come, the time for revenge.
A secret hand did away with Lejkin,[13] the police chief in charge of
the resettlement. The Jewish police are persecuted at every step.
Not only by the Jews—the Poles, too, demonstrate their hatred for
the Jewish police. The ex-Jewish policemen working on the streetcar
platforms are constantly persecuted by the Polish workers. In Rem-
bertow, even German soldiers persecute them. Many shops protested
against hiring policemen. One shop voted to have all former policemen dismissed. I know for a fact that ex-policemen in one outside
work detail wear their caps until they reach the watch at the Ghetto
Wall, because a cap is a sign of importance in the Ghetto. Once
outside the Ghetto, they take their caps off, because they are afraid
of the Polish populace, who hate the Jewish Law and Order Service
for what they did during the resettlement. A man recognized a policeman who had taken away his parents in the street, and attacked

[13] Lejkin was probably assassinated on October 20 by a member of the
Jewish resistance movement.

him. In Hallman's shop the relief committee distributed dole to a sick ex-policeman. The furor against the relief committee cannot be imagined. This happens everywhere—ex-policemen are persecuted at every step.

People keep bringing up instances of the Jewish police's brutality during the resettlement. They tell this story: A Jew was killed at 50 Leszno Street. His body lay there in front of the gate. Two undertakers came along in a wagon to remove the corpse. That day, the police were scurrying around like poisoned rats, because their quota for the day was five "heads." If they didn't meet it, they and their families faced the threat of deportation. Without thinking overlong, the police took away the two undertakers, leaving the corpse to lie untended in the middle of the street. Another incident, that took place at 24 Leszno Street: A sixteen-year-old baker's boy beat up a policeman who was trying to take away the boy's mother. The boy tore the policeman's short coat. He was taken to the courtyard of the police headquarters, and there given twenty-five stripes, as a result of which he died.

Still another, no less horrible, instance: A policeman enters, or rather, to be precise about it, breaks into an apartment. All the tenants are hiding somewhere or other, leaving only a three-month-old baby in his cradle. Without a moment's thought, the policeman calls the German who is supervising the operation in from the courtyard. The German makes a face at being offered such a victim. He beats the policeman up badly and shoots the baby. A number of people have assured me this is true.

There are any number of horrifying stories about the conduct of the Jewish police at the Umschlag. To them, nobody was a person, only a "head" that could be blackmailed. The only way to escape was by buying the police off with money, diamonds, gold, and the like. The price per head varied. At first it was 1,000 or 2,000 zlotys. Later it went up, until it reached 10,000 zlotys per head. The exact sum depended on a complex of subjective and objective factors, into which the Jewish police had sometimes to draw "Yunakes" as partners, as well as the Letts or Ukrainians who were on service in the Umschlagplatz. The Jewish police were without mercy. You could be the most worthy of persons, if you didn't have ransom money, or relatives to pay the asking price, you would be sent away. There are known cases where the police, in addition to money, demanded payment in the form of a woman's body. My friend Kalman Zylberberg knows the badge numbers of the policemen, and the names of the women who paid for freedom with their bodies. The police had a special room in the hospital for this purpose. As a general rule, the police were beside themselves during the resettlement. They were always furious at the recalcitrants who refused to allow themselves to be resettled. The police themselves were continually threatened with being sent to the Umschlag with their wives and children. And then, they were demoralized from before the resettlement. Those seized for the Umschlag, particularly the women, put up resistance. All these things created an impossible situation for the police, who reacted like beasts.

Dec. 14

Hiding Places

Now, in December, 1942, hiding places are very popular. Everyone is making them. Everywhere, in all the shops and elsewhere in the Ghetto, hiding places are being built. Their construction has actually become a flourishing specialized craft. Skilled workers, engineers, etc., are making a living out of it. Hiding places go back many years. People began to hide out when the Germans entered Warsaw, in October, 1939. People hid themselves, hid their goods. On Franciszkanska and Nalewki Streets, cellars were walled up, attics, special rooms, stores of merchandise—because the Germans used to confiscate everything, removing complete truckloads of goods. Even then there were scoundrels who made it their business to knock down the walls of these hiding places. These were the professional informers, who recruited themselves for the job. The majority were porters. They used to uncover stores of goods which the Germans would otherwise never have found. The details of the removal of whole wagons full of leather worth millions from Franciszkanska Street have stuck in my memory. Days on end large military trucks removed this merchandise from the hiding places.

And then people used to hide themselves. In those days, during 1939, 1940, and part of 1941, people would be seized for forced labor almost every day—so the men hid out in the shops, under bench beds, in mezzanines, cubbies, cellars, garrets, etc. Some of the apartments were so arranged that a room could be set off for the men to hide in—usually behind a shop, credenza, or the like. The Germans knew the location of such hideouts, thanks to their Jewish informers, who accompanied them and pointed out the hiding places. Pious Jews, wearing beards and ear locks, used to hide out, too—showing yourself bearded [in the open] was perilous, because there were often Gestapo agents, or just mean Germans, who couldn't bear the sight of an "uncivilized" bearded Jew. They would shave off the offending beard, or just rip it off, skin and all.

During the time when there were blockades, the resettlement

period, hideouts assumed a new importance. People took special pains to build good hiding places, because they had become a matter of life and death. Old folks, children, and women hid out there. The men were not afraid to go to all kinds of selections because they had a chance to get various work certificates and exemption papers.

In those days the hideouts were more refined, better concealed. My family, for example, used to hide out in a subroom in an old house, on the third floor. It consisted of the few steps of another house [?]. Entry was through a trap door in the floor, which the wife of a policeman, who was not afraid of any blockade—policemen were safe at the time—used to cover with a rug and a table on top of it. In another place, they used a secret tannery, specially built into a cellar, for a hideout. A third place used a clandestine grain mill, marvelously disguised. Air-raid shelters were also used as hideouts. In one courtyard the air-raid shelter was underground. Entry was through a trap door, which the men used to cover with boards. In many apartments, people set aside special rooms, masking the entry a number of ways; for example, the entry would be through the next-door kitchen. They used to lift out the tiles to enter. Entry to the sealed-off room would be through the water closet, a trap door in the next room, or in the room above, which would be connected to the hideout by a ladder. In some places the entry would be masked by a movable block of tiles, so that, in case the walls were tapped, there would be no empty hollow spaces. If the hideout was in a cellar, people made sure that it was very far away, in some distant corner, where there were no windows.

These hideouts were given away by accident, very often by a child's crying. I know of a case on Nowolipie Street where several dozen people were hiding in two walled-up rooms. The Ukrainians blockading the house threw a party in the next room. They were about to leave when they heard a child crying. They chopped down the wall and found one of the rooms, with twenty-six people in it. They shot six of them on the spot; the rest bought the Ukrainians off and went to the Umschlagplatz. The second sealed room was not discovered.

In 90 per cent of the cases it was the Jewish police who uncovered the hideouts. First they found out where the hideouts were; then they passed the information along to the Ukrainians and Germans. Hundreds and thousands of people are on those scoundrels' conscience.

After the selections—for deportation or forced work—when things calmed down a bit in the Ghetto, a new chapter in the story of hideouts began. The populace had by this time learned to distrust the Germans. It was obvious that so long as the present system continued there would be a new operation against the Jews sooner or later, and in the end the Ghetto would be liquidated. Two events contributed to the popular refusal to accept the mollifying statements of the Germans at their face value: first, the continuing massacre of Jews in Treblinka and other camps; and second, the fact that 800 people were seized in the shops and deported toward Lublin. Nothing has since been heard of them.

Consequently, the populace has begun to plan how to secure their lives in case of danger. The richer people have begun to cross over to the Other Side. Others, less fortunate, are planning hiding places. During November and December, there was a feverish activity in the construction of new hideouts, differing completely from those built during the summer, during the time of the "operation." In the first place, they had to be usable in cold weather; secondly, they had to be furnished for people to be able to live there months on end. The reasoning was that if all the Jews of Warsaw were to be liquidated, those who had hideouts would go into them and stay there until they were rescued. The new hideouts were built in one of three places: cellars, underground, or on the floor of an apartment. The present hideouts are . . . equipped with gas, electricity, water, and toilets. Some of them cost tens of thousands of zlotys. They contain food supplies sufficient to last for months (preserves, sugar, and the like). Since there is the fear that the Germans might stop the water passage, as they did in a number of the houses where the "wild people" are living, people have stocked up on supplies of distilled water, buried in barrels in the hideouts. Or else, special artesian wells are dug. Of course, only the well-to-do can afford such luxuries. I know of one case where for 3,000 zlotys a water-works man connected the water pipes of a hideout with the water pipes of an Aryan factory, so that the people in the hideout would continue to have water even if the water was shut off in the house.

The Jewish brains that are working on problems of this kind have worked out a brilliant scheme to insure against the shutting off of water. They'll creep out of their hideout at night and set fire to the next house. They say the firemen will have to open the water connections then, and those in the know will take advantage of this to put in a fresh supply of water to last for a time.

Jewish craftsmen have also thought up a way of seeing to it that there is no shortage of gas and electricity—the plan is known supposedly only to them. The idea is to steal gas and electric current from the next house. Naturally, this is only possible when the gas or electricity is cut off in one house, not in the whole street.

Some hideouts are built into apartments. They locate an alcove or room corner and wall it in so that it can't be noticed. The chief trouble with such a hideout is that windows always betray its existence. A few weeks ago, a special police division of the Property Collection Agency[14] came to Warsaw and used this technique: They counted the number of windows on each floor, and then sent that many policemen up to each floor and ordered them to stick out their heads. It was easy to find out whether there were any disguised rooms, and where they were.

As a general rule, walling up windows is the hardest problem. In one courtyard, the tenants concealed the walled-up window of the basement by placing a garbage can in front of it; elsewhere, the window was concealed by steps.

As everyone knows, modern apartment houses are so constructed that all the apartments in the same line have the same layout. Walling up an alcove in one apartment does not provide an adequate hiding place, because it is quite easy to find the same alcove on a higher or lower floor in the same line of apartments. The way out of this dilemma was for all the persons living in the same line to wall up their alcoves. In one house, the residents all walled up one corner of a room, built an entry through a bakery oven, and put in a passageway from one floor to the next through a chain of ladders pushed through holes cut into the floors. An impressive hideout like that accommodates up to sixty persons.

The most important problem in any hideout is masking the entry. Every day sees the invention of new solutions, each cleverer than the previous one. What is involved is seeing to it that when the German detective taps the walls, he doesn't find any empty space. On the other side of one walled-up room, tiles were pasted into a frame, and the whole thing was pushed aside when people wanted to enter the hideout. In another place, the entry was through a water closet, in a third through a bakery oven.

Communication with the outside world is another basic problem. Arrangements are made in advance with a Christian, who looks after the needs of the Jews in the hideout on the days when they go into hiding. A few shops have hideouts so built that they have an underground connection with the Other Side. This [of course] is

[14] The S.S. Werterfassung agency, which confiscated the property of Jews who had been deported from the Ghetto.

only possible where the shops border on the Aryan Side. Building that kind of a tunnel is one of the hardest things to do. A good deal of earth has to be dug up and removed surreptitiously. This is far from easy; consequently, the diggers make it a rule that only those who have worked on the tunnel may use the hideout.

It is said that Germans have used hounds to search houses from which Jews have been driven out, to ferret out the hidden survivors. Thus far, no way has been found to put the hounds off the trace. Lysol is said to be effective. But there is danger that, smelling lysol, the Germans will know that Jews are in hiding in that particular house.

Besides supplying Jewish craftsmen with a source of livelihood, the hideouts have become a business for gangs that sell places in them for thousands of zlotys. This includes food supply.

There is altogether too much talk about hideouts—more talk than action. The Jewish Gestapo agents know about them, so, inevitably, the Germans do, too. There was even an informer in Hallman's shop who informed on a large hideout there. The argument runs that if the Germans know about Ghetto hideouts, they have lost their value. So, a few people maintain, the best thing to do is to build a hideout on the Other Side. Find a Christian family willing to rent a large apartment, wall up a room where Jews can be concealed, and, naturally, give the Christian family proper financial satisfaction. But the populace is afraid that at the crucial terrifying moment the Germans will discover some clever way of turning to nought all our efforts at self-rescue. Whether this is true or not, only the future will tell.

1952

A Warsaw Diary

by Michael Zylberberg

Faith

It is spring, 1943. I have now been acting the part of a Catholic among Catholics for a number of months. Unwittingly one grows further and further away from one's previous environment. It is interesting, however, that right now I see in my mind's eye all the Jewish characters of former times. Particularly the religious Jews, who, till the last, believed that there was some order, some pattern in life, that everything was not chaos. They felt there was a deep meaning in their suffering and death which would be perpetuated in Jewish history. These people seem more real to me every day. I feel that they accompany me wherever I go, indoors or out, even to the church which I visit so frequently.

Of course any religious Jew who saw the sufferings of his people was tormented by doubts. He saw the sorrows of the children and the old and the ill constantly around him. Often, in this nightmare, one felt this to be a world of neither laws nor judges, and one often felt compelled to ask one's self, "We lived by the Torah, and is this the reward?" The religious Jews tried to dispel their doubts by strengthening their beliefs, which were even stronger, perhaps, than in pre-war years. The Yeshivot were full to overflowing with eager students at that time.

As the situation deteriorated daily, so the religious Jews sought hope in the supernatural, turning to a new cabbalistic[1] interpreta-

[1] *Cabbala*—the major work of medieval Jewish mysticism.

tion of words from which a shred of comfort might be drawn. This tendency had begun in 1941 and the tortured searchings were even more intense in 1942. For example: a Rabbi reinterpreted the quotation, "When the Sabbath comes it brings with it peace." The Hebrew letters are used as numbers and the letters of the word Sabbath are 702. In the Hebrew calendar the year 702 coincides with 1942. This, they said, would be a year of peace, this year would see the end of the war. The extermination programme started in that year.

I often had to visit the Gerer Rabbi's[2] grandson, Rabbi Naftali, in Twarda Street, and his brother in Muranov Street. They both accepted the tragedy philosophically. They sat self-contained, quiet and impassive, showing neither fear nor capitulation. They seemed almost to accept their fate as a punishment, not of Divine but of human origin, because society had allowed barbaric men to rule the world. In the early days of the deportations the Gerer Rabbi's brother once appeared in the street. He ran quickly towards a street in which people were being arrested by the Germans. I shouted at him to warn him of the danger and begged him to go home. He did not seem to recognize me. He looked at me in a bewildered manner, but remained silent. The sorrow of previous generations of Jews spoke through his eyes.

When, in the spring of 1942, we started to hear terrible reports from the countryside, a student from the Gostynin Yeshiva came to Warsaw with a letter to the Rabbis. It came from his colleagues. They asked whether they should escape and hide in the nearby woods. The answer was that all the young people should leave the town, and, though it was dangerous, should hide out in the forest. They were warned to be careful of attracting too much attention as the majority of the Jews had to stay put.

In the early days of the catastrophe, at the end of July 1942, we usually stayed in the Jewish community archive office in Grzybowska Street. We thought and hoped that this building would protect us. In one corner of the archive room sat a famous elderly Rabbi, Rabbi Kanal, always with his prayer book and reciting psalms. He avoided human contact and talked to no one. When he was once asked what fate had in store, he said quietly, "So many Jews have died in God's name that one more old man can make no difference." A few days later he faced the Germans, refusing to get into the train which was transporting the Jews to Treblinka. He was shot then and there.

[2] Prominent Chassidic dynasty of Rabbis of the Alter family whose residence was in the town of Ger (Góra Kalwaria), near Warsaw.

It is difficult to forget something which happened at the end of 1942. It was bitterly cold in the offices of the Judenrat building in Zamenhof Street. Some people were sitting in one of the rooms, most of them religious. Among them was Professor Mayer Balaban. People talked of the day's events and the uncertainties of tomorrow, but the professor sat silent. One of the group, Jehuda Orlean, the well-known educationist and Aguda leader, said he avoided religious services as he did not want to be questioned. He had no comforting answers to give. Also, he did not want people to see him without a beard. Rabbi Schreibman, on the other hand, said that this was the time to tell people that it was not the end. Times were bad, but one must have faith and not despair. Without faith there could be no life. I heard him say the same thing a few days later at a wedding. In the few months before the total destruction of the ghetto there were many marriages between young couples recently bereaved. They would ask the Rabbi for words of hope, and Rabbi Schreibman would repeat his comforting message.

On another occasion, when the Orthodox leader Isaac Ber Eckerman was present, we discussed the tragedy again. Eckerman asked about some of his friends, and when he was told that they had already disappeared, he called out, "No one is left. This is our fate; not one of us will survive." Another Rabbi in the room answered, "Is survival important? One thing matters—the defeat of the enemy. You must surely believe this. Their defeat is so certain that this must be our comfort."

On Rosh Hashana, 1942, after a massive selection of victims in the ghetto, everyone felt extremely ill at ease. No one knew if the selection—which had started some days previously—had come to an end. People crept out of hiding and asked each other, "What is happening in the streets?" The streets were empty and silent. Suddenly a Jew appeared complete with beard and side-curls, accompanied by an exhausted woman. Both of them could hardly totter. They were covered with feathers and had obviously just crept out of a mountain of bedclothes where they had been hiding. The man kept raising his clenched fists to heaven and the poor woman who led him wept uncontrollably and shouted, "My husband has gone mad." "Jews," he called, "collect large stones and throw them up to heaven! Why has God picked on us for this torment? Give me stones to throw in defiance of heaven!" His wife was shocked at the blasphemy and tried to apologize for him, saying, "He has had neither food nor water for days. He is terrified. He is not responsible for what he is saying." The scene spelt the disintegration of a deep religious faith.

Many months have separated me from that scene, but I always hear the cry, "Stones, collect stones!"

Zygmunt the Cripple

I often wondered what happened to Jews who hid in the woods. And what about those in concentration camps and other ghettos? But perhaps those who acted out the tragi-comedy of being Poles and Catholics suffered most. It is hard to imagine the life of such a Jew, mixing freely with everybody, and being easily rebuffed by the expressions on people's faces; above all the constant role-playing, like an actor in some old classic play. I say constant, for one continued to act even at night. One groan, one word spoken in sleep would have betrayed the Jew. The smallest error of judgment in movement or in speech led to death.

These were my thoughts after a harrowing experience in the district of Czerniakow. It occurred in the main thoroughfare, Czerniakowska Street. In the summer of 1943, after the Ghetto Uprising, I again had to return to living with my secret in Czerniakow. I worked at 113, Czerniakowska Street, in a shop which sold spirits and provisions, owned by an elderly man, an engineer called Kantorski. I knew the shop well when my wife and I were living in the house on the common; I went there a number of times to buy various articles of food. Kantorski lived in Zyrardow, just outside Warsaw, and he travelled in daily. I often chatted with him and felt that, as a patriotic Pole, he could be trusted.

After my experiences at Skolimow and Chylice, I remembered this man and the trust I had put in his patriotism. The days were long, bitter and empty, and so I thought I might try to get a job as a salesman. I prepared a story for him. It was that I was a Polish officer in extreme difficulties in Warsaw, a deserter from the army who had refused to register with the Germans. I had come from Poznan and was now desperate for work. Of course, the whole business of tricking him was very risky, apart from the fact that the area was notorious for the thieves, hooligans and other delinquents who roamed around.

When Kantorski was alone in his shop I told him my tale in confidence and asked if he needed someone to help him. He was very sympathetic to my story and, as a patriot, felt he should employ me. However, he made one condition. He wanted a cooked lunch, to be prepared daily in the room behind the shop. He felt this would suit both of us. Smilingly, I readily agreed, saying, "This is indeed divine providence. Before the war, when I was in the army, I was a chef and head of the Army Catering Corps." In reality, I had no clue as to how one set about preparing a meal. I just relied on my memories of the taste of food and the sight of my mother cooking at home when I was a child, and the hope that some miracle would happen.

Kantorski never for one second suspected that I was a Jew. The way I spoke, my military bearing, and the confidence with which I had expressed myself were far from Jewish traits at that time. I started work, taking care to avoid talking about Jews, not only with him but with the customers who came to the shop. Friends of my employer often came in. They were mainly journalists, writers and former civil servants who all cursed the Nazis. But one often heard, too, that the one good thing the Germans had done was to rid Poland of its Jews, and for this one should be grateful. Incidentally, this was also the opinion of Mr. Kantorski. I need not say how I felt in the company of these people. I was always silent and never entered into any discussion, but did my work diligently and my employer was very pleased with me, since profits rose and the business was thriving.

Mr. Kantorski was also pleased with my cooking and said the lunches I prepared were better than those he got at home. I cooked the things I knew and liked: pea soup, fruit soup and steaks. There was no need to cook ham and pork, for apart from the fact that I did not know how, he did not ask for it. I made chopped farfel soup which delighted Mr. Kantorski and he always said, "Where did you learn to make such wonderful savory dishes?" In the end, he said he must bring his wife and daughter to one of my lunches, so that they too could learn about good food. They came, ate and asked for recipes. After this event, I took the liberty of asking Mr. Kantorski if I could invite a friend of mine and he consented gladly. Thus, on one solitary occasion, my wife, acting the complete Catholic stranger, dined with us.

All would have been well, but the summer sun and the long light days were my enemies. Twenty-four hours of uninterrupted night would have been paradise. The streets were filled with lay-abouts who, in these days of war, were having great success at earning money without working: overfed drunkards who cared for no one, and revelled in the situation. They awaited any odd turn of events which they could use to their advantage. I feared them constantly. The leader of the gang was a one-legged man who called himself Zygmunt. He spent an hour or two every day selling the Nazi paper *Nowy Kurier Warszawski* and hung around the streets the rest of the time, the spokesman for the crooks. He and his friends had an off-licence they always used and did their drinking there. They never came to "our" shop.

I always tried to keep off the streets. Eventually, I used to spend the night in the shop without the boss's knowledge. I slept on the stone floor, and managed cautiously to open the shop in the morning and lock up at night without his guessing that I stayed there. I was terrified of falling into the hands of the street gangs. My luck lasted for eight weeks: then, one afternoon, it happened. I went out of the shop—and bumped into Zygmunt. He just looked at me and that was enough to make me quake. We went our separate ways. But that night in the shop was sleepless for me.

The next day I saw Zygmunt limping towards the shop. He came in, greeted us and asked for half a bottle of vodka. I was busy with other customers, so Mr. Kantorski served him. I pretended not to see him. He stood there and, glancing in all directions, started to complain about present circumstances. At one time, he said, it was all different. When there were lots of Jews around, life was better, especially the year before they were put into the ghetto. His language was colourful. He remembered an old religious Jew coming out of the synagogue; there was snow everywhere, and he had thrashed the Jew soundly. The bright red of his blood had trickled across the white snow—this was his favourite picture. He even remembered the spot where the incident had occurred. Those were the days! But now, nothing like that came his way. My boss smiled and I did too. Zygmunt walked out.

My head was throbbing. What was the point of these stories of his? Was he getting at me? I met one of my Polish friends who knew of my true identity and asked his advice; he thought that it was idle chatter and I had nothing to fear. I thought otherwise, but what could I do? I had to stay put. The days passed and each seemed like eternity—till one warm August day when I was alone in the shop and noticed two men approaching—Zygmunt and an SS officer. They both came in and the officer asked for a bottle of vodka in German. I asked Zygmunt to translate. Both laughed and the SS man repeated the request in German. Another customer came in and I served her. While I was doing this, the German took out a camera and took a snap of me. I pretended to act stupidly and kept quiet.

The two men sat down at a table in the shop, ordered drinks and said I must have one as well. What next? I kept my head and Zygmunt said, "It's odd, all the kids in the street say this shop is owned by a Jew and we should boycott it." I replied, "The things kids say! They will say anything. They say you are a collaborator with the Gestapo." Zygmunt and the German looked at each other and did not know how to react to this. Zygmunt pressed on. He took a packet of pornographic pictures out of his pocket and showed them to me, one after the other. I fell in quickly. He knew that normally a Jew would shudder at this, but I carefully examined them all and expressed delight. I looked in my pocket and fished out a picture of myself taken in 1937 with a group of Poles. It had been taken while I was in the hospital and the others, like myself, were all patients there. When Zygmunt saw it he screamed, "Here you look like a real Jew!" I pretended not to understand. A few of Zygmunt's friends, who had been waiting outside for something to happen, came in. They went into a whispered conference and I stood around, for all the world interested and attentive.

Zygmunt and the SS man got up and paid, and they all went out together. They were pretty sure I would not try to escape; they had assessed me accurately, and now simply needed the opportunity to finish me off. I stood alone in the shop but came to a decision fast. There was a back door leading into the yard. Slowly, I went out and stood quietly in the yard; there was a cabinet maker's factory there and the workers greeted me as I ambled past. It was a former Jewish prayer-house and I could see, through the open windows, the Hebrew inscriptions on the walls. In the street I caught a bus into town. I never returned to the street or the shop.

Later, when I risked 'phoning him and arranged a meeting in town, Mr. Kantorski told me what had happened afterwards. The day after I left, a car stopped outside his shop and two Gestapo men got out. They came into the shop with two sub-machine guns and arrested him, being quite certain that he was the Jew! He was searched and questioned for hours at the police station before they finally realized he was not the man they wanted. They also saw from the snap the SS man had taken that they were mistaken. When they asked him for my address, he did not know what to reply as I had carefully avoided giving him one. They released him, with one request: as soon as I reappeared in the shop, he was to let them know. He gave me one last piece of advice: never to come to Czerniakowska Street again.

Zygmunt in 1945
There is a post-war sequel to the Czerniakowska Street story and Zygmunt.

It was the winter of 1945–1946. I was again in Warsaw, working and busy, and one day I was hurrying to keep an appointment at the one undamaged hotel left, the Polonia in the center of town, which had become a meeting place for visitors from all over the world.

It was cold and frosty, and snow covered the ruins of the city; it was just growing dark. There were plenty of people around and among them I suddenly saw, as if in a dream, a figure who reminded me of Zygmunt of Czerniakowska Street. I could hardly believe my own eyes. I stared—and it was indeed he, one-legged Zygmunt, quite unchanged. He stood in front of the hotel, chanting, "I buy old gold, golden coins, currency, etc." The tone was the same as when he had called out in 1943, "*Nowy Kurier Warszawski, Nowy Kurier Warszawski!*" The old horror flowed over me and in my mind's eye I saw his entry with the SS officer into Kantorski's shop; I remembered the verbal cat and mouse game. I was bewildered and did not know what to do, but I felt something had to be done now. A Polish army officer was walking by. Without thinking, I went up to him and said that the dealer in gold outside the hotel had been a German collaborator, and I asked him to request to see his identity card. I did not know the surname, but I asked him to look and see if his Christian name was Zygmunt. If it was, the officer should take him to the police station at once. The officer was most courteous and quietly asked to see the one-legged man's identity card. He looked at it, tucked it into the cuff of his coat and escorted Zygmunt to the police station which was in the same street. I followed at a distance, since I too would have to make a statement. The police officer in charge of the station asked to see my identity card, and then enquired why I had petitioned for the arrest of the other man. I quietly told him about the role that Zygmunt had played during the war. The officer listened gravely and said this was the concern of another special department whose head office was around the corner. He would dispatch Zygmunt and I was to walk around and ask for formal proceedings to be established. When I asked for the return of my identity card, he said it would be given back to me after some investigations had been made.

I did not particularly want to go with them to this special department that dealt with crimes like collaboration, so I went along alone. Zygmunt was escorted out by two plain-clothes men. It was only five minutes' walk. Arriving there, I sat and waited one, two hours. Still no sign of Zygmunt or the two policemen. After two and a half hours the detectives appeared alone, and blind drunk. They said I was under arrest! Two policemen on duty there asked why and they said, "Because he has accused an innocent man of crimes which he never committed." I summed up this farcical situation and I asked again for the return of my identity card, hoping to get out as quickly as possible. But they would not hear of it. They went on repeating drunkenly, "He must be arrested." The place was in an uproar so I demanded at the top of my voice to be taken to the head of the section. A senior officer appeared and asked what was hap-

pening. I begged him to give me a private interview so that I need
not talk to him in front of the two detectives.

I told him the whole story of Czerniakowska Street and described the recent farce. Finally I asked again for the return of my
card. The official got it back for me and, in my presence, severely
reprimanded the detectives. He promised me that he would have
Zygmunt arrested that evening and requested that I come in the
morning to present the facts to him. I was there in good time, waiting for Zygmunt to be brought in. When they did bring a prisoner in
he was a complete stranger to me. He had both legs and was not in
any way connected with my story. It seemed to me that the two detectives were having their own back on me, and that anyhow Zygmunt had bribed them well. The senior officer lost his temper and
warned the detectives that if they did not produce Zygmunt they
would have cause to regret it. He asked me to telephone the following morning and said that when he had Zygmunt there, he would
ask me to come again.

I telephoned a number of times and was always given a mud-
dled noncommittal answer. After a few days, the official told me that
the matter was out of his hands. All he could do was to give me
Zygmunt's address and, if I wished to follow the matter up, I could
get in touch with the Public Prosecutor. I thought long and seriously
and finally decided the whole thing was best left alone.

Zygmunt went on plying his trade in front of the Polonia hotel
and I avoided him like the plague. I began to feel afraid of him
again, and also of the two detectives whom I often saw in the street.
Whenever I saw them, I hid in a doorway. I was automatically repeating the pattern of the occupation.

1969

Golus-Jew

by Hayim Greenberg

Translated by Shlomo Katz

The Yiddish which was my mother tongue, and which we often called *zhargon,* used the term *golus*[1] to denote an unfortunate "accidental" condition. The accident, it is true, had lasted for two thousand years, time enough for a great civilization to be born, mature, and disappear—but an "accident" none the less. The related concept, *golus-Jew,* thus became a term of derision. When we youngsters wanted to insult one another, we could find no more humiliating appelation than *golus-Jew.* I remember clearly how one day one of our Gentile friends heard us use this term and asked to have it explained to him. One of us gave him a literal translation which proved entirely inadequate. He was told that *golus-Jew* meant a Jew in exile, and he could not understand why this term should carry any opprobrium. Another then informed him that the term carried connotations of ridicule: *zhidok,* or *zhidionok* (little Jew) as one might say in Russian. When we said *golus-Jew* we had in mind a pitiful creature, weak, ill-mannered, without pride and lacking in manly dignity, one who was willing to humiliate himself before those stronger than he, even fearful and self-deprecating before the *goy.* True, we were descended from these miserable creatures, but to make up for this we had Zionism which aimed to end the *golus* and transform the *golus-Jew* into an equal among equals—to make him a "normal Jew," as we phrased it.

My boyhood is now far behind me, and I have largely rid myself of my one-time *zhargon.* I have crossed oceans and come to know continents which formerly I knew only by hearsay. Before my

[1] A Hebrew word pronounced *golus* in Yiddish and *galut* in Hebrew.

eyes a new generation is growing up—a generation to which I have contributed of my own flesh and blood. And again I hear the concept *golus-Jew* being used, though now in a different language, with different intonation, with less contempt but still with a good deal of derision. I recall that most Jews to whom the expression *golus-Jew* would most naturally apply, died in Treblinka and Buchenwald, in forests and fields, on gallows, in gas chambers . . . and that with them ended also their talk and their mannerisms, their manner of speech and manner of thought, their "bad habits" and good ways, their great sorrows and small joys. When I now hear the term *golus-Jew* used derisively, I have the feeling as if graves were being desecrated, the graves of near ones—the nearest we ever had.

Bialik once said: "A people has as much sky over its head as it has ground under its feet." I frequently quoted this aphorism, and it always made a great impression on people not close to us. I still think (perhaps more than ever before) that there is much truth in this statement—but not the full and absolute truth that is valid everywhere and at all times in the life of a people. Even when he made this statement Bialik knew, far better than those against whom he directed it, that for some two thousand years Jews had not a square inch of ground under their feet but much sky over their heads. More than once we were hated, and efforts were made to undo us precisely because our sky was bluer, and clearer, and deeper, and more starry on dark nights, than the skies of other nations possessing "real estate." A skyless people could not have created the Talmud and the Midrashim, Kabbala and Messianic movements, the Shulhan Arukh and Hasidism. Perhaps the true measure of the sky owned by a people is its capacity for martyrdom. Should this be so, then there has not yet been born the Homer capable of voicing the heroic epic of the *golus-Jew*.

I realize I am stating banalities. But fresh, pure country air is also "banal"; only smelly or weirdly perfumed air is "original." And after one drinks many outlandish and interesting concoctions, one finds refreshment in "banal" fresh well water. My aim is not very ambitious: all I want to do is revise a few expressions in our vocabulary or, more correctly, to leave the expressions as they are and only to change the intonation with which some of us say them. The term *golus-Jew* must cease to be a word of insult and disdain for the recipient and an expression of superiority for the one who uses it.

Today, more than ever before, we have reason to negate the *golus*, to seek ways to end it, to reject any justification of its continued

existence, to rebel against it. But this should in no way affect our
evaluation of its inner worth and of its uniqueness in the past. Most
important, this negation must not influence our moral and esthetic
evaluation of the *golus-Jew*.

Golus is the sum total of a combination of circumstances—evil,
harsh, oppressive, humiliating circumstances. But the *golus-Jew* is
the man who lived, struggled, suffered and functioned under those
circumstances, and we must judge him not according to the circumstances in which he lived but by the way he adapted himself to
them, or adapted them to himself. Did he become a slave under
those circumstances or did he, despite all compromises, defeats and
attempts at imitation, master those circumstances?

Not every prisoner sold into slavery becomes a slave and loses
the image of a free man. The man who is brutally deprived of his
freedom to act as he wishes does not thereby become slavish in character. Only the one who becomes reconciled to this condition, and
renounces his will and his right to make his own decisions also gives
up his personality. Napoleon on St. Helena was a prisoner and not a
slave. Rabbi Shneur Zalman in his Russian prison was a captive but
not a slave. A prison is torture and humiliation. But we know that
prisons contained the freest spirits of the world, precisely because
freedom was the passion of their lives, and they did not become
slaves behind bars.

The distinction between spiritual freedom and the lack of it is
a simple one: whether one is capable of clinging to one's own values
in the midst of oppression and enslavement, whether one is capable
of fighting for those values under the whip of the oppressor, or
whether one loses his values and becomes incapable of suffering for
their sake. The matter of pride and humility, too, is reduced to the
place assigned by an individual or a nation to their values and
sanctities. Humility has its limits. If one is capable of humbling
himself under pressure of brutal circumstances in a hundred small
ways (or in a hundred ways which he, *according to his own scale
of values*, considers small) but is prepared to suffer martyrdom out
of loyalty to values which he believes to be crucial, then it would
be the height of injustice to consider such a person a slavish nature,
a man without pride. The pseudoemancipated Jew (and Zionism,
too, is not a guarantee in all cases against such pseudoemancipa-
tion) may speak contemptuously of the Jews of Poland of the past as
people without self-respect because they submitted to the humiliation of the Polish nobility, but even he cannot escape the fact that
the Polish Jew humbled himself only for the sake of his livelihood,
to escape a beating, or not to be driven from his home. These he

considered unimportant, small matters, on the rim of his existence
and not central to his life. But whenever the same Polish Jew was
asked to renounce that which he held high in his scale of values, he
was capable of great stubbornness and resistance and demonstrated
a talent for martyrdom.

Some years ago, Sholem Asch aroused resentment with his
story, "Yisgadal Ve'yiskadash." Asch, it was then said, insulted us.
He wrote sympathetically and affectionately of a Jew who displayed
slavishness and humility in a Nazi concentration camp, who cring-
ingly and with a smile on his face obeyed all the commands of his
overseer. He shamed us all, it was argued, when he obeyed the command to say of himself: "I am a swine; I am a dirty Jew," in order
to save his life. These criticisms of Asch stemmed from our inability
to judge people in the context of their own values. (Basically this
showed a lack of artistic imagination.) Asch's critics did not stop to
think for a moment that this humble obedience to all commands
contained much contempt for the tormentor, who failed to notice it
only because of his own absolute degeneration and dullness. Proud
as we may be, not one of us will be insulted by an animal. Humiliation can be inflicted only by someone who belongs to our species.
Itche Meier of Asch's story (like other cringing golus-Jews) considered that his Nazi oppressor belonged to another category of
beings than his own.

It is this profound contempt of the golus-Jew for the beast-
liness that surrounded him, as well as his intense sense of self-
importance, that often accounted for his submission to a thousand
humiliations in matters that he considered trivial in his scale of
values; and also for his pride, self-assertion, and devotion to supra-
personal aims which he manifested whenever his sanctities were at
stake. This was the secret—to use Heine's metaphor—of the golus-
Jew's weekday cringing and Sabbath pride.

One must be quite color blind—and blind to the true sense of
events—not to see that the golus-Jew's self-effacement often concealed his contempt for those before whom he apparently crawled
in the dust. He fawned on those who were alien to him and stronger
than he, but he did so feeling that he and they had no common
standards (temporarily?) for deeds and behavior, that they spoke a
language other than his own and therefore could reach no understanding, or exert a normal influence on each other.

The golus-Jew's fawning was therefore frequently no more humiliating, no more "opportunistic" than his efforts to placate a vicious dog by throwing him a bone, or calling him the endearments
to which his master had accustomed him. This, too, was the "oppor-

tunism" of the *shtadlan* who accompanied our *golus* history for many generations (not to mention those numerous instances when the *shtadlan* was basically a kabbalist, and his activities served him as a form of descending to the lower depths of uncleanness in order to redeem the few sparks of sanctity hidden there).

The *golus-Jew's* life, feelings and behavior were often consonant with Hillel's dictum: Ascend downward. Situated at the very bottom of the social structure he could conceive it as ascent. The Gentile world, occupying the highest rung of the social ladder, lived according to the superficial concept: Descend upward. In his more frenetic moments when he was obsessed with the idea of the Superman, Nietzsche contemptuously characterized this as slave morality and slave esthetic. In his more honest and clear moments, he admired and was intrigued by the *golus-Jew*.

The *golus-Jew* is the greatest spiritual adventurer and anti-fetishist in human history. He took a plant born in a specific country (better still, one born contrary to the laws of nature in the desert, where nothing grows) and said: "I will make this plant thrive in all soils and under all skies, and feel at home everywhere. Thorns might wound it, but it will live forever, nor will its wounds drain it of its life sap." The *golus-Jew* tried to believe that his plant would not be affected by climate—climate would have to obey the gardener.

What was the significance of *Shema Yisroel* for the *golus-Jew?* It was a form of signaling: You and I and others like us know a secret, the secret of everything. A wireless broadcast the secret formula far and wide, from one isolated Jew to another.

During the early days of his religious rebellion, Luther was asked: "Where will you be if the Church expels you?" Without thinking too long he answered: "Under God's heaven." The *golus-Jew* was a chronic expellee for many generations. But he was not "outside." "Heaven," he said to himself, "is also a roof; better still, a bridal canopy."

The *golus-Jew* walked through a world of darkness (at least, he thought of it as such) carrying a lantern in his hand. He still has the lantern but the oil is running low. Now the *golus-Jew* is beginning to live "outside" with a lantern that has gone out. Hence the crisis, the self-alienation, the uprootedness and the yearning after roots.

Are we about to conclude this great and Quixotic chapter in our biography? It is likely. But Israel must not become the land of Sancho Panza. The tensions of the *golus-Jew*, some of his ability to vault chasms, elements of his piety, and his constant sense of guilt should become part of the new way of life.

And let us remember: *Golus* was tragedy, not just a series of misfortunes. One is justified in wanting to escape tragedy (if one can)—but why be ashamed of it? Only a clod is ashamed of tragedy. Should you meet a man of sensibility who says he is ashamed of tragedy—do not believe him. It is probably not the only libel he invented against himself.

1945

VI

Yiddish: Language and Literature

It would be impossible to end a book like this one without a word about the fate of Yiddish culture and the Yiddish language. But we have chosen to avoid the more formidable essays—exhortatory, polemical or lugubrious—which have accumulated during recent years. Max Weinreich's essay is a scholarly contribution to a major theme in the study of Jewish languages. The piece by Jacob Stern-berg, a distinguished Yiddish poet living in Russia, does battle in behalf of Yiddish against commissars and their agents who would suppress or truncate it, and the piece by Abraham Koralnik is a wry —though not, thereby, any the less significant—comment on the mazl, the luck, of Yiddish in the modern era.

Internal Bilingualism in Ashkenaz[1]

by Max Weinreich

Translated by Lucy S. Dawidowicz

The title promises "facts and concepts," but I am interested essentially in concepts. Facts on the subject are available in abundance, some already researched and referable, others still requiring researching. But here I will introduce facts only for the sake of illustration. That will make it easier to evaluate the picture I will draw.

First, I must explain that "Ashkenaz," in my usage, does not mean Germany, nor even the Jews in Germany, but all Ashkenazim, both in Central and in Eastern Europe, as a community. Until the Haskala, all Ashkenazim spoke one language, Yiddish, though in several variants.

"Internal bilingualism" also needs explaining. Ashkenazic Jews were always a minority vis-à-vis the non-Jewish milieu and, consequently, had always to be bilingual. Not all members of the community in the same degree, but every Jew to some degree had to know the language of the coterritorial non-Jewish population. I have designated this situation as external bilingualism. We will certainly not minimize it, since for the development of Yiddish it was quite important which age categories and which social strata had at various times the widest contacts with the surrounding society. In this area we can tie in directly with research into language contact, which has made considerable progress in recent years. But here I am interested in bilingualism *within* the community; in other words, the symbiosis of Yiddish and Hebrew throughout Ashkenaz's entire history of more than a thousand years.

[1] This article is based on a paper presented at the Conference on Yiddish Studies in New York in 1958. The sources and bibliographic references have been omitted in the translation.

Vis-à-vis the coterritorial population, both were Jewish languages and among Jews themselves were quite intertwined. This interrelation expressed itself not just in the belief held by children and simple souls that Moses himself spoke Yiddish on weekdays and the Sacred Tongue only on the Sabbath. Definitely no later than the fourteenth century an illustration of a hare hunt appears in Ashkenazic Haggadahs, which turns out to be a mnemonic device to memorize the order of the benedictions when Passover falls on the Sabbath night: *yayin* 'wine', *kiddush* 'sanctification', *ner* 'candle lighting', *havdala* 'dividing the Sabbath from the workweek', *zeman* 'season'. What is this all about? The initial letters of the benedictions are y'k'n'h'z and in Yiddish—not in Hebrew, mind you—these letters sound like *yog n'hoz,* "chase the hare."

Even the names of both Jewish languages were not fixed definitely. When, at a Jewish meeting where the speechifying has all been in another language, a speaker in Yiddish comes on, an auditor can then sigh with relief: "At long last one hears a Yiddish [Jewish] word." But "His mouth doesn't touch a Yiddish [Jewish] word" means: "He doesn't pray," and praying as everyone knows is done in Hebrew.

Such sociolinguistic situations of internal bilingualism in which both languages are differentiated, not community-wise but functionally, occur not only in Ashkenaz. First, we do have analogous situations in non-Ashkenazic communities, and then we recall the position of Latin vis-à-vis the vernaculars in the Middle Ages and in the Age of Humanism. But the Ashkenazic situation has so many specificities that it is preferable to dwell just on that. I will cite only a few examples from elsewhere.

First: How are both Jewish languages related phonemically? In Ashkenaz II, that is, in Ashkenazic Eastern Europe, complete phonemic integration had certainly already been attained by the end of the Old Yiddish era (ca. 1500): in Whole Hebrew[2] there is not even one phoneme that is not encountered in Yiddish. At first glance it would appear inevitable: A self-sufficient Hebrew phonemic system must have ceased to exist when Hebrew was no longer a spoken language. But it can be proved, I think, that the Hebrew of the Western-Laaz speakers did indeed have phonemes which Western

---

[2] By "Whole Hebrew" I mean the traditional Hebrew of running texts (Scripture, liturgy) which are read or recited from memory. This is in contrast to "Merged Hebrew," which became part of the fusion language Yiddish—in other words, the traditional Hebrew component of Yiddish.

Laaz itself did not have.[3] In theory, a scale can be constructed for different Jewish communities, based on the degree to which their Whole Hebrew was phonemically integrated with the spoken language.

Let us ponder on the place of Yiddish and Hebrew in the household of Ashkenazic culture.

When European languages began their self-confident attack on Latin as a school language, they began to boast of their vitality. After the Haskala there were also people keen on counting Hebrew among the dead. Today, knowing about Akkadian or Numidian, we need to redefine the role of Latin up to the seventeenth century. If the Latin language had been dead, it would not have continued to develop and it could not have so strongly influenced the development of so many modern languages. How much more so must we abandon the contrast of dead as against living when we speak about Ashkenaz. The Sacred Scriptures are in Hebrew; we pray in Hebrew —why is this sphere of life less alive than the hurly-burly of daily life?

Traditional Ashkenaz, we must conclude, had two *living* languages, one that was immediate and the second mediated. A mediated language can be understood, can be quoted, can be sanctified, but people do not use it in their everyday life for communicating with one another or for expressing their feelings. You surely remember the anecdote of the Jewish lady who was in labor. Her first groan was the French "Mon Dieu!" then the second, in Russian, "Bozhe moy!," but when the doctor heard *"Got in himl!,"* he knew that the real throes had begun. When the Hebrew language ceased to be unmediated, and that happened many centuries before Ashkenaz was born, its growth was affected: its chief accretion was no longer from below. Yet Hebrew in Ashkenaz survived in the hothouse of Yiddish for specific functions. Which functions?

The term *loshn-koydesh*—the sacred tongue—suggests where to look for the division of functions between Ashkenaz's two languages. Some observant Jews will not utter the word *Shabes* 'the Sabbath' in

[3] "Laaz" is used to designate those languages brought to Loter (Lorraine), along the Middle Rhine, by migrants from Romance-speaking lands. These settlers were to found the Ashkenazic community starting in the ninth century. They came from two directions: a greater part from Eastern France (their language is called Western Laaz—Judeo-French) and a smaller part from Northern Italy (their language is called Southern Laaz—Judeo-Italian).

the bath or toilet. They will say "the seventh." Yet we should not be misled into thinking that because the elder language of Ashkenaz is the sacred tongue, the other is the secular tongue. In traditional Ashkenaz, as Heschel put it so beautifully, Jews strove to introduce into each mundane act at least a trace of sanctity and, consequently, there was no utter mundaneness. There were only gradations of sanctity. And so when maskilim began to transgress the Law, observant Jews did not regard Mendele's Hebrew novel *Ha'avot vehabanim* as less "secular" than his Yiddish one, *Dos kleyne mentshele*.

Why look for detailed proof, when the focal difference between Yiddish as Jews used it and the mother tongues of Christian Europe in the Middle Ages and in the Humanist era is so striking? In the Latin schools, students had to speak Latin exclusively even during recesses and were fined for uttering a word in the vernacular. With Jews, the whole of religious learning, from the *heder* for the youngest children through the yeshiva up to the casuistry of the greatest Talmudists, was conducted exclusively in Yiddish. Using the vernacular in religious study was not an Ashkenazic innovation; the pattern was already completed in the experience of the Babylonian and Palestinian yeshivas, from which the Gemara emerged. Through its function as a language of instruction, Yiddish became a medium of expression for a complicated juridical-moral philosophic conceptual world long before German, Polish, etc., became accepted media for similar purposes. Talmudist Yiddish, the Yiddish of the learned pious Jew, still requires systematic research. Sociologically we must note that practically all boys attended *heder* and that learned men were the highest status group in Ashkenazic society.

The distinction in function grows clear when we recall that the same rabbis who discussed Talmudic problems in Yiddish as a matter of course corresponded about these same problems, also as a matter of course, in Hebrew. In general, people wrote letters in Hebrew, if they had some knowledge of it. A question on a rabbinical matter and the response to it were written in Hebrew, except when one wanted to cite a witness's words verbatim. On the same principle, the Lithuanian Council ruled in 1679 that an individual's complaint against the community ought to be recorded in Yiddish. As a rule, nevertheless, the scribe recorded the community council's decisions in the minute book in Hebrew, though the language spoken in the Council chamber was Yiddish. Sholom Aleichem's moneylender surely did not speak Hebrew with his clients, but in his notebook he recorded *natati, kibalti, hivtahti,* 'I gave, I received, I promised.' Now we discern the principal distinction between Yiddish and Hebrew in the Ashkenazic cultural household.

Yiddish is the spoken language. In it one says what needs to be said and with it one fortifies Judaism. That is why we hear Rabbi Meir Katz, father of Shabbetai Ben Meir Ha-Kohen (SHaK), say that, with God's help, all Jews in White Russia will speak Yiddish. But Hebrew is the language for recording. Nahman Bratzlaver may instruct his disciples to pray only in Yiddish, but when he tells his amanuensis to record his stories, Nathan understands what he means and records them in Hebrew as best he can. Even the Dubner Maggid's great Yiddish oratory has come down to us only through a filter of Hebrew.

Linguistically the closeness of both languages created lots of problems: phonemic integration, borrowing, calquing, purism, style, and stylization—all beg to be studied through the Yiddish-Hebrew material. The learned men of Ashkenaz created neologisms like *mohel* 'circumciser' or *khalef* 'slaughtering knife'. With such redefinitions like *tseylem* from the Hebrew 'image' to the Yiddish 'crucifix', *bilbul*, from the Hebrew 'confusion' to the Yiddish 'false accusation', *shibush* from the Hebrew 'mistake' to the Yiddish 'trifle', we are at the borderline between both languages, and that holds for the formation of expressions on the pattern of *meshana mokem meshane mazl*, 'who changes his place changes his luck'. But when we turn to the large categories of word formations like *baln balones*, or *baldarshn*, or *katsoves*, we are no longer on a borderline, but in a wide frontier belt with a condominium over both languages. In this shared linguistic territory, names like Hirsh, Wolf, Leyb, Ber, and the like were first translated into their Hebrew equivalents Zvi, Zev, Aryeh, Dov, and, thus translated, they became elements in the Hebrew component of Yiddish.

Ideologically a balance was created by demarcating the functions of the oral and the written. The primacy of Hebrew in principle was not questioned. It had to be that way in a universe where Scripture ruled.

This was the theory; in practice the balance was bound to be upset.

Sometimes Hebrew broke into the domain of Yiddish. There were even instances when Hebrew was spoken, for example, with a visitor from a non-Ashkenazic community. Or, when the recitation of the mealtime benedictions could not be interrupted, the speaker would make do with such "sentences": *Nu, melekh* 'salt', *lekhem* 'bread' or *Ay, o sakin* 'knife'. Even as late as the end of the nineteenth century we hear of Jews who heeded the ARI[4] and did their best to

---

[4] ARI—Isaac Luria (1534-72), founder of the modern Kabbda.

speak Hebrew on the Sabbath, and, if they could not, preferred to keep silent.

Yiddish transgressed its bounds much more frequently: the spoken word has a momentum of its own. Women in their letters had to switch to Yiddish right after the Hebrew salutation. The scribal style of mixing languages in the community minute books is, I think, a compromise between the necessity to record in Hebrew and the urge to express oneself in Yiddish. What may originally perhaps have been an individual stylistic whim gradually gained prevalence as a very popular macaronic style which had considerable influence on both languages. Yiddish became chancellerized by the accretion of the Hebrew *makhmes* 'on account of', *heyoys* 'whereas', *kefi* 'according to', *mitsad*, 'on the part of', and so on; scribal Hebrew, for its part, was enriched by calques from the spoken language.

Yiddish showed very strong expansionist tendencies on two fronts: (1) in penetrating into prayers and benedictions, and (2) in establishing its own literature. Shulman, Niger, Zinberg and others have collected much material on this, but the underlying issues still require elucidation. The conflicts were variously resolved. In liturgy and ritual the Yiddish language seized new areas for a while, but finally had to retreat to the originally demarcated boundary of vassalage. Within the compass of literature Yiddish won a position of equality and sovereignty.

Social and linguistic realities inhere in these military-political metaphors.

In the matter of praying the basic conflict is immediately apparent. On the one hand: praying without understanding is unsatisfactory. The frequently quoted sentence from *Sefer hasidim* that the heart must understand what the lips utter in prayer is merely a repetition of an old truth. How else can one interpret " 'Shema' in any language you understand"? But it is an equally established fact that the prayers are transmitted from generation to generation in their sanctified version and that they are in Hebrew. Quite early, then, a compromise was reached that in addition to the fixed prayers the individual ought to add a plea from his own heart, and the term *tehina* for this individual outpouring of soul to the Almighty occurs as early as the Book of Daniel, about two hundred years before the destruction of the Second Temple. We may surmise from this model that the *tkhines* originated in Ashkenaz in Yiddish; certainly they are much older than the oldest extant printed texts of about 1600. Systematic study on the content, form, and language of the tkhine is still a desideratum.

Time was when some Yiddish speakers would not settle for this compromise. Perhaps it is more than mere coincidence (though the intellectual lines of communication are not clearly visible) that precisely in the period from the end of the fifteenth century to the beginning of the seventeenth, in the era of the Christian Reformation movements, there are so many penitential prayers, prayer books, festival prayer books—all in Yiddish, without the Hebrew original. In Cambridge there is such a handwritten festival prayer book, dated 1481.

The fact is that at least in some places people uttered the Yiddish words for "Almighty God" at congregational services. Therefore I agree completely with J. A. Joffe that the purely Yiddish texts were not just translation aids, but people must have actually prayed from them. It may even be quite likely that some worshippers recited the prayers in Yiddish not only when they prayed alone, without a congregation, but also at communal services. But it did not survive, and Yiddish remained at the threshhold of the liturgy. We can list the instances: reciting part of the Passover Haggada in the vernacular (perhaps the whole Haggada in some places?), a practice which gradually fell into disuse; the "Girls' Benediction" (on arising in the morning); God of Abraham, "night reading," Scripture verses for names (also for names of non-Hebrew origin), and the formula *Raboysay, mir veln bentshn* ("Gentlemen, let us recite the benediction"). That is the sum total. When the *Liblekhe tfile* and *Libsbriv* appealed at the start of the eighteenth century for all prayer to be in the mother tongue, they were defending a lost cause. Their request was fulfilled a hundred years later by German Reform, but Reform chose German, not Yiddish, and its social outlook was something entirely different.

Zinberg hypothesizes that masses with a lyric disposition defended Yiddish against community leaders, Masters of the Law, but that dry rationality prevailed. The thesis seems to me simplistic. What the masses really wanted, they got. Hasidism in one short century occupied most of Eastern Europe. But even Hasidism did not challenge the Hebrew liturgy; the ARI's version of the service was adopted, but not praying in Yiddish, Levi Yitzhok and Nahman Bratzlaver notwithstanding. Here the sociolinguist needs the sociologist of religion. For comparative purposes, let us mention the fact that despite tremendous pressure the Catholic Church did not abandon the Latin service. Without further ado, I venture to say that Yiddish as a language of prayer lost out not to the community, but to the individual. The rabbi, too, wanted conviviality, but the common man also yearned to do what the Torah commanded. In the individual's heart the scales oscillated and Hebrew outweighed Yiddish. A Christian principal of a Frankfurt *gymnasium,* named Schudt, at the very outset of the eighteenth century, relates that he asked two Jewish women how they could say their prayers in Hebrew without understanding the meaning of the words. One replied: When a doctor writes a prescription for me, it doesn't matter that I cannot read it, as long as the apothecary can read it and supply the right remedy. The second one replied even more pointedly: Indeed I don't understand the meaning of the words; but the Lord of the Universe does.

With regard to recording laws and customs in the spoken language, the authorities were ambivalent. Since Jews have to know how to behave, Yiddish books on customs became an accepted fact. Since Jews have to understand what they are reciting while performing the commandments, no less an authority than the MaHaRiL, Jacob ben Moses ha-Levi Molin, translated the passage "All leaven" from the Passover preparations, into Yiddish around 1400 and his text was preserved and reprinted for hundreds of years. But the counterprinciple comes into play with the same MaHaRiL when he condemns poems on the unity of God and the Thirteen Principles in Yiddish, because they may encourage the notion that one has discharged one's obligations by reciting the poems and is therefore exempt from performing the commandments themselves. Other rabbis ruled even more strictly. Shulman and Zinberg report—details are lacking, but perhaps they can still be tracked down—that rabbis "once" ordered a Yiddish translation of the Shulhan Arukh burned; the Law had to be in Hebrew. That happened, I think, at the end of the eighteenth century. Finally, as we know, the Yiddish *Hayye adam* became entrenched in Jewish homes. To compromise: an unofficial abbreviated version for utilitarian purposes can do no harm.

But no prohibition at all could halt the rise of Yiddish creative literature. There were no serious objections to the glosses and glossaries, even to the literal translation of the sacred Scriptures. Studies by Shtif, Leibowitz, and Noble show that these were unambitious teaching aids, auxiliary in character, and Ashkenaz had before its eyes an old pattern, reading the Hebrew text of the weekly portion twice and the Targum once. The liturgical translations did have higher aspirations, but they were shown their place. Nevertheless, the literature itself had proved to be unconquerable. It provides both artistic satisfaction and inspiration. It is an expression of the innermost strivings which demand to be heard. Hence, religious lyricism increased and the MaHaRiL's opposition was ineffective. Hence, *Shmuel-bukh* and *Maase-bukh* were bound to appear in Yiddish;

hence, even a first-rate Hebraist like Elijah Levita blossomed forth with a *Pariz un viene* and a *Bovo-bukh*.[5]

Perhaps the literature in Yiddish would also have been muzzled in the name of a canonized text, but traditional Ashkenaz had no belles-lettres in Hebrew. Yiddish literature challenged no one. Basically the space was unoccupied. Besides, Yiddish literature was ideologically a function of Ashkenazic culture, and had in the main a conservative outlook. Therefore, warfare against Yiddish literature was not very frequent or overt. But it was always denigrated, and writers in Yiddish put up with the dominant value system without protest. The rationalization was: We write only for women and for men who are like women, that is, who are unlearned. In this way Yiddish literature managed to survive—one can say, to get by like a "tolerated Jew"—and, though curbed, it developed until the new era which we call Haskala gave it the chance to cut loose.

But curbed or free, the fundamental fact is that Yiddish had attained the level of a written language. When a language system has both the spoken and the written, each formation influences the other and the sum total of the language is never again the same as in the days before the written form.

Since the Haskala the relationship of these forces has kept changing and new factors, sociolinguistic and linguistic, have entered.

Yiddish becomes an object of more conscious and deliberate refinement, though even Mendele apologized as late as 1864 for switching to Yiddish in order to serve the people.

De jure recognition came much later than *de facto* recognition, and up to the Holocaust the struggle against Yiddish never halted. In the newly risen secular sector the struggle was no longer on behalf of traditional Hebrew, but on behalf of modern Hebrew. At the same time, however, we note a phenomenon that is important also linguistically: a good number of Jewish writers are bilingual.

New combatants joined up against Yiddish on behalf of another new factor—the coterritorial non-Jewish language. In the West both

[5] *Shmuel-bukh* ("Book of Samuel"), a Yiddish poetic paraphrasing of the Bible, first published in Augsburg, 1544; *Maase-bukh* ("Book of Stories"), tales from the Talmud and other rabbinic literature popularly recounted in Yiddish, first published in Basel, 1602; Elijah Levita (1468–1549), Hebrew grammarian and poet, who introduced the secular romance into Yiddish literature, *Bovo-bukh*, first published 1507, was translated from an Anglo-Roman romance; *Pariz un viene*, translated from a medieval French romance, has survived in a late version published in Verona, 1594.

Yiddish and Hebrew were devoured by the languages of those countries. In the East the external language was internalized by a portion of the Jewish community and internal bilingualism became trilingualism: Hebrew, Yiddish, Russian or Polish. Owing to the reinforcement of the secular sector, the more or less linguistically assimilated intelligentsia became a new status group and, as a consequence of the new social movements, both modern Yiddish and modern Hebrew were noticeably modified.

The balance which at the outset of the Haskala was upset was never redressed. It can be said that our whole language struggle of the nineteenth and twentieth centuries, our entire cultural development in that period is essentially a striving for a new balance in Jewish society. The strength of Yiddish in the nineteenth and twentieth centuries grew enormously, but at the outbreak of the Second World War the scales were still swaying and the postwar era must stabilize anew our bilingual cultural household.

We should not copy the past, even if we could. Besides, which century would we copy? But we must learn from the past, the better to understand where we stand today.

1959

Tradition and Revolt in Yiddish Poetry[1]

by A. Tabachnik

Translated by Cynthia Ozick

A few bits of information about Yiddish poetry in the United States should help the reader of the following essay:

The first major group of Yiddish poets to appear in this country, during the last two decades of the nineteenth century, were called the "labor" or "sweatshop poets," since their work was exhortatory and dealt with the life of immigrant workers. Among the main poets of this group were Morris Rosenfeld, Joseph Bovshover, David Edelstadt.

There followed a number of "transitional" poets writing in the early decades of the century: Abraham Reisen, Yehoash, Rosenblatt.

About 1908 there began to cohere one of the major groups in American Yiddish poetry, "Die Yunge" (the Young), who repudiated the social didacticism of the "sweatshop" poets and, under the influence of Russian and German literature, advanced the idea of a poetry that would be esthetically self-sufficient. The main figures in this group were Mani Leib, Zisha Landau and, for a brief time, Moishe Leib Halpern and H. Leivick. The latter two, as Tabachnik notes, soon went off in other literary directions.

In the early 1920's there was formed another brief-lived group called "In Zich," or Introspectivists, who pushed Yiddish poetry in the direction of modernism, free verse, personal statement. Its leading figures were Jacob Glatstein and A. Glantz-Leyeles.—Eds.

[1] A paper read before the Conference of the Yiddish P. E. N., held in New York, December 16 and 17, 1950, in honor of Yiddish literature from 1900 to 1950.

Only the last two words of my title are really important—"Yiddish poetry." Ultimately all titles, themes, approaches, points of view are no more than a pretext for talking on and on about Yiddish poetry— perhaps our last remaining bit of consolation. The progress of Yiddish poetry, its development, its achievement—this after all is our *noblesse,* our miracle: to put it with Talmudic pointedness, "more is glory." The "more" of our poetry is no longer limited, so my lecture will have to be a quick outline rather than a detailed portrait. Nevertheless the title is no portmanteau: tradition and revolt are genuine events in literature, relevant to the dynamic of its evolution.

It is true that today we no longer hear of revolt in our poetry. Unfortunately we are already past the hour of literary revolutions, the scrambling and striving after new forms. We have new powers, but of new movements, in the formal sense of the word, we hear nothing. In general, the period of new movements did not last long among us. Poets who began as fashioners of the modern school in Yiddish literature have long since grown beyond that school. The "Yunge," for example, were at the start a group of poets with a definite image. Some thirty-five or forty years ago you could more readily speak of the character of the group as a whole than of the achievement of its individual members. But later this was reversed. Not only H. Leivick (though he joined it somewhat later) and Moishe Leib Halpern grew out of this group, or, rather, rapidly outgrew it, but also Y. Y. Schwartz and Joseph Rolnick. And even Mani Leib and Reuben Iceland, who are to this day the official image-bearers of the Yunge, have traveled a considerable distance beyond it.

The same is true with regard to the "In Zikh" poets—the Introspectivists. What sense does it make today, for instance, to speak of Jacob Glatstein as an Introspectivist? Glatstein's verse has not simply outgrown the theories and credos of Introspectivism; his very conception of poetry is now different. His critical articles contain scores of definitions of art and poetry and a multitude of comments on the tonality of the word and the formation of the poetic image, all of which are as far as possible from either the theory or the practice of the erstwhile Introspectivists.

On the other hand, the older poets, like Yehoash, who became caught up in the new movements grew, as it were, younger. And even A. Liessin, a poet who never ran after fashion, wrote his most artful verses after the storms of the revolution were over. In their later years both Yehoash and Liessin became not merely riper and more elegant, but more modern. Liessin even has a poem called "Imagistics." And Abraham Reisen, in many respects the father of the modern Yiddish lyric—didn't he learn something about craft from those who began as his disciples, or even as his imitators? So it is impossible to speak here of revolt and tradition in quite the same way you would use these terms for other peoples and languages. In general, you cannot classify our poetry according to the categories of other literatures, or measure it by their criteria. Our poetry developed with shortcut speed. In some fifty or sixty years we have had to experience as much as other literatures have in two or three times that span.

It must not be forgotten that we have only very recently begun to mold the language of Yiddish poetry, and the process is still far from complete. Because of this, wherever we acquired a movement at the same time as, or under the influence of, movements in other literatures, it came to signify something entirely different for us. What was considered decadent for others was our renascence; what was decline for others was our upsurge.

Things turned out differently for us even with poetry having an explicit social tendency. When Nekrasov came into Russian poetry with his bourgeois motif and journalistic style, there was an outcry from Tolstoy and Fet that he was making a shambles of the Pushkin tradition. Even if this was not true of Nekrasov, the gentile nations still regard didactic or tendentious poetry as a debasement of artistic standards. But can the same thing be said about our socially conscious poetry? Surely not about the poems of Rosenfeld, Liessin, Frug, Peretz. Not even about the work of Winchevsky, Bovshover and Edelstat—since from whom, actually, could these poets represent a decline? Had anyone written better before they came along? They were in fact the very poets who tore apart the vernacular for us and made it into a literary language. The difference shows in the matter of tradition as well. Can it be said, for example, that the fathers and forefathers of our poetry have exactly the same significance for our present-day poets as the fathers and forefathers of non-Jewish poets have for them?

Do we have anything resembling a Shakespeare tradition or a Pushkin tradition? When Itzik Manger, for instance, says that he traces his tradition to Velvl Zbarzher or Abraham Goldfaden, is it the same as when Eliot says his tradition is derived from the English metaphysical poets? For Manger all this is more a game than a serious intention, a question of stylized archaisms rather than adherence to an established tradition.

But if the younger poets did not have anything to affirm and continue, they did have something to turn away from; if there was nothing for them to bind themselves to, there was certainly something for them to shake off. By the time the "Yunge" were beginning their revolt, the older Yiddish poetry already comprised an impressive body. There was something to compete with, to gird one's loins against. Whatever the view we now take toward our older poets, we should remember that for the poets as well as for the critics and readers of that era, theirs was valid, genuine, "true" poetry. Under the title "The Songs of Yehoash the Poet," Y. Leontieff published in the *Tsukunft* a review of Yehoash's first book, *Collected Poems*. True, he pointed out certain shortcomings, but he did not doubt for a moment that Yehoash's verses were "songs" in the most exalted poetic sense of the word. Yehoash's "unsung song" was at that time considered a masterwork of form and diction.

So we have to remember that, historically, the "Yunge" were matching themselves against poets whose work was then regarded as the loftiest and last word in the art of poetry. It hardly seemed possible to imagine that anything better, or more beautiful, could follow the lyrics of Rosenfeld and Yehoash. Hence the "Yunge" had to struggle and put up with the greatest mockery and persecution. They were thought of not merely as "decadents," but as plain barbarians and defilers of the Yiddish word. Still, in the long run the "Yunge" were triumphant, and their successes were of an epoch-making nature: they altered forever the character of the Yiddish poem. After them it was impossible to write the way one had written before. The linguistic daring and poetic freshness that Moishe Nadir, Moishe Leib Halpern, Mani Leib and Zisha Landau introduced into the Yiddish lyric were, compared to the poetics of earlier versifiers, not merely a more productive, but a more modern and radical, achievement than the novelty and boldness of the "In Zikh" group when compared with the poetics of the "Yunge."

The revolt of the "Yunge," though it set forth artistically pure goals and zealously marked itself off from social questions, was nevertheless essentially an expression of deep social changes in Jewish life. Before the revolt of the "Yunge" could occur, Jewish life had to gather up new strengths and open up new sources of spirit while revivifying ancient ones; there had to be deep changes in the relationship between the individual and the community, and the ripening of a new sensibility; new cultural needs had to come about, and a fresh look at the meaning and purpose of life. Still, an artistic revolution is not the same as a social revolution. Often the more radical artistic revolutions are nothing short of reactionary in their social import, while by contrast the reversion to ancient traditions may turn out in fact to be progressive and democratic, indeed folkish in character.

What certain of our Marxist critics have called "reaction and darkness" was really with us an immersion in a thousand-year spiritual heritage, a maturing of artistic sensibility, a refinement of perception, and an emancipation and elevation of the individual. It was an infusion of religious folk-movements expressing high exaltation and a poetic imagination enriched by the visionary elements of folk-art. Literary or other spiritual movements which enhance people's lives are not reactionary. Yet just as our modern literary movements did not bring "reaction and darkness," so they also failed to bring dadaism or nihilism.

On the contrary, the history of our literature declares something else: that as Yiddish poetry became more modern, as it increasingly adopted such subtle and sophisticated movements as symbolism, impressionism, neo-Romanticism, as its very texture became more refined and sophisticated, it also began paradoxically to draw nearer to those crevices in the Jewish soul that harbor the "Hidden Light," the undisclosed, or—as David Ignatov, one of the chief leaders of the "Yunge," called one of his pieces—the "Buried Light." And on the other hand, wherever our poetry remained didactic, old-fashioned, conventional, unsophisticated, that was exactly where it turned out to be less Jewish in its artistic particulars (rhythm, symbol, imagery), and where it failed to give rise to any expression of our Sabbath-life or even our weekday life—that ordinary dailiness which later poets like Y. Y. Segal elevated to a poetic Sabbath-sanctity: to the beauty and holiness, in fact, of a sacred legend.

You may ask, was Liessin removed from the deeper sources of Jewishness? Liessin the great national poet, the fiery patriot, who mounted the scaffold with every martyr? Or Yehoash, Talmud-scholar, translator of Scripture, composer of tens if not hundreds of poems on Biblical and Talmudic themes? And what of Morris Rosenfeld, who wrote so many flaming national hymns? In the first place, we must remember that Yehoash and Liessin later on became a part of modern Jewish poetry too. Secondly, Liessin's somewhat dated poetics, his rational-declarative method, his resoundingly hammered phrase, often came into conflict with the hushed, mystical and metaphysical elements of his spirit. Thirdly, we are not speaking here of theme, or of national orientation, or even of national hymns or odes to the Jewish folk, but of something finer, deeper, something not to be expressed declaratively, in the manner of a credo, but which makes itself felt in form rather—better yet, which is form itself.

Take, for example, Yehoash's poems on Biblical and Talmudic themes. How do they differ from verses on the same themes by the now half-forgotten Russian poet Lev Mei? What Yehoash and Liessin did, sometimes successfully, sometimes not, was to paraphrase a Biblical or legendary episode. But how far they were from the vision, the poetry, the style, of legend! Contrariwise, compare a verse or poem on a Biblical or Talmudic theme by a modern Yiddish poet with verses on similar themes by our older poets; compare Leivik's stanzes on Rabbi Akiva with Liessin's declamatory poem on the same subject. Leivik's poems about Saul, Cain and Abel, Joseph and his brothers; Glatstein's about Saul, Ezekiel, David and Abishag; Manger's Bible-poems—measure any of these against the Scriptural poems of Yehoash, and see who is nearer in spirit and imagination to Midrash. There is a point to Manger's calling one of his volumes *Itzik's Midrash.*

As Yiddish poetry grew more modern, even modernistic, as it grew freer in rhythm, subtler in tonality, more artful and sophisticated in imagery, it also grew more Jewish—I was almost going to say more Hasidic, in the Reb Nachman Bratzlaver sense of the word. The very first revolt in Yiddish poetry, that of the "Yunge," was expressed in a turning back to origins—origins which Peretz calls "barely experienced"—to the religious vision of the Jewish people, its sorrow and rapture, its Messianic longing and redemption-mythos.

You can see this not only in Leivick, but also in Moishe Leib Halpern, that mutineer and blasphemer. It is apparent in his images, the free skip of his apocalyptic fancies, his grotesquerie which contains so much of Yiddish Purim-theatricality, his bright rhythms redolent of traditional Gemara-tunes. And not only in Leivick and Moishe Leib—there is the same spirit in Mani Leib, that master of Yiddish idiom whom some like to consider not, God forbid, a Jew, but rather a sort of Russian in disguise. Certainly no one can deny or minimize the influence of Russian poetry on Mani Leib. Nevertheless no one else has set forth a poetry of Jewish faith in Mani Leib's particular manner and with his beauty and artistry. If we count Leivick (in verse only, of course) in the tradition of those cabalists who were not satisfied to await the Messiah but wanted to wrest him forth by force, then Mani Leib must be the poet of quiet folk-piety, the poet of belief who finds his expression in the common people's faith that God will not abandon them, that the miracle is not far off and can occur at the last second.

In Mani Leib, Elijah apears exactly as the common people conceived him—not the Elijah who flies up to heaven in a fiery chariot, but the one who secretly wanders over the earth, often disguised as a peasant. And who takes on still another incarnation in Mani Leib. "Only another whistler," Mani Leib calls himself—but who and what is he if not comfort-bringer, consoler, singer of lullabies? He is almost an Elijah himself. Look how the two resemble each other:

> Love and sorrow fill his eyes,
> Love smiles on his lips.
> Among the poor, in peasant's guise,
> From house to house Elijah slips.

And the poet goes among the same houses and "whistles like a wondrous flute the ballads of the poor," and as he whistles "[Jews] stand and hear, and in the stillness swallow tears, and their hearts rejoice that they are poor." Rosenfeld had sung "On a mute word hangs my people's dream." Modern Yiddish poets have lifted the dream out of muteness and given it tongue.

What was true of the "Yunge" (and I refer to the "Yunge" in Europe as well, whose major figure was David Einhorn) was also true of the "In Zikh" group in America and the so-called Expressionists in Europe. The "In Zikh" poets, notwithstanding their modernism, indeed because of it, were in the main oriented toward Jewish spiritual tradition. Their achievement was less sublimated than that of the "Yunge"—what they did was done in a direct, open, Jewishly-conscious manner.

The most important exponent of Yiddish Expressionism in these twenty years was Moishe Kulbak. Kulbak's Expressionism went hand in hand with an immersion in Jewish myth—David Einhorn rightly said of him a while ago that it was he who finally succeeded in finding the Jewish landscape, the specifically Jewish image. Kulbak saw even the Russian Revolution as a "bloody giant with golden Tablets." And as for Aaron Zeitlin, one of the modernists, it is not only his themes or his religio-mystical concepts that are Jewish, but the sharp Talmud-like distinctions that zigzag through the poem, the exactness of phrasing, the nuances, the feverish hairsplittings, the astonishingly brilliant similes. It seems to me also that Uri Tsvi Greenberg, an important representative of Yiddish modernism in these twenty years, is no exception to the rule: the more modern our poetry became in form, the more Jewish it became in spirit.

Melech Ravitch, however, is something of an exception. His stress is more on universal ethics than on the specific Jewish moment. Not long ago he called himself "a realist and a rationalist." Essentially, though, he is a kind of cross between an ancient Essene and a present-day Duchobor.

Although Peretz Markish was in Poland at the start of these twenty years, in terms of his origins he belongs to the Kiev group. His earliest poems came under the influence of Russian futurism and

imagism—this did not prevent him from being Jewish in style as well
as theme. Disheveled and gushing though his early poems are, they
already show a timelessness and authenticity. In his "Train Com-
partment" and in other work of that period, there is plainly a striving
toward Jewish tone in figure and image. In general it is worth noting
that the Yiddish poets who were under Yesenin's influence built their
sometimes stilted and overintellectualized images out of elements
common to Jewish liturgy and ritual. If Yesenin's intoxicated images
glistered with the gold of priestly robes and rang with the brass of
church bells, our imagists, by contrast, blew the ram's horn, wrapped
their language in phylacteries, decked it out in scroll-covers, ark-
curtains, vestments fringed and striped. Even more than in Markish
—though more refined, tamed—you can feel the striving toward a
Jewish style in the older poets, David Hofstein and Asher Schwartz-
man, and even more quietly and directly in Kvitko, Finenberg, Res-
nick and Steinman.

Indeed none other than Professor Y. Nusinov—who actually became an official Soviet critic—said in a lecture about the Kiev group
held in the first years after the Revolution:

> It must be emphasized that though the Kiev group adopted as
> its literary criterion the forms of modern world literature, still
> Yiddish literature has seldom achieved the kind of national and
> historical scope attained just now in the work of Bergelson,
> Nistar, Steinman, Hoftstein and Asher Schwartzman. The latter
> three combine the nationalist past with the Revolutionary future
> in a distinctly noteworthy way.

Bergelson in his literary articles of that time laid stress on
"Jewish elements" and in this regard pointed to Der Nistar as an
example for the younger Yiddish poets of that epoch. But as soon
as the poets of Kiev, Minsk, Kharkov, and other groups were poured
into the one and only stream of Soviet Yiddish poetry and, in the
words of a poem of Kvitko's "quarreled with their grandfathers and
fathers," the situation changed. It is beside the point to dismiss
Soviet Yiddish literature with a wave of the hand. The very fact that
among the Yiddish writers in the Soviet Union there were a number
of the most talented poets we have ever had necessitates a serious
and thoughtful frame of mind.

Soviet Yiddish poetry is a record of important accomplishments
not only in the freer first years, but in the later ones. We must know
how to read Soviet poetry: it is often a Marrano poetry. Between
one or another hymn to Stalin in a good Soviet poet you can fre-

quently find precious lyrical passages. And even from the standpoint of *yidishkayt* not everything is so simple. What appealed to scholarly, religious, even nationalist Jewish tradition nevertheless fulfilled the social tradition of the Jewish masses. "Common people from Nyezhin," to quote Mani Leib, "who study Torah with Vilna seminarians" are also Jews. In the work of Izzi Charik, especially in an early piece like "Minsk Mud," the collective energy of the Jewish mass explodes in protest over its bitter lot—an energy previously given blazingly subjective expression in some poems of Morris Rosenfeld and, more artfully, in some of the stories of Itche Meier Weisenberg.

In Itzik Feffer's earliest poems there is something of Sholom Aleichem. Feffer made a huge leap from his *shtetl* into the turbulent forces of the Revolution the way Motl Peisi, the cantor's son, sprang out of the closeness of his father's sickroom into the spring air. Feffer rejoiced in the Revolution and its Red Army regiments and blond Komsomol members on the front just as another boy in Sholom Aleichem rejoiced in a Passover-eve emigration.

However many virtues can be ascribed to Soviet Yiddish poetry, which by the way has now become a Jewish estate without heirs in its own land, it is undeniable that when it "quarreled with its grandfathers and fathers" it more and more lost the fruitful soil from which modern Yiddish poetry developed. Ultimately it is a poetry of frontiersmen and frontiers without a hinterland—without that vast spiritual Jewish hinterland and reserve. In the last analysis a great part of Soviet Yiddish poetry lacks timelessness and durability. Out of the thousands and thousands of poems written by Soviet Yiddish poets, who knows how many can be salvaged for the general store of Yiddish poetry? To be sure, during the war, when Russian poets took to celebrating Minin and Pozharsky, Soviet Yiddish poetry was hymning Judah Macabee and Bar Kokhba. It is also true that in the period when it was permissible to laud the Jewish heritage openly and openly mourn the destruction of the Jews, the poetry of Markish, Hofstein, Feffer and, in part, Halkin and others, had greater substance, warmth, sincerity. But this point should not be carried too far. The Yiddish poet in Russia had already been too much terrorized, too much bureaucratized, too long kept in line for him to be able to breathe freely even in matters that deeply involved his emotions.

And what is true of Soviet Yiddish poetry is even truer of socalled proletarian Yiddish poetry in America, which was never noted for its talent. Nowadays it is enough simply to leaf through the couple of dozens of booklets by the proletarian poets to see how, with a few exceptions, the bulk of it is dated, obsolete—how gray, dull, and poor it all is.

Unfortunately I cannot dwell upon the generation of poets that came after the period of revolt and renewal. There are poets of genuine talent in this group who already have significant work to their credit. And I mean, of course, not only poets in America but those who came to maturity during these twenty years in Poland, Galicia, Rumania and other diaspora communities. Their number is too large even to list, let alone describe.

Considered broadly, it is a generation which arrived with no new artistic manifestos, fashioned no schools and overthrew nothing. Not every revolution, after all, is destined to make artistic revolutions, nor is such a thing necessary for the progress of literature. It is enough that poets have sprung up who can exploit and reinforce the new elements brought about by their predecessors. And that is what this generation of poets has done. It established what the previous generation initiated, with, to be sure, significant changes. What must particularly be kept in mind when we speak of this generation is the fact that it was preceded not simply by an older poetry, but by an explicit artistic tradition. And this brings me to the second point, or thesis, of my paper: that the true makers of artistic tradition in our poetry were not the classical figures, as in other cultures, but in fact the modernists; not the fathers, but the sons and grandsons.

The tradition is still young and there remain room and possibility enough for innovation and further elaboration. Already there are signs, however, that it is a tradition on the verge of becoming not merely crystallized, but fixed, rigid, in danger of becoming conventional and stereotyped, and of breeding epigones instead of stimulating new vigor. Observe, for example, how the turn toward Jewish spiritual tradition, once so penetrating and fruitful, begins to degenerate into tedium and hollowness, a "love-of-Israel" committed to nothing. We can only hope that today's Yiddish poets are not the last, and that poets may arise who will both invigorate and rebel against the artistic tradition of the last four or five decades.

I want to return for a moment to our pioneers and classical figures. Are their achievements in Yiddish poetry no longer worth anything to us? Perhaps no less than the modernists, they too fashioned a tradition. But it was not so much in the structure of their poetry, a good bit of which is alas permanently out of date, as in the spirit and ideals that animated them. The older Yiddish poetry is obsolete in form but fresh and robust in spirit. It exhibits a faith in mankind and humaneness, a healthy optimism, a hope for a brighter future, a trust in human reason; it is distinguished for its social passion, its lucid rationalism and positive view of life. These are all things which we are very much in want of today.

And when, as we never cease to hope, new Yiddish poets arrive who feel the need to return to a sober and critical consideration of things, they—weary of hidden complexities—will be able to turn back to the unambiguous clarity of our older poets. Thanks to the artistic renovations of the modernist tradition in Yiddish poetry, they will be able to bring the refinements of modernist craft even to plain and secular motifs.

1962

At Goodman and Levine's

by Reuben Iceland

Translated by Nathan Halper

In the basement of the Yiddish newspaper, the *Day*, where nowadays
you find the mailing department and presses, with the smell of ink,
lead, paper dust and mailbags, there—many years ago, before the
Day was born—one used to meet a smell of roast herring and cooked
fish, sour borsht, fried pancakes, bad coffee, scalded milk, as well as
other odors so intermingled that it wasn't easy to say which was
which. On the couple of steps which go down to the cellar from
East Broadway and which nowadays are used only in the hours
when the newspaper is mailed—in those years there was traffic from
early morning till deep into the night. For here, in this cellar, was
the dairy restaurant of Goodman and Levine and to it used to stream
all of the young Yiddish writers who were at that time in New York.
Not because, God forbid, they had such a fondness for dairy dishes,
but because it was the center of *Di Yunge*.

This was where you might recite a poem or hear one—where
you might listen and discover something about poetry or stories, because the talk on literary topics never came to a stop. Here you might
meet the handful of young writers whom either chance or talent had
raised up above the rest, so that they were famous while some of
the others were still unknown. It was also where you waited—with
a beating heart—till you were able to hear how you were currently
rated as a storyteller or poet.

The general public did not know about this place. The public, if
it had any interest in Yiddish writers, knew that on Division Street
there is a coffeehouse once known as Herrick's Cafe, subsequently

as Sholom's, and that this is where the older writers gather, those who appear in the papers. That there are others as well as these, the public did not know. And if it had known, it would not have been impressed.

This coffeehouse of our elders was known even in the "provinces," for almost all of the patrons at Sholom's were considered people of importance. Once, in Cleveland, near the end of 1914, when I happened to mention the name of a certain writer, telling how I got involved in a bit of argument with him about contemporary writing, I sensed that they began to wink at each other behind my back. "The fellow is bluffing!" If those people are still alive and remember the occasion, I am sure that to this very day I have remained in their eyes as nothing but a boaster.

There were two reasons why *Di Yunge* chose to carry on by themselves in a separate cafe. One was purely financial. The coffeehouse on Division Street was too dear for young writers, most of whom either were poor workers in a factory or had no job whatever. To spend these hours at Sholom's they would need at least a quarter in their pocket and—in those days, for these young men—this was a sizable sum. If even ten cents were lacking—which was not unusual —they would order a glass of coffee or tea with cookie or roll and would sit there the same number of hours for no more than a nickel. The other reason was snobbish. Our spokesmen simply felt that it was beneath us to pass the time in the same cafe as our elders.

There was a bit of immaturity in this snobbish exclusiveness. Nonetheless, it also expressed a healthy instinct. *Di Yunge* had found something that was new and personal and they felt that, for this to survive, they must isolate themselves from the old and established writers. It was therefore forbidden to have any dealings with the papers and magazines in which the others printed their things. One would be obliged to make compromises there and become subject to the will and taste of the elders. If what one has in mind is literature as such, one should have nothing to do with papers or their scribblers. And if one really wants to be careful, one must even avoid a cafe where they set the tone. Writers must have a place in which to get printed. They must also have a place in which to gather. To avoid dependence on the newspapers, we began to print our own journals and anthologies. Not to be under one roof with the older writers, we isolated ourselves in a separate cafe.

On a literary level, this brought excellent results. In other ways, however, it had its comic aspects and, not infrequently, some that were also tragicomic. One scene comes back with particular sharpness. It happened in the early months of 1915, a short time before the

Day moved from Pearl Street to the building at East Broadway which it still occupies. The days of the cafe were numbered. A few weeks later, Goodman and Levine's was closed and we, *Di Yunge*, had to give up our own place and mingle with the older writers who, at that time, had moved from Sholom's Cafe to L. Shapiro's Restaurant, also on East Broadway, near the corner of Rutgers.

It didn't take us long to see that the move was not a bad one. The food was better, the coffee certainly better, and at these new tables we felt just as much in our element as at the old ones in Goodman and Levine's. We also quickly realized that we no longer had any reason to fear the harmful influence of our elders; we were now sufficiently mature to be able to have a harmful influence ourselves. We had also gained enough literary prominence so that they, our seniors, were no longer able to dominate. It was we who took command in any place we entered. Still—before we left the cellar, we played a trick like this one.

About ten of us were sitting that night in Goodman's cellar when there entered a disciple of one of our most famous poets. He intoned a chant: "Come on! Banquet at Shapiro's! Fellows—you're invited. All of you are invited."

No one had to tell us for whom the party was held. The famous poet had in those days a habit of giving banquets for himself. A new book—a banquet. Two books? Certainly a banquet. No book or anniversary—he would think of some other occasion. Today I realize that all of these banquets were only a pretext for festivity, to dispel a passing gloominess or simply because of a longing for a drink in company. But in those days we had a feud with this poet and in such a case whatever the enemy does you see only his bad intentions. In these little banquets we saw merely a striving for more status and acclaim and, on this night, we decided, "Enough! We won't help him in his plans." And no matter how much his disciple urged, no one got up from our table. The famous poet's disciple left just as he had come—alone.

The poet was mortified. Is this possible? He is having a banquet, they have been invited. How can they refuse to come?

One delegation after another came to us in the cellar. Who was not included in these embassies? The most distinguished personages of the time. Yet no one got up from our table. The delegations returned just as they had come—without us. Secretly we were rather ashamed of our performance. Our stubbornness began to look foolish and arrogant. But the more embassies there came, the more our stubbornness increased. Only one of us got up. All of the others refused to stir. For a long time, we accounted this as a very heroic episode.

Only four or five of the tables in this cellar were "reserved" for writers. These stood in a corner to the left of the entrance, between kitchen and buffet.

No good came to us from either direction. From the buffet, we would be stabbed by the large, hostile eyes of one of the partners, especially if the restaurant was full and it didn't occur to these beggars that it might be the decent thing to leave the tables to more respectable customers. And out of the kitchen we would always get fumes, a bad smell of frying, a clang of tableware and the clatter of dishes getting washed. Our eyes would frequently smart because of the smoke that, beating through the kitchen door, would gather under the low ceiling: to which there would be added the reek of numberless cigarettes. Summer was frightfully hot. In the winter, one's feet would often freeze from the cold which blew along the floor or came in from the street when the door was opened. The food—as in most East Side eating places of the time—was barely endurable. The coffee simply horrible. The comments that you heard about yourself as writer were frequently enough to curdle your mother's milk—yet the cellar drew us. It drew us like a magnet.

I have already mentioned that in those days the majority of the young writers were shop workers. To miss a day's pay often meant not to have money to buy a pair of shoes for your child or be short three dollars toward the rent. Nonetheless, whenever you came into the cellar, you would find a crowd of people who, as you knew, were supposed to be in the shop. Several of *Di Yunge* were paperhangers and painters, and it wasn't unusual for them to get off the ladders in the middle of a job and come into the cafe in spattered work clothes which had once been white and with streaks of color on their face and hands. For a long time I used to have my lunch in the shop, fearful that if I went down to a restaurant I would not have the strength of will to complete the day's work.

Once on a Saturday in summer, when I worked only half a day, I came home and, after having my lunch, went to a barber to be shaved. In the evening, I was going to take my wife and six-month-old daughter to see one of our relations. I lived on Fourth Street, close to Avenue B; the barbershop was somewhere on Houston. In the chair, however, I suddenly felt the call of the cafe and was hardly able to wait for the barber to finish my shave.

It did enter my mind that it might be sensible to go home first and say where I was going. But my feet already were turning toward East Broadway. The day being hot, I expected to find only a couple of my colleagues in the cafe. For this reason, if no other, I would probably stay only an hour or two. It turned out, however, that the cellar was full. Out of a sea of faces and the clouds of smoke, there began to emerge the image of Mani Leib—a finger rocking in front of his nose like a pointer—his green, visionary eyes squinting at the homely, freckled, yet vital and insolent face of Moishe Leib Halpern.

I no longer remember what subject they were so passionate about at the time I came in. All I know is that in a moment I was in the midst of it myself. And it continued to boil—an hour, two, three. From one topic we would leap into a second, from a second to a third. Soon we were back at the first, each trying to prove a point with a quotation from an essay or a poem. In the same fashion, others tried to prove the opposite and for this purpose were also able to find crushing statements from a different authority.

Some left, others came. More of the writers left—and others took their place. We kept moistening our throat with coffee or with tea, at the same time nibbling on pancakes, on *blini*, cookies, rolls— especially on cigarettes. Hours flew. Night fell: no one noticed. Half the crowd had vanished; yet we, the other half, continued to sit there. The sweat kept pouring: yet we sat—talking. Goodman, at the buffet, sent sharp and contemptuous glances. Not seeing him or his eyes, we continued the discussion. Finally, Goodman exclaimed, "Even in Hell there is a time when they rest. Go in good health!" But it sounded like—Go to the devil!

It was already two in the morning. Those of us who were left set out through the tiny Seward Park to Delancey Street, from there on Essex until Avenue A, over Tompkins Square on to Avenue B, and from there—on Tenth Street—to the river, where one of us knew a wonderful place, near a lumberyard, which was very lovely and cool. Back to Tompkins Square, then on the numbered streets. And all the time our tongues never stopped. We kept finding topics that ought to be discussed.

At long last, the group started to get smaller, till only two of us were left, Mani Leib and I. It wasn't far from my house but he lived in Brooklyn and began to feel gloomy about having to go back, so he asked me to walk him as far as Delancey Street, where he would take the trolley that would bring him home. On Delancey, he decided to walk me back to my house. Then, in the middle of this, we turned again on Delancey.

Our literary conversation had run down. It was just before sunrise, yet we now had reached the haunting wistfulness of sunset.

We began to speak about the workday week, about the hardship of that life, about the fretting and yearning that fills the nights at home, and how all this, these long and boring talks, are at bottom no more than an escape, an attempt to hush the yearnings in oneself. He told me that when he comes home late at night he gets into his apartment not by way of the door, but climbs up to the roof and from there moves down the fire escape to a window in his flat, and that he creeps into his house life a thief—so his wife shouldn't hear him; and that, once, he happened to get lost and opened the window of a neighbor, an Italian, and how the other, thinking he was a thief, attacked him with a knife.

When Mani Leib finally got on the streetcar, the sun had already risen on the Brooklyn side of the East River. Only now did I realize that I'd stayed away the whole night, that I had not told my wife I might be delayed, and that we were supposed to visit a relation. It was with a troubled heart that I began approaching Fourth Street. When I came to the building in which I lived, the grocery downstairs was already open and the grocer, standing by the door, looked at me severely and said, "Young man, wasn't it your wife who ran to the police to look for you?"

1954

Yiddish Literature in the United States

by Joseph Opatashu

Translated by Shlomo Noble

It is now more than a half century since a new Yiddish literature has been in the process of development in the United States; new in its range and forms of expression, new in its outlook upon life and the world. This American Yiddish literature is quite different from Yiddish literature of earlier times. Both of course have their sources in Odessa, Warsaw, Kiev; also in the thirteenth and fourteenth centuries, the heroic period in Jewish life which produced *Shmuel-bukh* —an original creation of a purely Jewish theme, expressed in a mature and highly traditional manner. American Yiddish literature, organically connected with these sources and still nourished by them, has nevertheless a very different character. Indeed, those who had formed their literary taste on a reading of earlier Yiddish writings must find the work of American Yiddish writers both eccentric and alien.

What is the explanation for this phenomenon? For it is not merely the result of the new environment or the new climate; nor can stress be placed simply upon the thematic material. The fact is that the past half century has witnessed a literary revolt in the United States not only among writers in Yiddish but among writers in English as well. The rebellion among the latter began a decade later, lasted longer, and was carried on more intensively and widely. These American writers suddenly realized that they were living a life not their own. They found themselves nearly suffocated by the

Reprinted by permission of YIVO Institute for Jewish Research, New York, from "Yiddish Literature in the United States," by Joseph Opatashu.

prestige and centuries-old traditions of English literature. Overnight these young Americans of 1910–12 gave up Shakespeare, Byron, Shelley, Dickens, and Meredith. They refused to follow the trodden English path. Instead they insisted on making their own way in world literature.

The United States had great writers before 1900. Poets such as Poe and Whitman helped to create "schools" in France and added their idiom to world literature. Yet there was no distinctly American literature. Neither Poe nor Whitman, who have enriched world poetry, were fully recognized in their native land before World War I. It was then not easy for an American writer to establish his own way; it was even more difficult for him than for a Jew in the time of the Gaon of Vilna to be either a *hasid* or an agnostic. This was particularly true of Poe and Whitman who had refused to follow England's trodden literary path. By seeking to express themselves in their own way, however, they laid the cornerstone of contemporary American literature. Their youthful successors in the twentieth century deliberately discarded English tradition and began to write about themselves, about their America. In the process they gave birth to a new language: unpolished words, lively, full-blooded, that drove out the genteel and rigid diction of the English.

Almost the same situation, on a much smaller scale, occurred among the immigrant Jews in the United States. It was no imitation, of course, since this process of Americanization among Yiddish writers had begun a decade earlier. Migration readily improved the economic status of the Jewish newcomers. Once the immigrants lost the fear of hunger and the morrow and accustomed themselves to a degree of comfort, they became aware that they were cut off from their old home. They felt uneasy at the thought of having given up so much of their Jewishness—for they continued to feel the strong tug of the threads that tied their new life to the old.

When the immigrant had gorged himself with American abundance, even delicacies ceased to appeal to him. He became homesick and began to look back across the ocean as if there, in Poland, in Lithuania, in the Ukraine, in Rumania and Hungary, were the Heavenly Tabernacle where he had abandoned his soul and as if here, in America, he had found the Devil that knows of no Sabbath, no Holy Day, just work and nothing but work.

The yearning of these immigrants for their spiritual heritage—the synagogue with its study groups devoted to the psalms and other holy writings—caused them to become critical of things American. The old-country cucumber seemed to them infinitely superior to the local variety. With their homes unsanctified by *mezzuzas* at the door, the evil spirit invaded the Jewish quarter. A superficial anarchism and an equally superficial socialism began to propagate free love, mixed marriages, Yom Kippur balls, and warred constantly not so much against God as against everything the Jews cherished.

Yet at the turn of the century all this had just the opposite effect, serving as a sort of inoculation against dissoluteness and cheap cynicism. Instead of attending Yom Kippur balls many Jews began to form societies and gathered on Saturday and Sunday evenings to ease their longing for the old country. On those occasions they steeped themselves in "the good old days" of the towns of their birth. They refused to make peace with life in America, where children, growing without guidance and looking like rowdies in knickers, laughed at their parents for speaking incorrect English, played ball all day, and appeared bereft of the traditional filial piety.

Meantime the hurly-burly of American life wound itself about the necks of these immigrants like a hangman's noose. To protect themselves from this danger that lurked in the streets and even in their own homes, they began to transplant their "Cities of God" to their mundane surroundings. Soon in all larger American cities there appeared cultural microcosms simulating their native towns in Poland, Lithuania, the Ukraine, Rumania, and Hungary. All over the Jewish quarter there sprung up signs announcing improvised synagogues for the natives of Zamość, Lublin, Vilna, Kovno, Jassy, Pressburg, etc.

These organizations were formed not only for religious prayer but also for burial purposes. Jewish cemeteries were divided into sections, and each section was enclosed by an iron fence with a carved gate. The gilt letters on these portals made known that Jews clung to their native towns not only in life but in the hereafter. Here on the cemetery it was obvious that these Jews failed to take root in the United States; that they worked hard, very hard for the devil, but their souls remained in their native towns. One became fearful at the thought that their yearning did not subside even with death.

The environment of the 1880's and 1890's and even of the first years of the twentieth century was hardly conducive to the development of an American Yiddish literature. Jewish life was too turbulent, confused. There was no tranquility, no distance between the writer and his book. Most of all there were no roots, no ancestors. Jews had fled their countries for fear of arrest, military service, poverty, over boy-girl trouble. Those who had some tradition either had cast it overboard or had simply lost it on the way. In their new home they neither would nor could strike roots. Their aim was to save some money and return. They felt no affection for America or even for their own home. Workers kept changing jobs, and each shift usually meant moving to a new tenement. There was no time to settle down, to learn to appreciate one's own home. And what was true of the shop workers was equally true of the peddler, the merchant, the craftsman. Life was feverish, temporary, an interlude ending with their going back. The popular song, A *brivele der mamen* ("A Letter to Mother"), was typical of those that were sung in the streets and at home and often brought tears of longing to their listeners.

Such an environment could not bring forth a Yiddish literature. An isolated poet or novelist appeared to claim attention, but the only bond among them was the fact that they wrote in Yiddish. When they did resort to American themes, they concentrated on the immigrant who dreamt of escaping from the United States. This newcomer was depicted as ascribing all his woes and difficulties to the "bad" and turbulent America. He felt no love for his new home, no ties to the new soil. The writers followed the patterns established in Odessa, in Kiev, or in Warsaw, and were notably lacking in merit. Reingold, Sharkansky, Edelstat, Bovshover, Winchevsky—their work was a medley of socialist and anarchist propaganda in verse and fiction. That was the literature of the period, and the radical journals of the day boasted of its greatness.

In the preface to the first issue of *Di Zukunft* in 1892 the initial sentence read: "Our program may really be expressed in three words: We are Social-Democrats." The editor further explained why a serious monthly periodical was being established in the Yiddish "jargon": "*Di Zukunft* is being issued for Jewish workers who would like to educate themselves but have no opportunity because until now the Yiddish 'jargon,' the only language they can read, was used only for shoddy novels and folk drolleries."

In 1892 when the editor of *Di Zukunft* wrote with such authority about the shoddy writings published in the Yiddish "jargon," he apparently did not know that Mendele had already composed *Dos kleyne mentshele* ("The Little Man") in 1866 and *Fishke der krumer* ("Fishke the Lame") in 1869. As much as a quarter of a century earlier, therefore, Mendele had proclaimed, "My soul cleaves to the Yiddish language and unites with it forever." There had also appeared Sholom Aleichem's and Peretz's *Biblyotekn* ("Libraries"), but these were seemingly unknown to the Jews of New York. These immigrants spoke a poor Yiddish, with the pride of innovators; by comparison the Yiddish in *Di Zukunft* was a step upward, a kind of renascence.

The Jewish-American pandemonium of the 1880's and 1890's

brought forth its poet—Morris Rosenfeld. In his verses are to be found traces of America, of a Jewish America. He went to the workers' quarter with a bass drum to pound out his songs. His satire had not only molars but incisors—and still has them. In a time of confusion and false prophets, when Jewish life is turbulent and thorny, satire is the most appropriate form. Rosenfeld's prose is therefore as significant as his poetry; perhaps even more so to the historian seeking to familiarize himself with the Jewish life of that period.

The critics say that Rosenfeld was an oak. But one oak does not make a forest, as nine men do not make a *minyan*.

Kobrin and Libin appear. Bovshover blazes up. Yehoash arrives in America, then Liessin, Rosenblatt.

David Pinski's arrival brought forth good short stories about life among the workers. He was the first to depict their joys and sorrows, their simplicity and courage. That was something new in Yiddish. Endurance is the real criterion of a work of art, and Pinski's stories of workingmen possess the same freshness now that they had when they were first written a half century ago. Literary aspirants sensed this quality in him and were grateful for his ready hospitality and encouragement.

Only in 1905, after the failure of the Russian revolution, did a new type of immigrant set out for America, one who had destroyed all bridges behind him. And in his destruction lay his essential creativity. Almost at once these newcomers, disappointed in the Russian revolution, caught on to the American rhythm and to American spaciousness and they began to love their new home. Influenced by such writers as Joel Entin, Alexandrov, and later Zhitlowsky and Borukhov, they perceived that destruction confronted the Jews who did not live as Jews; that under those circumstances the written word shed its creativity, fell away from Jewish tradition—which was and must be a constant re-creation, a constant accretion of layers over the old, hallowed generations.

Our way of life and our literature ought to be and are our Halacha and Haggada. In each creative work we ought to detect the essence of past generations and of their culture. In Peretz's work you feel the echo sometimes of Isaiah, sometimes of Jeremiah, sometimes of Job. In Sholom Aleichem of Elijah the Prophet, not the Biblical figure, but as the folk literature conceived him, turning up in a time of trouble for Jews. This essence of past generations is the only criterion that determines the Jewish character of a creative work. For Jewish creativity is not a stagnant water overgrown with bog grass, but a running water that does not cease to flow, does not cease to stream into eternity.

By "the essence of generations," I do not mean the essence of warmed-over sentimentality, the aroma of the *tsholent* pot so to speak, which Dineson and to some extent Mendele introduced in our literature. In Peretz, who wrote hasidic stories in a folk style, that particular *tsholent* aroma was never there.

With the new immigrants came the new writers. They went into the factories and on the farms and at first did not even dream of making the written word their life's pursuit. Having burned their bridges behind them, these young writers never considered returning to the land of their birth. They immediately sought to strike new roots and unwittingly created a new Yiddish literature. This orientation was an inner process, an organic union of Yiddish literature with its new environment. Because this new literature developed very rapidly, it quickly overtook and outgrew the average reader. Indeed, for a reader who smacked his lips over a trashy novel by Zelikovitch, what enjoyment could he get out of a quality novel like Raboy's *Her Goldenbarg?*

Outwardly the writings of *Di Yunge* were a protest both against Odessa, Kiev, and Warsaw and, even more, against the haphazard state of Yiddish; against the American Yiddish press, whose leaders looked upon Yiddish as a means soon to be discarded; against the process which eliminated the savory kernels of Yiddish speech and left only the empty chaff. Besides, the sentimentality had to be smoked out. Among our Yiddish writers, the trees swayed too often in afternoon prayer, the sky was too often enveloped in a prayer shawl. And, to go from the sublime to the profane, the yellow press had one stock female: "She was like a 'baby doll,' but strong as an animal. When she lifted a leg, all the men drooled."

Protests of this kind united the young writers. Their trees ceased to sway in prayer, their skies ceased to be pure-blue prayer shawls. That was the only way to emancipate Yiddish literature from traditional sentimentalism. And once emancipated, the authentic Jewish strengths which had been tightly pent up in every genuine writer began to surge anew.

It first showed itself as a strong love of America. The neighborhood into which these young writers gravitated was largely populated by Germans, who had a decade earlier replaced the Scottish pioneers. The latter had entered the uninhabited section of Greater New York in the 1860's and 1870's, cut down trees and built themselves two-storied wooden homes with broad verandas. Each one had his cow, his horse and buggy, his dog. Their cows grazed where later were located Tremont Avenue, Jerome Avenue, the Grand Concourse. In time there arose a German brewery with its tall chimney belching smoke day and night. Others were built, and they soon served as fortresses to the German newcomers who began storming the neighborhood, establishing their beer saloons and taverns. Fifteen years later not a Scotsman remained in the vicinity.

Jews began to lay siege to this German fortress around 1903. They came from Manhattan's East Side and fought the Germans for years on end. It was at first dangerous for a Jew to pass a house occupied by a German and guarded by large vicious dogs. Blue Teutonic eyes became green with hatred for the invading Jews, but the latter persisted in their siege. Private homes were torn down and the rocky foundations were dynamited in preparation for the erection of large apartment houses. Pneumatic drills chattered deafeningly and bulldozers and tractors added to the pandemonium. But out of this hellish hubbub soon emerged the most beautiful section of the Bronx—the achievement of energetic and enterprising Jews. In this neighborhood, while still quite rural, young Jewish writers conceived their songs, their stories, their novels. And if they felt gratified to cleave to the soil, with its flowers and living creatures, they were even more pleased to associate with the dynamic men who were building homes, streets, cities. This joy in nature and this dynamism enlivened their writings. Soon Yiddish literature in the United States, though far from its source of origin, assumed an artistic form in many respects superior to the work of the first masters; reminding one that the great Polish works of Mickiewicz and Slowacki were written not in Poland but in France and Switzerland.

More. The idea of redemption, which found its highest artistic expression in Poland in Peretz's work—not the Baal Shem Tov's idea of redemption, since he had never stressed it, but that of the hasidim who had preceded him and who had confusedly stressed the "end" —took wing in American Yiddish literature.

Most of these young writers had great love toward Peretz and Sholom Aleichem. They were critical of Mendele because he had forced a beggar's sack upon "Yisroel" and cut down the wings of those who sought to rise upward. What Kriev, after World War II, pointed out about Mendele in his essay, "I Want to Relieve My Mind," Di Yunge had already stated in 1914. Not all members of this group of course were protagonists of this idea of redemption. It should be remembered that Yiddish literature in America had no "schools." Di Yunge was no literary school; nor were the "Introspectivists" a cult. The fathers of the "Introspectivists"—Leyeles, Glatstein, and Minkov—would have felt just as much at home among the members of Di Yunge—and vice versa. All of these writers were united in their protest against the mediocrity and irresponsibility existing among their fellow Jews.

Di Yunge included poets who regarded themselves as "song-birds," as esthetes emphasizing playfulness and those who believed that a writer must always seek the tie between his milieu and the past generation, for only then does the artist sense new vitality. The split between the two wings came in 1914. The esthetes—Zisha Landau, Mani Leib, and David Ignatov—took over the periodic anthology *Shriftn.*[1] I. J. Schwartz, Joseph Rolnik, Chaimowitch, Fradel Shtok, and I published *Di Naye Heym.*[2] Later Leivick and Boraisho joined us.

Morris Rosenfeld was a fine poet. But just compare some of his best poems with any poem by one of *Di Yunge* to see with what momentum the artistry of Yiddish moved ahead in all ways—in diction, in world view, in artistic expression, in form. What did this difference consist of? Yiddish literature ceased to be a means of enlightenment and became an end in itself. Its criterion became an artistic criterion. Subject matter ceased to be all-important, since it of itself did not make the writer.

A literature may be replete with traditional paraphernalia of long coats and hasidic hats, yet not be Jewish; thus the *Dibuk* and *Yoshe kalb* are pseudo-Jewish. Leivick, on the other hand, wrote his poems of Siberia in New York, yet each line pulsates with Jewish woe. Raboy lived on an American farm and wrote about cows and horses and the wild prairie, and every line breathes Jewishness. So it is with Yehoash, Liessin, Halpern, Mani Leib, Boraisho, Leyeles, Siegel, Glatstein, and Auerbach. It is a question of expansiveness, scope, rhythm.

There is a rhythm in America that is alien to Europe; not the external rhythm that is only skin deep, but the inner rhythm that comes from getting to be at home in the country, with the average American, of whom one out of two traces his ancestry back to four or five peoples—not so much generations as peoples. American avenues extend their asphalt or concrete surfaces as far as the eye can see—and the distance draws one on. One has the feeling that if one picked up and threw a flat pebble, it would never stop. And if these particulars are considered superficial and unimportant, the answer is that a multiplication of these particulars results in the breadth and beat of life, even as a multiplication of atoms makes up the entire material world.

It is a mistake to judge an important writer by a narrow esthetic criterion. Artists like Peretz cannot be measured that way. Their characters are gushing springs, where human souls are cleansed and

[1] Published 1912–1914 and later 1917, 1920, 1921.
[2] Published 1914.

rejuvenated and where human fate appears in all its tragedy. Those who do not probe the sources of their own life—whose lives are spent within the ready-made folk forms—will never appreciate the differences between a poet like Peretz and a great writer like Mendele. For the problem is not one merely of talent. Every artist must be talented. But talent alone is not enough. It is a question of depth, of spiritual effort.

Every people creates spiritual resources; folk resources are created haphazardly. Out of these folk resources artists who can see and listen, with alert senses, create order. Mendele was the greatest among these artists. But there are artists who do not depend upon the resources of the folk. These are insufficient for them. Such artists seek to fathom the power that creates a people, they want to discover if that power is also within them as artists. I know the universe to which Mendele and Rosenfeld belong. Peretz's universe, however, as it seeks to discover and liberate itself, is not that easy to grasp. This spirit which strives to liberate itself was always present among Jews, whether in Judah Halevi or Peretz, poets of genius who sought and found their justification in Jewish life. The American Yiddish writers of whom I am speaking—Yehoash, Liessin, Pinski, Halpern, Rolnik, Mani Leib, I. J. Schwartz, Leivick, Boraisho, Leyeles, Glatstein, Siegel—all sought and found those depths of Judah Halevi and Peretz.

The Holocaust notwithstanding, Yiddish literature in America is still a multibranched tree that sheds its withered leaves and grows new ones, fresh ones. The Holocaust ought to be a summons to continue the work of earlier generations. Let it be said that the concept of continuity is a Jewish one. Continuity in world history is a new idea, born with the French Revolution. Until then historians believed that historical figures, world conflicts, and above all God Himself more than once disrupted continuity; whereas with the Jews, God's people, God Himself kept repeating: "Remember the days of old, consider the years of many generations," and arousing national historical remembrance: "so that the generation to come might know them, even to the children that should be born."

That was the foundation of American Yiddish literature in the last half century. It was laid between those two pillars—Rosenfeld and Yehoash. Story upon story has risen upon that foundation. These stories are inhabited by Yehoash's Yiddish translation of all the books of the Bible. The sacred books animate American Yiddish literature—Liessin's ballads about the Baal Shem Tov, Halpern's *Goldene Pave* ("The Golden Peacock"), Mani Leib's poems for children, I. J. Schwartz's epic poem *Kentucky,* and Leivick's two poetic dramas of the redemption, *Der goylem* ("The Golem") and *Di geule-komedye* ("The Comedy of Redemption"), Leyeles's work on the theme of redemption based on the life of Shlomo Molko[3] and Glatstein's *Shtralndike yidn* ("Radiant Jews"). Then comes Boraisho's *Der Geyer* ("The Wayfarer"), whose Elijah is not the prophet of the Bible, nor the Yiddish folktales, but the Elijah of Habad hasidism.[4] All these Elijahs proudly carry on their shoulders their wares which they gathered and fashioned on their way, ascending from story to story, as they fashioned consummate epics, flawless lyrics, masculine prose, fashioned life and people, fashioned the structure we call Yiddish literature in America.

1949

---

[3] Shlomo Molko, ca. 1500–1532, a Marrano cabalist and visionary who proclaimed himself the Messiah's forerunner. He was condemned to death by an ecclesiastical court in Mantua.

[4] Habad hasidism was founded in White Russia by Rabbi Schneur Zalmèn of Lyady (1745–1813). HaBaD is an acronym for *hokhma* (wisdom), *bina* (understanding), *da'at* (knowledge). In contrast to the hasidic dynasties that were entrenched in the Ukraine and in Poland which stressed spontaneity and joyousness, Habad combined its founder's original philosophic system with rabbinic learning and mysticism.

Words, Language, Style

by Jacob Sternberg

Translated by Samuel Mintz

A little skill in Aesopian reading should help to illuminate the power-fully charged issues behind the surface of this essay. Its author Jacob Sternberg (1890–   ) is one of the most gifted Yiddish poets of the twentieth century; he has lived in the Soviet Union since the Second World War. He writes here, in his old age, as a wily opponent of a Soviet Yiddish linguist, M. Shapiro, who has served as an official political-cultural tone-setter for what little remains of the Soviet Yiddish literary world. Ostensibly their dispute concerns the relationship of the Hebrew component of the Yiddish language to its other components; but actually Sternberg is making a vigorous case for the autonomy of the writer in general and the Yiddish writer in particular, as well as for the historical integrity and international character of Yiddish culture. All of these issues have long been debated and fought over in the world of Soviet Yiddish.

It will help the reader grasp the urgency of Sternberg's argument if he recalls that in the late twenties and thirties, as part of the cultural terror of Stalinism, the Yiddish commissars demanded that the vocabulary of the Soviet Yiddish writers be purged of its Hebraic elements, thereby, it was argued, cleansing it of both its traditional religious associations and its links with "bourgeois" Yiddish literature throughout the world. That these issues, in a somewhat muted form, still agitate and oppress the Yiddish writers of the Soviet Union becomes clear from Sternberg's essay.—Eds.

You may recall, esteemed comrade Shapiro, that in the third number of *Sovyetish heymland*,[1] in my article "Introduction to a Dialogue Concerning Literary Criticism," I raised the question: "Where do we stand today with respect to language, considered from a purely artistic standpoint?" As you see, the second half of my question went beyond a consideration of the spoken language only; it took up the problem of our cultural language, the medium of our literature. I further developed my question as follows: "Does the present generation of Yiddish-Soviet writers live only on its heritage, or does it bring with it fresh new layers of language, as had been done by virtually every one of the founders of Soviet-Yiddish literature? Is our Yiddish literary language innovative or static?" Moreover, I added that "concerning this important question not only the linguist, the grammarian, but also the literary critic must have his say."

Today, in the wake of the language symposium organized by *Sovyetish heymland*, to which your paper was the chief contribution, a paper in which could be heard a number of language directives for the guidance of our literature—today not only must the linguist have his say, but so too the writer. Not because we writers do not, God forbid, trust you in your entirely significant enterprise of language research, but because when discussion arises concerning language and literature, it frequently happens that you, the linguist, speak of words whereas we, the writers, speak of language. Or to be more precise: you speak of language and we—of style. And as Belinsky had already demonstrated in his controversy with the Russian grammarian, Gretsch, concerning Gretsch's attacks on the language of Gogol, language and style are not "one and the same." "Between language and style," wrote Belinsky, "is the same immeasurable distance as between the inert, mechanical skill in draftsmanship of an untalented dauber and the vital, original style of a gifted painter."

Here then is one ground of our dispute. The second is your habit of assuming for yourself the right of ultimate authority in *all* questions of language. No doubt you make this assumption on the strength of your expert knowledge and your unexcelled gifts of research, but these credentials lose some of their power, it seems to me, when you as linguists take it upon yourselves to legislate, to correct both the general public and the writer, to correct, that is to say, those who are the actual creators of the language.

Let us however get closer to our dispute. Notwithstanding the fact that you had consciously attempted to be more-or-less elastic,

---

[1] *Sovyetish heymland* is a political-cultural Yiddish magazine published in the Soviet Union.

not rigid or pedantic or dogmatic, nevertheless the inner person (as I would put it) took over; so that in spite of your erudition and your own attractive, even somewhat elegant literary style, you remained in essence the same consistently "dry linguist" (although you had claimed to have separated yourself from him)—the "dry linguist" who forgets that for the purpose of literary creation one must first and foremost approach the work as an aesthetic experience, keeping before one's eyes what is *sui generis,* that which is unique and from which one cannot under any circumstances be separated.

My chief complaint against you is: Your undoubtedly valuable polemic seems to me almost to have been delivered by two separate persons and where one of them thinks in a dialectical manner, the other quickly intervenes and draws the first back to tired platitudes. We see this particularly when you speak of "the lexicon of Hebrew elements in the Yiddish language."

On the one hand you characterize as "ultra-leftist" what etiquette requires me to call a conclusion of Nokhem Shtif's, namely, that "the old Hebrew vocabulary is now for the most part redundant," although you are correct when you say that Shtif's statement is "understandable in the context of the last twenty or thirty years." Even more, you are in agreement, touchingly so, with the observation that "to cut oneself off from words or experiences of Hebrew origin is to make Yiddish bloodless!" On the other hand you come in powerfully and say, "One must not take delight in words or compounds (of Hebrew origin), which are not only incomprehensible, but are also tied to associations absolutely alien to the younger generation. We must also keep in mind those who understand the oral Yiddish work and who show an urge to teach themselves how to understand also the printed word." First, why, esteemed comrade Shapiro, are you so harsh as to deny us the small "delight in words and compounds"? Is it possible that there are other, sweeter delights for a writer who must, insofar as he has literary gifts to do so, enrich the popular language? Yes, his "words and compounds" may on occasion be "tied to associations absolutely alien to the younger generation." What, therefore, do you advise the writer to do in such a case? Evidently neither more nor less than to separate himself from these associations. Do me the kindness to consider this matter more carefully: can one and ought one demand of a writer that he re-route his associations, whether they be close or remote? Would this not be the same, to put the matter figuratively, as advising a peacock to pluck out its feathers—even though its feathers give a peacock its glory? Truth to tell, you have adopted such an argument; the proof appears in your own unsatisfactory explanation: "We must also keep in mind those who understand the spoken Yiddish word and who show an urge to teach themselves to understand also the printed word." So allow them, begging your pardon, to develop their "urge," as you express it, and truly to learn not only the oral but the cultural language. Who prevents them from doing this?

Rather than bring the writer down to them, why not raise them up to the writer! The person who has put no effort at all into learning the basic language should certainly not become its guardian; he should not be placed at the shoulder of the writer to guide his pen! From such an appalling state of affairs to Abe Cahanism[2]—Abe Cahanism which you yourself detest—how short is the distance. This particular question is not only purely linguistic or nationalistic; it has also a deeply ethical character. Every person of more or less culture who lives for a long time among very remote ethnic populations feels an obligation to master their language, and not only for utilitarian purposes, but much more out of inner respect for the human environment in which the circumstances of his life have placed him.

Thus I must say that certain of your recommendations—whether consciously or not—sound a note of compromise, of negotiation as between a lender and his soon-to-be bankrupt debtor. . . . Such an attitude cannot fail to shock when applied to language, which is, after all, the dearest, the noblest creation of the people, that which claims to be and is in fact a folk memory, the enduring treasury of the spirit. Consequently your quixoticism amazes me, when you come forward to argue categorically which sort of Hebraisms have remained in the Yiddish language—that is to say in the folk memory —and which sort not, and even to make a kind of bookkeeper's account, a schedule of recommended and not-recommended Hebrew elements. As you put it in your own way: words and idioms that have been naturalized and those that are alien to the language. For example, the Hebrew "bereyshes" ("in the beginning") yes and German "ibl" no, although this latter word which you regard as fabricated has been naturalized into the whole vocabulary of Yiddish literature and is even used by poets who seldom draw their vocabulary from the so-called lexicon of learned words. Similarly, the Hebrew "ekhes" ("quality") yes, but the Hebrew "oykets" ("thorn"

---

[2] Abraham Cahan (1860–1951), editor of the *Jewish Daily Forward* in New York and one of the most influential figures in the Yiddish-speaking world of his time. In trying to make his Yiddish style accessible to the ill-educated reader, he introduced many English words and eliminated much of the Hebrew component. Sternberg is here hinting at the charge that was frequently leveled against Cahan, that he corrupted the standards of Yiddish writing.

or "point") no, although this "oykets" is entitled to celebrate its ju-
bilee, being used as it is in the publications of all the Jewish settlements, while "point," which is a word of Romance origin, is surely
more odd to the Yiddish reader and more easily understood by the
outsider than "oykets," for whose meaning no word of Germanic
origin exists in Yiddish.

To rule and dispose in this way, to pluck from a printed sentence one or another Hebrew word or expression and accept it or
reject it, granting a visa to one but denying it to another, leaving out
of the picture the context of the word, this is no *modus linguae*—no
language can be learned in this way! A diamond is not a diamond if
we cannot see the finger against which it is set or the ear of the
lady on which it hangs. There cannot be a *sine qua non*—a *khok-
veloya'aver,* an inviolable law to use an expression permitted by
you—a table of words and idioms permitted to *all* writers. Some
words are appropriate for certain writers but not for others. One
needs a word that another rejects. The Jewish scholar S. Halkin
seems to have managed with practically no Hebraisms at all and
this had absolutely no ill effect on his nuance-rich, lyric-melodic,
attractive, and if I might have your permission to say it, even aristocratic Yiddish prose style. Halkin, rather than use learned words
or idioms, endeavored to transplant into Yiddish words not of Hebrew descent but of the old Yiddish culture, and he achieved this
frequently by the use of archaisms—not words of the sacred language, but archaisms of Yiddish itself. Yet Peretz Markish, who was
not so learned in Yiddish as Halkin, ardently pursued expressions of
Hebrew origin. And how did Moishe Teif manage to knead into his
delicious folk-Yiddish those Hebraisms which for him might as well
have been plucked from the air? This means that one or another
lexical element is closely tied to the individual style of this or that
writer, to his language structure, to his instinct for language taken
altogether. Compounds—these are after all affinities blessed by
God. And if they are not God-given, then they come out of the ir-
reverent love of language itself. It is well know that in making a
match, in conducting a courtship, outsiders ought not to meddle. Let
us therefore apply this dialectical principle to the marriage of words.
Which leads to the conclusion: all language streams are equally
legitimate and important—the language of the ignorant as much as
the language of the learned, and vice versa. Certainly each depends
on questions of degree, the proper dosage of words, if you will. But
this becomes a question of our feeling, of our sense of propriety, of
our taste, not of "clericalism" or "archaism" or similar horrendous
attributes.

You never cease to remind us that *our language has lost its memory*. But it is my deep conviction that no one has a moral right to dogmatize so categorically at a time when hundreds of Yiddish writers scattered across the globe create works of literature for tens of thousands of readers in a language which they are continually polishing, pampering, dandling, and enriching. I will return to this point, but meanwhile I want to say that with such a declaration as yours ringing in his ears, no Yiddish writer, including yourself as a linguist, can stay for long at his desk. Unless—his purpose is to compose a laundry list. Mendele, the grandfather of us all, seated at his worktable, searched for his "yidele"—for him a most necessary word —searched even under the table: please, he said, do me a favor, come out of your hiding-place. . . . So it is a delight to read Elyah Spivak's characterization of Mendele's style: "In Mendele we see expressed for the first time, and with the most remarkable artistic energy, the *historical* lexicon of Yiddish cross-fertilized with the system of the contemporary language. In his work is vividly manifested the historical language-memory. It arises in its ancient source (Bible, Aggada, Halaka), it gathers strength from closer historical sources that cut through channels into the present time (storybook, *taytsh-khumesh*, Purim-drama, vernacular women's prayers, sermons)."

So I ask you simply: Is it permitted to the grandfather but not to his grandchildren? And if you say that every one understood Yiddish in Mendele's time, then you must recognize that Yiddish literature at that time did not have the many-branched cultural intelligences it possesses today. But in this connection I want to remind you of H. Leivick's famous remark that if only one reader of Yiddish had remained in the world, Leivick would be determined to write for him in Yiddish. In this there is not a tincture of what we call "language-fetishism," but rather *high morality*, which has its source in the deepest respect for folk culture, that culture whose juices nourished you and which in turn you nurtured with your own vitality. And be assured, even in this tragic situation—one writer writing for one reader—Leivick would have written on his own level, making no concession whether in matters of content, form, or language. For how can a writer do otherwise? How can he pay his literary debt except through the mobilization of all his resources?

Returning to our primary theme, I want to say that not only such literary personalities as Mendele or Leivick, but every one of us who seats himself at a desk must hear the sounds of the links in the golden chain of the language that he is creating. And not only the writer, also the good reader cannot survive as a reader if he is cut off from all the associations, both intellectual and emotional, that are called up by his reading.

In the course of your demand that the language be *accessible* and *comprehensible*, you introduce the following argument: "It must be understood that a measurable number of the now active Yiddish Soviet writers learned Yiddish in the Soviet Yiddish school only; even the Yiddish high school of that time afforded them no knowledge of Hebrew." Quite correct. But how can you not see the evidence of a serious tendency among these same writers more or less to acquire such knowledge?

And since you raise this point, cast your eye for the sake of argument on Soviet Russian literature, especially its poetry, and you will be astonished to see how many loan-words and sophisticated language practices drawn from *all* sources enrich the lexical treasury of contemporary Russian writers. These writers also evince a certain kind of "knowledge" which they did not acquire in the Soviet Russian schools. But you threaten us with another sort of restraint: "Not society for the language, but the language for society." Society, however, is not a static concept. It cannot be regarded as one thing only. "The October Revolution, as is well known, from the very beginning placed the Jewish cultural activist face to face with the broad proletarian masses—with the Jewish laborer, the artisan, the young, the working woman—and therefore it was necessary for the new printed word, the new oral word, the tribunal word to be comprehensible to every one, and especially to the unlearned as much as to the *Gemara*-scholar." This proposition of yours is entirely correct, but the October Revolution (of blessed memory) has already passed its fiftieth anniversary. And in this half century, Soviet society has been radically changed. So that whereas fifty years ago all cultural activity went forward on a broad front, it now proceeds in depth. Apparently therefore you may personally permit yourself the delight in that "vigorous, expressive, Hebraic idiom *khok veloya'aver*," without inquiring whether one remembers such a phrase or not. For according to your own strict logic, the Yiddish expression *a fester gezets* ("an ironclad rule") would do as well.

And now—concerning your categorical opposition to Max Weinreich's thesis. Weinreich wrote: "We should preserve everything good that we possess from whatever corner of Yiddish it may come. Archaisms from the *khumesh-taytsh* retain still the possibility of being resurrected from the grave." It seems to me that you made no attempt to comprehend the meaning of what was just quoted; rather, taking aim at the author of the quotation, you launched an ironic shaft: "He seeks ever wider pastures for Yiddish even in the *khu-*

mesh-taytshn; that is to say, no longer satisfied with an archaic lexicon of Hebrew origin, he sends us to the archaisms of the Yiddish language itself." At last the villain has been found out: "Archaic"! This reminds me of the question asked by a member of our writers collective at one of our meetings: what sort of a word is "shtok" (*stark* or *total,* as in total darkness, total twilight)? Such a word, he said, was used about thirty years ago! Well, for such a "theoretician" it is apparent that language is a thing of fashion: does one wear the hat now in vogue or does one not. . . . But you, esteemed comrade Shapiro, know very well that *ivre-taytsh* [the archaic Yiddish used in the translation of Scripture] is the literary stream of Yiddish into which not only our mothers but also we ourselves shed many tears of joy in our childhood. You know very well that the Hebrew archaism is the most intellectual, the richest in associations, and at the same time the most laconic language element, whereas the archaism of the vernacular is the juiciest but also the most lyrical, containing as it does the atmosphere of poetry.

And on the same point: listen, for the pleasure of it, to the way in which the young, immensely talented Andrei Voznesensky plays the most expansive, broadly Russian notes in his poem recently published in the "Literary Gazette." [*There follows a passage of verse in Russian which the author uses to illustrate his point.*]

A heavy use of archaism. But you will doubtless say—these are youthful *jeux d'esprit.* Nevertheless those who permit themselves to write poetry in this manner stand at the very center of the present generation of younger Soviet Russian poets. So here is another question for you: what sort of fate would one of the classics of Soviet Russian prose meet at your hands—Leonid Leonov, for instance, with his thoroughly archaic language, his difficult syntax, his entirely over-burdened stylistic structure? Ought he not to be grateful that he was not a Yiddish writer? Well, let us return to our own narrow circle. Suppose it had happened that the villain had actually been resurrected from the dead, that is to say that the language of the *taytsh-khumesh* had been revived and had marvelously enriched the language of Yiddish poetry. True it would have happened more likely abroad than here, where the process of integrating archaisms proceeds more cautiously, although recognizably. But today we do not turn a cold shoulder to Yiddish literature outside the boundaries of our land. You yourself acknowledge clearly that the appellation "Soviet Yiddish" "is never to be taken as a new species, as a literary language different from the literary Yiddish that is employed outside the boundaries of Soviet Russia." And you also recognize a certain revival of the archaic word among ourselves. Nevertheless you took the trouble to put together a list—by no means complete, but almost so—of permitted and not permitted vernacular archaisms, and according to my deepest conviction, this time also a quite arbitrary list. Thus for instance you prohibit "gedekhenish" (memory) and command that we use only "zikorn." Never mind that "gedekhenish" lives in the folk memory, the folk "gedekhenish" if you will, and that it has long since been naturalized into the Yiddish literary language: never mind that the choice of the words in question depend upon context ("gedekhenish" is lyrical and soft, "zikorn" direct and hard)—it is all the same to you as you excommunicate "gedekhenish."

You give the same treatment to such a dear, succulent, poetical word as "nayert" (*but on the contrary*) which is more impressive than the dry, monochromatic "nor." Why shouldn't we allow ourselves two words for the same meaning, a practice that enriches every language? After all, a certain nuance is added. Why do the Germans say "nur" and "sondern" while we are forbidden to use both "nor" and "nayert"? The answer you give is that you are defining "the unique lexical features of a uniform literary Yiddish in the Soviet Union." But here you commit once more, or so it seems to me, your basic error: instead of speaking about *language*, you speak about *words*. The unique features of Soviet Yiddish are not to be seen in *individual words* but in its total linguistic intonation—the melody, the voice of the language. Nor is "Soviet Yiddish" a frozen concept. By enriching itself with fresh contents and new themes, it expands its borders so that today we have assimilated into our poetry motifs with which we were completely unacquainted twenty or thirty years ago. So it appears that we are permitted to enrich our themes but not our vocabulary, our store of words.

I summarize: theories are transient, but the tree of life endures forever, as Goethe said. Our folk language lives and therefore I advocate a perpetual renewal and enrichment of our vocabulary. Our Yiddish tongue lives, and great creative miracles are taking place by means of it. Let us therefore be objective, observe the matter carefully, and acknowledge that which is worth acknowledging concerning the Yiddish language even as it exists outside the borders of the Soviet Union. Casting our eyes over the whole contemporary Yiddish scene, we see that there is no place for motifs of "decay" which can only hinder us or bring us to a halt. There remain to us enough moments of joy. And in truth, how many resources Yiddish still possesses! We dare not, on the basis of doubtful theoretical blueprints, erect a barrier against these resources. How often do I say to myself: "Yiddish, the new, young language! One must learn how to master it, to dig down to its roots. Let us not muzzle it; let us untie its tongue;

let us hear distinctly the bustling voices in all their various sounds of our six million martyrs—what a holy task this is!"

And finally: when I observed you, my dear comrade Shapiro, laboring over the Yiddish-Russian dictionary, I remarked to myself: a true linguist is akin to the Biblical Ruth who does not tire when she bends down to the fields gleaning and gathering after the reapers among the sheaves. . . . So do not permit your scientific practice to come into conflict with your scientific theories.

1968

Without *Mazl*[1]

by Abraham Koralnik

Translated by Irving Howe and Eliezer Greenberg

You need *mazl* for everything. Even the Torah in the Temple, it's said, needs *mazl*. Perhaps the Torah most of all, since everything depends on who handles her, who translates and who explains.

Every scripture, everything higher and more significant than the grey dumbness of the earth—depends on *mazl*. Depends even more than does the material side of existence. You don't need *mazl* to get rich. Whoever really wants to be rich, becomes rich sooner or later. If a happy accident helps out, so much the better. But an accident isn't *mazl*. The accident is unexpected, unforeseen, and thereby not inexorable. If a man grows rich because gold has been discovered on his land, that still isn't *mazl*. It's just an accident. It has nothing to do with him, it doesn't reflect his essential being.

Mazl is something different and deeper. It is rooted in personality. It is the crux of our being, determining that we live in one way rather than another. It is character and talent. And in regard to these, no one is in command. No one can add a crumb or subtract a drop. Such is the fate of a man's portion, and no more. A man can't jump over his head.

Some peoples have *mazl*, others don't. The English have it, the Germans not. And that isn't an accident, it can't even be willed. The Germans wanted to be rulers of the world, they had their opportunities, but finally these were of no help. The English wanted nothing, but were destined, nevertheless, for a world mission. They

[1] The word *mazl* signifies in Yiddish both luck and fortune. To suggest the presence of both, we use here the original Yiddish term, transliterated into English.

carried it out even though all the odds—their lack of numbers, their
isolation, the lateness of their entry into world history—were against
them. English character was English *mazl*.

Languages too have their *mazl*.

One of those most blessed with *mazl* is Hebrew. The language
of a small people in a cranny of Asia, Hebrew became the holy language of the world, for thousands of years a reservoir of spiritual
potentialities. Everything seemed to be against Hebrew, even the
people who spoke it. But Hebrew overcame. The Jews loved Hebrew
so much, they didn't even want to approach her too closely. Whenever a great soul wanted to say something vital to his people, he
spoke in Hebrew. And if he couldn't find the right words, Hebrew
found them for him. It survived. The *Guide for the Perplexed* would
by now have been quite forgotten if it hadn't been translated from a
beautiful and flowing Arabic into the coarse Hebrew of the Middle
Ages. The unfelicitous translation outlasted the graceful original.

For Hebrew had *mazl*. It was a language with a Maecenas.
Whenever I hear that name, I remind myself of the words of Horace, in his verse about the first Maecenas, the Roman patrician and
millionaire who left behind him an immortal name simply because
he loved literature. Horace's verse goes:

Maecenas, you who stem from kings

He did in fact stem from kings. And because he bore kingly
blood and was an aristocrat with a respect for the past, he also had
respect for things of the spirit.

May this not be why the Jews have had such a Maecenas-like attachment to Hebrew? It was the only kingly language they had, the
only one that tied together past and present; the only aristocratic
element in their life.

Today, before our eyes—almost before our eyes—there is growing up a new Hebrew literature. And at the same time, parallel to it,
Yiddish literature. Two literatures, one people.

But one of them has *mazl*, and the other not.

Quietly and sedately, Hebrew literature continues on its course,
not broad but deep. Gradually: line by line, tome by tome.

It is a literature that has grown up purely on idealism. No one
has needed it. But that is precisely its strength. Not being needed
has become its necessity; poverty, its richness. Of all literatures Hebrew has been the most aristocratic because it alone has had no end
other than its own cultivation.

No one made any demands on Hebrew. Writers and readers
approached the language with a sense of the sacred. Theirs, they

felt, was a holy task. Hebrew literature was often naïve, euphemistic, old-fashioned—but only in form. Its essential feeling ran true and deep, and its creators saw themselves as sharing in the world-historical spirit. That is why Hebrew literature, for all its poverty of circumstance, could maintain itself more firmly and with deeper roots than Yiddish literature, with its richness of achievement and large audience.

Yiddish literature had readers. Hebrew had Maecenases, people who felt they were doing themselves honor when they approached its kingliness of speech.

A literature without *mazl,* Yiddish literature: too late on the scene and not penetrating deeply enough into Jewish consciousness.

Jews like antiquity. The older, the better. The new doesn't please them. They can't accept the new with ease, neither the new freedom nor the new affluence. And not the new language, either.

This can't be fought, it runs in the blood.

Still—it is to be regretted. A shame. I can imagine a time when Jews will regret that they behaved so frivolously and condescendingly to the Yiddish word. It will be a time when Yiddish will have "disappeared." Once "disappeared," it will have become old, dead—and interesting. The Jews of that time will grow nostalgic—the English-speaking ones, the Hebrew-speaking ones—for the tones of the language generations and generations of Jews had spoken. They will grow nostalgic for the sounds born in the Middle Ages and strengthened on the Slavic steppes, sounds of Jewish intimacy and loneliness, sorrows and jokes, sounds saturated with the heart's blood of a people.

They will regret it, those who come after us. They will yearn for songs that were not sung, the sigh that failed to become a symphony, treasures that were never used.

Perhaps a Maecenas will then appear in behalf of the dead and sacred Yiddish tongue. But it will be too late.

A language without *mazl.*

1940

Glossary

bris—ceremony of circumcision

Cabbala—esoteric Jewish mystical teachings

galut—exile

gaon—an eminent scholar

Gemara—section of the Talmud interpreting the Mishna

Haggada—prayers and songs recited on the first two nights of Passover

Halakha—the Law

Hasidic—refers to movement of Jewish pietistic enthusiasm that arose in eastern Europe during the eighteenth century (see Editors' Introduction)

Haskala—movement of Jewish Enlightenment during the late eighteenth and nineteenth centuries (see Editors' Introduction)

heder—elementary Hebrew school

khumesh-teitsch—early translation of the Bible into Yiddish

landsmanshaft—society of Jewish immigrants formed in the U.S. and consisting of persons from one town or region

luftmensh—literally "man of air," a colloquial expression signifying person with no secure or visible livelihood

maskil (*maskilim*)—an enlightener, one of the enlightened

melamed—teacher, usually in elementary school

mezzuzas—ritual objects posted on the door of a Jewish home, consisting of small parchment on which portions of the Pentateuch are inscribed

midrashim—homilies

minyan—a quorum of ten males for communal religious services

Mishna—the oral Law which is the basis of the Talmud

mitzvot—commandment

pilpul—a dialectical method of explicating religious texts

Shekhina—Divine Presence

shlimazl—an unfortunate, incompetent, ill-fated, doomed to bad luck, and with a character to match

shtadlan—employee of a Jewish community employed in Russia to intercede with gentile authorities

shtetl—small town

Shulhan Arukh—a Code of Law embodying the Halakha

tallis—prayer shawl

Targum—a Hebrew word meaning "literal translation," which has come often to refer to Aramaic

t'fillin—phylacteries

zhargon—disdainful expression for Yiddish

Contributors

ABRAHAM AIN (1888–1959), a Jewish communal leader in eastern Europe.

BA'AL MAKHSHOVES (1873–1924), pen name of Dr. Israel Eliashov, one of the first and still among the best Yiddish literary critics.

SHLOMO BICKEL (1896–1969), Yiddish literary critic and essayist, an editor of the literary journal *Di Tsukunft*.

JACOB GLATSTEIN (1896–   ), Yiddish poet and essayist, founder of the *In Zikh* literary group during the early 1920's, a major figure in modernist and contemporary Yiddish writing.

HAYIM GREENBERG (1889–1953), perhaps the most gifted among Yiddish essayists, notable for his forceful style and wide range of subjects, long identified with Labor Zionism and for a time editor of *Der Yiddisher Kempfer*, a cultural-political journal.

ABRAHAM JOSHUA HESCHEL (1907–   ), a distinguished theologian and memoirist of East European Jewish life in *The Earth Is The Lord's*.

REUBEN ICELAND (1884–1955), poet and literary critic, the theoretical spokesman for the group of poets and fiction writers known as *Di Yunge* and especially prominent in American Yiddish literature during the second and third decades of the century.

I. KOPELOFF (1858–1933), memoirist of early Jewish life in America, author of *Amol in Amerika*.

ABRAHAM KORALNIK (1883–1937), prolific essayist in Yiddish, especially notable for his belletristic and impressionistic approach.

ABRAHAM MENES (1897–1969), historian and essayist.

SHMUEL NIGER (1883–1955), the most prolific and authoritative critic of Yiddish literature.

JOSEPH OPATASHU (1887–1954), novelist, short-story writer and occasional essayist.

I. L. PERETZ (1852–1915), poet, essayist, short-story writer who, together with Mendele Mokher Sforim and Sholom Aleichem, was one of the founding masters of modern Yiddish literature.

331

EMMANUEL RINGELBLUM (1900–1944), Jewish historian and educator, perhaps the most notable chronicler of the martyrdom under Nazi rule in Warsaw and leader of the Jewish underground. His book is printed in English as *Notes from the Warsaw Ghetto*.

C. BEZALEL SHERMAN (1896–   ), essayist and sociologist, author in English of *The Jew within American Society*.

JACOB STERNBERG (1890–   ), Yiddish poet, essayist, and theatrical director, one of the few to have survived the Stalin murders.

A. TABACHNIK (1901–1970), poet and literary critic, best known for his modern aesthetic approach to Yiddish poetry, especially that of *Di Yunge*.

JEHIEL ISAIAH TRUNK (1887–1961), Yiddish historian and essayist, associated with the Jewish socialist Bund, and notable for his cultural history of Jewish life in Warsaw.

MAX WEINREICH (1894–1969), a major philologist and literary historian, author of a history of the Yiddish language, and until his death director of YIVO, the Yiddish scholarly center.

HAYIM ZHITLOWSKY (1865–1943), one of the major intellectual figures in the world of Yiddish, devoted especially to the idea of a distinctively Jewish socialism and a fervent defender of the values of Yiddishism.

ISRAEL ZINBERG (1873–1943?), literary historian and critic, author of the eight-volume *Di Geshikhte fun Literatur bei Yiden*.

MICHAEL ZYLBERBERG (1907–   ), has written a memoir of his experiences in the Warsaw ghetto, entitled in its English translation *A Warsaw Diary*.